£25·00

TV Scenic Design

To the Scenic Designers of
the BBC Television Service
past and present

TV Scenic Design
Second edition

Gerald Millerson

Focal Press
An imprint of Butterworth-Heinemann
Linacre House, Jordan Hill, Oxford OX2 8DP
A division of Reed Educational and Professional Publishing Ltd

℞ A member of the Reed Elsevier plc group

OXFORD BOSTON JOHANNESBURG
MELBOURNE NEW DELHI SINGAPORE

Previously published as *Basic TV Staging*, first edition 1974, reprinted 1979
Second edition 1982 Reprinted 1984

First edition published in 1989 as *TV Scenic Design Handbook*
Second edition 1977 as *TV Scenic Design*

© Gerald Millerson 1997

British Library Cataloguing in Publication Data
A catalogue record for this book is available from the British Library.

ISBN 0 2405 1493 9

Library of Congress Cataloguing in Publication Data
A catalogue record for this book is available from the Library of Congress.

Typeset by Keyword Typesetting Services Ltd.
Printed in Great Britain by The Bath Press, Bath

Contents

Preface
to the second edition

This is an exciting time in the growth of TV scenic design. Although initially television design relied on techniques garnered from theatre and film, people working in the medium rapidly built up their own unique solutions to cope with the pressures and problems of daily schedules.

Recent advances in video camera design, coupled with more flexible video recording and editing systems, are freeing the TV director from constraints that previously restricted production methods. The camera has become more mobile. Pictures are more stable and of consistently high quality. Scenes can be shot, rearranged and manipulated in ways undreamt of a short time ago.

All this has resulted in increased pressures for the television scenic designer. There is even less time and opportunity to create effective treatments than before. And, of course, there are those ever-growing problems of rising costs, tightly controlled budgets ... and the other innumerable hard facts of life that have to be resolved.

But while all this has been happening, sophisticated electronic processes have been developing which offer today's designer great new opportunities. Electronic treatments that were impracticable not so long ago have become routine. Many designers are turning to these chroma key based systems to augment built scenery or to provide complete *virtual settings* as an answer to their design problems. In the new Chapter 8, we shall explore the principles and practices involved, and discover their potentials.

Preface to first edition

First, a word of explanation.

For over a decade, an earlier book, *Basic TV Staging*, provided an 'anatomy' of the set designer's craft; discussing the tools, mechanics and techniques of scenic design in the TV studio.

But the television/video field has expanded considerably. So to suit current developments, we have extensively revised and widened the text, and this new re-formatted international source-book is renamed *TV Scenic Design*.

What is this book all about?

It is a summary of the principles and practice of scenic design. Here you will find details of design approaches, structures, and staging methods that can be used under a very wide range of conditions.

We are concerned here with the mechanics and methods through which the scenic designer expresses ideas and interprets the ambiance of a production.

Who is this book written for?

Whether you are creating scenery on a shoestring in a campus studio, developing an in-house project, or studying to work in a network TV studio, you will find that the principles covered here can be applied, even though there can be considerable differences in the relative scale, space, budget and organization involved.

How can the book help me?

This is essentially a *practical* book, showing you in detail *how* it is done. Materials are costly, and you want to make maximum use of your budget. So emphasis here is on developing effective staging at minimum cost; on getting the maximum effect with the simplest means; and on methods that allow variety and individuality in your techniques.

This source-book will serve you as a reminder of alternative techniques, to trigger fresh ideas and approaches, and to encourage style variations.

The design mechanics included here are widely used in TV/video/film production, but you will also find them in exhibition work, museum presentations, window displays, and all other similar areas of visual presentation.

Acknowledgements

The information in this book reflects the generously shared experience of many superb scenic designers in BBC Television over the years, experts who have demonstrated their sensitive skills in blending practical design with stimulating, persuasive visual presentation. Many of the ingenious methods they have devised have become the grammar of their craft. This text is really a distillation of much of their work.

My thanks, too, to the BBC for permission to include here photographs taken in London studios, demonstrating typical scenic treatment for a range of productions.

The author would like also to express his appreciation of the help of his colleague, the late Mr Stephen Bundy, former Head of Scenic Design, BBC TV Service (for many years a widely experienced and esteemed designer), who gave his encouragement to the manuscript of the original book.

Chapter 1

The background of design

1.1 The illusion of reality

When we sit enjoying a TV program or a film we have an impression of total reality. We seem to be there where the action is, seeing everything as it is happening. We don't give a single thought to the mechanics of the production but accept what we see and hear as natural and real.

That is as it should be, for a production team has combined their various skills to build up a carefully contrived illusion. Through a cunning blend of controlled camerawork, lighting, scenic design, audio treatment, script, performance, editing, costume, and make-up they have created convincing make-believe. The scenic designer is an important member of that team.

1.2 The designer's craft

A subject's background directly influences how an audience reacts to what they are watching. It affects their response to the subject, their interpretation of what is going on – even what they are looking at in the scene.

The art of devising appropriate surroundings for the action is in the hands of the *scenic designer* – also called the *set designer* or simply the *designer*. You will find that terminology varies from place to place, but, wherever possible, the most-used variations are included here. Even the scenery itself is referred to variously as *sets*, *settings*, or *décor*.

The designer is a key member of the production group. Until the staging has been devised and agreed, the director cannot develop ideas about the action or the camerawork, the lighting director cannot design the lighting treatment, and sound specialists and various ancillary crafts and services cannot organize their contributions.

The designer creates and develops the *staging* for the entire production – the scenic treatment *and* how it is to be arranged and organized in the studio.

The design process involves:

- Devising the scenery, its decoration, furniture, draperies, and other set dressings,
- Preparing plans and elevations showing the physical features and layout of the production in the studio,
- Organizing the selection and preparation of the scenery, properties, etc., and
- The erection (and eventual dismantling) of these settings in the studio.

The skill and experience required to develop décor must depend to some extent on the scale and complexity of the situation. In a small production unit the director might select a few items from available stock and devise a very satisfactory background without

Figure 1.1 The television studio
Most studios follow a similar basic arrangement: a central staging area, with cyclorama; sound-absorbent walls with lighting, sound, and power outlets; and overhead lighting facilities. The observation window of the production control room is set in one wall.

the assistance of a designer. But specialist training tells, and certainly for a production of any size, professional experience and knowhow is needed to create optimum results.

What is less obvious is the subtlety and sensitivity that underlies the craft of design. A skilled scenic designer may take a few unpromising items and weave visual magic on camera. Someone with less flair may construct elaborate, high-cost settings that appear on screen as little more than an uncoordinated jumble!

Scenic design is a broadly based craft, and the good designer is not only a creative artist but a resourceful craftsman whose feet are firmly on the ground. He or she works with an understanding of the other allied studio operations that are contributing to the total production, keeping a wary eye on the economics of the project.

1.3 The settings ...

Most scenic design is not a matter of creating *impressive* settings but an appropriate environment that will provide persuasive, meaningful pictures:

- These settings have to be suitable for the dimensions and facilities of the studio.
- They must be reasonably robust yet constructed so as to be manageable to handle, transport, and store.
- They have to provide a safe environment for the performers and studio team.
- The design needs to be related to the available production budget.
- The settings need to convey the right sort of ambiance or atmosphere. They must have a style that the audience associates with the subject, whether it is the bright, glitzy, eye-catching display of a comedy show, the reassuring businesslike appearance of a newscast, or the homely comfort and realism of a domestic drama.
- Where staging requires a number of separate settings or subsections we usually need to introduce a common overall design theme to unify them.
- Decoration and furnishing will normally be closely coordinated with the environment. Even in a stylized situation, we can spoil the unity if, for example, we seat a group of guests in odd, unmatched chairs.

Through the décor we can:

- Establish a particular place for the action,
- Give a production a special ambiance,
- Engender a certain dramatic atmosphere,
- More subtly still, décor can draw an audience's attention to certain features or characteristic of a subject, emphasizing its size, frailty, daintiness, etc.
- Scenic treatment can also be used to strengthen the impact of a shot. For instance, we can accentuate a low shot looking up at a subject by using forced perspective in the background.

1.4 ... and the staging

A design can be extremely attractive yet fail if it does not suit the *mechanics* of the production. Settings need to provide a practical working environment that offers optimum conditions for action, camerawork, lighting, and sound and enables the entire production group to work effectively. So the designer is directly concerned with the *staging* process, with the way in which the scenic elements are arranged and organized in the studio.

The design needs to be suitable for the *performer*. Seats must be comfortable... not hard benches or boards to sit on! Stairs must be easy to use... no steep, ankle-breaking staircases that may look impressive on camera but put the talent at risk! The doors of a room should open and close easily, but not so easily that they swing open with a life of their own!

The staging needs to be suitable for the *production treatment* the director has in mind. A series of slender arches may appear impressive from a distance (long shot), but if the director intends only taking close shots in order to concentrate on people's expressions these arches may simply appear as vertical poles on the screen.

Similarly, if the director is confronted with scenery that prevents him or her from getting the cameras in to take the shots required, it has failed.

If the TV/video cameras being used have any idiosyncracies (e.g. vertical streaking or blooming on bright highlights) the settings have to be designed to suit these characteristics or the pictures will have distracting blemishes.

Picture impact comes from a blend of lighting and design techniques. As the scenic design and the lighting are usually created by different people, these specialists need to closely coordinate their work. Otherwise there is the chance that one will unwittingly frustrate the other. The designer might provide a set that could not be lit properly. Inappropriate lighting might spoil the illusion that the designer has created.

The sound specialist will also need the designer's cooperation. Low-hanging scenery could prevent the sound-boom operator from getting a microphone anywhere near the performers.

1.5 Is it appropriate?

Once we enter the realms of 'good taste', 'stylishness', 'individuality', or 'preference', there are few reliable guides to help us. Styles and fashions change. A treatment that is very suitable on one situation may look totally out of place on another. The approach that appeared fresh and *avant-garde* yesterday can look tired and overdone tomorrow.

Some scenic devices appear over-used and 'old-fashioned' with time. Others have become the familiar 'standard' way to treat the subject.

Over the years, various stereotyped conventions have grown up to suit different types of production. In fact, if you try to use a new form of presentation it can seem strange and orthodox. We have, for example, become accustomed to newscasters sitting behind a desk in neutral surroundings or against a busy editorial office. But what would happen if we chose instead to have them sitting in an easy chair in a lounge set, apparently reading from a newspaper, with its illustrations coming to life? The information could be identical but, in all probability, the audience would feel uneasy, and we might well find that the news message had now lost some of its authority.

If we watch a cooking demonstration in what appears to be an actual kitchen, everything we see carries conviction. But present exactly the same demonstration in highly decorated, 'show-biz' surroundings and the entire ambiance of the program changes. Instead of serious instruction showing the audience how to make a particular dish, everything has now become something of a stunt, tricks producing delicious food 'out of a hat'.

Many types of program have developed a certain form of staging not because people could not think up other ways of presenting them but because their mechanics work particularly well. Games shows and quiz programs are a regular example. In fact one might say that they now only seem to 'look right' when staged in the traditional way.

Production techniques and the designer

How effective the décor appears on the screen is going to be considerably influenced by the way it is interpreted by the director, cameras, and lighting.

1.6 What does the camera reveal?

Let's imagine that we are shooting a setting consisting of a series of arches. Each pillar is decorated with a pattern of small flowers. In the wide view we see all the arches but the decorations are too tiny to be discerned. Only broad detail will be visible.

Move the camera closer or narrow the lens angle a little (zoom in) and we see only a couple of arches in the picture. Now the pillars seem to have some sort of decoration on them, but this is unclear.

Get closer still or narrow the lens angle further and the flower patterns are clear. But we can no longer see the complete arches – only the pillars.

Finally, in a close shot ('zoomed fully in') there is only part of one of the pillars in the frame and the detail of the flowers stands out clearly.

All this is obvious enough but it does remind us of the way the camera can reveal or overlook features in the design, depending on how it is used. What the audience sees will depend on the camera's viewpoint and the amount of the scene the lens shows them.

The décor can have a very strong influence on the way the audience reacts to the action. But if a director concentrates on closer shots most of the time, so that they see little of the set, its psychological impact will be very limited. The audience is mostly seeing a restricted, localized area of the background behind the subjects and little else. And even that may be defocused.

A setting's effectiveness really depends on how well the director 'uses the set'. If he or she only takes a wide shot at the beginning of a sequence as an *establishing shot* and perhaps another at its end to conclude the item there is little opportunity for the audience to get any impressions of the overall scene or little chance of building up an atmospheric effect or establishing a mood.

1.7 How are the cameras to be used?

If the director intercuts between virtually static viewpoints and uses repetitive shots the audience will soon get to recognize these limited view of the surroundings, and will have forfeited opportunities to develop their interest.

Where the camera moves around the setting the audience becomes much more involved in the action. The setting appears more real and more interesting. This is partly due to the subjective effects that come from a varying viewpoint and from the intermovement of scenic planes ('parallactic movement').

If the director favors very mobile cameras, shooting the set from many angles, there is always the danger that the audience will become disoriented. There is also a greater possibility that a camera may overshoot the set, a problem for which the designer needs to be prepared.

1.8 Advance warning

If a director wants to shoot through foreground pieces at some point in a scene in order to create a greater illusion of depth, it helps to be told beforehand, so that appropriate items are available that can be used for the shot.

The designer needs to be warned in advance about any unusual camera treatment. For example, when the director wants to take high shots looking down on the scene there are several methods: by locating one of the cameras up on a platform, by shooting into a suspended mirror, or by using a camera crane. The design will need to be arranged to take these high shots into account and ensure that they are going to be effective. Otherwise all we may see is an uninteresting expanse of bare floor, with lamps hanging in shot!

Perhaps the director has some great ideas for cameras taking upward-looking shots from floor level. Then we have to ensure that these low-angle shots do not inadvertently see over the background into the studio beyond.

1.9 The program's purpose

Some aspects of design are so self-evident that they can easily be overlooked. One of the first things to clarify is the program's *purpose*, for that usually decides the overall style and staging approach.

A program involving a sympathetic discussion between two people on personal problems is going to require an entirely different presentation from a celebrity interview before an enthusiastic audience.

Especially when a production is unscripted, its purpose and emphasis may not be self-evident beforehand. If, for instance, we mistakenly assume that a program about books is to be a series of lighthearted reviews and it turns out to be a secondary discussion, the 'toytown' set provided for the former would be embarrassingly inappropriate. Preliminary planning usually irons out misunderstandings, but this sort of dilemma is not unknown.

Again, if someone is bringing along a piece of equipment for a new industrial process we need general details beforehand and an outline of how it is to be presented in the show. It might be sufficiently small to go on to a table, but it could prove to be quite bulky and need special power supplies. If the director is only going to look at general features of the equipment and then turn to discuss the product that is one situation. But if we are actually going to see it put through its paces an entirely different scenic treatment might be necessary.

There could be a considerable difference in the time and effort involved in these approaches to the subject.

1.10 Economics

Planning cannot proceed very far without a firm idea about the scenic budget available for the program. One might spend a lot of time and effort only to find when part-way through preparations that the money has run out!

Will this costing have to cover, e.g.
Construction – materials, manpower/man-hours?
Hiring rates – scenery, properties?
Storage and transport costs?
Organizational costs?

It may be more cost effective to hire a particular item or piece of scenery than to make or buy it for a single show. On the other hand, it might be more logical to buy a set of furniture for a long-running series than to hire it regularly. This can call for careful judgement at times. Many a prop store has its 'lemons' that nobody wants to use!

Clearly, the aim is to *make the money show*! This can be done in various ways:

● Ensure that materials are going to *look* effective. An expensive

Figure 1.2 Production organization
This flow-sheet shows in outline a typical work pattern as services and facilities are organized and coordinated for a large production.

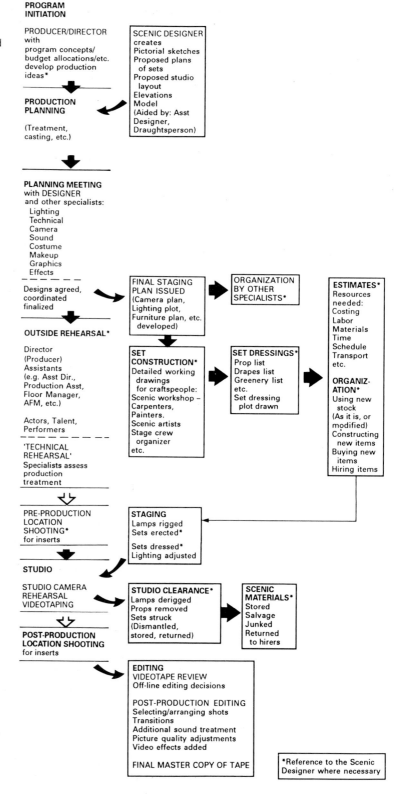

PROGRAM INITIATION

PRODUCER/DIRECTOR with program concepts/ budget allocations/etc. develop production ideas*

PRODUCTION PLANNING

(Treatment, casting, etc.)

PLANNING MEETING with DESIGNER and other specialists:
Lighting
Technical
Camera
Sound
Costume
Makeup
Graphics
Effects

Designs agreed, coordinated finalized

OUTSIDE REHEARSAL*

Director
(Producer)
Assistants
(e.g. Asst Dir.,
Production Asst,
Floor Manager,
AFM, etc.)

Actors, Talent, Performers

'TECHNICAL REHEARSAL'
Specialists assess production treatment

PRE-PRODUCTION LOCATION SHOOTING*
for inserts

STUDIO

STUDIO CAMERA REHEARSAL
VIDEOTAPING

POST-PRODUCTION LOCATION SHOOTING
for inserts

SCENIC DESIGNER
creates
Pictorial sketches
Proposed plans of sets
Proposed studio layout
Elevations
Model
(Aided by: Asst Designer,
Draughtsperson)

FINAL STAGING PLAN ISSUED
(Camera plan, Lighting plot, Furniture plan, etc. developed)

ORGANIZATION BY OTHER SPECIALISTS*

ESTIMATES*
Resources needed:
Costing
Labor
Materials
Time
Schedule
Transport
etc.

SET CONSTRUCTION*
Detailed working drawings for craftspeople:
Scenic workshop –
Carpenters,
Painters.
Scenic artists
Stage crew
organizer
etc.

SET DRESSINGS*
Prop list
Drapes list
Greenery list
etc.
Set dressing plot drawn

ORGANIZ-ATION*
Using new stock
(As it is, or modified)
Constructing new items
Buying new items
Hiring items

STAGING
Lamps rigged
Sets erected*

Sets dressed*
Lighting adjusted

STUDIO CLEARANCE*
Lamps derigged
Props removed
Sets struck
(Dismantled, stored, returned)

SCENIC MATERIALS*
Stored
Salvage
Junked
Returned to hirers

EDITING
VIDEOTAPE REVIEW
Off-line editing decisions

POST-PRODUCTION EDITING
Selecting/arranging shots
Transitions
Additional sound treatment
Picture quality adjustments
Video effects added

FINAL MASTER COPY OF TAPE

*Reference to the Scenic Designer where necessary

wall covering seen only in long shots may look no better on camera than less costly treatment. It may be well worth camera-testing samples beforehand.

● Don't build more than necessary. A photo blow-up may suggest distant features as successfully as actual construction.

● Designers are human! They can create a wonderful décor only to find that the director is not going to include a favorite feature after all. What the camera does not see is not there as far as the audience is concerned! Best check exactly what the director is actually going to use.

● Some directors plan shots and action with meticulous care. During rehearsal they will take opportunities and modify ideas, but they can be relied on to be systematic. Then there are the others who have only the broadest concepts, and cannot commit themselves until they have actually seen the shots on camera. The designer needs to be flexible and have sufficient 'standby' material (e.g. drapes, flats, props, furniture) to cope with unexpected variations that arise during rehearsal.

1.11 Time scale

Time is of the essence in television production. So many separate activities are involved; various work schedules must be estimated; and progress needs to be coordinated and checked.

We want a reasonably accurate idea of how long the various stages are going to take:

● The amount of time available to organize operations (get materials, arrange contracts, etc.) must be estimated.

● How long will it take to construct and decorate the sets (paint, paper, finish), to dismantle and store them and, later, to transport them to the studio?

● It can take quite a lot of time to search out suitable props and furniture for all settings (from stock, buying, or hiring). Supplementary material will also be needed, ranging from plants and grass matting to pencils and writing pads.

● How much time is available to erect the scenery in the studio?

● Is this a single production or one of a series? Does it have to match any others in a series? Will any existing stock sets be re-used?

● Is any special liaison needed with lighting, special effects, graphics, costume, etc.?

● Are any preliminary experimental tests needed (e.g. to check out a 'volcano' effect or confirm that a metallic-finish wall covering will not burn out on camera)?

● Are any parts of the show going to be shot *on location* before or after the main studio taping session? (The location tape can subsequently be edited into the main studio program.) Will that location shooting require any scenery? If so, does it have to match, or be part of, the studio staging?

These are typical factors that have to be considered as part of the design effort for the production.

1.12 Studio space

In most studios there seems to come a time when one runs out of space. The smaller the studio, the more ingenious we need to be to create an impression of spaciousness.

Because a studio is large, it does not necessarily follow that the staging for a production will be costly. We might, for instance, take a large area in front of a stretched cyclorama and, with the aid of a few stock columns and imaginative lighting patterns, produce very attractive décor for a ballet, at comparatively low cost.

A small studio teaches one discipline; to make the most of available space; to economize; and to be ingenious. It is possible, with forethought, to avoid any sense of restriction on camera.

As you will see in Chapter 8, one of the most effective ways of conquering a lack of space is to use *chroma key* to insert backgrounds electronically. If the director breaks the action down into a series of individually recorded shots, and the background is varied accordingly, it really does become possible with a little imagination, to 'squeeze a quart into a pint pot'!

Chapter 2

The basics of design organization

2.1 Practical design

Set design involves a shrewd combination of a sensitive imagination and a very down-to-earth outlook. Although staging is the fabric of illusion it must, above all, follow very practical lines. Design often has to meet a number of conflicting requirements, and at times these can take much patience and ingenuity to resolve.

The design effort involved in staging any production will depend on its size and complexity. Here we shall take a look at typical conditions that can be found in a television/video production.

2.2 'Off-the-cuff' design

This is design at its most rudimentary level – or so it first seems. But in practice, 'off-the-cuff' design requires the ability to make quick decisions, considerable adaptability, and a certain amount of opportunism to provide attractive results that work first time.

With no previous knowledge of the production, the designer has a brief meeting with the director on the general requirements of the show and then checks through available stock items (scenic units, drapes, furniture, and props) to decide what will be most suitable for the occasion. We can imagine the following sort of discussion:

> *Director:* 'John Doe has just inherited an old house, and he's going to show us some interesting things he has found in its attic.'
> *Designer:* 'We could re-create an attic perhaps by canting some large stock flats to provide the sloping roof of an attic room. We can fill it with props, including his discoveries. Or perhaps you want to suggest that we're in the living room of his house?'
> *Director:* 'The living room idea will be OK. Quite a small room, comfortably furnished. We'll need a couple of chairs for an interview, and a table to show various articles to the camera.'
> *Designer:* 'Will there be enough room on the table, or will we need some floor space, to show pieces of furniture? Perhaps there will be pictures that need to be hung on the walls.'

Director: 'Yes, we're not sure at this stage what he wants to bring, but let's allow for those sorts of things.'
Designer: 'I'll go and see what we have that might do...'

This is an oversimplification, of course, but it gives the general idea when dealing with impromptu design.

The designer checks through scenic stock and selects some suitable neutral-toned flats, a doorway, a window unit, drapes, rugs, chairs, table, wall pictures, or some vases that look appropriate.

Later, he or she contacts the lighting director concerned, discusses the staging plan, and confirms the setting position that will best suit the available lamps.

We meet this kind of 'off-the-cuff' design approach where there is little time or opportunity for elaborate staging and local organization is uncomplicated. In a daily magazine-type program this may be the only way to service current stories. Standards can be very high, but they do rely on the imagination and ingenuity of the designer and the range of stock scenery and properties available in store.

It is quite possible to improvise a setting... erect it in the studio... refurbishing where necessary... furnish and dress it... light... and start rehearsals in a couple of hours. Its success largely depends on the spontaneous skills of the people concerned. But this sort of pressure is a temptation for routine, 'safe' approaches. It's best restricted to emergency programs!

2.3 Design preliminaries

Most scenic design begins with careful preparations some time beforehand.

Having read any script and had a preliminary discussion with the program's director, the designer begins to form ideas about ways in which the subject can be treated. Rough sketches showing possible treatments will help the director and the rest of the production team to imagine the final effect.

The designer may have to do an appreciable amount of research before laying pencil to paper, building up details from a reference library about a particular historical style, and perhaps getting inspiration for fresh design approaches to a well-worn subject. He or she may have to check around, to see whether the particularly scenery, props, drapes, etc. envisaged for this production are actually available. It is also useful to have some idea of the costs involved. Clearly, no designer wants to sell an attractive idea to a director, only to find later that it is not practicable or is too costly.

2.4 The source of inspiration

So much depends here on the size and complexity of the production and the personalities involved. There are program directors who have very clear ideas about what they want to see on the screen, and give the designer explicit directives about the treatment they require. They may provide sketches showing the main features they want in the setting, a series of frames showing *storyboard* sketches of the main shots, reference photographs, or even rough plans. Here the designer has diplomatically to interpret and mold these ideas to suit the budget and studio space.

On the other hand, many directors expect the designer to provide them with visual inspiration, and to create a suitable environment within which the director (or the camera operators) can choose appropriate shots. In these circumstances the designer has a free hand to create the staging, even working out effective camera viewpoints and suggesting these to the director.

Planning

Production planning usually takes the form of discussion within the production team and the exchange of ideas and opinions. Although one does not exactly work through a checklist, in the end the designer does need to know the answers to a number of important issues that will affect the design approach.

2.5 Scale of production

Initially, we have to ascertain the *scale* of the staging operations.

How many settings are needed in this production? If it is a matter of only a couple of modestly sized sets there are unlikely to be any difficulties. But suppose a show calls for half a dozen or so? Then we have to consider priorities.

Rather than divide the space and the budget by the number of settings and give them equal portions, the rational approach is to find out the relative *productional value* of each. Generally speaking, money and space saved on a minor set become available to use on a major one.

If a setting is to be used for a number of scenes throughout the production it would be reasonable to apportion more of the budget and the studio space to it than a set used once for a brief gag. Which are the most important sets as far as the program's story-line or treatment are concerned? They will presumably require the most specific treatment.

Where a director is taking close shots throughout a scene, little working space may be necessary in front of a set. But if there are to be very long shots of action we may have to allow extra space so that cameras can pull back to a more distant viewpoint. Perhaps we will need to introduce masking of some kind to prevent one camera seeing another or inadvertently shooting into other sets or lights.

Where space is very limited the director may have little choice but to restrict the action or do without some splendid shots he or she had in mind. Now is the moment to work out the compromise solution. Action involving two people meeting in a sauna bath may in practice have to become a couple of flats and a bench, with wreathing dry-ice 'steam' filling the shot!

Will we be using any stock sets 'inherited' from a previous production – e.g. the 'living-room set' from last week's episode? If, for example, it had a large composite set do we really need to erect the complete set this time, or can we use just a section from it?

Are there any other productions in the studio sharing the staging area? In some production centers the floor space is divided between two consecutive shows.

There are also situations where a *permanent set* remains in position in the studio for regular daily or weekly productions, restricting the space available for other shows. Leaving it 'set and lit' saves the time and effort involved in continually striking, storing, and resetting.

2.6 Production conditions

Is the show to be *live* – i.e. transmitted or taped ('live-on-tape') as it is happening? If it is to be a 'straight-through' recording there will be little opportunity for major scene changes during the show, although a certain amount of quiet stagework may be possible at judicious moments (e.g. dropping in a cloth).

Working in 'real time' brings its staging problems, for the performers, cameras, and sound booms must be able to move around quickly, smoothly, and silently from one set-up to the next. If a camera is working at one end of the studio then has to get to the other end for its next shots this will take some time – particularly if there are any floor cables, scenery, or people in the way.

If instead the show is being *recorded in sections* the time this move takes will not be critical.

Is the show to be recorded *in sequence* ('running order') or *out of sequence* ('shooting order')? Shooting out of sequence may create *continuity* problems that have to be resolved.

Is there to be an *audience*? If there is, will they be seated in chairs on the floor, on platforms (rostra), or on special mobile audience-seating (audience rostra)? How large a group will they be?

Safety and efficient crowd-control are important whenever an audience is involved in a show. Very often, the regular position of a studio audience (near major exits) will determine where we can locate the staging. The setting(s) will usually consist of an open stage area, a series of conjoined box (three-sided) sets, or an in-line composite setting.

Will there be any *groups of people* in the set – e.g. a seated panel, standing guests? We need to anticipate their seating arrangements, how they will enter the set, the amount of room they will need, etc.

Are there any *musical groups or dancers*? These performers may have particular requirements. A pop group needs space for their activities, equipment, and electrical power. A tap dancer may want a special hard floor surface (tap mats) in order to be heard well. If a row of chorus dancers are going to perform on a raised area you would be well advised to strengthen it beforehand!

Is any special *care* required towards the performers – e.g. groups of children or access for the disabled?

By anticipating their particular difficulties and anxieties we can help to put them at their ease.

2.7 Construction

Here we have the routine questions about the *form* the scenery is going to take. We shall be looking at various types of design approach in some detail in Chapter 4.

The director may have preferences or preconceived ideas about the style and construction.

Will there be any *unusual shots* that affect the design? In a cookery program an overhead mirror may be desirable. In a drama, people may peer into a dark closet, which should be backless so the camera can watch them as they search.

Perhaps a camera has to move in very close to look at an object on a mantle-shelf, so an armchair and a rug may have to be sneaked out of the way unobtrusively as the camera dollies in.

This is also the time when we should find out whether there are to be any abnormal situations, such as a camera working from a high point (platform or tower), four-walled settings, or holes in the floor that require special design arrangements.

2.8 Action

Action can determine design. Instead of creating a set and having the action take place within it, we may need to work the other way round. Knowing the kind of action we are going to see, we build the set with the requirements of this action in mind.

A dance team may work in a tight group or have a routine in which girls jump from platforms into waiting arms below. A mime artist may sit in a chair throughout the act or dash around, making great leaps across the stage. A magician may only need a small card table or room for a performing elephant. We must be prepared (or let them know) if their routine will not be practicable.

Clearly, answers are needed to some very basic questions:

● *How is the set going to be used?* The general character of the show will dictate the design approach. Whether, for instance, we are demonstrating clock repair, how to make quilts, or modeling clothes must influence the form and character of the set.

Fundamentally, while clock repair may require only a bench and a stool, the quilting display must have extensive wall surfaces or screens to display the work. The dress models want plenty of floor space to demonstrate their attire.

- *What is the talent going to do?* This may determine how we furnish the set, props, or even its layout. If people are sitting in a bar the requirements are straightforward enough. But if the plot calls for a brawl to break out we now have a situation using breakaway tables, chairs, windows, plenty of space, and so on.
- *Where are they going?* If we know where people are likely to be moving in the set we can adjust the layout accordingly. If, for example, they are *not* going to use a staircase in the hallway of a house we can reduce cost (and transport) by installing a lightweight dummy version. If they are going to climb out of a window or batter in a door, it must be structured and supported to allow this.
- *Are the acting areas all accessible?* Suppose we decide to arrange a raised area for models to parade in a dress show. How would they get up there? Would they use decorative foreground steps or would they appear on the platform, having used hidden access stairs behind the scenery?
- *Is there sufficient space for the talent?* If, for instance, a group of musicians is to be seated on a platform they will need space to sit comfortably, with room for their instruments and music stands.
- *Will you be supplying any equipment for the performers?* A cartoonist may need a drawing board; ballet dancers, a resin tray; or the previously mentioned dress-show, a quick-change cubicle. A program on food preparation might involve a fully working cooking stove, but what equipment and utensils will the cook need?
- *Will they need any expendable items?* A cartoonist will need a supply of suitable drawing sheets, felt pens, etc. Will a cook be bringing the ingredients for the food preparation?
- *Will demonstrators be bringing equipment?* If so, will it require any particular supplies? General power is available, but what if they have to have compressed air, rapid drainage, or other special requirements (e.g. three-phase power)? Will their demonstration make a mess or be likely to damage the studio floor? Will it take long to set up and disassemble?
- *Will performers need any accessories or support material?* Perhaps they will require artwork, graphics, models, maps, or similar support material in the course of the action.

  In a play, action props are often necessary (e.g. a telescope with which to scan the horizon, a poker to stir a fire). Action may require an actor to drink or smoke, or pick a flower, or read from a book (which may have script pages pasted within it).
- *Does the set require any special built-in features?* A script may call for a bell-pull beside a front entrance; a sliding observation

panel in the door of a gambling den; or a wall-safe in which to place a document.

The questions that arise will obviously depend on the kind of show you are dealing with. But these are typical reminders of the need for forethought.

2.9 Special effects

Special effects really come into three groups:

● Those organized by the designer (e.g. snow, rain),
● Those needing the services of specialists for the sake of safety (fire, explosions, gunfire),
● Electronic effects such as chroma key, which needs special design arrangements.

For the first two, the designer may need to provide protective sheeting for the floor:

● To avoid its being damaged,
● To restrict wreckage debris, or
● To prevent water seepage.

Sometimes toughened glass panels will be needed to protect a camera from thrown water or missiles!

Electronic effects (chroma key) may need not only blue backdrops but similarly colored platforms, steps, or risers/blocks to suit the action. (See Chapter 8.)

Any kind of special effect is best planned well ahead in detail with the specialists concerned.

2.10 Graphics

In some organizations graphics are the responsibility of a separate group of specialists. In others the designer will also prepare or design the graphics used in a production.

Graphics can provide titling, decorative and pictorial illustrations, explanatory charts, maps, graphs, diagrams, etc. They can take many forms, including:

● Camera graphics and title cards, supported on an easel in front of the camera,
● Projected graphics displayed on screens in a setting (front or rear projected) or on an in-shot picture monitor,
● Graphics displayed within the set – wall maps, desk charts, etc.,
● Free-standing panels with large painted or photographic graphics,
● Graphics as scenic features – a wide range of applications, including titles on books, illustrations stuck into books, signs, posters, labels, logos, hanging cut-outs (e.g. lettering in plywood or styrofoam), etc.,

Figure 2.1 Preparations
Planning – the overlay rough. By
drawing a scale plan of each setting
on a tracing overlay you can readjust
positions for optimum camerawork,
lighting, and sound treatment.

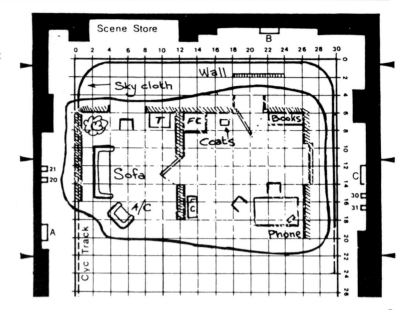

Planning – the sketch. Many people
have difficulty in envisioning from
plans and elevations what a proposed
setting is going to look like. A rough
sketch can help to coordinate ideas
and avoid misunderstandings.

- Three-dimensional graphics for demonstrations (e.g. showing
  an eye in cross-section), solid tiles, models of equipment,
  miniatures for use in drama productions (e.g. showing landscapes, buildings),
- Graphics inserts within the production (from slides, computer,
  etc.).

Exactly which of these are created, organized, or constructed by
the designer and assistants will vary with production groups. But
the designer certainly needs to be closely concerned with all
graphics relating to a show.

2.11 The scale plan

So much for initial discussions and concepts. Even the most atmospheric sketches have eventually to be turned into timber and paint.

Using a drafting ruler with a scale of ¼ in to 1 ft (or 2 cm = 1 m; 1:50), the designer draws a scale *plan* view of each proposed setting together with typical furniture on a series of *overlays* (plain or squared tracing paper).

Only by reliable drawing at this stage can one estimate true proportions and assess how much room is going to be needed. Fortunately, scale drawing becomes second nature after a while. It is not enough to *guess* that there is enough space for a group of people. It can prove very embarrassing to discover in the studio that there isn't! Or to find that someone cannot walk between a settee and a table, because everything is too crowded together. Never assume that it will be 'alright on the day'.

It is good practice to have the dimensions of all stock items listed, with a scale outline stencil for standard size items (Table 2.1). Otherwise it is wise to measure furniture beforehand to ensure that there are no last-minute surprises!

Table 2.1   Typical measurements

Furniture				
Tables:	4 ft × 2 ft 6 in;	2 ft × 2 ft 6 in;	1 ft 6 in × 1 ft 6 in	
	1.22 m × 0.75 m;	0.61 mm × 0.75 m;	0.46 m × 0.46 m	
Chair:	1 ft 6 in × 1 ft 3 in	/	0.46 m × 0.39 m	
Piano:	Upright	4 ft 6 in × 2 ft 3 in	/	1.37 m × 0.68 m
	Grand	5 ft × 6 ft 6 in	/	1.5 m × 1.98 m
	Baby grand	5 ft × 5 ft 3 in	/	1.5 m × 1.9 m

Studio equipment			
Camera mounting (pedestal, wheeled tripod)	5 ft	/	1.52 m diameter.
Picture monitor (on wheeled stand)	3 ft × 2 ft	/	0.914 m × 0.6 m
Loudspeaker (on wheeled stand)	2 ft × 2 ft 6 in	/	0.6 m × 0.75 m
Sound boom base	5 ft × 3 ft 6 in	/	1.5 m × 1.06 m

2.12 The studio plan

The next stage is to take these preliminary overlay plans of the set and arrange them on a blank copy of the *studio plan* (*studio plot*), taping them in possible positions to form a rough plan.

The studio plan is a standard printed scale bird's-eye view of the entire studio (again, ¼ in to 1 ft; or 2 cm = 1 m; 1:50).

It shows a great deal of standard detail:

● All studio dimensions,
● Studio entrances – access to scenery storage; storerooms; doors to make-up and to quick-change rooms; stairways to the control room; stairways to walkways, and the studio grid,
● Details of various available facilities located along the walls: e.g. technical supplies, cable outlets (lighting, sound, cameras, electrical supplies, water, etc.),

Figure 2.2 The studio plan
A standard printed plan of the studio
shows the staging area available,
with various features and facilities. A
typical metric scale of 1:50 (2 cm =
1 m) is replacing the widely used ¼ in
= 1 ft scale.

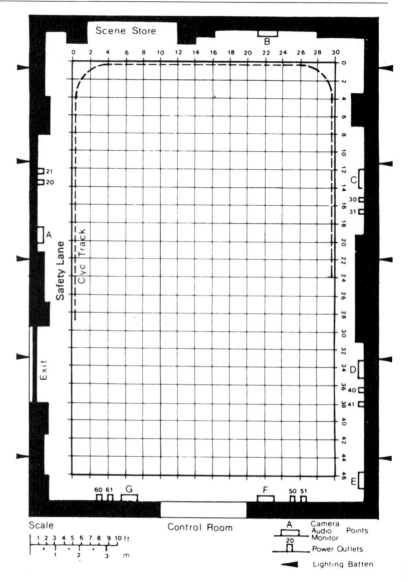

● Rigging facilities, hoists (scenic, and lighting), any stacking
areas, cyclorama tracks.

Most of the studio plan is taken up with a squared *staging area*
(*setting area*) within which you can position the settings. Numbers
along two of its edges correspond to a regular series of marks
(footage marks) painted along the studio walls. These help to
locate scenery accurately on the studio floor during setting.

Studio plans usually have small markers, showing where overhead
lighting battens (barrels) are located. These, too, are numbered,
and provide an extremely useful guide for exact floor location.

A broken line along the edge of the staging area shows where the
cyclorama or *cyc track* is available.

2.13 Safety lanes

Studios easily become congested and exits blocked. So it is good practice to have a *safety lane* or *fire lane* (e.g. 3 ft or 1 m) wide around the staging area (shown as a white border on the studio plan) in studios over 25 ft (7.5 m) wide.

This provides an escape route in case of any emergency. Without such precautions even quite a minor fire or power failure can become a disaster in a crowded studio. Nothing should be allowed to jut into or be stored in this safety zone. Any cables (cameras, lighting, sound) are best covered over with lightweight contoured boards so that people will not trip over them. Otherwise cables should be suspended. The safety lane also ensures that there is always access to the various wall supplies – a particular advantage compared with studios where scenery and equipment clutter the studio walls.

2.14 Elevations

Elevations show *side-views* of all the scenery to the same scale as the plan. The drawings include details of all vertical planes, walls, doors, windows, etc. and give information about their surface finish (e.g. moldings, painting, wallpaper).

Elevations not only guide the construction and decoration of the setting but help us to imagine what the actual staging will look like in three dimensions in the studio.

Where specific detail is needed (e.g. details of a decorative design for a scenic artist) this may be given on separate, larger-scale elevations (e.g. 20:1: 5 cm = 1 m).

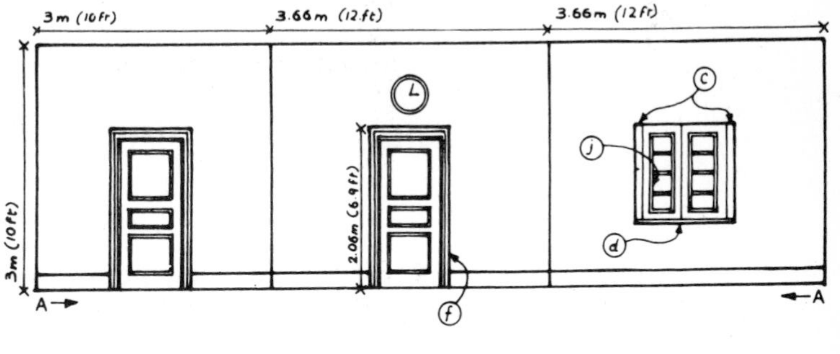

Figure 2.3 Elevations
A scale side-view of the settings, showing dimensions, detail, and treatment for scenery (normally to the same scale as the studio plan). Explanatory notes are written alongside features to guide construction, painting, carpentry, etc.; to identify stock units; and to indicate surface treatment, etc. (e.g. walls painted 'Dark Stone', windows void). Additional design points for carpenters, painters, and scenic artists are identified with lettered circles (e.g. (d) Fix plastic molding No. 27 here).
Extra detailed information on specific features may be shown on separate large-scale elevations.

2.15 Scale model

If these scale elevations are stuck onto thin card, cut out and attached to their respective studio plan they provide a simple *scale model* of the scene. Extra features (e.g. columns, stairs) can be added if necessary. This is a particularly useful idea whenever the staging is at all complex, for it helps everyone (director, specialists, lighting, cameras, sound, and staging crew) to imagine the final result. Using a miniature viewfinder one can even see the sort of shots possible from various camera positions.

2.16 The preliminary plan

Armed with rough plans, studio layout, and the sketches (together with a card model perhaps), the designer again meets the director.

Now the director has a scenic framework for the production, and begins to anticipate shots, to think out treatment:

The staging model
The card model gives a clear idea of the layout and extent of the project. It helps the production team to visualize situations and to plan accurately.

Director: 'As you know, this explorer is going to tell us about her travels. We could begin the scene with her coming into the room from the sunny garden.'
Designer: 'It was only going to be a painted drop outside the french doors [french windows], but if you want some garden outside, we can move this set over, and make this other one smaller.'
Director: No, let's keep the rooms this size; she has brought many interesting articles back with her. Instead, I can begin with her sitting writing at a desk in place of the round table shown here. If we make it "evening" we can keep the drapes closed and you won't need a backdrop. That will leave more room for cameras in the next-door set. And we can have several table lamps, and a standard lamp lit. We can develop a cosy welcoming atmosphere.'

They probably go over these ideas, modifying, improving and rationalizing, and the designer adjusts the rough plan as necessary. After the meeting a preliminary working plan is drawn.

2.17 The production planning meeting

In the long run, good planning saves time, money, effort... and tempers. An early meeting of the principals of the production

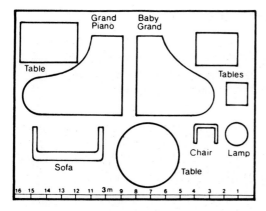

Figure 2.4 Equipment stencil
Scale stencils can be used to mark standard-sized furniture and equipment on the floor plan.

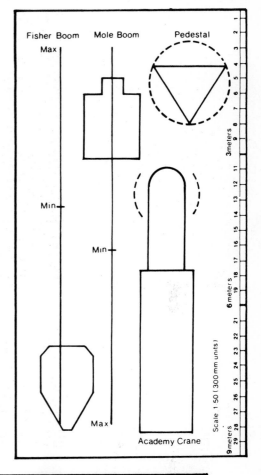

Figure 2.5 Staging plan
This master plan of the studio shows all settings with their major furniture and dressings, together with additional scenic features, floor treatment, etc. From the staging plan other specialist plans are developed (camera plan, lighting plot).

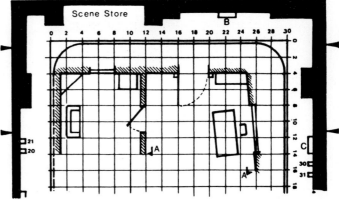

team is an essential preliminary for most productions. Here the proposed working plans are introduced to the specialists responsible for technical facilities, lighting, sound, costume, make-up, graphics, and special effects.

For the average show this is a straightforward coordination exercise. The director explains what the show is all about and how

Figure 2.6 Camera plan
The main working positions of each camera (1A, 1B, 1C, etc.) and sound boom (A1, A2, B1, B2) are marked on the staging plan to provide the 'Camera plan'.

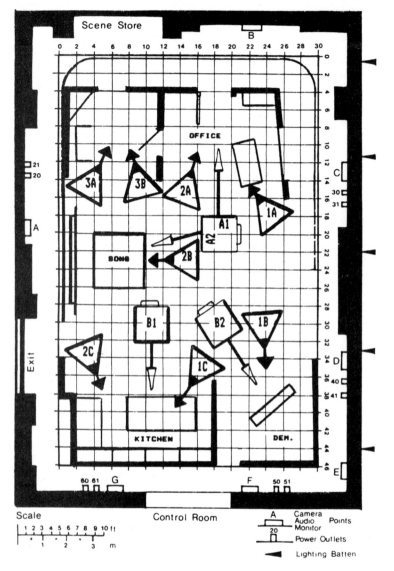

he or she expects to shoot it. The designer talks about the setting, its features, wall finish, colors, and so on, so that everyone can visualize the treatment.

The group discuss any potential problems they can see, and, if necessary, the staging or production treatment are modified. Improvements made at this stage help to avoid hang-ups and wasted time during camera rehearsals. With this information the specialists disperse, to organize their own particular contributions.

The designer then produces a final staging plan, incorporating any changes and including accurate details of:

● Each setting (flats, doors, windows, platforms, stairs, or arches) and its furniture, large props, drapes, etc.,

● Additional scenic features (trees and bushes, statuary, street furniture, etc.),
● Floor treatment (painting, carpets, etc.).

To this master plan the director adds outlines showing the main camera and sound-boom positions for each set. (This *camera plan* guides the camera and sound crew during rehearsals as well as forming the basis for a *lighting plot*.)

A series of very detailed *furniture/prop plots* may also be prepared (one for each set) to assist in set dressing and to show any furniture moves or alterations that are to be made during the course of the show.

2.18 Major productions

Where we are dealing with a sizeable production in a large studio careful anticipatory organization is essential. Otherwise we could have the lighting crew walking over a newly painted studio floor; or find that part of the scenery has to be refitted and upsets the lighting; or the wrong drapes have arrived; or furniture has been stored in the way of a camera; or a pool is leaking... or the thousand and one problems that can beset a busy studio!

As well as the main production meeting the director may have a series of separate meetings with individual specialists in the team: consultations on details of the costume/wardrobe performers will wear and approving music or recorded sound effects.

The designer and the lighting director will need to get together to consolidate their visual treatment, for lighting and scenic design are closely allied (see Chapter 12).

Now the designer's work is increasing daily. Various departments in the organization require information and guidance. Contracts and schedules have to be arranged for the construction of scenery. Detailed drawings and references will be needed by carpenters, painters, scenic artists, and kindred trades who are making or refurbishing the scenery. Properties have to be located, selected, and hired. Transport will be needed. Special effects (e.g. rain outside a window) need to be organized. Stagehand crews must be alerted. There can also be those endless additional chores concerned with safety, union arrangements, labor requirements, man hours involved, insurance, and so on.

2.19 Pre-studio rehearsals

Few TV organizations can afford the luxury of extensive rehearsals in the studio. Studio time is expensive and the facilities may be required for other productions.

However, for a complex production, such as a soap opera or drama, the director needs to *block out* (arrange) performers' positions, grouping, and action to suit the production treatment. So this is done away from the TV studio, in public halls, rehearsal rooms, or similar locations, some time before the actual studio date.

Pre-studio rehearsals
In the rehearsal hall full-size outlines
of settings are taped to the floor.
Poles in stands show major
architectural features and help to give
a sense of dimension. Stand-in
chairs, benches, and tables provide a
mock-up of the actual furnishings to
be used by the actors.

Here the director rehearses the show in sections: the cast becomes familiar with their lines, practising performance, moves, and business until the entire show runs smoothly, ready for its studio debut.

These *pre-rehearsals* are carried out in a full-scale mock-up of the settings. Chalk lines or colored tape stuck to the floor show, in outline, the main features of the sets (walls, doorways, arches, fireplaces, stairs, etc.). Vertical poles or chairs mark the limits of each room, and help to give a sense of dimension. Dummy doors or frames can be used to simulate the real thing. Substitute furniture and properties (e.g. telephones, tableware) help the actors to become familiar with their surroundings.

Standing at each camera position (perhaps using a small viewfinder), the director can adjust the action and positions to suit the anticipated shots.

When pre-rehearsals appear to have reached a final state, a *technical walkthrough* (*tech run*) is called, attended by the specialists concerned with the technical operations (lighting, cameras, sound), make-up and costume, who check and anticipate problems while envisaging camera and sound-boom treatment.

It is at this stage that the director may discover that certain unexpected changes are needed in the setting: an extra flat perhaps, where he or she is likely to shoot past the edge of the setting in a cross-shot. A visit by the designer helps to smooth out such problems before they arise.

At this time the designer will be checking on the workshops that are constructing the scenery, making sure that things are working out, offering advice, and confirming that everything is running to schedule.

Now the final *staging plan* (*floor plan*, *ground plan*, *setting plan*) can be prepared and issued to various groups responsible for the studio operations and staging.

2.20 The studio setting period

Arrangements for erecting the settings in the studio vary with the size of the production and local practice:

1. *Immediately before* the camera rehearsal (e.g. early morning setting),
2. *The day before* camera rehearsal,
3. *The night before* the camera rehearsals ('overnight setting').

Each arrangement has its advantages, but clearly, the more time there is to complete the job, the better.

During the *setting period* the designer is extremely preoccupied, as the staging begins to take shape:

● Guiding the stage hands who are building the sets,
● Checking that the sets are accurately located at the planned floor positions ('on their marks'),
● Checking the condition of the scenery (i.e. no visible damage or dirtying during transport from storage),
● Seeing that no items are missing,
● Supervising the set *dressing* (i.e. positioning drapes, furniture, ornaments, wall decorations, flowers, and the general bric-à-brac that clothes the scene),
● Checking the safety of the structures (i.e. sufficient bracing, ample suspension arrangements),
● Looking out for any unforeseen problems, obstructions, for cameras, lighting, sound,
● Guiding scenic artists and others who are involved in floor treatment, and last-minute touch-up of paintwork, walls, disguising the joins between flats, etc.,
● Adding those indefinable finishing touches to the scene that give it a coordinated, lived-in look (e.g. adjusting the hang of the drapes, the position of a vase, smoothing out a table covering, distributing some magazines on a side-table).

2.21 Lighting the setting

Fundamentally, once the lighting director has devised the *lighting plot* (after planning meetings and any pre-studio rehearsals) the next stages are:

1. Rigging the lamps,
2. Setting the lamps,
3. Final adjustments, or changes.

As you will have realized by now, the people designing and lighting the show could all too easily frustrate each others' efforts.

The designer might provide a low ceiling that prevents the set from being lit! Or the lighting might entirely destroy the impression of distance outside a window. There needs to be similar cooperation during the setting period.

2.22 Rigging the lamps

Probably the best arrangement is to complete the main *lighting rigging* while the studio floor is empty – *before* the setting period.

This method allows all the overhead lamps to be hung in their plotted positions on the *battens/barrels/lighting grid* more quickly, safely, and without hassle. In many studios, suspended lamps can be lowered to around chest height, cabled to their outlets, diffusers and color gels added, and rough-set, avoiding the restrictions of rigging from ladders/treads. When this has been done lighting is raised out of the way and the scenery can be erected. (Lamps can be pulled down to their working height after the set has been built.)

Any lamps that are to be fitted to floor stands or to rest on the ground (e.g. lighting a background) can be added after the setting is complete. It is essential, of course, that the sets are subsequently built *exactly on their planned floor positions*, or the lighting rig will not match the sets!

If a set is built *before* lamps have been positioned this usually prevents lighting battens from being lowered. Consequently, all hung lamps have to be added, moved, removed, or plugged while standing on high steps. This can be a very precarious exercise in a crowded set, whether you use folding ladders or wheeled-base types (which are safer but clumsier). The same problem arises, of course, if the lamps are suspended from a fixed lighting grid.

Close liaison between the crews lighting and setting the show is essential.

Where, for example, scenery is high or there are overhanging pieces (e.g. ceilings, large arches, or tree branches) these can *prevent any lighting barrel or lamp in that area being used at all*, for they are now out of reach! Given cooperation, though, it is quite practicable for setting and lighting to take place at the same time, to mutual advantage.

2.23 Camera rehearsals

The setting is built and dressed and the lighting has been completed. Now the *camera rehearsal* begins.

Production activities are really divided between two major areas: the studio itself and the nearby *production control room*, which is the nerve center from which the director controls operations.

The director sits in front of a number of *picture monitors*. These preview pictures continuously show the separate outputs of all the cameras – whether they are on-shot or not. Other monitors show any additional picture sources (videotape, film, slides).

While watching these different shots the director can use the *production switcher* (*vision mixer*) to select the particular camera required at that moment. This selected picture is switched 'on-air', and appears as the *studio output* on a *master monitor* (*line, main channel, transmission*). When the recording session is scheduled, this video, and its separate audio channel, will be routed to the videotape recording system.

The director in the control room communicates with the production team through an *intercom* (*talkback*) *system*. In the studio the crew (cameras, sound, lighting, stage crew) follow instructions on earphones – unheard by the performers or studio microphones.

Also on the studio floor the busy *floor manager* (*FM*) is following the director's intercom instructions: guiding and cueing performers, slightly adjusting furniture positions to suit shots, and generally ensuring the smooth running of studio activities.

2.24 The designer during rehearsal

Rehearsals give the designer an opportunity to catch and correct any unsatisfactory features in the design: to detect whether anything has gone wrong or not worked as expected; or to alter things to suit changes the director has now made in the camerawork or the action.

Figure 2.7 Staging distractions
Various accidental effects can distract the audience.
 1. Puzzling object intruding into the shot.
 2. Cable in shot.
 3. Damaged flat (e.g. torn or dirty).
 4. Shadow of someone out of shot.
 5. Wall-picture not straight.
 6. Reflected light in picture glass.
 7. Table picture reflecting camera.
 8. Multiple wall-shadows around lamp.
 9. Distracting hot spot.
 10. Wall mirror creates accidental 'halo'.
 11. Wrinkle visible in wallpaper.
 12. Camera is overshooting the set.
 13. Obtrusive foreground prop.

As far as the designer is concerned, the camera rehearsal period is an important opportunity to:

● See exactly which shots the director is going to use,
● Check pictures on preview, to confirm that the effect is as anticipated (i.e. tonal relationships, unity of design, ambiance, etc.),
● Discover whether there are any design defects (e.g. an overbright tablecloth) or features needing correction (e.g. a wall that shakes when a door opens, a wrinkled skycloth),
● Check for floor clutter: standby scenery, unused furniture, properties, rugs, wrappings, treads, etc. getting in the way of

cameras or performers (the floor manager and an assistant will usually be keeping a watchful eye on this situation,

● Consider possible improvements in the set-dressing or the overall scenic effect,

● Devise solutions to those odd unanticipated staging problems that inevitably arise (e.g. a decorative plant 'growing out of someone's head'),

● Generally liaise with the director, lighting director, cameras, sound, wardrobe, special effects, etc.

First rehearsals, in particular, are an essential opportunity for the designer to check, correct, and improve. He or she is as likely to be 'on the floor', organizing and supervising, as in the production control room watching rehearsal pictures.

The designer lists any changes that seem necessary and makes these alterations when there is an opportunity – personally, an assistant, or the scenic crew. Much depends on the way the show is organized for rehearsals and recordings. Some changes may be made quietly, during rehearsal, when cameras are shooting another set.

Although it may only take a moment to put a lampshade straight in a wall fitting or to reposition a vase, other alterations can require much time and effort. It could, for example, need a substantial break in rehearsal (e.g. a meal period) to modify a setting, repaint a floor design, or investigate why a room door keeps sticking. If some foliage looked unconvincing or an item has been broken accidentally it may take some time to find a substitute.

It is important that the alterations the designer makes do not inadvertently upset some other aspect of the production which could remain undiscovered until the next rehearsal – or even the videotaping session!

Let us look at the sort of things that can happen.

> Seeing shots on the monitors, the designer decides that part of the painted backing outside a window looks unrealistic, so positions a large bush to hide that section. The result is successful. But unfortunately this bush now obscures a lamp (not lit at that stage) that is going to provide 'moonlight' in a later scene.
>
> During a meal break the busy designer scatters tanbark over the bare-looking studio floor. The result is great.... but now a camera operator slips when pushing a dolly into position!
>
> A chandelier was barely visible, so the designer has it lowered. Director and designer are delighted... but the boom operator can no longer stretch the sound boom arm into the set to pick up the action!

To be fair, things also happen the other way round! An excellent design feature can be ruined by the wrong lighting or lost altogether because the camera operator reframes the shot. Inappropriate sound can destroy a pictorial illusion. Ill-chosen lighting can turn the most imaginative settings into crude-looking travesties.

Certainly teamwork is essential.

Table 2.2   Problems discovered during camera rehearsal

Watching shots during rehearsal you may discover features that need correction.

Shooting off	● Camera sees past setting into studio: at the edge of the setting; over the setting; through windows or doors.

Hot spots	● Small areas of setting appear overbright.
	● Surface is too light,
	● Tonal contrast is too high,
	● Glossy surface finish (specular reflections of lamps),
	● Localized overlighting:
	    Overbright 'spotty' lamp;
	    Patchy lighting;
	    Lamps 'doubling' in that area;
	● Picture is overexposed.

Surface appears too dark	● Insufficiently lit, ● Tones are too dark, ● Tonal contrast is too high, ● Area is in shadow, ● Picture is underexposed.
Distractions	● Reflections (e.g. of cameras, lamps, people), ● Lopsided wall pictures, lamp shades, ● Flickering candles (trim the wicks), ● Cables in shot (e.g. floor lamps).
Detail is too prominent, too faint, unclear	● In wall treatment, ● In backings.
Setting appears too empty	● Insufficiently furnished, ● Furniture is too dispersed, ● Insufficient items in middle distance, ● High camera emphasizes open areas, ● Unrelieved light tones can result in an empty, 'open' look, ● Absence of foreground subjects.
Setting appears too crowded/fussy	● Overfurnished with large pieces, ● Furniture is too crowded, ● Too many items in middle distance, ● Low camera emphasizes foreground areas, ● Absence of foreground subjects, ● Unrelieved dark tones can produce a 'closed' look.
Condition of setting	● Damaged walls/cyc cloth (dirty, fingermarks, tears, blemishes), ● Wrinkles/folds visible (in backdrops, cyc), ● Gaps visible between flats, ● Unstable wall, door, fence, handrail, etc., ● Sticking door, casement window, etc., ● Floor decoration is damaged, worn, unconvincing, ● Drapes or cyclorama are damaged, badly hung, creased, wrinkled, too long/short, ● Floor joins are overprominent, distracting (where cyc, backdrop, or flat joins floor), ● Scenic supports are visible.

Table 2.2 *continued*

Unconvincing effect	• Backdrop (photo, painted) tones, drawing, perspective unsatisfactory, not level, unstable, • Poorly painted wood, rock, brick, metal effects, • Floor painting (e.g. cobbles) appears crude in close shots, shining in backlight, • Unrealistic fire in fireplace, campfire, • Unrealistic sound from action on scenic 'stone, rock, brick, paving, stairs', • Insufficient foliage in some exteriors, • Dead-looking flowers, grass, foliage unconvincing.
Properties	• Inappropriate, too many, too few, look too 'arranged', • Disproportionate (too big, too small, not seen), • Too prominent (too light-toned or reflective, overlit, wrong color), • 'New' items appear damaged; worn out, used-looking, • Hanging light fittings too low or too high for shots (e.g. chandelier).
Furniture	• Inappropriate style, • Uncoordinated styles, • Overprominent, • Unstable, • Too low or too high, • Too heavy to move easily, • Unsatisfactory surface tones or finish, • Uncomfortable for performers, • Produces unattractive shots of people.
Water effects	• Unconvincing effect (at the edge of a 'natural pool', simulated 'wet surfaces'), • Leakage hazards!

Methods of production

2.25 'Live' and taped production

If a production is live there are no opportunities for retakes. Everything has to work properly first time.

In some cases there may be a temptation to simplify the live production to reduce the likelihood of things going wrong, but few directors are willing to reduce their shows to the mundane just to play safe. Instead, it is up to the production team to anticipate, to rely on their expertise, and to coordinate their efforts... and get through.

2.26 No rehearsal

TV rehearsals and recordings can be organized in several different ways. The method the director uses can have a considerable bearing on the designer's opportunities and difficulties.

In the worst situation there is no camera rehearsal! After preliminary discussion the set is built, dressed, and lit. The director gives the crew a brief outline of the expected action (cameras, sound, lighting, switcher operator) and the unrehearsed production is then transmitted 'live' (as it happens) or videotaped without editing ('live on tape').

Everything relies on the experience, skill, anticipation of the production team, and a large element of good luck. The designer has no opportunity to alter anything! The unchecked staging has to work – and any defects accepted.

Even when faced with a situation that cannot be rehearsed (e.g. insufficient time, talent has not yet arrived), it is far better to set up typical shots beforehand, looking at performers or stand-ins in main action positions (e.g. sitting at tables, standing on the pre-arranged floor marks performers will use during the show). In this way, you can check the setting, lighting, and shots, and correct them as necessary.

2.27 Stop–start rehearsal

In this regularly used method the director rehearses the show, in the order in which it will be transmitted/recorded (i.e. 'shooting order' is in 'running order'). The camera rehearsal is stopped whenever corrections or improvements are needed. There is no complete continuous 'run-through' rehearsal.

The production is then transmitted or recorded 'live on tape' at the scheduled time. If taped, any unsuccessful parts or improvements may be retaken and edited into the videotaped program.

Here the designer seeks to correct problems as they arise, during any breaks in rehearsal, or before taping is scheduled ('transmission time').

2.28 Stop–start and dress rehearsals

The show is rehearsed in sections as before. Then after a pause during which the director gives notes to performers and crew, the entire production is rehearsed again, straight through without any stops ('dress rehearsal'). This way, everyone gets an accurate idea of continuity and timing.

Finally, the show is performed straight through, as it is taped or transmitted. There may be some retakes of any unsatisfactory parts afterwards (e.g. to correct a bad shot or poor sound). These are edited into the final version.

This method gives the designer ample time to improve results progressively throughout rehearsals until they reach the optimum for the eventual recording.

Any alterations can be made while the cameras are rehearsing in another set or during breaks that arise during rehearsal and meal breaks.

Where a large production is in the studio for several days a set that has been 'rehearsed and taped' can be removed overnight ('struck') and a new set erected in its place for the next day's scenes. Overnight resetting periods may provide further opportunities to readjust existing sets.

2.29 'Rehearse/record'

In this approach the production is tackled section by section or scene by scene. Each segment is rehearsed and then immediately recorded. Sections may be shot out of order and edited together later into their final sequence.

So instead of moving from one setting to another the director may shoot all the scenes in, for example, the inn, one after another, irrespective of where they come in the story line, then go on to another setting.

At first sight this may look like regular film-making practice, but in fact it leads to many compromises due to tight time schedules. Instead of having the opportunity to discover a lighting or staging defect on camera and then correct it while the crew is rehearsing the next scene, problems have to be rectified immediately, as the director is eager to take (record) the scene and press on to the next.

2.30 Retakes and continuity

Whenever an action sequence or a scene is unsuccessful during recording the obvious thing is to shoot it again immediately. But there are situations where this is not practicable: for example, where the setting becomes damaged or even destroyed in the course of the action (a fire, an explosion, a gunfight, wrecking, or thrown water).

You can anticipate retakes, and have substitutes or identical replacements available in case they are needed. Otherwise it will be necessary to tidy up and reuse existing items, replacing them in their original positions.

Most drama productions involve action – people change their positions, things get moved around, food and drink are consumed. With the passage of time we would expect a calendar in a setting to move on, flowers to wither, people to grow older over the years, and so on.

So we need to keep an eye on the apparent passage of time in settings – the *continuity*. Otherwise there is the danger that the audience will notice that the hero has been wearing the same shirt over several years; has spectacles in one shot but not in the next; or is apparently dry after coming in from a storm. Amusing, but distracting!

It is very easy for continuity errors to arise if the director is shooting scenes *out of order* or is *retaking action* in a scene where changes have taken place during the action (e.g. finished eating the food on the table or a candle has burned down).

The floor manager and assistants will probably check on such routine matters as 'Was the fire lit in this scene? Were the drapes open or closed? Was she smoking? Hadn't he moved that chair by this time? Shouldn't the table lamps be on?' But the designer will ensure that the appropriate props are at hand, and deal with any major scenic changes (e.g. seasonal variations, weather effects, or rebuilding 'collapsed' structures).

There are some regular effects, such as snow and rain, that need careful organization to avoid wasting a considerable amount of studio rehearsal time. Also, of course, it is always easier to shoot an 'exterior' setting showing a 'fine sunny day' and later shoot scenes or the same location in rain or snow than it is to do the reverse!

2.31 Clearing the studio

The videotaping session is completed and the floor manager has announced that the studio is now 'cleared'.

The cameras on their mountings are moved to a storage area and their cables tidied away. The sound equipment (microphones, booms, cables, and loudspeakers) is similarly stored. Other units such as floor picture monitors are removed. The lighting crew remove any floor lamps and their cables.

Now the process of *striking* the settings can begin. A good crew of stagehands does this quickly and efficiently. Much of the scenery will be used again in one form or another. Some may have been hired and has to be returned undamaged. Drapes need to be detached and folded. Furniture is removed and stored. Properties are collected together. Floors have to be cleared and cleaned.

Within a surprisingly short time the studio is empty, and no traces remain of the concentrated effort... except a videotaped record of hours, weeks, or months of work. If it was a live production there may not even be that!

For the designer, though, there may still be the processes of sorting, classifying, and storing materials, scenic units, properties, etc., so that they are readily available for the next production. Some items may be junked. For example, there is little point in using valuable storage space for a mammoth sign announcing 'JOE'S PLACE' unless we can re-use it in another episode in the near future. Perhaps it can be dismantled and its panels refurbished for another show.

Chapter 3

Scenic construction

Most television settings are devised by connecting together a series of more or less standard component parts. In this chapter we shall look at how these units are made and what they can do.

Figure 3.1 The cyclorama

Curved cyclorama. A shallow C-shaped hung cloth background, used on large staging areas, to produce a spacious or panoramic effect.

Wrapround cyclorama. Form of cyc widely used in TV, video and photographic studios. Corners should be gently curved (e.g. 9 ft or 2.7 m radius minimum).

The cyclorama

3.1 The 'cyc'

Even the smallest studio can make use of the *cyclorama* – or *cyc* as it is usually called (pronounced 'sike'). This is simply a suspended cloth hung from a straight or curved track to form a background along two or more walls of the studio.

3.2 Materials

Various materials are used for the cloth cyc, including canvas, muslin, duck (linen or cotton cloth), filled gauze, shark's-tooth scrim, felt, and even velours. Which is most suitable will depend on your particular purpose.

Some materials are more durable than others. Some are delicate and easily creased, others are pretty rugged. Some shrink badly, others get dusty or grimy. While scrim is relatively cheap and expendable, velours, with their velvet-like nap, are very costly and long lasting.

3.3 Size

The cyc itself can be anything from 9 ft (2.74 m) to 20 ft (6.08 m) high, depending on the size of the studio. It may be from 20 to 60 ft long (6.08–18.25 m). If there are several cycs round a studio, gaps or overlaps will be needed to provide safety exits.

3.4 Hanging the cyc

The cyc usually hangs at the edge of the staging area, leaving access along the safety lane (fire lane) which is located around the walls of the studio.

It may be left hanging in position, or kept stored and hung when it is needed. You can suspend the cyc by tying its upper edge to a series of hung wooden battens or tubular pipes. But the most flexible system is undoubtedly the *cyc track*, *curtain track*, or *cyc rail*.

This consists of one or more permanent rails, usually suspended from the ceiling grid or supported at the height of the studio gantry/walkway. Runners, which move freely along the rail, are hooked into eyelets in the upper edge of the cloth cyc.

With this arrangement you can leave the cloth cyc permanently suspended. To store it out of the way when it is not wanted, just draw the cloth back along the rail, bunching it to an unused part of the rail. Later, pull it to where it is required and stretch out a sufficient amount.

The cyclorama can be used hung in folds or pleats. But for most applications it is stretched taut by wrapping the lower edge round a batten or pipe or bottom-folded and weighed down.

3.5 Colors

A whole range of colors is used for cycloramas, including off-white (60% reflectance), light gray, mid-gray, dark gray, black, light blue, dark blue, and blue (cobalt) or green for chroma key effects. Although you could, of course, use any other colors for the cyc, you may not find them as adaptable as the usual range.

If the studio is fitted with a multirail cyc track it is possible to hang a selection of cloth cycs (e.g. black, light blue, off-white gauze) and select them as needed.

3.6 Paper cycloramas

In a small studio you can use *seamless paper* to form a cyc quite economicaly. The paper comes in rolls about 36 ft (11 m) long and 9 ft (2.7 m) wide. Available in a number of colors and tones, it can be stapled to a run of flats or suspended at one end and draped down and along the floor, without any *floor join*.

Figure 3.2 Paper cycloramas

Background paper may be hung and draped along the floor.

Unfortunately, seamless paper has its disadvantages. It is easily marked, which is fine if you want to decorate it with background patterns but too liable to show footmarks and scuffing. It takes several overlapping sheets to cover a wide area, and unless their edges are stuck together (e.g. with double-sided adhesive tape) joins are easily torn.

You may find that you have lighting problems with seamless paper, as light bounces off its smooth surface. This can make it appear noticeably lighter from some directions than others, and it can be difficult to get really dark background tones due to light scatter.

3.7 Hardwall cycloramas

Permanently installed *hardwall* or *board cycs* are used in some studios, at one end of the staging area. These are made of plywood or prepared board and have certain advantages. You will certainly

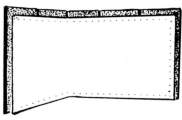

Or stapled to a run of flats as a continuous background.

get none of the wrinkles, tears, or stretching difficulties that can plague cloth cycs! You can attach quite large lightweight decorative features to a board cyc.

Its surface is normally painted in an even, mid-gray tone. Because extremely smooth finishes show hot spots from lamps, the hardwall/board cyc is best roughened slightly with a sawdust coating.

It is possible to vary the apparent tone of a mid-gray cyc, from near-black to brilliant white, simply by adjusting the overall lighting intensity – provided that other lighting nearby does not spill onto it. For a dead black background, though, it may be necessary to hang a black cloth over the hardboard cyc temporarily.

At times it can be inhibiting to have a permanent cyc in the staging area – whether you need it or not. But as it can be incorporated into many forms of setting, in practice this does not prove too limiting.

However, the hardwall cyc can adversely alter sound quality. Its hard slightly curved surface can produce disturbing sound coloration at times, as sound waves rebound from it. This is particularly noticeable if you are staging 'exterior' scenes, when this hard, reverberant sound will seem unnatural.

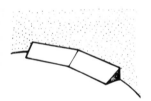

Figure 3.3 The floor join

Concave cove. Formed from plywood, fiber-glass, or plastic sheet on a timber framework. The merging cove/ground cove provides a curved plane between the floor and the cyc background to prevent any abrupt join being visible.

Straight cove. A similar simpler device, using a flat sloping plane. Less effective, as it tends to be overbright, reflecting suspended cyc lighting.

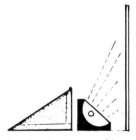

Cyc lighting. A row of lamps may be hidden behind the cover to illuminate the cyc from below (see Figure 12.9).

Ground rows

3.8 The floor join

Normally, the point at which the cyc and the floor meet appears in the picture as a horizontal line, however carefully the bottom of the cyc is rolled. This join may not matter; but at times it can be quite distracting.

There are several ways of overcoming this situation.

You could drape the background cloth so that it continues along the floor, as we saw earlier, when using seamless paper. But this is not practicable when the cyc is curved. Also of course, you will not want the cyc material damaged or dirtied by feet walking over it.

Instead, it is preferable to paint the floor an identical color and tone to the cyc (using special water-soluble paint) and use some intermediate 'cove units' to disguise or hide the join. These units are universally called *ground rows*.

Unfortunately, the *same term* is also used for low scenic planes (Section 3.10)! Also the strip lighting (*troughs, cyc units*) used at the bottom of a cyc to light its surface from below is frequently also referred to as a ground row!

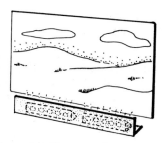

Figure 3.4 The ground row

Vertical planes. Vertical boards used to obscure the floor join and floor lamps lighting the cyc.

Profiled planes. Decorated, edge-profiled vertical planes used to suggest landscape, buildings, etc. and create an illusion of skyline or intermediate terrain.

3.9 Cove units

This is a regular, very effective method of hiding the ground join. Each unit is typically 6 or 12 ft (1.8 or 3.6 m) long and consists of a sloping surface of plywood or fiber glass sheet, supported at e.g. 45° on a hollow framework. The coving is repainted as necessary, to match the floor. It is easier to blend the light intensities of the floor and the cyclorama if the cove surface is slightly concave rather than flat.

3.10 Scenic planes

Another form of 'ground row' used to hide the floor join consists of a series of plain vertical plywood boards. Generally around 2 ft (0.6 m) high, these are usually self-supporting and can hide ground lamps lighting the cyclorama.

A ground row can be profiled with an irregular outline to represent hills, rooftops, distant buildings, treetops, etc.

3.11 Cyc cloths

A *cyc cloth* is a large painted scenic cloth hung as a cyclorama. Photographic versions are occasionally used but are generally too expensive. The cyc cloth customarily shows a distant view of some kind, such as a landscape or a town scene.

Flats

3.12 The basic unit

The commonest scenic unit is unquestionably the *flat*. There are two forms: *softwall* and *hardwall*. Each is basically a faced cross-braced wooden frame. It can be used singly, but more often a series or 'run' of flats is fastened together to form walls to settings.

3.13 Softwall units

Usually referred to as 'canvas flats', the *softwall* flat has canvas, hessian, calico, burlap, duck, or unbleached muslin stretched and glued to its wooden frame. The material is brushed over with size or a diluted plastic glue containing a waterproofing agent. Fire retardants are applied to the finished unit. The flat can be painted or papered and decorated.

Softwall flats are conveniently lightweight and inexpensive – but not particularly durable. Because the flat's surface is rather flimsy it will not support hung objects readily, and may not look convincing if used to provide 'walls' for a realistic setting.

However, they are certainly useful for less exacting applications:

- In a studio production they can provide *backings* outside windows and doors or be used as ceiling pieces.
- In *rehearsal halls* they can augment floor outlines to provide a dummy layout of the studio setting.
- For *production training* the softwall flat allows one to construct mock-up settings quickly and easily for exercises.

3.14 Hardwall units

In the traditional studio hard flat, a surface of plywood, prepared board (hardboard, fiberboard, composition board) about ¼ in (6 mm) thick is attached to the wooden frame. It is then faced with stretched hessian, burlap, or lining paper.

Other types of hard flats are used occasionally, with outward or inward curving surfaces (convex and concave 'sweep' units) and heavy-duty wood panelling.

3.15 Stock flats

Most studios keep a supply of *stock flats* of several kinds, which can be adapted to any production. These may be plain, molded (e.g. as brickwork or stone walls), or paneled in various period styles.

Some have two categories of stock flats:

- Those that may be repainted or decorated as required,
- Those that are 'dedicated', and must not be modified or treated in any way apart from periodic refurbishing. These may include mid-gray general-purpose flats (useful for many routine purposes); period paneling (e.g. linenfold); and specially decorated units.

3.16 Frame construction

As we saw, all flats are based on a framework. The standard frame is typically made of 3 × 1 in (76 × 25 mm) lumber. Heavier units may use 4 × 2 in (100 × 50 mm). In Figure 3.5 you will see the general form of the flat and the names of its parts. The top and bottom *rails* and the central *stretcher* or *toggle* rail are screwed and glued to the vertical *stiles*. Reinforcing *corner blocks* and *keystone* pieces are glued at the joins. These are formed from ¼ in (6 mm) plywood, which is screwed or nailed onto the structure. The clout nails should be driven through the wood and bent over (clenched/clinched) on the front side to secure these supports.

Diagonal braces (*corner braces*) across the rear of the frame, help to strengthen it and prevent warping.

Another unit, sometimes called a *box flat*, has a different form of frame. Faced with canvas, plywood, or ⅛ in (3 mm) masonite, it is used primarily for large window backings.

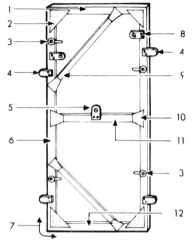

Figure 3.5 The flat

Flat construction. Most standard flats take the general form shown, although the number and position of toggles/stretchers and braces will vary with size and shape. There are also preferences in the attached hardware.
1. Top rail.
2. Corner block.
3. Lash cleat.
4. Stop cleat (to align flats).
5. Brace cleat (brace eye).
6. Stile.
7. Frame (1 × 3 in pine).
8. Lash eye.
9. Diagonal brace (corner brace).
10. Keystone.
11. Toggle rail (stretcher).
12. Bottom rail.

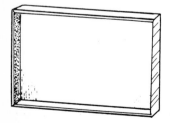

Box flats. A simple board frame structure that may be bottom weighted or braced. Effective, but bulky, heavy, and cumbersome.

3.17 Flat heights

While taller flats of 10–12 ft (3.0–3.6 m) are found in large studios, 8–10 ft (2.5–3 m) high flats are more common in studios where the ceiling is lower and the camera is less likely to overshoot past the tops of the flats.

In large studios, flats 12–15 ft (3.6–4.6 m) high may be used at times (e.g. for walls alongside a flight of stairs), but handling and safety problems increase considerably at this scale.

In many settings, lamps are positioned just over the top of the flats. So if flattage is high it usually forces studio lighting to a steeper vertical angle and degrades facial modeling.

3.18 Flat width

The widths of flats again varies between organizations and according to the use of the flat. Frame flats can be anything from 6 in (152 mm) to 12 ft (3.6 m) wide. But common sizes are 4–6 ft (1.2–1.8 m) wide.

Flats up to about 4 ft (1.2 m) wide are quite convenient for one person to move around. Above that, it generally needs two people to carry or run them (Chapter 9). However, if a set were constructed from a series of narrow flats, the frequent joins between the units would be obtrusive, unless they were disguised by careful 'stripping' (Section 9.23).

Flats of around 1 ft (0.3 m) wide are mostly used as *returns* (*jogs*) to position a flat in front of or behind its neighbors. In this way, we can suggest depth in a structure. Similarly, we can use a small return at the end of a wall to imply thickness, particularly where a camera is going to move past it while following action.

The narrowest flats (e.g. 6–9 in or 152–228 mm wide), used to give depth to a doorway or a wall, may be formed from plain timber planking (wood board).

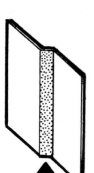

Figure 3.6 Wall construction

Returns. By introducing a return in a stretch of wall one can provide a more interesting effect and disguise joins between flats. (See Figure 5.3.)

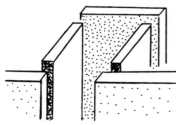

Concealed joins. The prominence of joins between flats can be reduced by the way in which they are positioned. (See also Figure 8.12.)

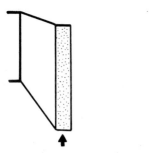

Wall thickness. The thickness of a wall can be implied by using narrow returns.

3.19 Hardware

Over the years, a variety of scenic fittings have evolved to join, support, and suspend all types of scenery. Sometimes there are several devices that do the same job.

The most important fittings attached to a flat are:

- *Lash eye.* Holds the knotted end of a length of permanently attached line (*lashline, lashing line*). This is used to fasten one flat to another.
- *Lash cleat* (*tie-off cleat*). A projecting lug around which the lashline is wound to pull two flats together.
- *Throwline cleat.* A general-purpose cleat, mainly used to run the line around when lashing two flats together.
- *Brace cleat/brace eye.* The curved hook at the end of an adjustable *stage brace* (*scene brace*) fits into the hole in the brace cleat.

- *Stop cleat.* A flat plate fitting behind the vertical stile of an adjacent flat to help keep the two units in line.

In Chapter 9 we shall look in detail at the way flats are supported and aligned

3.20 Surface finish

Flat, even-toned surfaces can look pretty dull. So a lighting director often introduces uneven, patchy illumination, shading or shadowing surfaces, to produce an attractive visual impact. Similarly, a scenic designer will select surfaces and finishes that lend variation and interest to otherwise plain areas.

It is worth bearing in mind, though, that some surface finishes bring problems, as we shall discuss more fully in Chapter 11. We can summarize these as:

- Very dark matte surfaces easily appear unmodeled and detailless.
- Even when strongly lit, dark-toned glossy surfaces such as polished, dark wood paneling often remain unmodeled, apart from prominent reflections of lamps.
- Metallic surfaces (metal, metalized plastic film, foil, or paint) reflect strong speculars from lamps. These not only distract the eye but can cause electronic problems.
- Some wall coverings have attractive metallic ornamentation (e.g. gold motifs). Unfortunately, this can usually only be seen well on camera from certain angles. When a lamp is directly behind the camera the pattern may be very pronounced. But at other angles this detail becomes much dimmer, and may even vanish into the background altogether. So you may find it appearing and disappearing as shots are intercut.

Surface formation

3.21 Illusion through paint

Apart from any contouring built into them, most scenic units have smooth, even surfaces. The simplest treatment you can apply is a *flat lay-in* – a plain untextured finish in distemper or casein-prepared paint.

However, there are a number of ingenious ways of using paint that can suggest texture or surface relief quickly and economically:

- *Spraying.* A skillfully used spray gun or even an aerosol paint-spray can is useful in providing shading effects, pseudo-contouring, dirtying, or simply unevenness over a surface. Lighter tones appear to advance from a mid-toned background and darker ones to recede, creating a depression.

- *Dry-brush work*. Here we overpaint a dry flat ground color with a nearly dry brush so as to leave a sparse pattern of brushmarks across the ground color. The result suggests metal, wood, stone, or fabric.
- *Stippling*. Using a coarse brush, a sponge, wrinkled paper, or cloth, a series of small close dots or patterns of color are applied on a different ground tone. The finish resembles earth, cement, or stone.
- *Puddling*. On a horizontal surface wet colors are allowed to flow together and intermix, to give random variations. The effect suggests ageing plaster walls, earth, etc.
- *Daubing*. Using a rolled rag, paper, or sponge, dabs of color are patted irregularly over a surface to give varying density of tone.
- *Scumbling*. Here a transparent coating of a dark tone is applied over a lighter one to create shadowing texture.
- *Glaze*. This is achieved by selectively dry brushing a lighter tone onto a background color to suggest highlight sheen.
- *Scuffing or dragging*. The brush is applied very lightly so that it just skims a surface, leaving any textural depressions in it unpainted.
- *Wash*. A thin coating of a lighter or darker tone is applied to the background (body color) to simulate highlights or shadows.
- *Rough-cast*. By sprinkling a powdered material such as sawdust or sand irregularly over a freshly painted surface you can introduce random changes in tone or texture.
- *Spattering or dottling*. This is carefully controlled but random mottling, obtained with brush-thrown splashes or a spray gun at low pressure.
- *Wood grain*. This effect is achieved by applying a dark-toned paint over a light background, then combing and brushing it in patterns similar to natural wood graining. A light varnish gloss can provide a controlled sheen to the surface. Apply it more generously, and the surface looks wet.

Using these techniques we can produce a wide variety of finishes that look extremely convincing on the screen.

At a distance the camera cannot detect the difference between actual relief and carefully painted imitation. So the scenic artist can create a range of effects that are indistinguishable from the real thing.

Let's imagine the scene as a camera looks around a setting depicting a ruined house. We see a plastered wall, where part of the surface has broken away to reveal the brickwork beneath. Gilded molding decorates a once-beautiful paneled room. The rich colors of a stained glass window fall evocatively onto mellow stonework. Beyond a lancet window, trees are stark in a winter landscape. On a distant wall an ornate mirror hangs broken.... But in truth, we are really looking at plain stock flats, transformed by the magic of the brush. It is a reminder that the camera can be fooled effectively.

How successfully one can do so depends on several influences: the skill of the artist, how strongly the surface is lit, how close the shot is, and the shooting angle.

We need also to take care that lighting angles do not reveal painted detail as false. If a shadow is cast over a surface by something nearby or the direction of painted shadows and shading does not correspond with the real light direction the eye will recognize the trick.

Some subjects (e.g. drapery, foliage, water) are seldom really convincing when painted on the flat, although they may get by if the painted details are partly obscured by other scenery or only appear as an incidental part of the total scene.

3.22 Surface coverings

Ever-changing selections of wallpapers, vinyl designs, and wall fabrics offer a very wide selection of tones, textures, and patterns. The main problem here is that the range tends to relate to current fashion, so it may be difficult when staging a drama to find one that looks contemporary with that period.

It is worth remembering the various photographic wallpapers that are also available. Extremely realistic brickwork (new or weathered), stonework, various wood-finishes, roughcast, pebbles, and tiling can look like the real thing on camera. They not only save time and effort but do not require skill to apply. Surface details can be painted or attached to the wall, and, where necessary, the covering can be judiciously brushed or sprayed to create ageing effects.

Finally, of course, you can simulate a decorative wall covering. After preparing the surface with plain paper or a flat lay-in you can:

- Use a patterned printing roller,
- Apply stenciled ornamentation (brushed, or sprayed),
- Stick on paper, plastic, or photographic motifs.

It is possible to stick many sorts of materials onto flattage to give it an unusual finish, including carpeting, fabric, wire netting, plastic mesh, tanbark, cork chips, and tiling. When sprayed or brushed, these materials take on quite a different appearance. But remember, it may not be easy to clean up the flats afterwards for other use!

3.23 Attached contours

A number of materials can be used to form three-dimensional modeling to convincingly simulate brickwork, stonework, weathered wood, surface molding, carving, tiling, cornices, paneling, tree bark, etc. At best, the results are virtually indistinguishable, even up to fingernail-scratching distance!

Typical materials include:

- *Plasterwork*: heavy, brittle, but able to reproduce fine detail,
- *Papier mâché*: easily made, durable, lightweight; more suitable for general forms,
- *Canvas on wire mesh*: built up on a timber framework to imitate rocks or to form a foundation for other materials (turf, peat, sawdust),
- *Carved wood*: carved pieces attached to the face of a flat (e.g. to form a corbel),
- *Plastic forms*: plastic extrusions providing finely modeled 'carving' or molding to stick to flat surfaces,
- *Fiber glass*: for general or detailed modeling – lightweight, durable, flexible,
- *Molded rubber*: used to form durable detailed surfaces (e.g. tree bark),
- *Styrofoam/expanded polystyrene*: see Section 3.24,
- *Shell moldings*: see Section 3.25.

Fiber glass moldings
The fiber glass moldings providing the tree-trunk walls of this log-cabin and the rough-built stonework are convincing up to fingernail-scratching distance!

3.24 Expanded polystyrene/styrofoam/jabolite

This is a white plastic material, now widely used in molded form for equipment packaging. It can be bought in both block form (8 × 4 ft (2.4 × 1.2 m) and as boards. Its low cost, lightness, and versatility make it a valued material for scenic design.

Typical ways of treating the styrofoam include:

- *Cutting* with a very sharp blade, a jigsaw, or a special hot-wire tool,
- *Surface burning* with a blowtorch/flame-gun to create a craggy, weathered effect,
- *Dissolving* the surface away with paint-thinners, acetone, or carbon tetrachloride, using a brush or spray,
- *Painting* with oil-based paints or aerosol paint sprays, the surface will partially dissolve.

The material is easy to work and sections can be strengthened or held together with hardwood dowel rods or stuck with suitable adhesive.

To tone or decorate surfaces, they can be painted with emulsion or latex-based paints. But remember to experiment with some waste material beforehand, to ensure that your paint will not interact with the polystyrene and discolor, erode, or melt it completely.

Surfaces can be smoothed off with abrasive sheet (e.g. glass paper), while for a hard-glazed finish resembling natural rock, gently applied flame can work wonders.

Among the many merits of expanded polystyrene is the ease with which you can create very convincing rock and stonework without the weight and dangers of the real thing. This is particularly welcome when people in a drama are victims of earthquakes, landslides, collapsing houses, thrown rocks, falling statues, explosions, and similar mayhem.

Styrofoam also lends itself to very sensitive sculpting, and even quite large set pieces (pillars, fountains, arches, decorative blocks, statues) can be carried quite easily by one person.

Cut-out styrofoam board gives great opportunities for solid-looking signs, lettering, motifs, 'wood planking', and 'rafters'. Unlike wooden versions, these lightweight units only need a light line to hold them in position (e.g. fishing line). Although even double-sided tape may suffice at times, there is always the danger that it may fail at the wrong moment!

But, of course, this wonder material also has its drawbacks:

- Although there are fire-retardent grades of polystyrene foam one must take precautions when using large pieces in the studio. Some organizations specify that fireproofed muslin or cheese-cloth must be applied under the finishing coat of paint to improve fire resistance. Certainly keep these materials well away from lamps or hot surfaces!
- The material is fairly fragile, and crushes, cracks, or crumbles (although it will support a surprisingly high downward load). So those delicately stenciled hanging decorations are going to need careful handling and transportation if they are to survive.
- Because the material is so light, items may blow over or sway in the breeze from studio air conditioning. So free-standing structures may need support lines and bottom-weighting for greater stability.
- Noxious fumes are given off when treating or burning the expanded polystyrene, so work must only be carried out in open, well-ventilated areas.

3.25 Shell moldings

Some really outstanding effects can be produced using shell moldings. Thin plastic sheets of PVC are laid over a specimen

Figure 3.7 Shell moldings
Three-dimensional shell moldings
vacuum-formed from thin plastic
sheeting can be cut out, attached to
flats, and decorated to suggest brick
walls (new, worn), rock face,
stonework, roof tiling, architectural
features, etc.

surface in a special apparatus and drawn onto it by a vacuum to
take up every crevice and cranny.

These vacuum-formed sheets are typically up to 8 × 4 ft (2.5 ×
1.25 m), and provide realistic contouring shells resembling rock-
face, carved wood panels, wooden moldings, stone walls, brickwork, tiling, mullioned windows, carved stone, pebbles, escutcheons, armor, pistols, even fish.

You can use an entire panel (or cut out parts of it) and staple it
to any scenic unit, and you can paint and decorate its neutral
surface as necessary. The molding is low-cost, featherweight, and
adaptable. Given care, it can be reused but it is liable to be
crushed out of shape if manhandled.

3.26 Contoured flats/plugs

When architectural features such as windows, doors, fireplaces,
bookcase recesses, or niches are required in a room, one sometimes uses a complete fully constructed feature. But such a unit
can be heavy and cumbersome to transport.

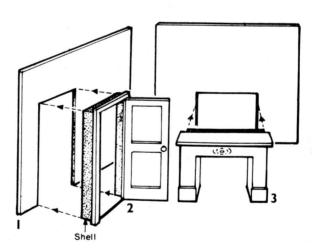

Figure 3.8 Contoured flats/plugs
Contoured stock flats (1) are shaped
to allow a variety of door (2), window,
or (3) fireplace units to be inserted as
plugs.

So for many purposes it is much easier to use *contoured flats* or
frames instead. Here the flat is shaped or cut out to receive a
separately constructed sub-unit – the *plug* or *shell*.

Apart from weight advantages, the component parts are more
adaptable and easily stored. A single profiled flat, for example,
can be designed to take a wide variety of different doors: interior,
exterior, solid, paneled, glazed, etc.

The *plug* (*shell*) representing the fireplace or whatever can be a
hollow wooden structure, made of fiber glass, or formed from a
plastic shell. The plug bolts into position and can be painted to
resemble wood, brick, marble, stone, masonry, tiles, etc.

3.27 Door flats

A *door flat* consists of a complete framed doorway, permanently attached within a flat. A *sill iron* (*saddle iron*), in the form of a narrow strip of metal, is fitted across the bottom of the door opening at the lower edges of the architrave, to give added stability. If this brace becomes distracting in close shots of the floor it may be removed temporarily.

Scenic doors are not normally fitted with working locks. Instead ball-catch inserts are used to secure the closed door and appropriate handles are attached for each production.

3.28 Window flats

Here the complete window frame is permanently attached within a flat. Although bulkier, this arrangement gives the unit greater stability.

Fitted glass is not only vulnerable but dangerous. Glazing also reflects lamps and cameras, so it is not popular with lighting directors. If, for some reason, you *must* use glass an old motion picture trick is to position the panes slightly off the vertical to divert reflections downwards.

Windows in scenery can be treated in several ways:

● Leave them unglazed – the normal practice.
● Fit sheets of transparent plastic in place of glass.
● Screw a large transparent plastic sheet on the back of the glazing bars.
● Stretch and stick a large sheet of gauze at the back of the glazing bars.
● When windows have to be broken in the course of action use special plastic sheet or (exceptionally) very thin glass. (Have standby sheets for replacements after rehearsals.)

3.29 Single and double cladding

Most scenery is intended to be shot from just one side, so only that face is normally decorated. On the rear, untreated side is the hardware for supporting it and identifying labels.

However, there are times when the camera is going to see the same wall from either side (e.g. adjoining rooms). Then we have the option of using two back-to-back runs of one-sided flattage or double-clad units, which are decorated on both faces. The latter are bulkier but more stable.

In any single-sided door flat, where the door is practical (i.e. can be opened) both sides of it will need to be decorated and a timber *reveal* will give the impression that the wall has thickness. (We use the same subterfuge at the end of single-flat walls to fool the camera as it is moving past the end of a solid structure.)

When we are shooting both sides of a doorway or window one face may have a brickwork treatment (exterior) and the other an interior wall finish (e.g. wallpaper).

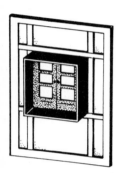

Figure 3.9 Cladding

Single cladding. Most scenery is only decorated on the side that will be seen on camera – 'single-clad'. Any 'depth' is created, as in this window flat, with a false reveal.

15cm
(6 in)Spacing

Double cladding. Where cameras are going to see both sides of flattage the 'wall' may be given 'thickness' by using back-to-back flats with appropriate spacing structure. Window and door flats may be constructed in single- or double-clad form or as 'plugs'.

3.30 Dummy features

Instead of using regular scenic pieces it is sometimes more convenient, cheaper, and easier to use dummy replicas. If a wall closet is only an architectural feature in a room but not needed in the course of the action why not have an indistinguishable imitation – a pair of doors on a frame or a plastic shell bolted to a standard flat? Similarly, a fireplace or a room door can be simulated by a surface dummy.

Staircases can be suggested by a suspended plywood shell.

You can devise a 'window' simply by bolting a batten to a wall and hanging appropriate drapes on it. No actual window is needed. There are even situations (such as the end of a corridor) when a painted or photographed window can be quite convincing!

In fact, you can go further and do away with even these, and project a light-pattern of a window, doorway, or balustrade, and have no structure at all in the studio!

Set pieces

The catch-all term *set pieces* (also called *built pieces*, *solid pieces*, *rigid units*) generally refers to any free-standing scenic structure, from screens or modular units to arches, platforms, and stairs.

Figure 3.10 Arches
Arches can be made in several forms:
1. Single-clad, with a thin board reveal to give it thickness.
2. As a complete double-clad structure. Heavy and bulky, but very stable.
3. As individual columns, with a separate *arch head* which rests on them. (Often suspended over them, just touching, without putting weight on them.)
4. Often, the arch needs only to be indicated rather than built complete. A *half-arch* provides free camera and sound-boom movement beneath.
5. An arched brace implies vaulting.
6. Corbels suggest an overhead arch or beam.

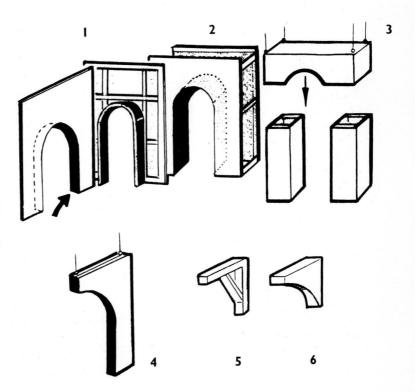

3.31 Arches

The simplest arches are single sided and require rear support. They can be in the form of an arch plug inserted into a profiled flat or made by fitting a reveal around its opening, to give the impression of wall thickness.

The double-clad arch is more robust, and is formed between two profiled flats. It may be self-supporting, but by attaching securing lines (ties) from above one avoids any danger of its overbalancing.

Large arches are usually constructed in sections around a framework and built up in the studio. The *arch head* is made as a separate structure that is suspended and appears to rest on e.g. flats or it may be supported on columns (round or square section).

Sometimes the camera's distance or its viewpoint prevent it from seeing the entire arch. Then a *half-arch* may be all that is needed. It gives better access to cameras and sound boom yet looks just like the real thing. The unit is supported by lines from above and attached to a wall flat (e.g. by pin hinges).

3.32 Buttresses and pilasters

To form a buttress in a wall you can either interrupt a run of flats and build a projection from narrow flats or use a stock square-section column against the wall. Shallower projections such as pilasters are usually formed from a wooden shell, which is bolted onto the wall flat.

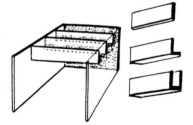

Figure 3.11 Beams
Where environmentally appropriate, beams can be fitted across a set (without unduly inhibiting lighting) to prevent overshoot and suggest a low ceiling.
Distant beams may be formed from single boards, but L- or U-shaped structures are more convincing in closer shots.

3.33 Beams

As ceilings inhibit lighting treatment and alter the acoustics, they do not often form a major part of studio settings. However, where the ceiling is low and any beams would be clearly visible there are three approaches:

- Fit a series of lightweight beams across the set (e.g. made of moulded polystyrene over thin wood shells) and lay a ceiling over this framework.
- Suspend a series of flats across the set to form a vertical surface (e.g. 2 ft or 0.6 m high). A narrow horizontal board attached along its lower edge serves as a soffit. This arrangement has the advantage that it allows light to be directed between these *cutting pieces* to illuminate the scene beneath.
- Beams will look more authentic if their ends appear to rest on corbels (braces) or arched braces attached to the wall. These can be timber shells.

3.34 Columns and pillars

These were formerly constructed from thin plywood bent around a timber framework. But lightweight versions using plastic sheet or fiber glass are now more usual. Typically, from 6 in to 2 ft

(152 mm–0.6 m) in diameter, maximum heights range from cylinders of 2–4 ft (0.6–1.2 m) high to full-size versions 8–12 ft (2.4–3.6 m) or more high.

The *capitals* of columns seldom appear in shot but, like their bases or *pedestals*, they are constructed separately and attached when necessary.

Raised areas

3.35 Blocks/step blocks/apple boxes/risers

Where we need to raise the height of a piece of furniture slightly ('block it up') or provide a step to increase an actor's height for a particular shot, a portable plywood-faced box can prove useful. This *block* (also called a *step block, apple box, pancake, or riser*) may be made as an enclosed cube or left open on one face.

In sizes from 1 × 1 ft by 6 in (0.3 m; 152 mm) deep up to 2 × 2 ft (0.6 m), blocks can be pressed into use for many everyday applications; as a step to a low platform; to build a display stand; to create uneven ground; decorated as building blocks in a children's program; or as a base (plinth) for a column.

3.36 Platforms/parallels/rostra/risers

Larger areas are built up with *platform* units – another of those items with several names. ('Riser' is, strictly speaking, the term for the vertical face of a step or structure, but is now used for the complete platform unit and for blocks.)

Figure 3.12 Platforms and blocks
Demountable platform structures (parallel(s), rostrum/rostra) come in a range of sizes and are extremely adaptable. Platform shapes can be varied by introducing triangular sections ('cheese pieces').
Very low platforms, or half-height variations, can be formed from small, rigid blocks (risers).

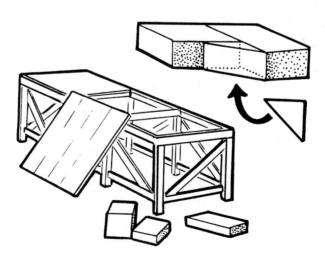

Typical platform heights are: 6 in, 1 ft, 1 ft 6 in, 2 ft, 4 ft, 6 ft (152 mm, 0.3 m, 0.46 m, 0.6 m, 1.2 m, 1.8 m).

Tops have an area of e.g. 2 × 4 ft, 2 × 8 ft, 4 × 4 ft, 4 × 8 ft (0.6 × 1.2 m, 0.6 × 2.4 m, 1.2 × 1.2 m, 1.2 × 2.4 m).

A shallow platform (6 in or 1 ft or 152–300 mm deep) is built as a rigid permanent shell, but larger platforms are normally dismantled into separate top and base units.

The detachable top for a platform locks into a supporting base frame. It is constructed from a timber framework faced with boards or heavy plywood (½ in or ¾ in; 13 mm or 20 mm). This may have *cladding* added in the form of a decorative or protective sheet to suit a particular show's décor.

The main support frame of a platform can take several forms:

● Permanent sub-frames of e.g. 2 × 4 in (50 × 100 mm) lumber which are bolted together,
● A corner-hinged lumber frame that folds as a trapezium,
● A frame in which the end sections are centrally hinged to fold inwards for storage,
● A skeletal metal framework built up from slotted steel L-sections bolted together (e.g. 'Zircon' scenic metal or 'Dexion').

The sides of the platform base may be left open and clad with compressed board or plywood when needed or left permanently faced.

Groups of individual platforms can be tied or bolted together to form a large elevated area, and by joining units of different heights, extremely interesting variations become possible.

Where platforms of different areas are used together, small three-sided units ('cheese pieces') may be fitted, to 'round off' the corners of the structure.

Stock platform units may be painted mid-gray or black for immediate use. But they generally require decoration and cladding (in compressed board/hardboard/colorboard) or carpet to improve their appearance.

3.37 Stairs

A staircase can be formed in several ways:

● By joining together several parallels (rostra) of increasing height. If their height differences are too great, you can position appropriate *blocks/step blocks* to provide intermediate treads.
● By using *step units* (*stair units*), singly, or stacked. Several can be used side by side to form a wide stairway.
● By using a supported run of *treads*.

Step units/stair units are constructed on a timber or slotted-steel framework to form a group of two to four treads. Each has a 6 in (152 mm) step height (riser) so that the unit relates to standard platform heights of 1 ft, 6 in, 2 ft, 2 ft 6 in (0.46 m, 0.6 m, 0.75 m).

The step units may be stored with unclad sides to reduce weight, appropriate boarding being added as needed for a production.

Figure 3.13 Stairs
Standard step units are normally designed to suit standard platform heights. Where a few steps are required a three-tread unit (perhaps several side by side) may be sufficient. Continuation units can be added for additional treads.
Staircases ('treads') are usually constructed in the form of a flight of e.g. six-step units, which are suspended or fastened to other scenery at the upper end or 'legged up' on a timber structure.
Separate handrails, balustrades, or banisters are attached by pin hinges.

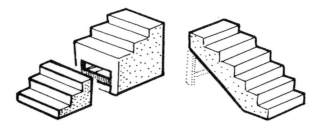

Alternatively, the unit may be built permanently clad to appear as a solid structure.

Treads are constructed as an unsupported flight of steps or staircase. The upper end of the treads can be secured to a platform by pin hinges. Alternatively, the top end of the treads can be 'legged up' with a timber framework.

Hallway with staircase
Built up on a platform to facilitate low-angle shots, the hallway is very fully dressed to suit a Victorian-style house. The upper part of the staircase is a dummy. A central hanging chandelier appears to illuminate the hall. A small spot clamped to the top of a flat keys local action.

Curved stairways follow a similar design to ordinary step-units/stair units or treads. But they may be built as a series of ascending sections for ease of construction and transportation.

If the staircase is only included as a structural effect, and the action does not call for anyone to actually climb it, you can use a much simpler structure and support its upper end with suspending lines. In that case it is a wise precaution to string a warning notice across its bottom end during the setting period and rehearsals, to ensure that no-one inadvertently tries to walk up it ... to adjust a lamp perhaps!

For larger staircases a properly constructed scaffolding foundation is essential, and this requires the experience of specialists. Scenic cladding is then attached to this structure.

Handrails or balustrades are necessary for most stairways. They are normally stored separately and are attached to each stair by pin hinges.

3.38 Getaway steps/offstage steps

Many productions provide us with a dilemma:

● Unseen by a studio audience, a group of musicians has to climb onto a platform to await their opening cue.
● Singing as she climbs a decorative staircase, the artiste reaches the top and bows, acknowledging the audience's applause as her number ends. The lights fade. How can she exit unobtrusively, without the anti-climax of returning downstairs or weaving her way through the dance group who are now performing there?
● An actor goes upstairs and the cameras continue to watch the action in the hall below. (He wants to move on to his next scene but seems to be marooned aloft!)
● An actor has to appear on a balcony or at the top of castle battlements in the studio scene. But there are no visible steps, for these would be inappropriate.

Here we have regular situations where *getaway steps/offstage steps* are needed. These are sturdy open treads, located out of sight from the cameras, allowing performers to get on and off an elevated area without being seen on camera.

Typically 4 ft (1.2 m) wide, the steps may be attached to the side of a platform by pin hinges. Timber handrails are bolted or nailed to their sides.

3.39 Ramps

When you need a sloping flat surface to reach up from the studio floor to the top of a platform a *ramp* is the answer.

This is reinforced non-slip boarding, braced with a timber framework. But for lightweight use, hardwall scenic flats may be suitable.

3.40 Wagons

Occasionally, one needs a *movable* platform, so that parts of the setting can be readjusted or wheeled out of the way during a production. Then the *wagon* (*stage wagon*, *truck*, or *float*) comes into its own.

These low-wheeled platforms have a boarded or heavy plywood surface, from about 3 × 6 ft (1 × 1.8 m) to 6 × 8 ft (1.8 × 2.4 m), and are around 6 in to 1 ft high (152–300 mm). Hidden beneath the wagon are four or six heavy-duty free-wheeling casters. These enable the unit to be rolled into place quite easily.

The casters may incorporate footbrakes with which to lock them off and ensure that the platform is secure once it is in position. Otherwise wooden wedges, stage-weights, or sandbags will be needed for safety.

Using drapes

3.41 Draperies

Drapery or *drapes* is the broad generic term for all types of fabric used in staging.

Strictly speaking, we should only refer to the material as *drapes* when using it as some form of static decoration and to *curtains* when it is movable, as on a curtain track; but distinctions become blurred!

'Drapes' include such diverse features as decorative cloths, scenic gauzes, black background cloths, tab curtains, cycloramas, velours, and chroma key backgrounds.

They usually form just a small part of a setting's dressing or decoration – the curtains at a window, a tapestry hung on a wall, the draperies on a four-poster bed.

A background of drapes can be used to set off groups of panels, screens, pillars, or other scenic elements set out in front of them.

Occasionally, the entire décor may be created with drapes which serve as background, wings, and proscenium curtain.

Figure 3.14 Drapes
Examples here show typical ways of suspending drapes:
1. Hung from a bar, batten, or curtain track.
2. Attached to a line across a flat, or tacked/stapled to its surface.
3. Hung on a drape frame (tubular or timber).
4. Hung from a timber *gallows arm*, hinged to the end of a flat.

3.42 Supporting drapes

There are many decorative methods of arranging drapes. For instance, they may be fully stretched, hung straight, with fullness, in folds, ruffled, scalloped, pleated, ruched, gathered, swagged, cascaded, festooned, looped back, pinch-pleated, etc.

The purpose and style of the draperies can influence how you hang them:

- *Hung over flats.* You can simply throw one end of the drape over a flat and let it hang. For a short run of roughly stretched black drapes this may be sufficient.
- *Timber batten.* You can tack the drape to a 3 × 1 in (75 × 25 mm) timber batten and either hang the batten over the top of the flat or suspend it with thin line that is secured behind.
- *Directly attached.* The drape can be tacked or stapled directly to a flat. Alternatively, it can be suspended on a string across it (using a pocket along the top edge of the drape or a series of hooks).

It is worth bearing in mind that these rudimentary methods of supporting drapes are liable to result in a lot of wear and tear (literally!), especially when removing them hurriedly on dismantling the set. So more sophisticated approaches are preferable:

- *Slung from a suspended batten or tubular barrel.* The drape is held with tapes attached to webbing along its upper edge, by special drape-clips, or by eyelets and string ties.

For lightweight drapes a length of rod in a stitched pocket along its upper edge may be sufficient support, but for heavier materials the amount of sag can be unacceptable.

● *Hung from a suspended overhead rail or pulley system*. This *traveler*, *tab-track*, *tab-rail*, or *curtain track* enables the drapes to be pulled along by a control cord – to one side or center closing.

To improve their operation, the drapes on a traveler are usually provided with a stitched pocket along the lower edges, fitted with chain or a series of weights.

● *Batten track*. A lightweight *runner* or *track* may be fastened to a wooden batten, which in turn is either fastened to the upper part of a flat or projects from brackets which hook over the top of the flat.
● *Drape-frame*. This timber or tubular metal frame can be used singly or coupled in two- or three-fold units. Drape frames may be braced from the rear, self-supporting, or suspended, depending on their particular design.

3.43 Auxiliary drapes

A *leg* is a narrow length of material hung on a frame, either with fullness or stretched, to mask off the wings and side walls of a stage area. It can also be used to hide a camera from the audience or from other cameras. By butt-joining or overlapping a series of these leg frames you can produce the effect of a run of drapes.

A *border* is a narrow length of material (usually black) suspended in front of an acting area to hide lighting bars, battens, etc. from the camera or from an audience. It will usually be hung straight, but if decorative, may be arranged festooned or swagged.

3.44 Choosing draperies

You can, of course, use *any* fabric as a background, but there are traps for the unwary. Here are some hints that may save you much disappointment.

If you have some untried material available it is wisest to camera-test it before using it extensively in a production. Hold it in front of a camera (preferably on a drape frame), and check its appearance with someone standing in front of it under typical studio lighting, in longer and closer shots, from straight-on and oblique angles. There is many a slip betwixt the eye and the camera, and a drape that looks great to the eye can appear nondescript or *overpowering* on camera!

Paradoxically, a genuine period tapestry in the background may look dull and uninteresting on the screen compared with a length of canvas carefully painted with aniline dyes.

Color
Avoid large areas of primary colors, unless you want a vivid, crude impact. Bright red and orange, in particular, are likely to appear noisy in picture (chroma noise).

You may also find that certain reds and bright blues change in value or hue on intercutting between cameras; e.g. looking lighter/darker or more orange/red or blue/green on different cameras.

Pattern
Whether you want a material that provides a plain unobtrusive background or something with visual interest will decide how much decoration you feel is desirable. However, a little decoration goes a long way.

Small patterns easily look busy, and become lost in longer shots as they merge with their background.

It is best to avoid thin vertical or horizontal stripes and close check patterns at all costs. Not only do they disappear in longer shots but they are likely to produce a dazzling, flashing, strobing effect at certain distances.

Big patterns can dominate and unbalance shots. Some very odd visual effects can arise when, for instance, people in an interview seem to be balancing background motifs on their heads or horizontal background lines cut through their necks. If the camera moves in an attempt to avoid the effect either the shot becomes radically changed or the distracting feature moves to another part of the frame and spoils the composition.

Note that striking background patterns get remembered by your audience! This may not matter in a daily talks show where they become part of the ambiance of that particular production. But it certainly limits their continual re-use as *stock drapes*.

Tone and finish
There is an element of luck when using drapes with a glazed or glossy finish. They may appear lively, dramatically modeled, or sculptural, or they may glare, lose detail, and be covered with distracting hot spots!

Very light-toned drapes easily lose modeling and *block off* to become white patches as the reflected light exceeds the camera's upper handling limits. Also, overlight backgrounds can affect the tonal quality of foreground subjects (see Chapter 11). Although reducing light levels on the drapes will usually improve the situation it may also rob foreground subjects of light at the same time.

With very dark-toned draperies – particularly light-absorbant velours – a great deal of light may be needed on them to reveal any sort of modeling. Otherwise they look flat and drab. Unfortunately, this extra light can spill onto other nearby surfaces and overlight them!

Very thin materials may look filmy and delicate but they do have disadvantages. They often drape badly and have a tendency to billow in air currents from ventilation/air conditioning. Also, you may find that any structure or framework supporting them (e.g. a drape frame) shows through, revealed by backlight, and spoils the effect.

3.45 Wear and tear

It is a sad fact of life that even slight dirtying, creases, wrinkles, folds, or tears often look far worse on camera than a casual glance would assume. Careful handling and storage is the only preventive (Chapter 9).

It is not always possible to put things right on the spot, but there are a few first-aid remedies that may save the day:

● Wrinkles in gauze stretched over windows and frames (used as substitute glass, decorative gauze): lightly spray with water and dry off (local lamps, hair dryer).
● Wrinkles in stretched cyclorama: readjust and tighten bottom weighting; re-tie suspension tapes more tightly; use 'cyc-stretchers' (Chapter 9).
● Dirty marks on cyc (footmarks!) through careless handling: lightly brush the area and chalk over judiciously.
● Localized tear in cyc (e.g. probably caught on a projection while pulling into position): use wide adhesive tape (e.g. gaffer tape) at the rear.
● Where you cannot make marks or tears less obtrusive, consider whether there is any chance of hiding them:

> By placing something in the foreground (e.g. a bush, a piece of furniture, or a wall picture),
> By adding a decoration (e.g. sticking a decorative motif over them),
> By adjusting lighting to leave the defect less fully lit or in shade.

Where you find that background tones are too light on camera it may be necessary to 'take down' overbright drapes by dipping them (lightly dying them), spraying them (temporary black coloring), or covering them with a black scrim (gauze).

3.46 Decorative screens and panels

Although they are quite simply constructed, screens and panel units can provide many extremely attractive staging opportunities.

A timber or metal framework is backed by a panel or grid. Where strengthening members (rails) are needed, they can be used as part of the pattern. The unit can be anything from 6 to 12 ft (1.8–3.6 m) high and 2 to 6 ft (0.6–1.8 m) wide, depending on its particular application and whether it is to be free standing or partly or fully suspended.

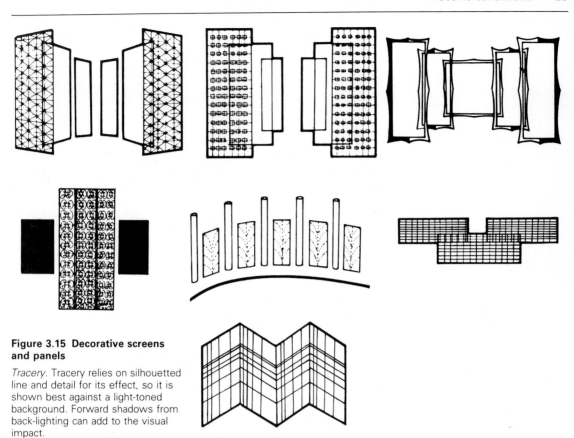

Figure 3.15 Decorative screens and panels

Tracery. Tracery relies on silhouetted line and detail for its effect, so it is shown best against a light-toned background. Forward shadows from back-lighting can add to the visual impact.

Textured panels. Edge lighting or top lighting can emphasize the texture and form of panels that have strong surface contouring.

Smaller screens and panels may be used singly, interlinked, or hinged in two- or threefold sections. Also, of course, they can be arranged singly, combined or grouped, in many variations.

You can use the frame as part of the design or cover it with a shaped cut-out border.

A wide variety of materials can be used to back the frames, including:

Figure 3.15 (continued)
Nets and mesh. Flexible nets can provide both tracery and texture, suspended or draped across scenic units.
Wire mesh can be formed into structural forms and combined with other units (drape frames, blocks). They can be sprayed, painted, stenciled, or decorated.

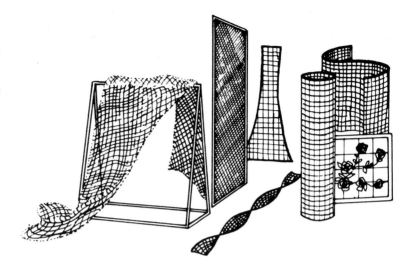

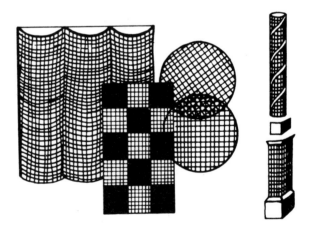

- Frosted plastic (forming a translucent screen),
- Plastic sheeting (clear, ribbed, beaded, etc.),
- Stretched gauze/scrim,
- Trellis,
- Perforated prepared board (hardboard stencils),
- Mesh (plastic, wire, expanded metal),
- Bars (wooden dowels),
- Straight slats (laths),
- Woven slats, rope, wickerwork,
- Plain or decorated board,
- Fiber glass sheet,
- String the frame with plastic string, rope, or wire,
- Stick-on shaped forms (e.g. egg packaging, cut-out styrofoam sheet, vacuum-formed moldings).

Figure 3.16 Flexible screens
These can be used singly (braced or unbraced) or combined in a variety of shapes. Decorated with stuck-on motifs, ribbons, or ropes or light-patterns, lighting color-changes, etc., they offer flexibility at low cost.

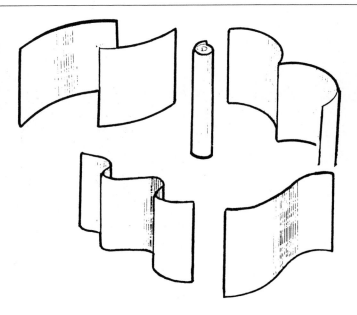

3.47 Flexible screens

Because flexible screens can be readjusted and reshaped easily and simply they offer unusual design opportunities.

They are made from hinged aluminum strips or from a series of close parallel wooden laths, fixed to a fabric backing. The design is very similar to the flexible security shutters used to protect some shop fronts.

These flexible screens are set up on edge, usually as self-supporting units, and can be arranged in various interesting forms – rolled up (to become pillars), unrolled (to wind in convex or concave curves), or S-shapes.

The screens can be used with other scenic units such as panels, and are easily rolled up and stored.

By painting either face with different tones or colors and adjusting lighting it is easy to introduce many variants. One can attach decoration, swag drapes or foliage over them.

Considering how simple they are, flexible screens lend themselves to a wide range of programs (e.g. talks, dance routines, demonstrations) in a decorative or neutral form.

3.48 Cut-outs/profiles

Watching a picture on a TV receiver we cannot tell whether the camera is looking at an actual scene or shooting a high-grade picture postcard someone is holding up in front of the lens. The eye can be fooled by a flat replica, and profile pieces rely on that fact for their effect.

The *cut-out* or *profile* is constructed from a sheet of plywood, prepared board, hardboard, or compressed card, attached to a

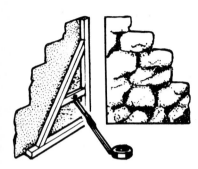

Figure 3.17 Profiles and cut-outs

Profiled flat. The board surface is cut around the edges to follow the features of the subject (e.g. rocks, brickwork, architecture). The effect can be naturalistic at a distance, particularly for photo-enlargements.

Cut-outs. Can be used realistically to simulate features (e.g. pillars) or as a stylistic effect (e.g. a boat).

timber frame or a stock flat. The edges of the sheet are shaped, to follow the outline of the subjects painted on it.

The unit is usually free standing, and can be held upright by a rear brace, a jack, or bottom weighted with a stage-weight or a sandbag (Chapter 9).

There are various ways of decorating the surface of the cut-out unit, including painting, attached contours (e.g. shell moldings), and photographic detail (e.g. stonework).

At first sight, one might assume that cut-outs are more suitable for the broader décor of the theatre than the more realistic scenery of the television studio. But in fact, with care, they can be used very successfully, particularly when intermixed with solid set pieces.

Suppose, for example, you need a ruined wall in a scene. Instead of a bulky structure you can create a convincing lightweight substitute in a fraction of the time at low cost:

> Stick some regular 'brick' wallpaper onto plywood or hardboard. Dirty it down and add details to suggest a weathered appearance (cracks, staining, damage). Cut out some individual bricks from spare sheet and stick these over, slightly askew, to suggest partial collapse. Finally, cut irregularly around the wall edges to give a partly ruined profile. If there is any prospect of the camera seeing the top edge of the wall a horizontal face can be added.

Cut-outs are successful for two reasons. First, as we have seen, the camera cannot detect their flatness unless an oblique viewpoint reveals the true thickness. Second, they enhance the illusion of depth.

They do this thanks to an effect called *parallactic movement*. Looking around the real world we see how nearer subjects overlap and hide more distant ones. As we move around, the amount of overlapping varies, and we come to associate this changing effect with varying distances. Cut-outs imitate this illusion in the setting.

Some cut-outs still look remarkably convincing in quite close shots. A cut-out of a photographed statue, for instance, may appear like the real thing. But let shadows of a tree branch fall across its surface and we realize immediately that it is flat. A cut-out pillar looks solid unless the camera reveals its true thickness. Then no-one is fooled.

Cut-outs can be used in several ways:

● As *decorative pieces* – tracery, slung motifs, escutcheons, banners, fantasy objects (e.g. giant toys, kitchen utensils),
● To resemble *architectural features* – balustrades, arches, stonework screens, fountains, or even complete buildings.
● As *wings* – to mask off the edges of acting areas (e.g. resembling foliage, buildings),
● *Ground rows* – to hide the bottom of a cyc; to hide lamps; or to suggest a series of distant planes (e.g. mountains, forests, skyline). (See section 3.10.)

Where ground rows are going to be lit with trough/strip-lights resting on the floor, keep them at least 6 ft (1.8 m) apart to allow space for the lamps and for the light to spread. Otherwise, it may not be possible to illuminate them evenly.

Pictorial backgrounds

Any technique that can create a realistic background effect in the studio, without building masses of scenery, obviously has a great many advantages. This is the aim of the pictorial background.

3.49 Backdrop/painted cloth

The simplest form is known variously as a *backdrop*, *painted cloth*, *backcloth*, or *canvas drop*. This is a wide roll of suitably prepared canvas on which a scene is painted. Its top edge is attached to a wooden batten or provided with tapes to tie it to a suspended barrel. The bottom edge is fixed to a batten or a round pole around which the cloth is wound for storage.

If the painted cloth is really large and is hung like a cyclorama it is known as a *scenic cloth*.

Painted cyc cloth
Scenic cloths can appear totally realistic on camera, as this excellent example of the scenic-artist's craft demonstrates.

The effectiveness of any painted background obviously depends on the skills of the scenic artist. At its best, the effect is virtually photographic and entirely convincing on camera. At its worst... it is better to tackle the situation another way!

3.50 Photomurals/photo blow-ups

Photographic enlargements are also used as pictorial backgrounds. They are prepared by sticking the wide strips of photographic paper onto a canvas backing, which is supported and stored in a similar way to a backdrop. Smaller photo backgrounds can be attached to flats or mounted in a box-frame.

A good *photomural/photo blow-up* can be completely realistic. Many designers prefer to use 'black and white' photographic backgrounds, which are then suitably colored by a scenic artist (e.g. with aniline dyes). Actual colored photographs are not only much more expensive to produce but on camera can appear to have oversaturated false color values.

You can mount a large color photographic transparency of a background scene on a translucent surface in the wall of a set and light it from the rear. Some studios make regular use of such *translucents* in permanent sets – behind newscasters, for example. The overall brightness can be controlled accurately and the result can be very convincing. However, they are vulnerable, of restricted size, and too expensive for more general use.

3.51 Adjusting the background

Both backdrops and photomurals need careful handling and storage. We have to avoid any possibility of creasing or cracking and hang the cloth as straight, flat, and free from bulges as possible.

When selecting and initially preparing the background scene check that its perspective and eyeline are going to make a reasonable match to the studio camera's viewpoint. Otherwise, some very strange spatial effects could develop (e.g. with the studio camera

Figure 3.18 Camera height and eyelines

Matching camera height. Ideally, the studio camera should match the viewpoint used to produce the background (height, tilt, lens angle) as in 2. Otherwise background and foreground will be incompatible (1).

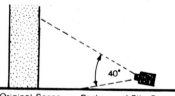 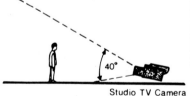 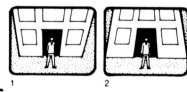

Original Scene   Background Film Camera

Studio TV Camera

Matching eyeline. Perspective will only be correct when the camera's eyeline (height) matches that of the background (1). If the background is above the subject eyeline (2) or below it (3) the result will be incongruous. (Raising or lowering the background may correct the situation.)

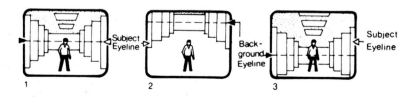

shooting downwards on the studio scene that has a background showing a depressed viewpoint!).

Normally, any slight discrepancies can be overcome by slightly raising or lowering the background.

The pictorial background's surface must usually be lit evenly, without any shadows, avoiding steep lighting that will emphasize any bulges. The exception is when you find that parts of the background are reproducing lighter or darker on camera than was expected (e.g. overlight skies). Then by judiciously shading off that area it may be possible to improve the overall effect.

There are not too many things one can do to a pictorial background by lighting adjustments. Some hopeful souls have used colored lighting on a monochrome background to simulate time passing (blue skies, sunsets) or seasons changing (from fields of snow to the greens of spring), but the results are unreliable. So, too, is any attempt to make a day scene look like night by taking the light off it! It may be better to drop a black gauze or drape over it to convey darkness, or close the window curtains at night so that the camera cannot see the unlit background at all.

To be plausible, the quality and characteristics of the foreground scene in the studio and those of the flat pictorial background should match reasonably closely. Ideally, the proportions, perspective, tonal range, overall brightness, light direction, color values, etc. should be similar. But in practice, there can be all manner of discrepancies as long as no-one notices them!

3.52 Re-using the background

Having gone to the expense of preparing a realistic pictorial background it makes good sense to get further use out of it later, in other productions. Of course, if its subject is particularly identifiable – the Taj Mahal perhaps – there are not going to be many opportunities. But if it shows typical local countryside or architecture then it could prove to be a useful background to keep in stock.

When a stock background is re-used in different productions even a regular audience is unlikely to recognize it unless there are some very prominent features that attract their attention. If the camera is only going to see part of the background through a window then, for all practical purposes, it becomes a 'new' backing. Even in a regular series a stock cloth could be used several times if repositioned so as to reveal different sections!

You can give a stock pictorial background new life by attaching new features over parts of the original or retouching it to suit the latest production. You may be able to hide parts of the background scene with foreground trees, bushes, or walls so that only parts of it are visible. Used in this way, what was at first quite costly becomes a very economical scenic item.

The studio floor

3.53 Floor care

At a casual glance the studio floor just appears to be a flat, even-toned neutral-colored surface with a matte finish, and we take it for granted.

But in most studios that floor is a precision-laid surface that is the result of a great deal of research and experimentation. It needs to be particularly flat and level to avoid picture bounce on moving camera dollies.

It has to be a hard-wearing, non-skid, quiet surface – no squeaks from wheels or shoe soles! Ideally, it should not dent easily or be affected by water, paints, solvents, oil, or chemicals.

A number of materials have been tried for this purpose, including rubber, plastic, and heavy-duty lino, laid over a hard asphalt foundation.

Now although scenic designers are not concerned with the technicalities of studio design it is as well to realize how important everyday *floor care* really is in the studio. It only needs one person to drop a heavy piece of scenery, score its surface as we drag a faulty flat across the studio, or ignore a water leak and the damage is done.

3.54 Floor treatment

Camera dollies need a smooth, clean floor if they are to move on shot without the picture bouncing around. The narrower the lens angle, the harder it is for the camera operator to avoid unsteadiness. If the camera is only moving while off shot the problem may not be so great. But even then we have to ensure that neither the camera wheels nor the operator's feet are likely to slip. And there should be no odd debris around that can get stuck onto the camera dolly's wheels. A rolled-up piece of sticky tape can spell disaster, and has been known to stop a camera from moving or cause it to develop a 'limp'!

So much for the problems. Provided we bear them in mind, the studio floor offers great design opportunities. As we shall see, it can be painted, decorated, covered over, scattered, and transformed in many interesting ways.

3.55 Floor painting

Using special water-soluble paints, there are several techniques for decorating the studio floor.

The simplest is an overall coating of even tone or color to match the general décor or to provide a special effect. Regular finishes include black, beige, light blue, off-white, and chroma key blue. This can be applied by roller, brush, or machine.

The result is quite hard-wearing and does not mark unduly. However, one must be particularly careful to prevent water or other liquids falling onto the finished surface. The result can be disastrous! Not only will the finish be spoiled and the damage probably spread around to adjacent areas but the wet paint can become extremely adhesive – sufficiently in fact, to have caused a motorized camera crane's wheels to stick to the floor and rip up the surface when it moved!

However, the great advantage of this paint is that it can be removed quite quickly and easily using a floor-scrubbing machine, after the scenery has been dismantled at the end of a production.

3.56 Hand painting

Using the same water-soluble paints, a scenic artist can modify the appearance of the floor considerably, using any of the methods we

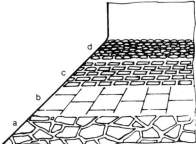

Figure 3.19 Floor treatment

Decorated floor. Decorative designs on the floor may be hand painted or stuck on.

Simulated surfaces. Floor painting (hand or machine) or suitable wallpaper designs can simulate surfaces that would be difficult to provide directly and unsuitable for camera movement.
a. Crazy paving.
b. Paving slabs.
c. Pavé bricks.
d. Cobbles.

Floor coverings. Floor surface unused by cameras can be covered with:
a. Sawdust.
b. Scattered peat or tanbark.
c. Dead leaves.
d. Rubber or plastic sheets of relief cobbles, bricks, etc.
e. Grass matting. Ground contours here have been changed by using (f) sawdust sacks or sandbags and (g) sack-filled platforms or blocks.

Floor cloth. Elaborate floor treatment can be pre-painted on a floor cloth.

met in Section 3.21. On camera, this will provide texture, shading, and tonal variations in its surface to simulate earth and other materials.

The brush (in skilled hands) can similarly imitate wood-plank flooring, parquet flooring, worn paving slabs, new slabs, cobbles, irregular stones, stone sets, crazy paving, tiles, broken earth – even carpeting.

A special protective varnish coating may be used to glaze the floor surface and give it a polished appearance.

To speed the process, where a large area is to be covered the scenic artist may use group stencils cut in plywood or plastic sheet. For decorated floor tiles, parquet blocks, and similarly detailed work this both eases the labor and helps to achieve consistent results.

There are also floor-printing machines available, fitted with large replaceable rubber rollers to provide routine floor decoration such as paving, cobbles, floor blocks, and planking.

3.57 Adhesive patterns

Tacky-backed tapes and designs in plastic sheeting can be used successfully to build up 'instant decorations' on the floor. If no-one is going to walk on them or cameras dolly over them there are few problems. Then you may even fasten regular wall coverings (wallpaper) to the floor with double-sided adhesive tape round the edges to simulate timber, bricks, or pebbles.

Colored tapes can be used to build up decorative floor patterns – particularly geometric shapes and perspective effects.

Like all floor treatment, it is safest to look it over after rehearsals to check whether it has been scuffed up or dirtied, or has started to peel, and needs refurbishing before the show is recorded.

3.58 Floor panels

Large panels of heavy-duty vinyl, rubber, or prepared board (e.g. around 3 ft (1 m) square) can be used on the floor to provide a temporary surface. (Rolls of material do not lie flat, so are best avoided.)

The panels can be anchored by double-sided tape or taped together at joins. Particular care is needed at the outside edges of such floor coverings if cameras are going to dolly onto them.

You can arrange simple checkerboard designs by alternating colors or tone. Alternatively, the panels can be decorated and treated by scenic artists before coming into the studio to form pictorial mosaics (e.g. a giant star motif, Chinese dragon, logo, program identification sign, map, etc.).

3.59 Floor cloths

Large, decorated floor cloths of hessian, duck, or other heavy-duty fabrics can be prepared away from the studio and laid before setting up the scenery.

A floor cloth has the advantage that it can be re-used. Also, unlike a directly painted floor, the cloth can resist water spillage and will actually protect the floor surface to some extent.

On the other hand, it is not easy to achieve a completely smooth, wrinkle-free surface with a floor cloth. Accurate positioning takes time and geometrical patterns distort too easily. Cameras can move over the surface without undue picture-bumping but are liable to pull and wrinkle the floor cloth in the process, even when the edges have been taped firmly to the floor by gaffer tape to try to overcome this.

There are times when one needs to provide real protection for the studio floor, to prevent its being damaged by *water* (during rainy exterior scenes), or *heavy staging* (scaffolding, audience plat-forms), or sheer *messiness* (sawdust, snow, tanbark, peat, leaves, etc. used in studio 'exterior' scenes). Then it is advisable to lay old sheets of prepared board of some kind (hardboard, compressed board), covered with floor cloths, tarpaulin, or heavy-duty plastic sheeting.

3.60 Scattering

Probably the quickest and simplest way of disguising the flat, smooth studio floor for scenic effect is to scatter selected materials over it.

Many studios have a strict list restricting the substances that may be scattered. They prohibit *sand* or *salt*, for example, in all scenic staging.

As a general guide, we can say that any material used should not be harmful to people or equipment. It should not be corrosive or abrasive, nor damage the floor. It should not blow around easily. It must not be unpleasant to handle, and it should not be flammable. Ideally, any material that might burn should be sprayed with fire-retardant solution.

Typical acceptable substances include:

● Tanbark and powdered peat, to simulate soil and dirty conditions,
● Sawdust, to imitate snow, sand, or earth,
● Cork chips, to provide quiet 'gravel', where real gravel would crunch noisily on mike and is liable to damage the floor,
● Expanded polystyrene granules or shredded paper to substitute for snow – although it may prove too white on camera and have to be sprayed down,
● Dry leaves, strewn to add conviction to exterior scenes.

You can get great effects by careful, strategic floor scattering. BUT you do need to take precautions.

First, confine the scattering to where it is going to show. Do not have it anywhere near camera or sound-boom positions, or floor areas where equipment is going to move around. It can foul up wheels, stick to their tyres, and make the floor slippery.

Second, remembering how easily materials tread around onto the clean studio floor, delegate someone to sweep frequently, return-ing it to the specified area.

Third, avoid water. Where this is not possible, confine it to a localized section which has protective floor sheeting.

3.61 Substitute surfaces

As we saw earlier, there are a number of floor surfaces that the skilful scenic artist can imitate surprisingly well. But they are only painted representations – impressions that will not really stand up to the scrutiny of close shots. Furthermore, lighting will often reveal the trick. The surface looks textured from some directions but smooth from others, as backlight bounces off the painted floor.

For a really convincing textured floor finish, large contoured mats of rubber or plastic are available. These are molded from real cobblestones, pave, bricks, tiles, etc. and can be completely realistic. Unlike the painted floor, cameras cannot move over them but they can be walked on quite safely.

Real paving slabs are far too heavy to use *en masse* in the studio and are likely to damage the floor. Instead, lightweight fiber glass versions can be used that look very like the real thing. Where they need to be raised to form a sidewalk they can be mounted on low platforms, which are filled with sacks of a sound-deadening material (e.g. sawdust).

Where grass is needed you have the options of using artificial grass matting or real turf. Most new, untreated grass matting is unrealistic. But if it is lightly and irregularly sprayed with black, dark-green, or brown paint and perhaps cropped in places it can become very convincing on camera.

Real turf is more expensive, difficult to lay convincingly, and is somewhat messy. It is heavy, deteriorates if walked on, and cannot be re-used. So turf is normally only used when the camera is going to take closer shots in the area. For large tussocks of tall grass you can use the real thing or clumps of dried grasses. Wherever real grass is to be used in any form it is advisable to protect the floor beneath with plastic sheeting.

Sometimes you cannot use substitutes of any kind. If the action in a drama calls for someone to drop a coin which rolls through a crack in floor planking it has to be the real thing. You will need to lay a planking floor (raised on a low platform perhaps) to get the right sounds and to satisfy close shots.

3.62 Rugs, mats, and carpets

Floor coverings not only add a 'furnished' look to a room but help to improve its acoustics to some extent. They reduce foot noises and suppress that somewhat hollow, 'live' sound quality, that can develop in box settings – particularly where ceilings are fitted.

Full-area carpeting is seldom found in studio settings, although large rugs (carpets) are regularly used in living-room sets.

It is a wise precaution to secure any floor covering with tape at the edges to prevent it from moving around or slipping from under people.

Although 'lightweight' camera dollies (rolling tripods) can move on carpets, rugs, and even mats, it is not advisable for them to do so, for they are liable to damage them.

In any case, because such floor coverings are too uneven to allow cameras to shoot while moving it is far better to either avoid rugs and mats in places where cameras are going to dolly around or remove them for a particular shot. Alternatively, they may be rolled back as necessary (on cue, perhaps), to allow free movement.

Floor light-patterns

3.63 Opportunities and methods

On the face of it, light offers boundless opportunities for the designer. Through lighting changes the entire scene can be transformed in an instant or varied almost imperceptibly over a period of time. Light-patterns can be developed and interswitched in time with music or altered on cue. Even if the scenic designer is not directly concerned with the lighting treatment, he or she should be aware of its potentials and limitations. So let's take a look at the practicalities of floor treatment through lighting.

There are several ways of creating decorative light patterns:

- *Directly from the lamp* – by restricting the spread of its light beam. A regular *fresnel spotlight* can be shuttered with its 'barndoor' flaps to form square or rectangular areas of light or fully spotted to give a circular pool. Alternatively, a *projection spotlight* (*ellipsoidal spot, profile spot*) can use internal blade-shutters to form square/rectangular shapes or an iris attachment to produce circles of light.
- *Cast shadows* – from a large stencil cut-out hung in front of a lamp.
- *Projected light-patterns* – from special stenciled masks (gobos) placed inside projection spotlights and focused onto the floor.

3.64 Direct patterns

To produce a sharp symmetrical light-pattern on the floor, the light-beam from a suspended lamp needs to point straight downwards. Otherwise it will be elongated and partly defocused. Projection spotlights may be fitted with a small mirror to divert the beam in any direction.

However, most studio lamps are not designed to be used pointing straight downwards. If they are used at a very steep angle the fitting can overheat and the lamp bulb fail. A warning, therefore, that if you want effective light-patterns on the floor make sure that the right fittings are available.

3.65 Cast shadows

Fresnel spotlights have a stepped lens that produces a *soft-edged* light beam. This is fine when we want to blend together a series of adjacent spotlight beams. But it does mean that any shadows

Figure 3.20 Cast shadows
Shadows cast across the floor (e.g. by a single, strong backlight) can produce 'natural' decorative patterns.

cast by these lamps tend to be slightly blurred (e.g. when a large stencil cut-out is hung in front of a fresnel spotlight). This may not be obvious in long shots. It might be just what you want anyway, to produce a subtle effect. Removing the lens from a fresnel spotlight will harden the light but spread the beam, reducing its intensity.

For a hard-edged *cast shadow* you really need a stenciled design positioned some distance from a small, intense point light source.

3.66 Projected light-patterns

Excellent projected light-patterns are possible, using finely etched stainless steel gobos, in ellipsoidal spotlights (profile spots). These are readily available commercially in a very wide range of patterns or you can make your own out of foil or steel sheeting (see Figure 4.4).

Projector spotlights do have their limitations, though:

● Their light output may be low compared with other lamps lighting the scene.
● When fitted with fairly narrow-angle lenses the pattern only covers a limited area. Increasing the lamp's distance (a longer 'throw') increases the pattern size but reduces its brightness.
● To obtain a bigger pattern at a given distance you can fit a wider-angle lens (shorter focal length), but this results in lower light output and increased distortion of the projected image.

3.67 Problems

Light-patterns are only successful on light-toned, matte, undecorated surfaces. It is a waste of time attempting them on dark, shiny, or heavily decorated areas.

Any lamp used to provide light-patterns must have a completely clear beam path. Scenery and other lamps must not get in the way. This is obvious enough, but is a practical difficulty in a crowded staging area.

Ideally, light should be projected at right angles to a surface to avoid any distortion or uneven sharpness. That is seldom possible.

Any movement of the suspended lamps will cause the floor-patterns to sway.

If people move into the overhead lighting producing the patterns their appearance can be transformed! Their features will be emphasized, with the skull-like modeling and sunken eyes that come from 'top-light'. Paradoxically, any other lighting for the performers may well spill over onto the floor light-patterns and degrade them.

Light-patterns can take time and patience to set up – and usually a lot of trial and error. An apparently simple request for a checkerboard floor-pattern in light could, in reality, require some 30 or 40 individually adjusted projector spotlights to build up the pattern over the whole stage. Having finally achieved this it takes only the briefest glance for somebody to point out where they can see one slightly out of alignment!

Ceilings

3.68 Frustrations

A ceiling gives a studio setting an indefinably complete, authentic look. However, in most cases designers avoid both the ceiling and the wall nearest the camera (the 'fourth wall'). These do not exist – except in the audience's imagination.

There are very good reasons for this practice. Most of the lighting for the actors is suspended just above the side and back walls of the set, and would be completely cut off by any sort of ceiling. (The setting is lit from lamps over the acting area.) Lamps could be arranged on floor stands instead – as we do when shooting interiors on location – but these get in the way of mobile cameras and come into shot.

Even if there is a ceiling over only *part* of the set, this might involve rearranging lighting solely to avoid unattractive shadows, rather than to suit the action or develop an atmospheric effect.

Sound quality can also change considerably under low ceilings.

3.69 The central light-fitting

You can create the impression that there *is* an unseen ceiling by hanging a central light or a chandelier somewhere near the center of the room so that it dips into the top of cameras' long-shots. If the sound boom is likely to get tangled up in it while following action or the fitting casts ugly shadows onto the actors or the walls you may need to relocate it further upstage, beyond the action. But, with care, those hazards can usually be circumvented.

3.70 The need for a ceiling

These are very practical reasons for introducing a ceiling as far as the director and cameras are concerned. Without it, a low camera could easily shoot over the top of a set and see lamps and the rest of the studio! If the designer increases the height of the setting's walls to prevent overshoot (assuming that is possible), they can appear far too lofty for the type of room depicted.

Also, of course, there are types of environment – particularly small, crowded rooms – that look less authentic or convincing without an obvious ceiling.

So what do we do about providing an effective ceiling without ruining the lighting or the sound? There are two approaches. In the first, we strategically introduce a ceiling across the set (or part of it). In the second, we fake it, and use a substitution method.

Figure 3.21 Ceilings

Part 1 *Complete ceiling.* Complete ceilings over a set are practicable, providing the action and camera treatment are compatible with lighting opportunities. The situation may be lit through windows, doors, lamps behind furniture, false returns, etc. Translucent ceilings may help, but usually look patchy and inappropriately bright.

Part 2 *Corner piece.* An abbreviated corner ceiling may be sufficient for cross-shots yet avoid restricting lighting.

Part 3 *Local ceiling.* To avoid overshoot in an isolated shot a small partial ceiling may be arranged (or put in).

Part 4 *Cutting pieces.* Instead of an actual ceiling, one or more cutting pieces (soffits, fascia) can be used to suggest beams obscuring a ceiling.

Part 5 *Scenic background.* If a scenic background (backdrop, photo-background, chroma key insert) includes a ceiling we can convey the impression on camera that it continues over the entire acting area.

Part 6 *Foreground matte.* A painted horizontal flat showing a ceiling can be hung in the foreground and included in the shot.

Part 7 *Camera matte.* A clear glass or plastic sheet (or cut-out graphic) supported in front of the camera can show a ceiling which merges with the rest of the set in the shot ('glass shot').

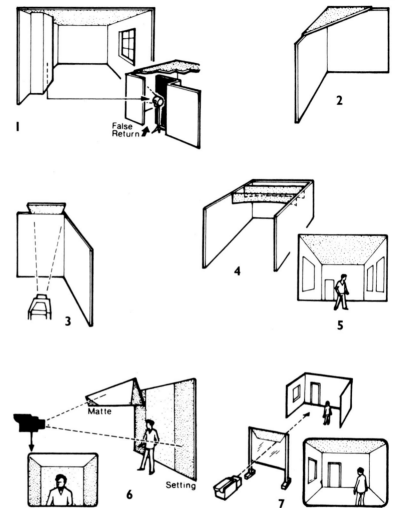

3.71 Complete ceilings

Whether a ceiling poses difficulties or not is influenced by:

● The action (what it is, where it is),
● The variety of camera viewpoints,
● Where lamps can be positioned,
● The opportunities to readjust lighting for different shots,
● The environmental effects required (time of day, mood, etc.).

Light from the camera direction alone ('frontal lighting') tends to reduce form and texture in the picture, destroy atmosphere, and create background shadows behind subjects. So although it illuminates the scene it may not be an artistic solution to the problem.

But where it is possible to light from an angle, through windows, doors, or wall-breaks in the setting, and to hide lamps behind furniture or scenic features, high-quality lighting treatment is quite practicable with a fully ceilinged set.

3.72 Partial ceilings

If a camera is only shooting upwards when it is in one part of the set you will need a visible ceiling for just that shot. For other viewpoints (where the camera is shooting level or downwards) no ceiling is necessary. This leads to the idea of providing *partial ceilings*, tailormade for specific shots.

Often, surprisingly little actual ceiling is required, and even that does not necessarily have to be horizontal.

Sometimes it is possible to carry quite a shallow ceiling right across the upstage part of a setting, either horizontal or angled upwards at the front, so that action there can be lit from under its open ends.

An overhanging flat may be attached to the top of a side wall of the set and provide just enough coverage for the shot.

A partial ceiling across the corner of a set ('corner piece') is often sufficient to prevent the camera overshooting.

3.73 Cutting pieces

Another technique, borrowed from the old idea of 'borders' and *teasers* in the theater, is to provide what are sometimes called *cutting pieces*.

The simplest is in the form of a *fascia board* with a shallow *soffit*. In this arrangement a vertical plane about 1–3 ft (0.3–1 m) high is attached to a horizontal board around 6 in–1 ft (152–300 mm) wide. This creates a supposed structural or architectural feature (*header*, *overhang*, *arch*, *cornice*) that breaks the line and prevents shoot-off.

Where it is appropriate, you can use a series of such planes suggesting beams, vaulting, or girders at intervals over the acting area.

3.74 Substitution

Another approach to the problem of providing ceilings is to sidestep the issue altogether and introduce a substitute in place of actual structures:

- *Scenic backdrop*. The action takes place in front of a scenic backdrop or a photomural, showing the walls and ceiling of the room in perspective. Although this technique is restrictive and requires correct camera positioning, it can produce impressive results for low cost.
- *Background cloth*. Here the walls of the setting may actually be lower than usual. Either a light-toned cyclorama or a large scenic cloth is hung behind the back wall of the setting. As the

camera shoots over the walls it sees the cloth, which appears in the shot to be ceiling. This arrangement allows complete freedom for lighting from the sides of the set. If the cloth has a perspective ceiling painted on it and the shot is correctly aligned it will blend with the setting to provide a striking illusion.

If a chroma key blue cloth is used instead, ceiling details can be inserted by that means (Chapter 8).

- *Camera matte*. This is simply a vertical board set up in front of the camera to appear in the upper part of the shot. It may be plain or painted with a perspective ceiling. This is essentially a deep-focus shot, so considerable depth of field is necessary (i.e. a small lens aperture), otherwise the camera matte will be too softly focused.

The perspective, scale, and tonal balance of the camera matte will need to relate to the studio scene, although this may not be unduly critical. Once the shot has been adjusted during rehearsal the positions of both board and camera should be marked on the floor to enable the shot to be set up again quickly.

A more sophisticated version of this trick is the *glass shot*, in which a precision matte is painted on a vertical glass panel positioned in front of the camera. Over the years it has been used widely in motion picture making to devise many spectacular scenic effects.

- *Electronic matte*. Here a picture of the ceiling is inserted into the picture of the studio scene by an automatic electronic switching process. Now certain problems of the camera matte are overcome, for depth of field is no longer critical and the masked area can be combined more accurately with the studio setting.

However, remember that the studio camera's picture is deliberately framed high to make room in its shot for the ceiling insert. So we need to hang a black cloth (border) in the camera's line of sight to prevent it shooting into lights and causing lens flares.

Greenery

General conditions in television studios are unkind to most plants and foliage. Tender plants are easily damaged, foliage wilts, and too often the appropriate flowers are not always available or in blossom at the time you need them.

So a number of approaches have developed wherever greenery is required, either to decorate a setting or to simulate natural surroundings, such as a garden or countryside.

3.75 Living greenery

Living greenery in the form of potted plants, shrubs, etc. can be used effectively, provided that it is periodically sprayed with water to keep it fresh. It can also help if damp sawdust, tissues, or peat are used as a base for the greenery to rest on. It is best to keep cut flowers out of the lights for as long as possible.

As we saw earlier (Section 3.61), you can join a number of turfs together to form a convincing sward, but the surface soon crushes and becomes battered-looking. If there are going to be lengthy rehearsals try covering the grass over with hessian or a similar material to save the surface. It is sometimes possible to restrict turf to areas that are seen but not walked on. Then you can either use tanbark, peat, or sawdust to simulate a path or introduce imitation grass matting where people are going to walk around.

Clumps of tall grasses, reeds, and bamboo transfer well to the studio, and are very useful where dense growth is needed.

Even a few large shrubs in containers quickly build up an impression of extensive growth. Their tubs can be hidden by grass matting, tufts of coarse grass, or mounds of tanbark, peat, or crushed bark.

3.76 Dead greenery

Here it is a matter of choosing the right sort of material from whatever is available. Branches cut from evergreen shrubs and coniferous trees may go on looking good for days afterwards. But other foliage is liable to deteriorate noticeably. Leaves quickly curl and fall, and the withered result can only be used at a distance.

Tree branches of around 2 in (50 mm) in diameter can prove very useful in studio settings. They can be suspended, dipping into the top of a shot to suggest the presence of a large tree, or you can support them vertically by short timber struts or a *tree-stand* to become a sapling or bush.

A *tree-stand* is quite a useful device. It consists of a vertical metal tube about 9 in (250 mm) long, fixed to a heavy metal base plate. The end of a branch is stuck into the stand, which is weighed down with a stage weight or sandbag. You can also use the tree-stand in everyday staging to support small flag-poles or laths and steady skeletal structures of all kinds.

For larger branches, diagonal struts or legs can be used.

Leafless branches can not only provide us with winter tracery but they can be sprayed in white, silver, or color for decorative usage. Fortunately, they also store well.

Various forms of ivy, creeper, and evergreen foliage can be used in dry form and, for example, fastened to brick walls, sheds, or house exteriors very convincingly.

Although specially dried flowers and grasses can be used successfully they are not generally very durable.

Figure 3.22 Greenery

Part 1 *Living plants*. Living foliage deteriorates under hot lights but is most convincing where greenery is to be handled or seen closely.

Part 2 *Tree trunks*. Simulated bark molded from real trees in rubber, plastic or fiber glass can be fixed to a timber frame (1). Natural tree branches are inserted in holes provided (2).

Part 3 *Natural dead greenery*. A natural tree branch (1) supported in a weighted *tree stand* provides a sapling or bush. Bare branches (2) (leafless, painted) create interesting decorative features. Dried clumps of grass (3) build up uneven terrain.

Part 4 *Typical 'plastic gardening'*. Artificial creeper (1) and ivy (2) arranged on fiber glass 'stone walling' (3) with plastic flowers (4) set in peat and scattered dried leaves (5) create a convincing effect.

Part 5 *Hedges*. An artificial hedge can be built up on a wire-mesh framework, using short branches of cypress, box, etc. (1). Vertical tree branches stuck in a wooden board (hidden under ground scatter) provide a realistic effect (2).

3.77 Artificial greenery

Such a wide variety of artificial flowers is available today that many designers use nothing else. Both fabric and plastic forms can be quite indistinguishable from the real thing on camera.

Artificial plants have endless applications. They can be used:

● In floral arrangements, to decorate settings from drama productions to talk shows,
● Planted in studio 'gardens' and 'exterior scenes',
● Attached to branches or greenery as 'blossom',
● Stapled on walls as climbing plants,
● Trailed around scenic screens and columns.

Although we cannot bring large trees into the studio they can be simulated very convincingly with structures made from fiber glass or rubber molds of actual bark, attached to a timber framework – or even a stock column. Holes can be left for real tree branches to be inserted.

There are two ways of making lightweight hedges. You can stick a number of short branches close together in a wooden board. Alternatively, you can attach a framework of expanded metal to a wheeled base and cover it with foliage such as box, cypress, or privet.

3.78 Mixed methods

Quite often, we can achieve the best effect by combining several techniques. Suppose, for instance, you have a scene with 'explorers hacking their way through impenetrable forest'. You might tackle it as follows.

> In the background a scenic cloth showing distant forest. In front of it cut-outs of trees. Then slung branches and branches in tree-stands. A hedge-frame perhaps, to hold more foliage. Nearer the camera are a number of large shrubs in tubs. And finally, leafy branches are hung in the foreground, for the camera to push through. Light the entire forest patchily to suggest dappled light from above, and on camera... we are in a believable tropical forest!

3.79 Street furniture

As we walk through the streets of a town or city many features become so familiar that eventually we are barely aware of them. Looking around, we see lamp-posts, mail boxes, fire hydrants, pavement signs, phone booths, litter bins, notices, wall posters, road signs, fencing, benches, bollards, statues, fountains, newspaper stands. Without them, any street scene would look quite unreal.

Many of these items have become so evocative that, simply by grouping two or three of them together, we can conjure up an environment on the screen. Some bushes, a bench, and a trash can, and the action is clearly in a public park. A lamp-pole, a post-box, and a sign, and we can believe that the people are waiting for a bus.

Larger studios keep stock versions of many of these regular items. Bulky or heavier pieces, such as fire hydrants, are replicas, made up in fiber glass or plastic.

Chapter 4

Staging techniques

From the basic structures and processes we turn now to ways in which they may be applied.

4.1 'Traditional' methods

Although we like to feel that our work is personal and hopefully original, we are all, nevertheless, conditioned and constrained by the medium in which we are working.

The very nature of television/video production results in certain design trends. To some extent, these methods are influenced by fashion or custom, but they are mainly determined by the fact that directors over the years have found that some approaches *work* and others *do not*.

Let's look at an example that crops up from time to time. A new director of a talks show wants to do something different, and decides to have speakers seated in a circle of easy chairs arranged around a central table.

He or she considers two possible scenic approaches. In the first they are surrounded by low flats, with cameras peering over from all angles. In an alternative set-up he has a surround of black drapes, with hidden cameras peeking through gaps.

At first sight, such treatments may seem a welcome change. They have the advantage of providing free, 360° shooting with no cameras in sight. They get away from the regular methods of staging a show of this type. Unfortunately, rehearsals reveal another side to the situation.

Where cameras are shooting over surround flats they all have high, unflattering viewpoints of the seated people. Cameras have to make considerable moves around the ring of flats to vary their shots. Where they are hidden behind black drapes they are virtually immobile.

With both methods, as shots are intercut, speakers appear distractingly to jump from one side of the screen to the other. Composition is often awkward and heads frequently intrude into shot.

Without laboring the point, the staging concept does not really work. Next time, the director will probably follow a time-worn approach that does.

It is no coincidence that all over the world there are marked similarities between the ways different countries stage certain types of program. These are methods that get the best results. They provide a good range of shot opportunities with successful lighting and sound.

Some staging approaches have become so 'traditional' that any radically different design could appear strange and unacceptable to an audience. A quiz show staged in a bar or a religious program in a factory would not somehow carry the same weight as in the surroundings we normally associate with these types of program.

Most people working in the medium on cameras, lighting, sound, etc. have a frustrating abundance of great ideas. There are those impressive camera angles, dramatic lighting effects, arresting sound treatments that they itch to use, given half a chance. But, regrettably, these would be inappropriate for the particular production they are working on at the moment! The scenic designer is no exception.

Despite these various constraints, the designer's task is to keep recurrent forms of presentation looking fresh, interesting, and eye-catching, and yet appropriate to the needs of the individual show, and that can be a challenge indeed.

4.2 Basic forms of staging

Most TV staging treatments are themes and variations on a few recognizable categories:

- Scenic background,
- Area staging,
- Open sets,
- Desk set-ups,
- Box sets/closed sets,
- Composites,
- Audience shows,

and, exceptionally:

- Two-tier staging,
- Enclosed sets.

4.3 Scenic backgrounds

Probably the most basic form of scenic treatment is the *single decorated flat*. Don't despise it! There are moments when nothing more elaborate is needed. Let's look at a few examples.

Situation: Night. Watcher in street waits for a room light to go out in the house opposite.
Treatment
Watcher: One brick flat for watcher in localized patch of light, looking upwards.
House: One window flat with rear-lit blind. (Photograph establishes the street location.)

Situation: Girl out marketing, phones home.
Treatment
Street set: Stone-faced flat with poster and public phone booth.
Home set: Wallpapered flat with phone on table.

Situation: Host in games show announces winning contestant.
Treatment
He stands in front of drapes frame; gold lamé, with overswagged red velvet.

Situation: Guide takes us on a tour of the Tower of London.
Treatment
He stands in front of a contoured stone wall flat. The tour consists of pieces of library (stock) film clips! Each time we return to the guide between clips the flat has been modified – adding different signs, handrail, bush, lighting changes, etc.

4.4 Area staging

This is the sort of décor used when there is to be large-scale activity in the studio – marching bands, ballet groups, orchestras, choirs, acrobats, etc.

Widespread action needs plenty of space, so we want to leave the floor as free as possible. The basis of most area staging is the cyclorama, left as plain tone or decorated with attached or hanging designs or lighting patterns.

Alternatively, you can use a *cyc cloth*, i.e. a large artist-painted cloth hung as a cyc, that serves as a total background. This could be:

● Realistic (e.g. a woodland glade),
● Stylistic (e.g. a dramatic 'theatrical' treatment for a Wagnerian opera),
● Decorative (e.g. the inside of a circus tent, complete with painted cheering audience).

You can develop the large open floor area in front of the cyclorama, using shallow scenic units against the cyc, or wings, or 'scenic islands'. Which is appropriate will depend, of course, on the sort of action in the show and how it is going to be shot.

Large pieces of scenery in the performance area would get in the way of the action. But it is usually possible to introduce some shallow free-standing units, such as columns, cut-outs, or screens, fairly near the cyc to give dimension to the background of the shots. Take care, though, to check that they can be lit effectively

Figure 4.1 Basic forms of staging

Scenic background. A single plain or decorated flat, a photo blow-up, or a painted scene provides sufficient background for limited action (particularly when chroma key inserted.)

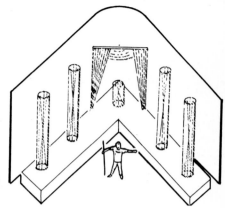

Area staging. Area staging is essential for broad action and widespread movement. Emphasis is on pattern and decorative effect.

Open sets. Economical and flexible, open settings are adaptable for stylistic and realistic situations.

Desk set-ups. Modular units or custom-built desks are adaptable to many regular show formats (Figure 6.2).

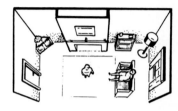

Box sets. The traditional three-sided set convincingly simulates rooms while providing maximum operational flexibility.

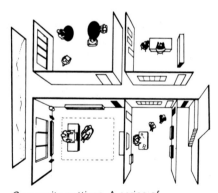

Composite settings. A series of interconnected or conjoining sets makes maximum use of the staging area.

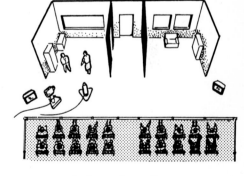

Audience shows. Sets are arranged to give the audience an optimum view of the action. The audience may be seen on camera or heard only as reactive background responses.

Two-tier staging. Very occasionally used where floor-level staging or subterfuges cannot be used. Requires well-designed scaffold framework for upper storey. Necessarily inhibits lighting, sound, and camerawork within the ground-floor setting.

without throwing ugly distracting shadows onto the adjacent cyc. This is a regular problem.

Paradoxically, if you are using *finely traced* materials such as bare tree branches or nets, their soft shadows falling on the cyc may actually add to the overall effect.

When cross-shooting a large performance area with several cameras the greatest problems lie in preventing the cameras shooting off onto the studio walls or inadvertently getting each other in shot.

The simplest solution is to provide a series of *wings* in some form. You can use a succession of hung drapes, drape frames, flats, profiled flats – anything, in fact, that matches the rest of the décor. For the 'circus' scenic cloth, for example, you might have giant clown cut-outs as wing pieces. If wings are not practicable then you can always hang drapes (black, velours, etc.) or a cyc cloth along the sides of the staging area to mask off the studio walls.

When there is sufficient space you could develop a shallow 'horse-shoe' setting across the width of the studio, built right up to the cyc. This arrangement often features entrance arches on either side, with slashed curtains of metalized plastic.

Where the subject is a large static group, such as a band, a choir, or a symphony orchestra, a series of scenic 'islands' on platforms, or one large central multi-level island, are possible treatments.

To add interest to longer shots you might decide to suspend groups of decorative latticework screens over the acting area. Similarly, there are opportunities for localized sloping 'ceilings' of open framework, box structures, or grilles. A succession of decorative cloth borders could be effective.

Finally, to unify the effect you may be able to introduce *foreground pieces*, with cameras shooting past people seated at small tables or groups of 'interested onlookers', or through a foreground tree. Not only does this create an additional dimension for the pictures but it avoids that 'decks-cleared-for-action' look that you find with some area staging.

4.5 Open sets

Open sets generally consist of a series of pieces of furniture or scenic pieces arranged in front of an open cyc to produce the impression of an environment. The result is 'a set without walls' – although their absence may not be obvious on camera. The result can be realistic, decorative, or even abstract, depending on what you do.

Take, for example, a white doorway, a white window frame, and a wall-mirror frame, and arrange them around a central white carpet. Against black drapes and floor we have created a symbolic room. But suspend a draped window and furnish the room more fully with tables, chairs, plants, sofa, table lamps, etc., and, although it has no walls, the result can seem on camera to be a real, three-dimensional room!

Abstraction can be taken a stage further, to the point at which we depict the bare bones of an entire building structure in the form of a decorative *skeletal set* (Section 4.31).

4.6 Desk set-ups

Several types of production use desks of some kind as an integral part of the décor (newscasters, discussion panels, games shows, debates, demonstrations, talks, etc.).

These desks are normally formed from modular structures (Section 6.9) – either refurbished stock units or units constructed for that show. Sometimes the top of a desk will have a hole through which the speaker can watch a small picture monitor (e.g. showing preview pictures of videotape or film).

The desks are usually located within some form of area staging (Section 4.4), often on a low platform to bring the speaker's eye-line up to a convenient camera-operating position.

4.7 Box sets/closed sets

This is the traditional three-sided arrangement used for many studio settings. It consists fundamentally of a back wall and two side walls. The front fourth wall is missing, although we may suggest it or even build it occasionally (Section 4.11).

Even when we are creating a realistic room environment the set will usually be rather larger than life in order to provide more space for actors and cameras to move around. This is not obvious on the screen, particularly when narrower-angle lenses are used.

When the set is small or narrow it may be helpful to angle the side walls apart slightly at the front ('splaying'), to give cameras a better opportunity to cross-shoot the action.

4.8 Composite settings

Most *composites* consist of a series of interconnected sets representing a group environment. So we may have:

● An office complex, with adjacent rooms around a central corridor,
● A street scene with a shop, including its interior and a store room at the rear,
● The entire ground floor of a house together with its backyard,
● A ship's cabins, companionway, and deck.

Occasionally, several small sets are grouped (although unrelated) in order to save studio space. Then, for all practical purposes, they form a composite.

When a *box set* is built there is usually plenty of room behind each flat to provide individual bracing from the rear. But in a *composite setting*, where several sets are built close together, there may be no space for normal bracing. Then, as we shall see later (Chapter 9), special precautions are necessary to keep the whole assembly stable (e.g. suspension points, corner bracing, or cross-braces between sets).

Composite sets also pose additional problems for *lighting*. When sets are arranged around the studio there are seldom difficulties in finding room to hang lamps or power outlets to feed them. But when lighting a composite we are liable to need a large number of lamps in a limited area of the studio, and this may strain local resources.

4.9 Audience shows

Whenever a studio audience is invited to watch a show being recorded we need special group seating. This can be arranged for the occasion on multi-level platforms or provided by specially designed mobile units, which incorporate all seating, treads, handrails, etc.

As far as the designer is concerned, an audience show has several special requirements:

- All seating arrangements must meet local fire and safety regulations respecting types of seats, density of seating, spacing, gangways, guard rails, stairways, exit signs, etc.
- Settings normally take the form of area staging, open sets, or desk set-ups. Where a naturalistic setting is required this can be designed as a large *in-line composite* facing the audience or a series of side-by-side box sets, arranged so that they can see all or most of the action. There are usually several slung picture monitors and local loudspeakers so that the audience can follow all aspects of the show, including any video effects, film, or videotape inserts.
- The audience platforms (rostra) and the operational area in front of the sets can take up an appreciable part of the studio floor space. So at times you may even find that there is insufficient room for all the settings needed. One solution to this dilemma is to pre-record sections earlier in the day, strike the set, and replace it with another for the scenes the audience is going to watch. (They will watch the taped section on the hanging monitors.)
- If the director is going to take shots of the audience it will probably be necessary to hang drapes at the sides and rear of the seating area to provide a background and to improve the acoustics (e.g. deadening random audience noise).

4.10 Two-tier staging

Even if a studio has a sufficiently high ceiling and the program budget can accept the extra cost, most television designers avoid extensive building above the normal floor level unless it is unavoidable, for it introduces many complications for the entire team.

If we want to indicate that there is another floor above or below the present one it is often a lot easier and more convenient to use a subterfuge than to build it. Fortunately, we can usually get round the situation simply by stimulating the audience's imagination instead!

Watching action on the screen, an audience makes a lot of assumptions. When, for instance, they see someone leave a room and later appear in a bedroom they assume that the person has walked upstairs, especially if the dialogue has indicated this. We do not have to show them actually doing so.

There are times when you only need an actor to look upwards, as if there is an upper floor, and leave the rest to the imagination!

You can convey the idea that there is a cellar just by laying a dummy trapdoor on the floor. When it is opened up the camera sees a square of black velvet which, on screen, looks like darkness below.

Again, light from a hidden lamp on the floor behind a flat can create the illusion that it is coming from a non-existent hallway below.

Actors have even walked behind a vertical flat 3 ft (1 m) high, progressively bending their knees and convincingly implying that they were walking downstairs!

But what if we cannot rely on editing, fake scenery (Section 3.38), or implication?

If the action calls for someone to go upstairs you can build the staircase up to the height of the top of the set (e.g. 10 ft (3 m)) and have a platform at that level with a dummy door flat. We see them climb but have only had to build a nominal amount at height.

But suppose the director wants the actor to climb the stairs and enter a room with the camera following and then look out of the window into the garden below? Now we are getting into a much more complex and demanding situation.

Cameras on the studio floor can only get a restricted range of shots from action a foot or so above floor level. Their viewpoints will be very low and they easily overshoot.

So unless the director is using hand-held cameras or camera cranes which can elevate to 9 ft (2.7 m) or more, camera mountings will also need to go up onto this raised area and that will involve extra precautions and floor reinforcement.

Scenery is heavy, and if you are anticipating erecting elevated castle ramparts, towers, upstairs rooms, etc. then standard platforms (parallels, rostra) may not be able to carry their weight. It may be necessary to use extra high flattage, which rests on the studio floor, the platforms being set up against it.

As a general guide, the upper load-bearing capability of a stock platform may be of the order of 100 lb per 4.28 ft^2 (45.4 kg per 0.39 m^2), depending on its construction and condition. (The treads of any stairway or steps leading up to it should preferably be around 8 in (200 mm) from nose to a riser, with a step height of 6–9 in (152–230 mm).)

Otherwise the staging now enters a different league entirely, and you will need to use carefully planned, expertly erected tubular scaffolding as a base for the elevated scenery.

4.11 Enclosed sets

You are not likely to meet four-walled sets very often – except on location. Unless the room is large, cameras can have difficulty in getting far enough from the action to take reasonably long shots. They tend to work with wider-angle lenses, and, ironically, exaggerate and distort the space (Section 7.3). Cameras may be able to shoot in through doors or windows to improve their shots.

Within the room, unless cameras are hand-held, space will need to be cleared for camera mountings and crew, and this may involve removing or rearranging furniture at intervals.

Where four walls are essential in a studio setting you can make use of *wild walls*, i.e. removable walls which are raised, hinged, or slid out of the way as needed, to accommodate shots.

A further approach is to include hiding places and peepholes for cameras through doors, windows, fireplace, false returns in walls, *camera traps* (hinged wall flaps behind pictures), pull-aside drapes, etc. (Section 5.15).

Considering the many compromises involved in four-wall staging, it is usually preferable to try to find another way of tackling the situation. It can, for instance, be a lot better to build the apparently four-walled set as two *separate* box sets, shoot the action in each, and edit the lot together later.

4.12 Style

There are a number of factors that can guide us towards the most suitable design approach.

Is the setting to be an integral part of the presentation, as in realistic drama? Or is it to provide an unobtrusive background that supports the action, without having any associated overtones?

Is the setting to appear neutral? Or is its main purpose to be decorative, creating a certain mood or atmosphere?

Are there aspects of the program itself that will influence the style of the setting? Perhaps, for instance, it is to reflect a certain historical period or a specific location.

It is easy to underestimate the importance of staging style. But the form we choose can considerably influence how the audience

Figure 4.2 Stylistic approaches

Neutral backgrounds
The simplest staging uses a plain non-associative background (1).

Realistic staging
This can take several forms:
(2) directly imitating an actual place;
(3) capturing the atmosphere of a location; or implying a location through selected elements.

Decorative staging
Decoration can be created through (4) abstract design; or (5) fantasy; or by concentrating on outline, as in the silhouette (6).

responds towards the program itself. As a rule, staging style reflects not only the program subject but the way in which the director intends treating it.

If, for instance, we are presenting a serious subject such as 'Tooth decay' to a gathering of medicos we would probably select a formal style to suit the occasion. But to get the attention and interest of an audience of small children a whimsical, entertaining approach would be much more appropriate. Choose the wrong style and the result can be embarrassingly unsuccessful! Humorous overtones in a seriously slanted program could appear coy or of dubious taste.

4.13 Basic stylistic approaches

Broadly speaking, we find that most staging falls into one of three stylistic groups:

1. Neutral, non-associative backgrounds,
2. Realistic staging,
3. Decorative treatment.

At times a particular treatment may have elements of each.

Neutral backgrounds

4.14 Plain tone

The simplest neutral background consists only of a plain undecorated single-tone surface behind the action.

You can achieve it using a cyc, seamless paper, a run of even-toned flats, plain drapes, scrim, a translucent screen, or electronically inserted tone.

Plain-tone backgrounds have their merits. Subjects will stand out very clearly against neutral-toned surroundings if you take care to select an appropriate tonal value.

It is undoubtedly the most economical way to stage any subject. But it can also be the dullest! For remember, this single tone will be appearing behind the subject in *every* shot!

4.15 Cameo staging

To create a *cameo* staging effect we need totally black surroundings: a black background and floor (floor cloth or painted floor). All the camera reveals will be lighter-toned subjects (people, furniture, scenery), standing out boldly, isolated in darkness. There is no impression of 'space', just a detailless void.

The technique's chief merit is that it concentrates the attention on the subjects. There are no distractions. At the same time, it disguises space. Whether the studio is tiny or enormous the result could look the same on the screen!

This technique does have its drawbacks. A visual illusion known as *simultaneous contrast* or *spatial induction* arises whenever we look at a subject against a strongly contrasting tone – particularly in longer shots, where the background dominates the picture.

A black background will cause the subject's tones to look lighter or paler than normal. It is possible to compensate for this impression to some extent by deliberately reducing the camera's exposure a little (stopping the lens down slightly).

Another very practical problem is the way in which we find dark tones and shadowed parts of the subject *merging*, and becoming lost in the black background. Looking at someone with dark hair we may find that we can see their face clearly – but their hair vanishes entirely!

You can actually use this unwelcome effect to produce visual tricks! Dress a person entirely in black and they will disappear altogether against the black background. Have them hold up a light-toned object and it will seem on screen to be suspended in mid-air – a useful phenomenon if you happen to want that sort of 'magic'!

You can reduce the tendency for dark subjects to merge with the black background by using strong *backlight* behind them. Unfortunately, however, although this prominent rim-light outlines their edges well it can look very artificial.

While very light subject-tones can appear crisp, fresh, or even startling against the black background, mid- to low-toned subjects can look very drab, somber, or dramatic.

Watching action against black backgrounds for any length of time can become very tiring, although some memorable low-budget dramas have been produced against black drapes in times past.

Black backgrounds are regularly used for 'exterior night' scenes in the studio. It takes just a few items (and the audience's imagination) to form a convincing environment out of little.

Plain black backgrounds are easy enough to achieve. Simply hang a run of black drapes behind the action. They do not need to be stretched carefully, for any folds or wrinkles will not show.

To ensure that the darkest picture tones are 'crushed out' and merge into a solid black background one can slightly reduce the exposure (*lens aperture*, *f-stop*) and/or adjust the camera channel's electronic *black level* (*batting down on blacks*; *set down, sit*). But take care not to overadjust the video, or tonal gradation in all darker tones will also be lost (Section 11.6).

If the camera is likely to see the floor in any shot it will also need to be black. It is simplest to spread a black cloth over this area. It takes only moments to put down and to remove afterwards.

However, there are hazards. Material laid on a smooth studio floor can be quite treacherous to walk on, and people are liable to slip. If cameras attempt to move onto it they will probably ruck it up, even if you tape the edges.

So clearly, the best solution is to paint the floor black. The limitations here are:

- The obvious nuisance of having to paint the floor (and wait for it to dry!) and later scrub it off again.
- Backlight can bounce up off the painted black floor, so that it appears lighter-toned and shiny on camera.
- Scuff marks from feet, camera dolly wheels, or sound booms may be visible, so that in time its surface needs refurbishing.
- Any water spilled onto the painted floor not only ruins the surface finish but makes it slippery, sticky, and dangerous.

You can use thick seamless paper to provide a continuous unbroken background and floor tone, but it is not very durable and, like painted floors, reflects bounced backlight and is easily marked by feet and equipment.

4.16 Limbo staging

Limbo effects make use of a plain 'all-white' background to provide neutral surroundings for the action, effectively isolating subjects, especially if they have mid- to dark tones.

The general effect of limbo staging is of 'infinite space', particularly if the floor is carefully blended into the vertical background. The result can be very attractive, delicate, and ethereal. On the other hand, it can be blank-looking, dazzling, or devoid of interest. As always, the coin has two sides.

The easiest way to stage limbo surroundings is to use an evenly lit open cyclorama, completely free, of course, from folds, wrinkles, or other blemishes. Failing that, an unbroken run of flats may suffice.

The floor area also needs to be white, its tone being merged into the cyc, with appropriate 'ground row' or 'cove' units.

Limbo staging is not without its hazards. Subjects tend to look darker than usual in front of very light surfaces. If we try putting more light on them to compensate, or open up the camera lens to improve exposure, the light background will become even lighter and 'block off' at *peak white* (i.e. the maximum level the television system can transmit). 'Superwhite' backgrounds are disturbing to watch.

In fact, you do not need very white background and floor surfaces to achieve good limbo effects. By adjusting the light intensity even cream or pale-grey tones can be lit to reproduce as white.

4.17 Electronically inserted tone

Finally, as we shall discuss in Chapter 8, we can use *chroma key* techniques, and electronically insert the entire black or white background at the touch of a switch!

4.18 Non-associative backgrounds

The purist might argue that no background can be truly non-associative. After all, most stimuli tend to promote associated ideas in our mind. Even plain tone is reminiscent of certain moods and conditions:

● *White* – with delicacy, simplicity, lightness, cheerfulness, sparkle, blankness, cleanliness, innocence, colorlessness, vigor, snow...
● *Gray* – with depression, gloom, monotony, inactivity, calmness, decay...
● *Black* – night, mystery, heaviness, somberness, ominousness, smartness...

Nevertheless, it is possible to devise backgrounds that provide pleasing, attractive surroundings for action and yet will not have conscious associations for the audience; surroundings that are neutral and non-representational. For example, an indefinite, vague pattern of light shapes and shadows can be used to effectively break up an otherwise bare, blank background without creating environmental or emotional overtones.

But if that pattern is focused to make it distinct and clear-cut it often starts to take on a particular pictorial significance. We now find ourselves reacting to the line, shape, mass, and tonal distribution we see.

For the designer, this change is more than an interesting academic nicety. It demonstrates how the impact of staging will vary, as one alters the prominence, clarity, and contrast of features in the décor.

4.19 Subject/background contrast

Occasionally, we deliberately limit the tones in both subjects and surroundings in order to develop a particular effect – an ethereal

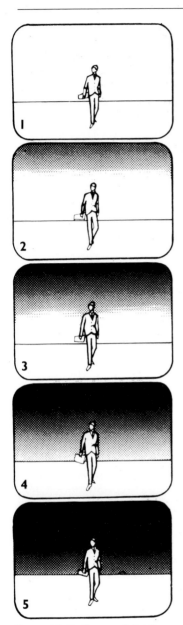

Figure 4.3 Background shading
As the background is progressively
shaded the picture develops a more
'closed-in' feel.
1. This open-air effect would usually
make an interior scene look artificial.
2. Typical shading for a lofty interior
lit by daylight.
3. Wall shading for a typical room in
daylight (8–10 ft (2.4–3 m) high).
4. Shading for an evening interior or
dramatic day interior.
5. Strongly shaded wall for restricted
surroundings (small, low-ceilinged) or
night effect.

atmosphere, for instance. But, generally speaking, we want
subjects to stand out from their background.

The closer the subject tones are to those of the background, the
more they will tend to merge. So dark clothing against dark tones
in walls, furniture, or foliage or light-toned clothing against pale
scenic tones are best avoided wherever possible.

A good contrast between faces and their backgrounds is particularly important. As a guide, remember that face tones typically
reflect 30–40% of the light falling on them. The preferred lightest
tone in the scene is around 60% (TV white) and the darkest about
3.3% (TV black). But as we can adjust the amount of light falling
on a background, or leave it in shadow, the effective value of any
surface can be altered over a wide range.

4.20 Flatly lit backgrounds

If a background is flatly lit so that its tone is even all over, we tend
to get an impression of openness, emptiness, or plainness. That's
fine if we want to create an open-air look, or to suggest the infinite
in limbo treatment. But it would hardly be appropriate to light the
walls of a room in this way with flat, unbroken light. The result
would be unsatisfying. The interior would look baldly artificial. It
might even cease to look like an interior at all!

Even if the designer is not responsible for the lighting, he or she
will certainly be concerned with the effect it is having on the sets!

4.21 Vertical shading

If we take a plain background and grade its tones so that it is
darker at the top and progressively lighter lower down some
interesting effects develop. It is unimportant whether this shading
is achieved through lighting or by judicious use of a spray-gun. We
find that vertical shading can have a strong influence on our
impressions of height and size.

Try this technique in an interior setting. It does not matter
whether its walls are plain or decorated. You will find that, as the
shading moves downwards and a greater area of the upper wall
becomes darkened, the room will feel progressively smaller and
the ceiling lower – even if there isn't one! Clearly, a lofty palace
scene would have walls shaded higher than a claustrophobic
cottage interior.

Graded background tones also have very practical advantages.
They allow us to alter how prominent various parts of the scene
appear on camera. We can throw some areas into sharp relief and
make others less conspicuous. Similarly, we can use wall shading
to emphasize the outlines of people, furniture, or parts of the
setting.

Wall shading does not have to be highly dramatic. It can be so
gradual that it is only really obvious in more distant shots (long
shots). But subtle shading contributes an attractive quality to the

picture that is totally lacking with flatly lit backgrounds. It is, in fact, a regular practice for experienced lighting directors to shade walls to an appropriate extent for most types of production.

4.22 Background light-patterns

Light-patterns on the background generally have one of two purposes: to simulate a *natural* effect (such as sunlight shining through a window) or to provide an attractive *decorative* effect. Sometimes a given pattern can be adapted to either: e.g. a realistic red-orange moving-flame effect becomes an exciting dynamic pattern when used with green or blue light for a dance routine.

For the designer, light has particular advantages over pigment when devising background patterns:

● They can be switched on and off at will.
● Their intensity can be changed slowly or rapidly.
● Light-patterns can be combined and intermixed.
● They can be sharply defined or softly focused.
● The hue and intensity of a background behind a design may be varied at choice.

Earlier, we discussed how light-patterns can be cast onto the *floor* to provide decorative effects (Sections 3.63–3.67). The opportunities for *background* patterns are even greater, for they are normally quite independent of action lighting.

You can create background light-patterns in several ways. Some are more convenient and more flexible than others:

● *Directly from the lamp.* By adjusting the beam spread ('spotting' and 'flooding'); by lighting a surface at an oblique angle the beam can be spread to create wedge-shaped light-patterns; by using accessories such as barndoors, cylindrical 'snoots', 'flags' (separate large flaps).
● *Cast shadows.* Any opaque material can be suspended in front of a lamp to cast shadows on the background (a tree branch, a window frame, a large cut-out motif, or a large stenciled sheet).
● *Projected light-patterns.* A projector focuses the image of a photoslide or a metal stencil (gobo) onto the background.
● *Reflected pattern.* Light is reflected from a mirror-plastic or metal-foil sheet, which has a design painted on its surface or is cut out in the shape of a design. You can get some very interesting random 'textural patterns' simply by reflecting light from uneven or creased cooking-foil.
● *Silhouetted shadow.* You can have the subject that is to be silhouetted unlit against a light background (which is illuminated from the front or the rear). Or you can place the subject *behind* the background, and cast its shadow onto the rear of the background.

Point several lamps with different light colors onto the same suspended pattern, reflection sheet, or silhouette and you will achieve some interesting multi-colored mixtures.

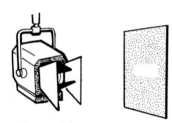

Figure 4.4 Light-patterns

Beam shaping. The spotlight's normal circular beam (adjustable with focusing control from *spot* to *flood*) can be restricted with barndoor flaps to give square or rectangular coverage – either to confine and localize light or produce decorative background patterns. When the lamp is 'flooded', coverage is maximum, light output is lower, and the shadow is sharpest.

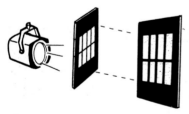

Cast shadows. Objects can be positioned in front of a spotlight to cast shadows on the background. The shadow is sharpest when the lamp-area is small (lamp fully flooded), when the subject is far from the lamp, and is distant from the background.

Figure 4.4 (continued)

Projected light-patterns.
A projector lamp (ellipsoidal spot; profile spot, effects spot) focuses the image of a stenciled metal plate (gobo) onto the background. Image size depends on the gobo, the projector's lens-angle, and its distance from the background.

A wide range of gobos are obtainable with realistic or decorative patterns. Simpler effects can be home-made in metal foil.

If the image is projected at an angle to a surface it becomes distorted ('keystoning'). However, this effect may appear quite natural.

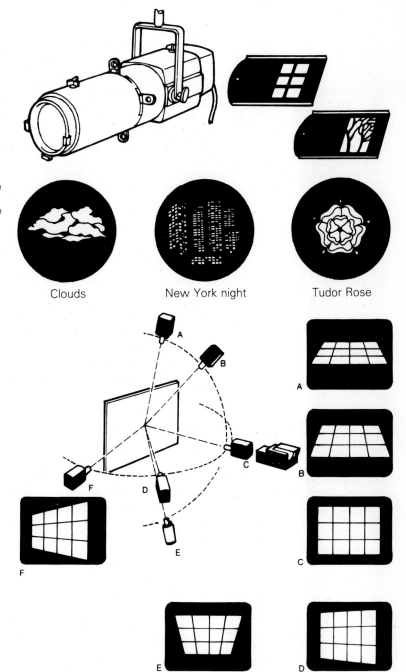

Clouds   New York night   Tudor Rose

Reflected patterns. Patterns on mirror, foil or metalized sheet can be reflected onto backgrounds. Creased/crumpled foil provides random reflections.

Figure 4.4 (continued)
Silhouettes. Silhouettes offer interesting background patterns, provided either by shooting an unlit subject against a lit background or shadows cast onto a rear-illuminated area.

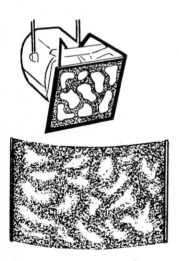

Figure 4.5 Dappled backgrounds
Random dapples on a background create interesting abstract effects suitable for a wide range of productions. Produced by cookies (dapple-sheets), cut-out color-medium, or projected patterns. Most effective when very defocused.

Here is a quick reminder of a few of the endless opportunities for light-patterns in staging: logos, lettering, stylized patterns (e.g. flowers, moon), window patterns (leaded windows, prison bars, circular windows, lancet windows, skylights), trees and foliage shadows, geometrical shapes, abstract reflections, clouds, stars, sun, signs, stained glass windows, skylines (day and night), decorative motifs (music, birds, geometrical, snowflakes, floral), etc.

And, of course, there are the moving light-patterns that can be produced by motorized projectors with animation disks: sea swell, flames, moving clouds, snow, water ripple, spirals, flickers.

4.23 Dappled backgrounds

An all-purpose shadow device, known variously as a *cookie*, *cuke*, *cucoloris*, or *dapple sheet*, has found regular use in all types of program.

There are two forms. The first is a solid sheet (metal or black plywood), which has been deeply cut away at its edges to produce an irregularly indented shape. This is held in a 'flag stand' in front of a lamp to produce a strong-shaped shadow.

The second form consists of a metal sheet in which a number of large, irregularly shaped holes have been cut to leave thick or thin ribs between. They may be designed with an open or a solid center.

These devices produce effects ranging from a subtle or pronounced dapple to sinuous veining, according to the proportions.

The open type of cookie has the particular advantage that it can be slipped into the bracket that carries the color medium in front of a fresnel spotlight, and with little effort will produce colored or white dappled light of varying density. You can even place several pieces of different colored gel in front of a lamp and obtain a 'stained glass' effect. Patterns from a series of lamps will blend together to cover an entire cyclorama for decorative effect.

Another worthwhile alternative arrangement is to staple together several sheets of different colored medium ('gels'), having first cut out a number of differently shaped holes in each. Their individual and combined colors will produce multi-colored random patches.

The open cookies are also invaluable when you want to introduce barely discernible dappling on walls (interior or exterior) to break up plain surfaces or to produce the strongly dappled light and shade of foliage.

Realistic settings

4.24 The illusion of reality

Most drama settings are designed to simulate a *real* environment. We try to create an atmosphere through staging and lighting that is so realistic that the audience is convinced they are actually there, eavesdropping on events that are taking place at that moment. For them, the place actually exists. That is the art of make-believe we are all engaged in.

Yet it is a paradoxical process. Sometimes a skilled scenic artist will paint a backdrop that to the eye looks a masterpiece yet on camera somehow seems theatrical. At others, quite a crude effect, such as a water ripple, is accepted as totally realistic, although in fact it bears little relationship to reality. Disturb a curtain by waving a piece of board or twitch a tree branch with a length of fishing line and we have a convincing spring breeze.

There are no 'rules for realism'. It is a matter of perception, of judging just what is right for that particular environment. The skill lies in placing objects around so that they look as if they have been left that way by those living or working there. The result may be an untidy scatter or a neat sense of order, but it is much more than mere imitation.

4.25 Forms of realism

There are several forms of 'realism' in practice:

- *Replica* – where we are aiming to re-create a faithful copy of a particular place,
- *Atmospheric realism* – where the setting is portraying a certain *type* of scene. It may, for example, resemble a 'typical Victorian drawing room',
- *Symbolic realism* – in which we create what appears to be a realistic environment by combining a few associated details.

4.26 Accuracy

When re-creating an actual place in the studio a lot depends on whether your audience recognizes the location and whether the camera reveals important visual clues that *they* associate with it. Certain 'standard' views of the White House, Niagara Falls, or Sydney Opera House are familiar worldwide. But take a different or closer viewpoint of these famous places and even videotape or film shot on the spot may not be identified.

If total accuracy is essential the obvious approach is to limit the amount of décor you are going to need to reproduce. It is one thing to replicate a doorway and quite another to build a full interior! Fortunately, there are tricks, such as camera mattes or chroma key, that can allow one to appear to do even that, combining a minimum in the studio with photographs of the location.

4.27 Authenticity

It is all very well to seek to re-create a 'typical Victorian drawing room' in an historical play but exactly what is 'typical'? Research in a photolibrary can reveal so many themes and variations that it may be difficult to detect common features.

Show the outcome of our researches to someone who has actually lived in a Victorian drawing room and, if we are successful, they may be astonished at the accuracy of the reconstruction. On the other hand, they may find it a caricature, a joining together of inappropriate pieces. They detect a wrong balance that destroys conviction *for them*.

Most people in the audience, however, will accept the décor as *authentic*, whatever its errors, and even assume that this indeed was the way people lived at that time. That has happened on many occasions in motion pictures, where imagination and 'poetic license' have been responsible for much misinformation!

'Authenticity' is partly a matter of conscious research, but it is also a question of whether one can get reasonably similar items to dress the setting. One may discover that in a grocer's store of the early 1900s they packed loose sugar in bags of stout blue paper... but do we need this touch to reconstruct 'reality'? If suitable items for such a shop are still available to hire will they not be either too battered to use or too precious to risk? Who is going to track them down?

Obviously, a lot depends on the sort of productions you are designing for and your resources.

4.28 Believability

Scenic backdrops, photomurals, and photographic chroma key backgrounds can be totally convincing – until we happen to notice that they are strangely still. Sea waves do not move, people remain poised, traffic is frozen.

The coaching inn
A totally convincing exterior setting. The floor is painted to simulate cobble stones, augmented with molded cobble mats and generously strewn with straw and powdered peat. The carefully selected props give the setting a 'used' look.

From another angle, the scene takes on added depth, thanks to the foreground pillars. Their brick bases are formed from moldings attached to a timber framework.

A closer view of the stone walls, the brick walls, strategically placed grass tussocks, and the scenic cloth of distant houses.

From behind, we see that the 'stone walls' are molded on low profiled flats. The 'weathered brick walls' are fiber glass moldings attached to timber framework, built up on platforms and supported by heavily weighted stage-braces.

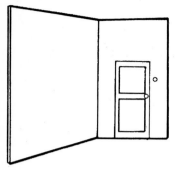

Figure 4.6 The 'lived-in' look

The raw finish. Freshly decorated scenery can have a new, artificial appearance.

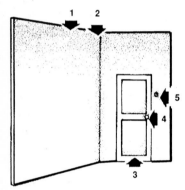

Subtle treatment. Selective after-treatment can give a setting a more authentic, lived-in look.
- Typically, the set is lightly sprayed ('blown down'), so that flats are darker towards the top (1), and towards the corners (2).
- Slight shading on door panels (3).
- Shading around handles (4), and light switches (5).

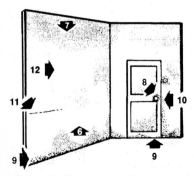

Ageing. If after-treatment is emphasized, the result is a dingy slummy look.

The obvious solution is to avoid having these givaway features in the photographs, but that is not always easy. You may be able to retouch the photograph, paste something over the unwanted items, or adjust the background's position so they are less prominent. Otherwise a foreground object in the studio camera's shot may be the solution.

Apart from that, as we saw earlier, you need to take care that the foreground scene in the studio matches the background reasonably well, and that no shadows reveal the trick.

4.29 The lived-in look

When freshly painted, a light-toned flat often has a raw, crude appearance that can give a setting a very artificial look. You can compensate for this to some extent by using uneven lighting, but if the surface is flatly lit, results may be very disappointing.

Most settings benefit from careful aftertreatment. Gentle shading or brushwork with black or brown water-paint can bring out surface modeling and the shape of structures. Plain flat surfaces can be given a texture that overcomes the blank, uninteresting finish of a completely even surface tone.

However accurately one re-creates an environment, it will still have false overtones if it is too fresh-looking and tidy. It needs to look 'used' – not *too* used, or it will seem slummy or dilapidated. But there is a subtle balance which depends on the occasion.

The technique (which is known variously as *dirtying down*, *antiquing*, or *blowing down*) imitates the wear and tear of everyday living. It involves gentle shading, discoloration, or highlighting that suggest grime and wear-marks where these would accumulate in actual locations. Typical places include:

- *Doors* – around the handle and nearby door edge (stile), kick marks along the bottom rail,
- *Walls* – rub marks and discoloration on walls from chair backs or passing people,
- *Fittings* – grime around light switches, discoloration around wall pictures, mirrors, etc. (particularly the surround marks left when these have been removed),
- *General* – corners, crevices, around fireplaces, niches, windows, etc.,
- *Floors* – simulating uneven wear, tracks worn by feet (especially inside doorways), litter.

Carried to an extreme, you will have a hovel or a ruin on your hands.

- Water staining on walls (6) provided by an uneven color wash.
- Heavier uneven spraying for random dirtying (7).
- Dark marks around handle and switch (8).
- Scuff marks (random surface damage) on wall and door (9).
- Rub marks from people pushing past the wall and door (10).
- Chair scrape on wall (11).
- Lighter patches where posters, pictures, etc. have been removed (12). (Made by covering over an area while dirtying down.)
(See Section 7.14.)

Acoustics and the designer

The acoustical characteristics of surroundings can have a considerable effect on the quality of the sound we hear.

Although materials such as stone, brick, and metal reflect sound waves most strongly, any rigid wooden structures, hardwall flats, or wooden panels in the studio (and, of course, the floor itself) are also very reflective.

When sound waves bounce off nearby surfaces they tend to reinforce the original sound-source, to produce a bright, strong, reverberant effect. Too many reflections, and the overall sound becomes confused. In more confined spaces sound can take on a harsher, boxy quality, perhaps resulting in a ringing hollow 'slap-back' effect.

Soft surfaces, on the other hand, absorb sound, particularly towards the higher end of the audio spectrum. Where there is considerable absorption (i.e. in very 'dead' surroundings) the resultant sound loses definition and becomes weaker, lifeless, flat, or woolly.

Sound is most strongly absorbed out in the open air. But upholstered furniture, drapes, rugs, and clothing all deaden their surroundings to some degree and reduce reflections.

For a good acoustical balance we want conditions that are neither too reverberant ('live') nor too 'dead'. Most settings sound better when they contain drapes, rugs, carpeting, or upholstered furniture, particularly underneath a ceilinged area.

A small room with straight parallel walls is likely to sound quite hollow. But by breaking up the walls with returns, alcoves, fireplace, furniture, wall cabinets, etc. you can considerably improve the sound quality. Even slightly splaying the side walls of a box set can reduce reflections.

Any hollow wooden structure such as platforms (rostra), staircases, or treads will resonate when walked on. The simplest way of reducing thudding feet and resonance is to clad the units with carpet, carpet underlay, or felt. It is a good general principle to treat any raised area in this way wherever people are going to walk or play instruments.

Where a low platform area represents a solid structure such as a sidewalk, hollow-sounding footsteps would be quite unrealistic. So it is advisable to place bags of sawdust, foam plastic, or expanded polystyrene beneath the platform to deaden unwanted noise. Occasionally, planks or light paving are used to give the passing feet a particular environmental sound quality.

When a person is seated at a desk or table (e.g. newscasters, anchor people) you can reduce accidental sound reflections by surfacing its top with a soft material (e.g. felt). Some desks have a hole cut in the top, at the edge nearer the camera, so that a microphone on a floor stand can be poked through. This avoids the thumps that a mike, resting on the desk, is liable to pick up.

A small musical group (e.g. a string quartet) requires an enclosed intimate sound quality, not the open sound of an empty studio. To reduce the amount of sound reaching studio walls, and being reflected as echo, you can introduce *acoustic screens/acoustic flats* around them.

Decorative settings

In this form of scenic treatment, emphasis is on *decorative effect*, for display, dramatic impact, or fun.

4.30 Symbolism

By extracting a few essentials from a scene we can often convince our audience that they are seeing a complete location. A desk and a chair in front of a plain background can be accepted as an office. A single window flat is assumed to be part of a complete building.

But we can go further, and select elements that then become *symbols* – of childhood, age, labor, progress, and so on. They may become decorative to a point at which they bear only a passing resemblance to the original thing, such as the 'rising sun' motif that symbolically represents 'dawn', 'hope for a new day', or 'Japan'.

Silhouettes too are a form of abstraction, and can provide extremely attractive decorative effects at low cost.

Fantasy can use deliberately distorted reality to create bizarre effects. Examples here range from cartoon to the madman's world of *Dr Caligari*. We find it typically in children's shows comedy, dream sequences, and horror. It is a world in which the artificiality of the flat cut-out and the broadly painted backdrop are acceptable substitutes for more elaborate structures.

4.31 Skeletal sets

With this decorative technique we are down to the bare bones of staging – almost literally! Deceptively simple, this treatment epitomizes the very essence of design abstraction.

Let's look at some variants that have proved very successful against an open cyc when coupled with sympathetic lighting design:

Figure 4.7 Skeletal staging

Skeletal treatment reduces a location to its essentials:
Using a series of isolated real/realistic picture elements.

Creating decorative symbolism.

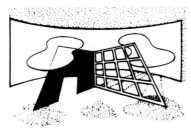

Developed abstractions.

- Suspended motifs – cartwheels, giant garden tools, cut-outs of heraldic shields,
- Vertical poles, looped with garlands of flowers,
- Suspended nets, swagged at ascending levels,
- Thick ropes forming a floor design ascend, to hang in an echoing design above,
- Whitened bare tree branches, set in floor stands, growing progressively smaller with distance to create a pseudo-perspective effect,
- Giant paper lanterns and streamers at different heights form a bower.

These were examples where, even on a low budget with few facilities, imaginative designers conjured striking, beautiful effects.

We could take a number of stock architectural pieces such as doors, give them a colorful new finish, and arrange them around the staging area as a decorative effect for a dance number.

As we saw in Section 4.5, we can position isolated units against a neutral background and fabricate an entire room in the imagination. This stimulating (and very economical!) approach has been used over a wide field of programs such as drama, talks, discussions, recitals and comedy sketches.

In the most ingenious form of skeletal staging, emphasis is on 'structural anatomy', and uses the outline and construction of a subject as a basis for a framework. So a 'house' might have symbolic windows, doors, balconies, staircases, and balustrades but no walls. Forest trees might be stylized as metal-frame outlines, with abstract tracery suggesting leaves.

Skeletal staging stimulates the imagination. But we need to avoid 'one-shot' design that only looks good from a particular viewpoint. To be really effective, skeletal treatment needs to be organized so that cameras can sectionalize the décor into a series of 'sub-skeletals'. Otherwise there is the danger, particularly in closer shots, that pictures may resolve themselves into little more than 'sticks growing out of people's heads'.

4.32 Translucent screens

Translucent backgrounds provide an extremely useful range of staging opportunities. In a small studio you can use them as general-utility backgrounds, which can be quickly modified for each production.

You can construct translucent backgrounds from a variety of materials, including stretched cloth or frosted plastic sheeting. It is preferable to use off-white or light gray materials with a matte finish, so as to reduce light reflections. But if these are not available a fine mesh black net over the face of a light-toned screen will help to achieve higher contrast.

There are various ways in which you can use a translucent background:

● As a plain background of adjustable brightness and hue (remember, any joins, supports, or stretchers will show through when lit from the rear),
● As a shaded background, lit from below at the front and/or the rear with strip lights (ground row, floor trough, cyc lights),
● For displaying light-patterns and shapes,
● Decorated by silhouetted ornamental screens, foliage, etc. placed behind it,
● To display projected pictures,
● As lit translucent paneling behind display shelves, skeletal scenery, etc.

Figure 4.8 Translucent backgrounds
A translucent screen can be used in many ways:
1. To provide a plain-tone background.
2. Bottom-lit as a shaded background.
3. To display light-patterns.
4. To provide ornamental silhouettes of unseen subjects.
5. For projected pictures.
6. As a lit background for silhouetting *foreground* cut-outs, skeletal units, shelf-units, etc.

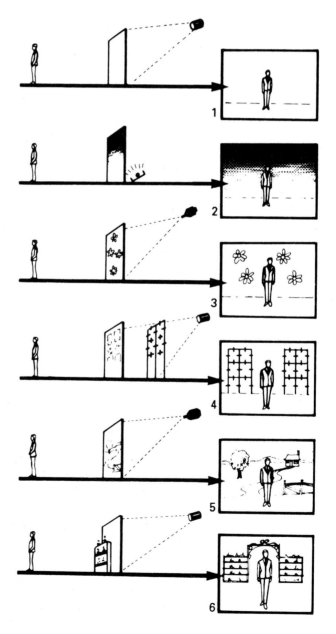

Any frontal light spilling onto the screen will dilute the density of the image or shadows cast upon it from behind. But some imaginative effects are possible by mixing both front and rear projection of different colors. Or again, you can gradually mix from rear to front projection, change the rear display, and slowly mix back to get interesting transformations.

Using scrim

4.33 Scrim/scenic gauze

Another of these terms that has acquired multiple use, *scrim* nowadays refers to both:

● The 'diffuser' that is placed in front of a lamp to 'soften' the shadows and reduce the light level, and
● The *scenic gauze* that, as we shall see, finds a number of uses in scenic design.

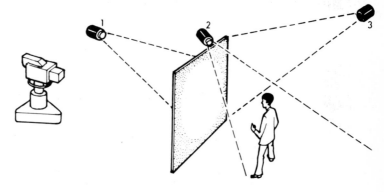

Figure 4.9 Scrims/gauzes
The effect of the scrim/gauze can be altered by changing lighting.
1. A light-toned scrim lit from the front alone appears to be a solid plane. Surface painting or decoration is seen clearly. Unlit subjects behind the scrim are invisible.
2. By reducing brightness of frontal illumination on the scrim and lighting subjects behind it the subject and setting are revealed, with outlines and contrast softened. Surface painting almost disappears.
An unlit black scrim virtually vanishes, while an unlit white one slightly diffuses the scene (see Section 7.11).
3. Rear-lighting the scrim increases overall mistiness and silhouettes any details on its surface.

We are concerned here with the latter.

Scrim/scenic gauze is basically a thin cotton or synthetic netting (e.g. rayon) with a mesh of around 1/16–1/8 in (1.5–3 mm) in diameter. Some types of mosquito netting and a fabric known as 'shark's tooth' are widely used. Scrim is available in black, gray, or white, and can be dipped or sprayed if necessary to different shades or colors.

It needs to be of sufficiently open weave to avoid excessive light absorption or obscuring subjects behind it. Yet it must be robust enough to stand handling and stretching.

You can drape scrim (although it creases easily) or arrange it in sculptural forms and stiffen it with sprayed adhesive, but in most applications it is usually stretched taut, without visible seams or wrinkles.

4.34 'Solid' scrim

The main feature of scrim is that its appearance changes according to the way it and the local scene are lit.

Lit from the front, stretched scrim appears as a solid plain surface:

● Nothing behind it is visible – provided that the light falling on the scrim does not pass through onto very light or shiny surfaces.
● You can project shadows or images onto the scrim from the front and, with less effect, from behind.
● With care, you can tape lightweight lettering, patterns, or designs onto the scrim.
● You can paint or spray the scrim (e.g. by stenciling), but, of course, this will usually prevent it from being re-used unless you want the same effect next time. Due to the way scrim stretches it can be more practical to add any surface treatment *after* the cloth has been hung and stretched, rather than decorate it beforehand and hope to hang it accurately.

4.35 'Transparent' scrim

If you leave a stretched scrim unlit (even a light-toned material) and light things behind it strongly they will be clearly visible. On camera the scrim itself will virtually disappear:

● If you are using a rather dense scrim, things in the distance will look a little softened.
● But you will need a greater amount of light than normal on the background scene.
● Any surface detail or painting will be silhouetted against the background under these conditions. So whether they are visible or not really depends on background tones.

4.36 'Translucent' scrim

The particular value of scrim is that by altering the balance between the amount of light falling directly onto its surface and the lighting on the scene behind it you can alter its apparent density.

Shoot a street scene in the studio, with an unlit scrim between the camera and the street, and everything looks quite normal. Add just a little light to the front of the scrim and the image softens. A little more, and the picture appears misty, even foggy, depending on the tone of the scrim.

A foreground scene shows a group of people at a party. A gradual lighting change, and the walls 'dissolve' to show their children back home. The camera dollies forward and we are in the next scene, with the children.

4.37 Scrim cycs

In some studios it is a regular practice to stretch a scrim over a taut cyc. As well as helping to disperse the light on the cyc and spread it more evenly this technique obscures any irregularities in the surface of the cyc, and can add to the illusion of infinite space.

You can eliminate wrinkles and creases in the scrim, after securing the top edge (e.g. with edge tapes to a batten), by weighting the lower edge under battens or tubular bars.

Sometimes the stretched scrim is pitched (sloped) away from the cyc at the bottom, so that ground lighting can be positioned between the scrim and the cyc. It is arguable how useful this practice is, for the lamps tend to be unduly close to the stretched cyc and so emphasize any irregularities there (through edge-lighting).

4.38 Substitute glass

When a room or shop setting in the studio has windows you have three options:

● *Leave the window framework void.* This saves work and expense, and is satisfactory enough for many purposes. However, the window tends to have a rather blank, unglazed look. If you want any signs or lettering 'stuck' to the shop window you will need to suspend them on black thread or line.
● *Glaze the window* with individual panes of clear plastic sheeting or secure a single sheet over the outside of the window. Results can be excellent, but the plastic may become scratched and smeary, and can buckle and reflect studio lamps. Too often one has to re-adjust the lighting or the shots just in order to get rid of the spurious reflections!
● *Staple a tightly stretched scrim to the outside of the window.* There will be no unwanted reflections. The scrim will also soften off the contrast and definition of the exterior scene and reduce its artificiality. It can even make a mediocre backdrop quite acceptable at times!

There is an added bonus, for this diffusion will help to create a greater illusion of distance beyond the window, even when a back-drop is only a short distance from the opening.

In everyday life we often notice how atmospheric haze progressively softens the detail and contrast of a scene with distance. (On sharp, clear days, distant things look much closer.) So when we see diffusion in the scene outside the windows of a setting it is not surprising that we tend to interpret this as 'aerial perspective'.

Incidentally, the scenic artist lightly spattering a painted backdrop with fine drops of white or gray paint, or gently spraying it over to reduce contrast, is following a similar principle.

Black scrim can be used as a glass substitute in the window of a shop. Not only is this extremely safe and trouble-free, avoiding all the embarrassing reflections of plastic sheeting, but you can still stick lettering or motifs to its surface. These will both establish the plane of the window and give added depth to the structure.

4.39 Contrast control

Where a scenic cyc cloth of open countryside or a townscape is used as a background to a scene it is sometimes helpful to stretch a black scrim over it, to reduce the 'rawness' by lessening its definition and contrast.

If you have the misfortune to find during rehearsal that some drapes are too bright or prominent, you can use the same idea and overcome potential disaster. The camera will not be able to detect the trick.

On location interiors black scrim has been used over windows to reduce the brightness and prominence of the view outside.

4.40 Painted scrims

Words cannot describe the beauty of the effects that can be achieved with painted scrims.

Nebulous shapes, vaporous trails, or glorious cloud formations can be sprayed or painted onto black scrim with a success that is achievable by no other means.

Castles, woods, mountains, buildings, painted on black scrim, are imbued with a magical quality, so appropriate for fantasy.

One memorable application of this technique was a drama in which the entire setting was painted on stretched black scrim. The material was mounted on a series of thin, black, self-supporting frames against a black floor. Under careful lighting the wall decorations, paneling, cornices, moldings, niches, arches, and drapes had a delicate but real quality, giving the production a slightly dreamlike atmosphere that was unique to this scenic treatment. Only the furniture was real. If one faded out the light falling on the scrim screens, the actors were left isolated, in pools of light.

Mobile scenic units

The idea here is to allow selected items to be added, removed, or rearranged quickly and quietly, even during recording.

The simplest example, perhaps, is the use of a quick-change table top – a board with table cover. One version contains the freshly set meal and the other has an identical layout with the dirty dishes – 'after the meal'. By swapping the boards during an intermediate shot we can suggest that time has passed.

Sometimes, just by adding wheels to a flat, a dummy hedge, or a large column we can simplify repositioning and add considerable flexibility to the staging.

4.41 Wagons

As we saw in Section 3.37, a *wagon* is a low-wheeled platform. It is also called a *stage wagon*, *truck* or *float*.

You can use a wagon to support anything, from an odd piece of furniture to a whole setting. There are several situations where this principle can prove particularly useful:

- When the area available for lighting is limited wagons can be prepared, stored to one side, and wheeled into position as needed.
- Similarly, when you have a chroma key area set up in the studio (e.g. background and floor coloured blue) you can wheel in prepared scenic elements or partial settings.
- In a large setting an essential part of the scenery (e.g. a fireplace wall) may prevent the director getting shots from certain angles. Built on a wagon, it can be repositioned or removed as necessary.
- Sometimes the action takes place in one part of a setting and then moves upstage to another area for the rest of the scene. Instead of removing individual chairs, desk, sofa, carpet, etc. by hand from the downstage area so that the cameras can move in, you could use a wagon for this section of the setting and slide it right out of the way in a few seconds.
- If a camera shoots past foreground subjects it can give a great impression of depth to the scene. In a restaurant, for instance, you might have a table with diners, a floral display, and a decorative screen filling the foreground. But this would all get in the way of camera movement. So you set them up on a wagon that can be wheeled away to clear the floor space whenever you need.
- In an audience show, one of the settings may only be needed for part of the production. A wagon allows it to be moved away and replaced by another, within range of the audience.

The main disadvantage of wagons is that you need a floor clear of cables (cameras, lighting, sound booms) and other impedimenta and space to put them in another part of the studio. If there is high scenery mounted on the wagon it could hit lamps in passing, so it may be necessary either to keep the lighting higher than normal in the route of the wagon or raise and lower lighting battens (barrels) for the move.

Although there is no point in using a wagon where you could simply remove a few pieces of furniture by hand, for more complicated or fully dressed inserts, where various props and set dressings have to be arranged, the ready-prepared assembly can save a lot of time.

4.42 Mobile areas

The larger the area to be moved, the greater the difficulties. So although it is possible to have sizeable turntables ('revolves') or mobile platforms carrying an entire orchestra they need to be very

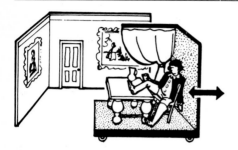

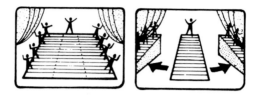

Figure 4.10 Mobile areas

Wagons. Part of the setting can be built on a low platform with swiveling casters to allow repositioning or quick striking during production.

Movable sections. Entire scenic sections may be built on wheels to enable them to be repositioned for effect. Here the large staircase splits to leave the soloist isolated.

carefully constructed if they are not to become cumbersome or even dangerous.

Much depends on how big the sections are, and whether they are low or built up:

● Will they be carrying only lightweight scenery (e.g. decorative screens) or more substantial scenery?
● Will there be people on the sections as they are moved?
● Are the units to be moved in shot or between scenes?
● Must it be one large unit or could you use a series of small ones?
● How far and how fast is the move to be?
● Will the units be pushed around by stagehands or motorized?

Unless the units are properly designed for the purpose they may well prove unwieldy and noisy to move, and the hiatus when one becomes immobile mid-route has to be seen to be believed!

4.43 Moving vehicles

There are some intriguing variations here. For some directors it is sufficient to sit a couple at the front of a horse-drawn carriage and have stagehands bounce it up and down on its springs. The floor manager shakes the reins and sound effects of horses' hooves complete the illusion.

Others, feeling that this approach is rather too basic, add extra touches. The rear end of a stuffed horse can be seen jiggling as it 'trots'; a little wind blows the clothing (a flapped board or a small fan); shadows move over the people from 'passing trees'.

To create a convincing impression that a vehicle is moving you may need to provide the audience with such clues as:

● Passengers being swayed or jogged,
● Parts of the vehicle shaking,
● Sounds of progress (engine noise, hoof beats, wheel noises, etc.),

Springs

Figure 4.11 Moving vehicles
By mounting a vehicle (or part of it) on a sprung platform or wagon, it can be rocked, bounced, swayed, to suggest that it is in motion.

- Lights or shadows passing over the passengers,
- Passing scenery,
- The road receding into the distance,
- Wind, dust clouds, blown leaves, etc.

There are few difficulties if you have a closed carriage at night. But an open cart moving hesitatingly through traffic in crowded city streets on a rainy day is quite another matter!

What seems, on the face of it, a straightforward enough requirement can need quite close coordination of sound effects, lighting, and the driver's actions. If the background is visible in the shot (using rear projection or chroma key behind windows), action in the vehicle should coincide with what is happening in the background scene. When the background stops, the rocking cart and the noises of hoofs or engine must stop too! (With rear projection an actor can follow the background in a mirror, but when using chroma key it is necessary to watch a monitor.)

4.44 Shots in cars

Any shots of automobiles have hazards:

- Lamps produce very strong localized highlights. Light reflected on the windshield and side windows is not only distracting but can prevent a camera outside seeing the occupants clearly. Some studios remove the windshield and lower the side windows as a regular practice for cars being used in studio drama.
- Not only the lights but also the camera crew will be reflected in the car's side windows and door panels. It is the fate of many a shiny new car to be sprayed over with dulling wax spray to kill the reflections!

A drama show that regularly needs a particular type of vehicle (e.g. a police car) may use just a windowless body shell on a wheeled frame. The hood (bonnet) may be removed to shorten the body and allow cameras to get closer.

Briefer still is the sawn-off rear half of a car, mounted with heavy springs on a wheeled platform. Unconvincing to the eye, it looks quite realistic on camera.

4.45 Ships and others

The *sprung platform* technique, when suitably handled, can provide realistic movement for a variety of transport, including rowboats, buggies, hansom cabs, and aircraft.

For violent movement (ships in heavy seas) much more radical methods are used, from settings built on rockers to platforms supported by hydraulic jacks. Many directors settle instead for cameras tilting or rolling, rising and falling keylights, and even actors swaying in unison, with a swinging cabin-lamp pulled by an unseen line.

Height and depth in floors

The flat studio floor is fine for most staging purposes but there are occasions when we want a raised area for some reason. Then, as we saw in Section 3.36, the *platform* (*parallel, rostrum, riser*) comes into its own.

4.46 Interviews/talks

It is a regular practice in many studios, when staging an interview, to place the seating on a low platform (e.g. 12–18 in or 305–455 mm high). This enables the cameras to shoot the seated performers at their eye level, rather than look down on them at an unflattering angle (Section 4.6).

This arrangement is particularly helpful where the cameras are mounted on wheeled tripods ('rolling tripods'), which have very limited height adjustment. 'Pedestal' mountings, which have a greater height range, can still work effectively where seating is at floor level.

4.47 Multi-level settings

By using platforms to vary the floor height you can give a setting an added dimension. Obviously there are several basic ways in which you could arrange these units, each appearing equally impressive on the screen in frontal wide shots:

1. As a series of low, isolated platforms,
2. As a series of isolated platforms of increasing height,
3. As an 'island', in which platforms of increasing height combine to form a central built-up structure,
4. As a similar 'island', with the highest platforms around the edges and back of the staging area and the lowest in the center,
5. As a line of platforms across the cyc, forming a series of steps.

What is not immediately obvious is that some give the director a good range of shot opportunities while others can prove very restrictive.

The points to bear in mind are:

● The camera cannot move in close to a subject on a platform. It can zoom in (use a narrow lens angle) but subjectively this squashes space.
● Because most cameras can only reach a maximum height of around 6 ft (1.8 m) they will usually be looking up at performers on the platforms. The closer the camera, the steeper its angle will be.

Remember, a person's eyes are about 4 ft (122 cm) above their feet when seated and about 5 ft–5 ft 6 in (152–168 cm) when standing. When we place them on a platform the camera has to reach those figures (plus the height of the platform) to take level shots of them.

So what does all this amount to in practice? Well, it depends on the type of program. In a fashion show or rock concert the continually low viewpoints may even help to give the presentation a visual importance. In a tap dance routine cameras could get fine shots of feet.

But suppose the cameras are shooting a symphony orchestra on these platforms and want to get close shots of a violinist's fingering, an over-the-shoulder shot of a tympanist at the back of the orchestra, a flautist in the middle of the group, or the conductor facing the orchestra? They may be unable to get meaningful shots.

You may find it an interesting exercise to look closely at each of these platform layouts and assess the shot opportunities they give from various directions.

4.48 High ground

When you want to create the impression that action is taking place on raised ground (e.g. a cliff-edge or a mountain top) the structure in the studio does not have to be particularly high. A low camera shooting upwards can make it look a lot steeper than it really is.

Figure 4.12 Heights
It can be safer and cheaper to simulate heights than to attempt to build them. Here the escaping fugitive climbs a cliff...but dislodges a rock and is discovered.

But all we need in the studio is:

A high camera shooting a gravel-strewn floor,

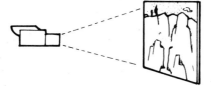

A picture of the cliff,

And a canted shot of a surface-contoured flat (using a mirror, prism, or camera on its side) to suggest vertical climbing!

The usual ingredients for realistic outcrops of uneven or rising ground in the studio are:

- Platforms of appropriate heights,
- Sloping ramps,
- Tightly packed sawdust sacks,
- Scenic blocks,
- Sandbags.

Platforms form the main structures, with sloping ramps leading from one height to the next. For localized humps, scenic blocks can be used. Sawdust bags fill in gaps.

If anyone is going to *walk* on this raised area sandbags can provide a firm foundation for an uneven path. But these are heavy, and, wherever possible, lighter materials are preferable.

As always, it does not matter how you achieve an effect. What is important is what it looks like and how safe it is. If, for instance, one needs a grass-covered mound in the background it might be a lot easier to use an inflated life-raft upside down as a foundation than to build the terrain piecemeal.

From now on it really depends on the type of terrain you are creating. The structure can be given an overall covering, such as a painted cloth or tarpaulin which has been finished to resemble earth, pebbles, sand, snow, etc. Grass matting can be draped and localized turfs added for greater realism. You can scatter tanbark, peat, sawdust, or leaves.

Grass clumps will give definition to the terrain, as will rocks made from shell moldings or expanded polystyrene. Also, of course, you can develop larger outcrops of rock, using traditional mesh-covered timber framework, with a heavy canvas or fiber glass skin. Given appropriate surface painting, the results can be very convincing on camera.

Finally, you may want to add small trees and shrubs to break up the overall contour.

If the director wants to move camera mountings around on this elevated area you will need to provide a suitable flat, level, reinforced, non-skid section for them.

Footsteps are liable to sound unnaturally hollow as they resonate on any platforms, but for an exterior scene this would be absurd. So to reduce noise to a minimum it is a good idea, wherever possible, to surface the tops of the platforms with felt, foam plastic sheeting, or cork-chip-faced bitumen felting. As we saw earlier, low platforms can also be loosely packed with sawdust bags.

4.49 Heights

Sometimes there are no ways round the situation. Our hero has to be seen climbing up the dangling rope, hand over hand, to the balcony above.

But in others you can fake the process, making it a lot safer – and less costly. You not only use a substitute for the real thing but *cheat* to make the audience believe that they are seeing a lot more than they really are!

Let's look at the balcony scene in some detail to see how simply the 'impracticable' can be achieved:

● The person at ground level is looking upwards, shot on a high camera.
● The person on the 'balcony' leans over a low stonework flat (backed by a flat), looking downwards towards a low camera.

The 'low' and 'high' cameras can be normal cameras taking mirror shots. It is very basic, but it works.

If you want to heighten the tension during the scene with details of the climb, you can either use:

● A ramp that has been surface textured and given suitable footholds, or
● A horizontal platform for them to crawl on.

With a hand-held camera on its side, a mirror on the lens, or video special effects the 'climber' can achieve the impossible.

Figure 4.13 Depth

Built-up ground. Holes in the ground are created within platforms (parallels, rostra). The ground can be covered with painted tarpaulin, shell rocks, grass, sandbag mounds, scatter, boards, etc.

4.50 Holes

Where only a shallow hole is necessary (e.g. for someone to dig out when uncovering buried treasure) a raised area about 2 ft (0.6 m) above the floor will probably suffice. On the other hand, if you require a sizeable hole for people to climb in or out of (e.g. a bomb crater or a well) it will need to be 3 or 4 ft (0.9 or 1.2 m) high.

So we come again to the question we discussed in Section 4.47. Can cameras shoot the action successfully when people who are 6 ft high stand on a raised area 4 ft from the ground?

Never overlook height limitations in the studio. It is an unforgettable experience to find on the day that lamps which are normally way above the acting area at 12 ft (3.6 m) are now almost touching the actors' heads! Can lamps be raised to get them well out of the way? Will cameras overshoot? With hindsight, one is prepared!

From holes in the ground let's turn to holes in the floor of a room. Now there are some additional complications. If the storyline calls for someone to lift a trapdoor and climb down into a cellar we could fake the move by using a dummy trapdoor (Section 4.10) and cutting to show them *in another setting*, descending the cellar stairs.

Simulated depth. It is simpler, and often just as effective, to stimulate audience imagination with hidden lamps and dummy exits.

But if the director insists that an actual trapdoor and cellar are essential we now have a two-tier setting, and the weight/floor-loading considerations we met earlier (Section 4.10).

Furniture

Apart from the more obvious needs to choose furniture of appropriate style, period, and so on, there are several very practical matters that one should not overlook when appraising furniture for a production.

4.51 Stock furniture

Most studios hold a stock of furniture for general use in productions. This includes chairs, couches, bookcases, desks, large and small tables, etc. Some become 'old favorites' that turn up regularly – sometimes too regularly. Ideally, stock furniture should be robust, easy to keep clean, without obvious scars from ungentle handling, easy to store, and of no obvious period.

As far as possible, there should be a selection of pieces that will blend together for single or group presentations. A talk show in which guests sit in chairs of different designs can look pretty uncoordinated.

The solution for many types of program is to hire furniture for the occasion that will suit its particular décor. For a regular series, though, one has to guard against hiring it so often that it would have been cheaper to have bought it outright!

4.52 Practical hazards

Are the seats comfortable to sit in? If they are not, you are likely to find inexperienced talent fidgeting, wriggling about, or sitting unnaturally as they try to adjust their positions.

Does the chair suit the performer? Too often one sees bulky men perched on light-framed chairs and small women lost in large armchairs. Actors are skilled in hiding their discomfort, but they appreciate carefully chosen seating nevertheless!

Is the chair fixed or are people likely to move it around and change its position? Swivel seats and armchairs that travel as one sits in them are really troublesome, for they can upset shots that the director has carefully arranged during rehearsal. What was to have been a frontal shot can become an ineffectual profile, because the chair has been moved off its floor marks. Lighting, too, will have been upset.

Low armchairs or sofas can be very difficult to get into or out of gracefully. They encourage lounging and very awkward postures. If you are stuck with such a seat it might be possible to use additional cushions to build it up and improve matters.

Armchairs that have wings or head supports can limit the range of possible shots and lead to unflattering lighting.

On the list of particular hates among types of furniture are:

● Wickerwork furniture, where the mike picks up the the slightest creak,

Figure 4.14 Furniture
Unsuitable furniture can lead to
uncontrollable situations. Here we
have:
1. The swivel-chair effect (the talent
moves around unexpectedly),
2. The low armchair (awkward shots,
and difficult to get out of),
3. The precarious perch (inelegant
and unsafe),
4. The hard surface (talent becomes
fidgety),
5. The rolling armchair (moves off its
marks and ruins shots),
6. Wing armchairs that hide the
talent and restrict the shots,
7. Cushions may make the talent
more comfortable and bring them
into a better position for the camera,
8. Where the furniture is too low for
the camera's shots it may be blocked
up (with care!).

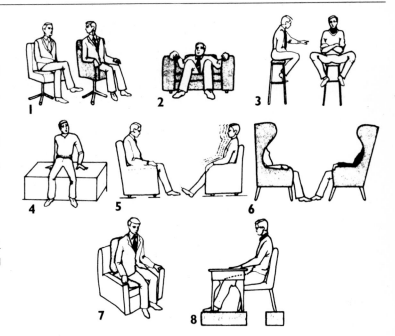

- Rocking chairs, which encourage people to move back and forth and frustrate closer shots,
- Flimsy or spindly furniture that is easily broken,
- Furniture covered with a fabric that is soon marked or damaged,
- Furniture with strongly patterned fabrics that will be overprominent on camera, or with close stripes or check patterns that will 'strobe',
- Heavy or bulky pieces of furniture (check whether large units (wardrobes, bookcases, etc.) can be subdivided for easy transport),
- Furniture with polished chrome features.

4.53 Taming the unruly

Polished surfaces are a delight in the home but a curse in the studio. They reflect strong highlights straight into the camera lens and cause distracting blobs or lens flares in the picture.

You can reduce the shine from any surface with a temporary dulling spray. Several types are available, including:

- *Matte* – which reduces the flare from most surfaces. Overused though, it will give the surface a dull waxed flat appearance,
- *Semi-matte* – which is similar but less drastic, so tends to reproduce the shape of curved surfaces more attractively,
- *Black* – which helps with overlight surfaces and reduces the transparency of glass and plastic surfaces.

When the shine from a table proves embarrassing you can often get over the problem by positioning something appropriate in the spot where the highlight appears – a book, table mat, blotter pad, or vase of flowers. Otherwise it might be best to put a table cover (table cloth) of suitable tone over the offending surface. Sometimes a piece of black scrim, cut to the shape of the table top, can help.

If orthodox furniture proves to be too low to suit a shot you may be able to overcome the problem by *blocking it up* with a small low platform of scenic blocks. Alternatively, you can place a wooden *furniture block* under each leg. These are square or cylindrical pieces of wood, about 4 in (100 mm) high, with a recessed top. (They can be disguised with dark cloth or paper tubes if they happen to appear in shot.)

Properties

4.54 What are props?

Properties, or 'props' as they are more usually referred to, are the furnishings of the setting.

Furniture is sometimes called *stage props* (chairs, tables, sofas, etc.).

The enormous variety of decorative features used to dress a setting are *set props* or *dressing props* (e.g. framed pictures, wall mirrors, vases, telephones, table lamps, rugs, flowers, books, etc.).

Personal props are any items worn or used by an actor. For instance, an actor may be issued with eyeglasses, a wallet, and money as personal props. (In certain circumstances they may use their own possessions – e.g. a pipe.)

Action props (*hand props*), on the other hand, are items that are used in the course of plot action, such as a telephone, drinking glasses, or a doorbell.

An item may be *non-practical*, which indicates that it does not function. You might, for example, have a film projector on a table in a laboratory setting. It is not used. It doesn't matter whether it is broken or simply not connected. It is non-practical.

If you want the equipment to work and project film onto a screen in the set then it needs to be *fully practical*, in full working order.

On the other hand, if you want to be able to switch the projector on and operate it so that it only *appears* to be working (although the picture on the wall screen is obtained by some other means) then it will be *practical* but not 'fully practical'. This distinction can be very important at times when you have apparatus that no longer functions and you need to 'dummy' its actions.

Also, of course, there is no point in making an item such as a telephone, refrigerator, oven, or gas-cooker fully practical if it is only being used as an incidental feature or a piece of set dressing.

Set dressing

4.55 Underlying skills

Fundamentally, *set dressing* is concerned with the choice and arrangement of the various items that 'clothe' the bare setting – furniture, drapes, decorative props, etc. The range of articles required will depend on the type of production and on the style of the décor.

The set dressing might be quite sparse, just requiring a few stock props. For an interview, two chairs, a central table, rug/carpet, water carafe, drinking glasses, and ashtray might suffice.

On the other hand, you might be designing a setting for a major drama – a printer's workshop, an antique shop, a hardware store, or a museum. These would probably involve a considerable number and variety of hard-to-find items. Tracking down and hiring the right sort of articles could be a time-consuming process. Some organizations use the services of specialists, who assist the scenic designer in this area.

Set dressing is a very personal art. It involves so much more than selecting and hiring appropriate props for the occasion. A skilled designer senses the sort of things the characters who 'live' in a particular setting would choose to have around them. Where would they leave things? Are they tidy? Such a convincing atmosphere is built up under sympathetic lighting that, for a moment, one forgets that this is a world due to be dispersed in a matter of hours.

You meet a similar situation with make-up and wardrobe. An actor playing the part of a hobo too often has a neatly dirtied face and neatly torn clothes, and fools no-one. But with an expert touch the grimy face and scruffy clothes look so realistic that people queuing with him in the meal break keep their distance, fearing that they might catch something!

4.56 Effectiveness on camera

When you are choosing suitable properties always bear in mind the all-important question – '*How will they look on camera?*' Certain materials can introduce difficulties. There may be times when you will not be able to avoid them, but at least you will be able to anticipate the situation.

Deep velvets and velours tend to look 'dead' and unmodeled. Lighting them more intensely may not be practicable or may overlight other objects in the vicinity.

White materials generally *burn out* detractingly on camera. But even when the camera manages to reproduce tonal gradation, such white surfaces are liable to catch the eye and prove distracting in the picture. Although you may be able to improve the situation by shading light off an overbright surface, this may leave other subjects underlit.

If you cannot avoid using very white materials it may be advisable to *dip* (dye) them to a very light coffee color, gray, or blue to prevent their exceeding the camera's upper limits or becoming too obtrusive.

Shiny materials are liable to cause troublesome flares, so watch out for shiny plastic or metal finishes and glazed materials. If they prove too eyecatching or create video problems (e.g. burn out on camera) a dulling spray may be necessary.

4.57 What the audience sees

Everyone involved in program making has a major problem for which there is no solution. We cannot stand back and take a detached look at what we have done. We cannot see our work with a fresh eye and assess it as our audience will be doing when they see it *for the first and only time*. We can but try to anticipate their first impressions.

After working hard on a project it is all too easy to excuse or justify shortcomings or to overvalue features that have taken a lot of time and trouble to arrange. It is easy to worry and fuss about something that they will overlook altogether, for they are concentrating on the dialogue and the action.

Similarly, we can forget that all our audience knows about the scene derives from what the camera is showing them. They cannot make a free visual selection. The camera emphasizes; the camera diminishes; the camera overlooks.

- If a beautifully carved statue does not come into shot, it is not there as far as our audience is concerned.
- In long shots, delicate patterns on a wallpaper are not discernible. As far as they can see, the wall has a plain surface.
- Quite a large item may be barely visible on the screen as it falls into shadow or is masked by other subjects. On the other hand, a small object that was intended as an incidental part of the set dressing may become prominent if it comes into the foreground of a picture.

4.58 Dressing density

It is surprising how few props are needed to give a setting a 'furnished' look if they are well chosen and carefully positioned.

The period and location in which a scene is set must influence not only the style of set dressing but how densely it is decorated. While a Victorian parlor was generously strewn with knick-knacks, a smart living room in the 1930s was often quite sparsely decorated.

The density of set-dressing can very subtly affect the ambiance of a setting. A laboratory scene, for example, can take on the appearance of a well-organized, modern, efficient workplace. But rearranged and overdressed, the same scene can become a very cluttered, confused, and disordered environment.

Where the décor is lightly furnished, with little decoration, there may be a feeling of openness, space, and elegance – or conversely, of poverty, neglect, and inadequacy. A densely dressed environment may suggest overabundance, fussiness, disorder, and confusion. We cannot generalize, for 'atmosphere' derives from many varied factors. But set-dressing is certainly a major contribution to the overall effect.

It is worth remembering, too, that dressing a set does not just involve the placement of ornaments and decorations. If a scene is

Figure 4.15 Set dressing
1. From the bare skeleton of the set – architecturally appropriate for the occasion...
2. A personalized décor is developed, suitable for the period, the characters, and the action. Carefully selected properties enhance the scene and give it conviction.
3. Excessive set dressing produces an overfussy effect, clogs the composition, and may impede the cameras. The location becomes confused and cluttered; perhaps just the effect you want to convey!

in a hovel we might be more concerned with a few dirty rags hanging from a broken shelf, torn cardboard stuffed into a shattered window, a floor strewn with screwed-up soiled paper, rusty tins, debris, or dirty straw. There might even be a stuffed rat or two! And these are all *props*!

Practical lamps

4.59 Practical problems

Practical low-wattage light fittings add considerably to the realism and atmospheric impact of interior scenes.

Some locations are continuously illuminated with artificial lighting (e.g. shops, supermarkets, corridors, etc.). This lighting treatment becomes such an essential part of those environments that we need to include (or suggest) it in any studio replica.

For many other types of studio setting, illuminated wall-lamps, table and stand lamps, chandeliers, etc. will usually be accepted by the audience as indicating that the scene is taking place at night.

To be effective, a practical lamp should not only appear to be lit but should seem to be lighting nearby people and the setting appropriately. Now although that is all very obvious, it is not always possible to achieve this under studio conditions.

If a person is wandering around in the dark with an oil lamp, for example, there may be too little light from it for the camera to produce good pictures. All we see is an isolated flame and a partly lit face. Change to a lamp with a stronger output, so that the subject is now well lit, and we shall probably find that the light source itself is far too bright on camera, producing unattractive portraiture.

Most practical fittings are of relatively low power and cannot compete with the stronger studio lighting. So the general technique is to have them appear suitably bright on camera and simulate their effect with studio lamps.

Some light fittings can take high-power lamps (e.g. overrun bulbs, such as photofloods) without overheating or burning the lamp shade. But, ironically, an uprated fitting often produces obtrusive light patches on nearby walls, so the remedy can make things worse.

4.60 Choosing practicals

When choosing lighting fittings there are several design features to bear in mind:

● *Bare-bulb fittings* generally appear overbright on camera and cause video defects (streaking, lens flares). If you dim them down until they are trouble-free the small localized blob of light that results is unconvincing. Frosted lamps provide a larger, more realistic light source.

● If a fitting uses a dark or opaque lamp shade it may look unlit from some angles, although its reflective white lining inside may be too bright for the camera.

● When studio lighting falls onto an opal glass lamp globe, or a light-toned shade, the lamp will often look lit, even when it is switched off.

4.61 Controlling practicals

Many actors are not used to lighting and adjusting oil lamps and hurricane lanterns. So they are liable to end up with a flame that is too small and blows out or a flaring wick that is troublesome on camera.

Battery-powered replicas have advantages, for their brightness is constant, but they are generally less realistic.

If a candle proves to be too bright, trimming the wick length will usually do the trick.

In a period production which uses gas fixtures (e.g. wall brackets, street lamps), electrical mock-ups are often more convenient. But where you *are* using a gas supply it is best to preset the gas flow, so that an actor does not have to adjust its brightness; only to light the fixture and turn it to maximum. Then there will be no chance of its being too bright for the camera.

Sometimes one can fake the whole thing. For example, the only wall-mounted gas fixture that could be obtained for a mysterious alley setting was irreparably broken. But after introducing a piece of shaped card resembling a gas mantle, 'lit' by a carefully adjusted spotlight, the gas fixture seemed to have sprung to life!

Decorative light fittings

4.62 Illuminated signs

Illuminated signs give life to a street scene in the studio. You can devise them in three ways:

1. *Directly* – by hiring the real thing or making a direct imitation. But even where this is practicable, the sign too often proves to be costly, bulky, and difficult to transport.
2. *Indirectly* – by using a painted translucent panel or a stencil, covering a light-box. With this method you can produce quite an elaborate 'multiple display' or a 'neon' sign simply and effectively.
3. *Simulated effect* – in which lettering and designs in highly reflective material (metal foil, plastic sheet, or white paper) are stuck onto a black, non-reflective surface (e.g. velvet or black flock-paper) and illuminated with a spotlight.

4.63 Multi-lamp displays

Strings of lamps can be used to decorate a setting:

● Arranged as bare lamps, along the edges of platforms, round arches, circling pillars, hanging in festoons, attached to poles or skeletal structures, etc.,
● Concealed behind edging boards, to provide an illuminated rim to flattage,
● Behind rear-lit translucent panels.

Installation can be a lengthy job. But it is important that it is done carefully and to high safety standards. The lamps must be accessible and well ventilated. Otherwise, apart from any fire hazards, individual lamps are liable to fail and create an embarrassing gap in the display.

Lamps may be left lit throughout a scene, groups interswitched, or color changes introduced. They may be flashed rhythmically or intermittently.

You can give the impression of *light movement* by switching groups of lamps in succession (*chaser lights*). Take a row of e.g. 10 lamps. Light lamps 3–10. Switch on 1 and 2 and switch off 3 and 4. Switch on 3 and 4 and switch off 5 and 6, and so on, and you will have the illusion of light continuously chasing around a group.

In a multi-lamp design, light group A, add adjacent group B, then group C, and you produce an effect of growth or expansion. Similarly, if you take a string of lamps and progressively light them the line will appear to grow.

Figure 4.16 Decorative light effects
In this selection of decorative lighting, we have:
1. Cyclorama lighting (barndoored spotlights on the floor shooting upwards),
2. Hanging festoons of decorative lamps (shaped bulbs),
3. A tubular metal skeletal frame with lamp sockets,
4. Lamps fitted to the edges of scenery (normally low-wattage bulbs in batten-fitted holders),
5. Reflective panels (embossed or stencil-painted mirror-plastic, sequins, etc.),
6. Internally illuminated treads and platform (e.g. plate glass panels with plastic facing),
7. Hidden strip lighting that edge-illuminates panels,
8. Slash curtains (reflective PVC strips) or tinsel.

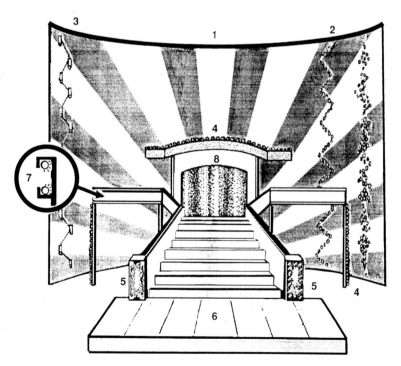

Although a certain amount of switching can be done by hand, continuous displays need to be controlled by automatic circuits that are computer programed.

Rhythmically flashing, pulsating, swirling light-patterns can produce spectacular effects. An increasing variety of gimmicks is available. But they can also become fidgety and distracting if overdone. If we are not careful the audience might pay more attention to the 'fireworks display' than to the performers!

Chapter 5

Staging practices

It is not enough to provide attractive décor. It has to be organized in the studio so that the productional mechanics work. In this chapter we shall discuss various factors we need to consider when planning scenic layouts.

5.1 Suiting the studio

Studios come in all shapes and sizes, and their dimensions and proportions can have important influences on the entire staging.

The *effective available height* in a studio is the distance from the floor to the underside of hanging lamps. (The exact amount of space taken up by any lamp will depend on its design and the form of suspension used.)

If a lighting grid is only 9 ft (2.7 m) above the floor then it is safest to consider the maximum height available for scenery as only around 7 ft (2.1 m).

The *shape and proportions* of a studio can decide how it is best used. If we take as an example a rectangular studio of 2:1 proportions (e.g. 60 × 30 ft or 18 × 9 m) major settings will normally be located at *either end* of the studio, along the shorter

Figure 5.1 Studio layout
Here are typical layout hazards one needs to look out for when staging a production:
1. A scenic backing in the safety lane (fire lane), obstructing a studio entrance.
2. A space-saving small set is too cramped for action. Overshoot into the next set is probable. The working area is restricted for cameras.
3. The large corner ceiling may limit lighting, and cause acoustic changes as action moves around the set.
4. The narrow hallway restricts camerawork and lighting. (Splay or hinge the right-hand wall flat?)
5. The foreground hanging light-fitting will probably be out of shot; may cast shadows on actors; could impede a sound boom.
6. Cycloramas and sets can limit exits or access round most of the staging area. (A potential hazard in an emergency.)
7. The setting should not be close to the cyc. (Difficult to light cyc, and possibility of damage to cyc cloth.)
8. The safety lane will probably be dark, as it is obscured from studio lighting by the setting and cyc. So illumination will be needed behind the cyc.

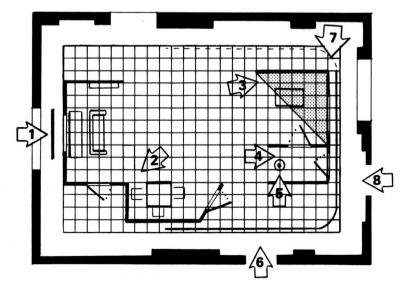

walls. The size of sets against the longer *side walls* will be restricted by the amount of space cameras and sound booms need to maneuver. Typically, they might be about 12–15 ft (3.64–4.56 m) deep at most. If sets are required along both of the long walls in this studio they will necessarily need to be quite shallow; even then, cameras may have to work with their backs in the sets along the opposite wall to get long enough shots.

Where the staging area is irregularly shaped, due to the structure of the building itself, access doors, staircases, storage areas, etc., this also can restrict the size and shape of sets.

Studio layout

At first sight one might assume that, provided a studio is large enough, distributing the settings around the staging area is a simple, straightforward process. It can be. But at times it can require foresight and ingenuity to avoid time-wasting tangles and frustrations.

Remember that initial planning process, in which we arranged the overlays of each set on the studio plan (Section 2.12)? Now let's look at *practical factors* that influence exactly where the designer positions settings.

5.2 Shooting order

During very quiet parts of any production it is possible to hear all manner of extraneous sounds – air conditioning, the sound of camera cables dragging across the floor as they move, footsteps.

If we position the settings around the studio in *shooting order* cameras and sound booms can move smoothly from one set to the next in turn, keeping studio noise to a minimum and saving a lot of time and effort.

When the show is being *recorded in sections* the time it takes to move equipment will not be so critical. But it is still a good general practice to avoid making operations unduly complicated.

5.3 Crowded studios

At times, even large studios can become extremely congested. But if a show demands a number of sets, or big settings, this may be unavoidable. Apart from ensuring that no space is wasted and that sets are no larger than they need be, the director can sometimes alleviate matters by:

● Recording all the scenes in a particular setting and then removing it ('striking' it), either to make more room to use adjacent sets or to enable a new set to be built in its place (e.g. an overnight reset),

● Pre-recording certain scenes (elsewhere or on another day), so that fewer sets are needed together in the main videotaping session,
● Using chroma key for backgrounds,
● Using space-saving staging techniques (Section 5.20).

5.4 Cyclorama limitations

In some studios the cyclorama is quite small and can only be hung at certain positions. This can influence the studio layout, for you need to give priority to any set that requires the cyc and position others within the remaining space. This situation is particularly true where the studio is fitted with a 'permanent cyc'.

5.5 Widespread action

Occasionally, a production will require the maximum possible area you can provide, to accommodate widespread action – perhaps a vehicle driving around the studio, a group of horse riders, or a marching band.

The first step is to arrange for this area to be near the main studio access door, perhaps the entrance through which scenery is brought into the studio.

It may be sufficient simply to clear the maximum floor space there. But cameras panning around the open studio are going to see the studio walls, equipment, crew, and other sets. This may not matter, but it could be distracting and irrelevant, and lose a sense of occasion. Furthermore, the audience might become more curious about what is happening in these 'behind-the-scenes' shots than the main action!

To avoid this you can arrange *masking* to limit the camera's field of view. Hung black cloths (borders) will hide lamps. Flats at the left and right extremes of the camera's viewpoint (gobos, tormentors, wings) can restrict the visible area. If there appears to be an excessive amount of floor visible in the wide shot, something placed in the foreground at the bottom of the frame (e.g. a trough of flowers or a balustrade) will disguise the expanse.

5.6 Studio audience

If a show is going to have a sizeable invited audience (Section 4.9) this will largely determine the scenic layout in most studios.

Special seating arrangements with easy access will be located near a public entrance to the studio.

The settings must be positioned to give the audience a good view of the action.

Given these requirements, there are usually prescribed staging arrangements in most studios, where audiences are invited regularly.

5.7 Production control room

The studio's production control room is usually separated from the studio itself by a large soundproof window through which the director and others can have a clear view of activities.

A brief glance through the window will often help to resolve rehearsal problems that would otherwise mean leaving the control room and going into the studio, so wasting valuable rehearsal time.

Without this overview the director has only the pictures on the cameras' preview monitor screens to show what is happening in the studio. Understandably therefore, many directors prefer to have major sets located immediately opposite the window of the control room, wherever possible, to give them a clear view of studio operations.

5.8 Sharing the studio

In a busy studio it is not unusual to find two separate productions sharing the staging area. If they are going on air consecutively the studio will probably be divided into two sections.

In a small or crowded studio some of the lighting in the center of the studio may have to be reset, to serve each program in turn. When space is really tight it may be necessary to make room in one of the settings by temporarily removing furniture, so that cameras can back up to get long shots of the other sets.

Where part of the staging area is regularly occupied by a *standing set*, left there from another show (Section 6.14), this will usually be cleared of furniture and props when not in use to avoid items straying. Also, sections of the set may be dismantled or stacked to allow maximum floor space for other shows to use.

It is good general practice to mark the positions of all pieces of furniture and scenery that are likely to be moved with clear but unobtrusive *floor marks* at their corners, especially if items are going to be removed and reset later. These marks can be in chalk, crayon, or adhesive masking tape, but it is important that they can be cleaned off easily after the show.

5.9 Storage

In most productions one finds an assortment of items that need to be kept ready for use in the staging area:

● Standby or replacement props,
● Pieces of equipment needed in the program,
● Pieces of scenery that are to be removed or to be positioned during the production (e.g. mobile units, wagons, breakthrough doors, camera mattes, wild walls).

So when planning the layout of settings it is as well to set aside storage space for this purpose rather than hunt around hopefully on the day, as too often happens.

5.10 Facilities

In some studios, supply points for water, drainage, gas, and electrical power are only available in certain areas. It is worth bearing this in mind when positioning a set (e.g. a fully practical kitchen for a cookery show) that needs these facilities.

5.11 Lighting and layout

In many studios lamps are hung from a series of suspended battens, bars, or barrels. They may be moved along these supports quite easily, but it can be quite laborious – or even impossible – to place lamps at intermediate positions between them.

In fact, the more the position and shapes of settings relate to the overhead lighting system, the greater the opportunities for precision lighting.

When positioning settings, therefore, it is most helpful if back or side walls of sets can be located underneath lighting battens, rather than mid-way between them.

There are also situations where settings may need to be arranged to allow a clear unobstructed path for lighting. Regular examples are where light is to shine through a window, to cast a light-pattern onto a wall, and where a projector is to provide patterns on a background.

Again, if backings are placed too close to windows or doors it may not be possible to light them properly.

Although lighting problems may be the other fellow's worry it is the appearance of *your* sets that is affected!

5.12 Proportions and shapes of sets

Limited space and budget usually preclude sets from being much larger than they need be. In smaller settings action is more restricted, but where you need a spacious effect you can often achieve it by using a *wide-angle lens* to exaggerate distance.

Lighting treatment is less flexible in small or shallow sets, where the performers and the set cannot be lit separately.

As you can see in Figure 5.2, the proportions of a setting can modify camerawork, lighting, and even sound quality. Narrow corridors are particularly troublesome.

5.13 Wall formation

Although scenic flats are available in a wide range of sizes they must necessarily be limited to what can be handled and transported with reasonable ease. So if you want a wall of more than a few feet it becomes necessary to join several individual flats together, side by side.

Long, straight runs of flats can be uninteresting, and, even where there is no obvious architectural justification, most designers prefer to introduce irregularities in the shape of settings.

Figure 5.2 Proportion and shapes of sets

Typical size. Typical dimensions for a twofold set (book-wing; book-flat), and a threefold (box) set.

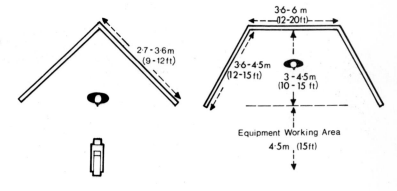

Cross-shooting.
1. Cross-shots easily overshoot on flat backgrounds. The set lacks depth and solidity, but occupies little space. (It can be stacked or nested.)
2. A slightly improved arrangement but liable to look disproportionately wide in cross-shots.
3. Very satisfactory proportions for general use but oversplayed.

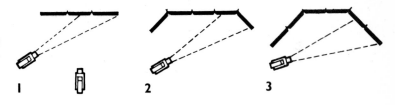

Set proportions.
1. Walls may be splayed slightly to improve camera access; but can exaggerate room size in cross-shots.
2. Right-angled corners are realistic but may restrict camera angles (especially with two or three cameras and a sound boom working into the set).
3, 4. As sets become narrower, the working area is reduced and only straight-on shots are possible. Sound pick-up becomes 'boxy' and lighting often steeper.

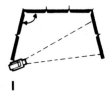

Staging height. The height necessary for backgrounds depends on the longest shot to be taken (A), the lowest camera position (B), and the subject height (e.g. action on a staircase). See Figure 5.6.
A 10 ft (3 m) flat is adequate for general use but a 12 ft (3.6 m) one is needed for larger settings. High flattage tends to cause steepening of lighting angles.

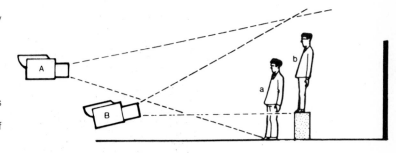

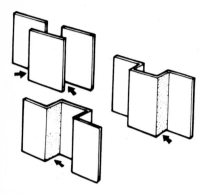

Figure 5.3 Wall formation
Where possible, long runs of wall flattage are best avoided. Instead, breaks or returns can be introduced to provide a more interesting effect, disguise joins, and improve acoustics.

Breaks are arrangements in which a flat is displaced, standing in front or behind its neighbors. In a decorative setting the effect can be very attractive. It has less application in architectural sets, but may be quite acceptable where the gap between the flats is not evident on camera.

Most familiar of all is the *return* or *jog*, in which the run of a wall is interrupted by an apparent buttress or recess. This is formed from narrow flats (e.g. 3 in, 6 in, 9 in, up to 2 ft (76 mm, 152 mm, 229 mm to 0.6 m)) lap-joined at right angles. The result is not only more interesting visually but acoustics are somewhat improved.

5.14 Working areas

One gets very accustomed to making accurate judgements when working on a scale floor plan (e.g. ¼ in = 1 ft; 2 cm = 1 m). Nevertheless, even an experienced designer continually uses a scale measure to ensure that dimensions in the studio are going to be realistic. There is little point in scribbling a row of chairs on a plan only to find that in the studio set there is insufficient room for them. Furniture that looks great in a sketch may leave little room for actors to move around in an overcrowded set.

Even more important, perhaps, is the need to design the settings and the staging layout so that cameras can get the shots the director envisions and sound booms can operate successfully.

For many kinds of production, cameras and booms work within an area across the front of a setting. If the cameras are semi-static, and are only changing their shots by varying lens angles (i.e. zooming in and out), quite a limited working area may suffice. But if cameras are going to move around to different viewpoints they will need the space to do so, whether this is *around* the set or actually *within* it. The bigger the camera mounting, the more room is needed for it to maneuver.

Many experienced directors always use scale-size cut-outs of camera mountings, attached to thin cords (representing the camera cables), to work out their shots and to check that there is sufficient room for cameras to move about. This practice has avoided many a problem and has saved wasted rehearsal time.

5.15 Restricted viewpoints

If a camera is going to move up *into* a setting you have to make sure that there is sufficient room for it to do so, and that there are no obstacles. This is simple enough in an open set but in a typical domestic setting, such as a living room or a bedroom, it may not be very practicable to leave over 6 ft (1.8 m) gaps for the camera dolly to pass through. If you remove furniture to make space, the set can look unnaturally empty.

Side walls are often splayed or 'opened up' at their downstage end to improve camera access, but if overdone, this will upset the proportions of the setting.

Figure 5.4 Restricted viewpoints
Working within a room the camera tends to be too close to subjects and have limited movement. Instead, it can often get better shots from selected vantage points:
1. Through a window,
2. Using a hinged flat for temporary access ('swinger'),
3. A camera trap in a wall (disguised as a wall-picture, mirror, panel, etc.) opened when necessary,
4. Shooting through a false-return (gap in the wall),
5. Shooting in through a backless cupboard,
6. Shooting in through a fireplace,
7. Hidden temporarily behind a screen, furniture, buttress, etc.,
8. Shooting in through a doorway,
9. Hidden behind a pull-aside curtain.

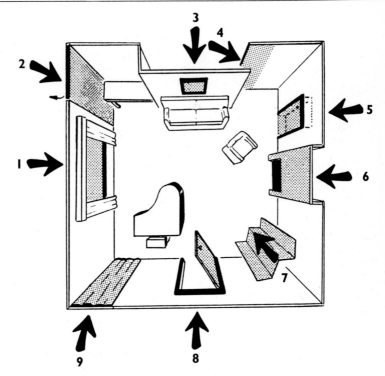

The typical dilemma for a camera inside many room settings is that it cannot get far enough away from the actors to get a range of shots. Because it is just a few feet from them it can only provide close shots, and little else. Also, in a multi-camera show there is the danger that other cameras will come into shot.

One solution is to construct the setting with 'peepholes' that allow cameras to get shots from positions that would otherwise be inaccessible. There are several effective methods (Figure 5.4):

● A camera may look into the room, through a *door* or *window*.
● A *hinged flat* ('flipper', 'swinger') may be used that can be opened to give access for certain shots. Inside the set the flat becomes part of the regular wall. A caster on the bottom of the flat will allow it to be repositioned quickly and quietly.
● The set may include a *wild wall*, which can be removed easily, to allow camera access. This wall is not attached to neighboring flats but is 'run' (i.e. lifted and manhandled aside), wheeled away, or 'flown' (raised/hoisted out of the way).
● A *camera trap* may be used, which is in the form of a panel in the wall of the set, disguised to look like a picture, a mirror, or a row of books. This is hinged or slid open for a camera behind the set to take selected shots.
● Using a *false return* in a wall, which leaves a gap or 'break' in the flats that is not visible from other camera positions.
● A camera may be *hidden* behind a piece of furniture (e.g. a cupboard, an ornamental screen) or an architectural feature (e.g. a buttress).

- A low camera can shoot into a room *through a fireplace* (having removed any fireback).
- *Pull-aside drapes* can give the camera access. These are often hung on a short hinged 'gallows arm' that may be swung to one side. Alternatively, you can use a fixed batten, fitted with a curtain track, or a swag-cord that loops the drape to one side.
- The camera may shoot the subject via a *wall-mirror*.

Backings

5.16 The need for backings

Staging is usually arranged so that the camera sees what is intended and no more. But wherever there is an *opening* of any kind in a setting, such as a window, a doorway, or an arch, there is always the danger that the camera might see through accidentally, and reveal other parts of the studio beyond (overshooting, shooting off). There are several things you can do:

1. You can *mask off the openings* by:

- A window – fit a blind over the window or close the shades.
- A door – avoid opening the door. If it is in a side wall opening inwards towards the room hinge the door on the downstage edge, so that it opens away from the camera. For an outward-opening door, hinge it on its upstage edge.
- An arch – hang a drape across all or part of the arch.

2. You can *continue the setting beyond the opening*:

- Outside a window – provide bushes, trees, brick walls, sky cloth/cyc.
- Outside a door – build a hallway, perhaps indicating a stairway with a just-visible set of treads.
- Beyond an arch – have part of a room, or similarly appropriate feature on the far side.

But if these extra settings are not needed for the action, or there is no space for them in the studio layout, or we are trying to keep the budget down, these are hardly viable solutions.

3. The simplest and cheapest answer is to introduce a scenic *backing* of some kind, a backdrop, a drape, some flats to restrict the shot and obscure whatever is outside. Not only is this method economical but it effectively conveys an impression of space and distance beyond the opening.

- Outside a window – for night, a black drape and a bush perhaps. For day, a light-toned drop (sky cloth) or a scenic cloth.
- Outside a door – a flat, perhaps with wall decorations (mirror, picture), a half-table, or a chair.
- Beyond an arch – swagged drapes at the sides of the arch to reduce visibility through it and a similar abbreviated treatment to the hall. Or instead, a pictorial background, a photomural of an interior to suitably extend the setting.

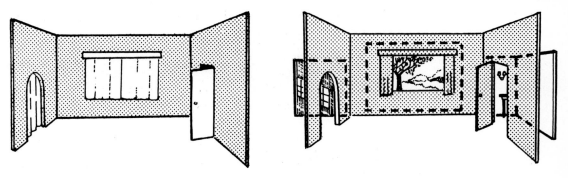

Figure 5.5 Backings

Avoiding backings. Blocking off openings prevents the camera overshooting and no backings are needed. However, backings do create extensions to the setting and give it a greater realism.

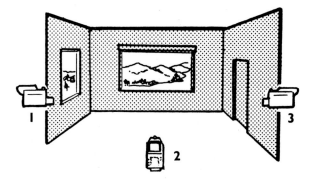

Effectiveness of backings. The backing behind a rear-wall window is clearly visible from all camera angles, so it continually reminds the audience of the location.
A side-wall window is unseen on Camera 1, edge-on to Camera 2, and fully visible only on Camera 3. So its effectiveness is limited on the screen.

The value of backings.
1. A blank window simply implies that it is day or night, but tells us nothing about the location or the environment. With the window curtains drawn the room becomes a closed box.
2. An obscured window (frosted panel) with a tree-branch shadow suggests that it is daylight and that nearby trees are in leaf (bare branches for winter); but nothing more.
3. A scenic background can give a setting considerable realism, for it reveals the location and sunlight on the wall 'connects' the room with the external world.

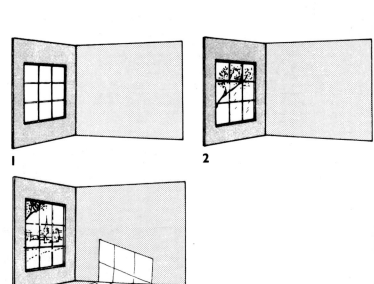

5.17 Positioning backings

In purely mechanical terms you need to ensure that any backing really does mask off the scenic opening from all camera angles. It may, for instance, work for a camera shooting across the set but not for another shooting more obliquely to the opening.

There are several regular problems:

- Backings that are too small, or too far away, so give insufficient coverage,
- Badly angled backings, allowing cameras to overshoot the upstage end,
- Backings that are too close to the opening; e.g. so close to a window that the backing cannot be lit evenly, causing room lighting to cast shadows onto the backing and preventing external lamps from shining in through the window (i.e. as sunlight or moonlight),
- Objects (e.g. trees) placed close to the exterior backing, casting shadows onto it.

5.18 Window treatment

There are a number of ways of blanking off a window so that there appears to be daylight outside yet the camera cannot see through. You can 'glaze' it behind with stretched scrim or use frosted or obscured plastic sheeting or ornamental sheeting (hammered, ribbed, molded, etc.). Inside the room you can fit light drapes (ninons, sheers, lace curtains), venetian shutters, or roller blinds.

With such arrangements you will not need a backing of any kind. Light can shine onto the window from outside, perhaps casting a branch shadow to suggest a nearby tree, and convey an impression of the weather and time of day (e.g. bright sun, evening, sunset, night).

An obscured window is mechanically convenient, but a *backing* outside a window does have distinct advantages. It can create a more complete environmental illusion. Now we have the opportunity to see where the room is located. It is not just 'daytime'. We can see that there are mountains out there, and it is spring. The sunlight is coming through the window and casting shadows on the wall. The branch we see outside has fresh leaves that are rustling in the breeze. With background sound effects we have an added relationship between the 'outside world' and the room, making it seem more real.

5.19 Overshoot/shooting off

Whenever a camera shoots past the limits of a setting there is the choice of either readjusting the shot or modifying the set in some way.

There are regular situations where cameras *overshoot/shoot-off*, i.e. when:

Figure 5.6 Overshoot –top of setting

Causes. If the background is insufficiently high the camera may shoot over, even on close shots, with the camera level, using an average lens angle (24°).

But the camera is particularly liable to see over the set when:
1. Shooting from a low viewpoint,
2. Dollying back for a longer shot of the scene,
3. Using a wide lens angle (zoomed out),
4. Tilting up, to shoot a high or tall subject.

Remedies. There are regular ways of preventing overshoot (apart from modifying the shot itself):
1. Using higher flats, topping-up with extra flattage, or hanging a border/teaser behind them,
2. Using intermediate vertical masking at the top of the shot,
3. Using an intermediate architectural feature (arch, beam, etc.),
4. Introducing a fascia,
5. Introducing a ceiling.

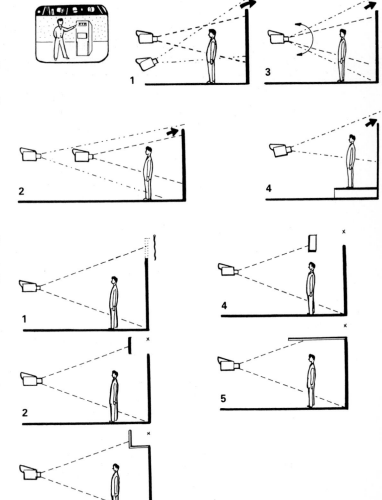

Figure 5.7 Overshoot –shooting past

Where the camera shoots past the edge of a set we have the options of:
1. Extending the flattage,
2. Adding a wing (return flat),
3. Introducing an intermediate masking piece (e.g. a screen, furniture). The nearer it is to camera, the smaller it can be.

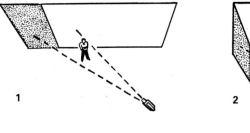

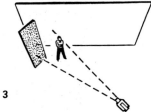

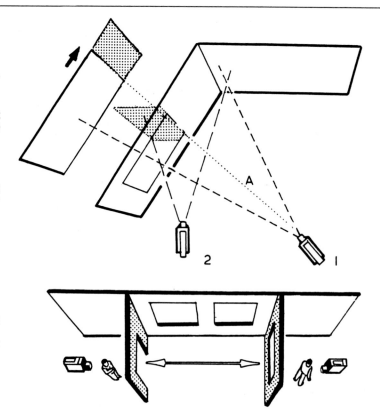

Figure 5.8 Overshoot – shooting through
Wherever there are openings in a setting the camera is liable to shoot through and see whatever is beyond.

Windows. The normal solution is to provide a backing. This may be adequate from Camera 1 position (at A) but insufficient from another angle (Camera 2). Repositioning the backing may be the solution (or modifying the shot). Alternatively, a larger backing may be needed.
It may be easier to introduce masking instead (e.g. an external wall flat), to prevent Camera 2 shooting off. (Sometimes even closing the window drapes a little may be sufficient.)

Composite sets. In a composite setting cameras and sound booms working in another part of the setting may be seen through arches, windows, or doors if masking has not been anticipated.

- Cameras are shooting at oblique angles on a shallow set,
- Flattage is too low relative to the camera's shot (the camera may be low, on a wide shot, or using a wide-angle lens),
- The camera is looking up at subjects (e.g. people on platforms or stairs),
- Shooting downstage action from an upstage camera position,
- Shooting into a set through a window or a door,
- Windows, doors, arches, openings, etc. are inadequately backed,
- Offstage areas are reflected in mirrors or reflective surfaces.

As you can see in Figure 5.6, there are standard solutions to these situations. They are all simple enough, but it is far better to anticipate during planning, and avoid last-minute remedies wherever possible.

5.20 Space saving

To make the maximum use of space in small studios you need to use the same staging area several times over in the course of a production. There are a number of well-tried ways of doing this.

Flat scenic backgrounds are comparatively cheap, and take up little space. In the form of flats or backdrops they can be plain,

Figure 5.9 Space saving
Where there is insufficient room for
conventional staging, various space-
saving subterfuges can be helpful:

 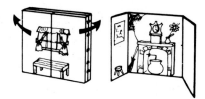 

1. *Wall pack*. A series of decorated
flats can be laid in a pack and
removed in turn to reveal the next.

2. *Bookwing flats*. The painted flats
are hinged open to show the next
scene; a method adaptable to
comedy and realistic situations.

3. *Nesting sets*. Placed one within
another, the inner set is struck to
reveal the outer. Lighting may involve
two separate rigs or use a common
set of lamps.

 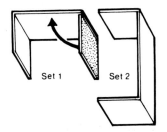 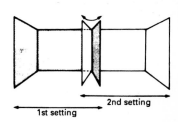

4. *Reversible sets*. This wagon
shows the interior of a Victorian
police station...but turns, to become
part of an elegant drawing room.

5. *Overlapping sets*. The wall of one
set (1) may be moved aside to give
access to a different set (2) nearby
(hinged folds, wheeled aside,
manhandled, flown).

6. *Hinged walls – total*. A common
wall may be repositioned for easier
access to each set in turn.

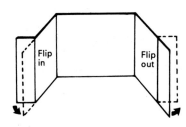 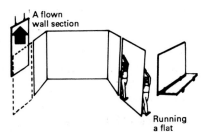 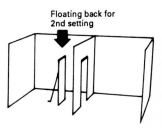

7. *Hinged walls –part*. Sometimes
hinging part of a wall (in or out) will
improve shot opportunities.

8. *Removable walls*. Parts of a wall
may be flown, man-handled, or
wheeled away to improve access.

9. *Inserted backings*. Backings take
up valuable floor space. Here, instead
of two separate sets, each with its
own backing, they have been
combined and a 'floating' backing
inserted when necessary.

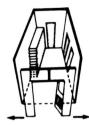

Figure 5.9 (continued)
10. *Breakthrough pieces.* The camera shoots a foreground doorway, which parts as it dollies through into the hall (breakthrough piece). As a result, quite a small hallway looks extensive. (See Figure 7.1, Part 2.)

11. *Revamping.* The appearance of a set can be changed by *revamping*, i.e. altering the set dressing, rearranging the scenery, changing lighting.

decorative, or pictorial. But they do have the disadvantage that camera movement is restricted.

How large a background you need will depend on the shots to be used. For waist shots or closer, a 6 ft (1.8 m) wide background will suffice. But for full-length shots, where a person is standing sufficiently far away from the background to avoid throwing shadows on it, a background twice or three times that width may be necessary.

- Several flats can be stacked in a *pack*. As the top flat is removed it reveals the next underneath. Backdrops can be dropped in and flown out, or unrolled (tumbler cloths) one over another to change the background.
- *Hinged flats* in the form of 'book flats' (pairs) or 'wing flats' (threes) can be decorated differently on both faces.
- *Nesting sets* are arrangements where a smaller setting is erected inside a larger one. The inner set is shot first, then removed ('struck') to allow the outer one to be used.
- *Wagons* allow scenic sections or small sets to be repositioned (Section 3.37).
- *Revamping* will change the appearance of a setting to create a new locale (Section 6.11).

Two sets will take up less room if they share a common side wall. If necessary, this can be hinged to move aside (splay) and improve camera access.

Where space is very limited you can even have the hinged side walls of a small set folded inwards, to be opened out when it is time to shoot there.

A further space-saving approach is to allow one set to strategically *intrude* into an adjacent setting. After action has been shot in the first set, part of it is removed, to give access to the second. Where two or more flats are battened together to form a removable wall this 'french flat' can be either flown or 'tripped' (see Glossary).

Finally, you can sometimes provide a *temporary extension* to a setting by using a 'floating' unit that is put in just for that scene to suggest that the set is much more extensive than it really is. Typical examples are temporary backings and temporary foreground pieces.

5.21 Elevated cameras

There are occasions when the director wants to use a high camera viewpoint to look down on the action.

The camera mounting can be set up on a reinforced platform (rostrum, parallel) of suitable height (see Section 5.24 on Safety).

Alternatively, you can use a special demountable tubular *camera frame/camera tower* (e.g. 7–9 ft square (2.1–2.7 m)).

Where space is too limited for such structures the camera may be able to shoot up into a large overhead mirror to get the required shots.

General staging treatment

Looking over plans prepared by several designers it is interesting to see commonly recurring themes in their designs and furniture arrangements for interior settings. There are good reasons for these similarities. They are appropriate and practicable.

5.22 Typical rooms

Most buildings follow recognizable architectural conventions. If we disregard these familiar forms when designing settings the result will either be *architecturally improbable or strangely unconventional* (e.g. a spiral staircase in the center of a room).

A room without architectural features has limited visual appeal. It relies entirely on the set dressing and furniture to create any sort of atmosphere. So although you can have simple three-walled box sets (closed sets) without doors or windows, most designers would aim at a more interesting structure.

The design details of a set must be influenced by the action and the camera treatment. Although it would be possible to have people enter and leave a room past the camera, going through an 'unseen door' in the 'fourth wall', this would be unconventional and could leave the audience confused. A door seen somewhere in the set avoids ambiguity. Rooms can be windowless, but where windows can be introduced, as we have seen, they do help to create a more convincing spatial illusion (Section 5.18).

5.23 Room layouts

If a set's layout is to be successful it needs to:

- Be appropriate and convincing (in period, style, and ambiance),
- Be suited to the action, allowing the actors' moves and business to be carried out easily,
- Readily provide the shots the director wants,
- Be suitable for appropriate lighting and sound treatment.

To see how a room layout might evolve let's imagine that the scene is a Victorian room – the study of Sherlock Holmes. It is very fully furnished, just as in the original story, which features a fireplace, windows looking onto the street below, and a door to the hallway.

The scene begins. We hear the sound of a carriage arriving. Holmes goes to the window and looks out...

So where is the window to be?

Is the window a background incidental? Do we only see Holmes's back as he looks out? Then the window could be located anywhere in the set.

The director indicates that she wants to see Holmes's reactions as the carriage stops.

So do we watch him from *outside* the window or will he have one shoulder towards the window and be shot from *within* the room?

No, this is not a pedantic question! In the first case, the camera needs floor space to get into position outside the set, between the backing and the window (e.g. backing 9–12 ft or 2.7–3.6 m from the set), and the window flat may need to be double clad. Shot from inside the room, the window is single clad, and its backing need only be 6 ft (1.8 m) away. The director has settled on an exterior shot.

If the window is located in the *upstage wall* of this box set the camera will need free access to move right round the set (using valuable staging space just for that one shot), and it will be shooting down towards the open front of the set. (A temporary insert backing may be necessary.) So it is best to avoid this situation.

It would be better to have the window in the *left side wall*, where the camera will have easy access. (Check whether the camera will overshoot the far wall 20 ft or 6 m behind Holmes.)

The fireplace, too, is an important acting point. It cannot go in the window wall, so it must either be in the upstage wall or the right side one. Several sequences show Holmes sitting beside the fire, so it had better be located in the right-hand wall; then cameras can easily get shots of the action there. The upstage area of any set is less easily reached.

As the doorway to the hall is unlikely, architecturally, to be in the window wall it must either go on one side of the fireplace or in the back wall... The set is beginning to take shape.

Figure 5.10 Safety
Accidents happen all too easily! Handrails/guardrails (1) are needed for platforms 2 ft (600 mm) or more above floor level. This handrail may be restricted or complete, and is typically at least 2 ft 3 in (685 mm) above the platform, with vertical supports at e.g. 4 ft 6 in (1350 mm) intervals.
The edges of the platforms should preferably have battens (e.g. 1 × 2 in (25 × 50 mm)) – either horizontal (3) or vertical (4) – to prevent chairs, etc. sliding off the platform.
Vertical boards ('kicking boards') (2) of around 1 × 5 in (25 × 127 mm), fixed to the inside of guardrails, prevent items (or people!) from slipping under the handrail.
Wherever possible, handrails should be fitted to stairs and steps. Where access steps are needed for a platform, but not seen on camera, lightweight open-tread types (5) can be pin-hinged to the structure.

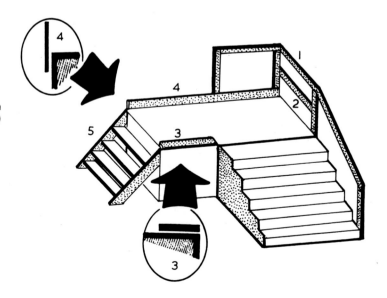

Table 5.1 Safety precautions

'Regulations' are a bore! But check through these 'do's and don'ts', and imagine if... They *all* relate to accidents that have really happened. Some were fatal.
- *Safety exits and safety lanes/fire lanes* around the studio should always be left clear. They should not be blocked or used for storage. Scenery should not intrude into these areas.
- 'Walkover boards' stop people tripping over floor cables in the safety lane.
- *Treads/steps/ladders* should not be rested against studio walls or flats. Do not use them partially open. Have someone stand on the lowest step. Do not stand on the top one.

- No wheeled units (wagons, wheeled flats, wheelable lighting ladders, vehicles, etc.) should be allowed to *run over cables of any kind* or *hit suspended lamps*.

- Whenever studio lamps are not in use, overall 'house lights' (working lights) in the studio ceiling should be lit.
- No *areas behind scenery* should be left unilluminated.
- If studio lighting is only illuminating the setting being used at the moment (to save power and reduce heat), other areas should be left with working lights.

- All scenery should be *thoroughly braced and secure*.
- *Unused flats* should not be rested against built scenery.
- Any slung scenery should have *more than one suspension point*. Safety bonds should be included in any heavy hung scenery.
- Make it a regular habit to consider *what would happen* if any piece of scenery fell or overbalanced. Where would it fall?

- Keep all scenery, suspension lines, and brail lines well away from lamps. Although a lamp may not be switched on now it may be lit later. Avoid covering lamps with drapes, backdrops, etc.: they can catch fire, despite fireproofing. Ropes will burn and weaken.
- All scenic materials should be sprayed with flame retardant.

- Leave *clear space between sets* for people to move through, unobstructed by scenic braces or jacks.
- Only store items such as props, furniture, or rugs in *agreed storage areas*.
- All stairs, getaway steps (offstage steps), and high points such as platforms/rostra should have security handrails. Platforms should have guard rails, kicking boards, battens, or edge-strips where appropriate. This is a regular area for serious accidents.
- When scenery is being erected, keep the area clear of people working on other jobs (e.g. lighting). Their preoccupations may prevent their being alert to any hazards.
- Handling scenery is not just a matter of strength. It requires controlled techniques to avoid personal injury (Chapter 9).
- Leave floor painting until last and put signs and guard barriers around the wet floor.

- *Avoid water spillage on floors*, particularly if they have been painted. After spillage or floor washing, have wet floors dried immediately to prevent surface damage and people slipping. If necessary, cover them over and arrange barriers.
- Regard all water as hazardous, particularly in any volume (e.g. tanks, pools).
- No water should be allowed near lamps, power points, cables etc. (Beware water spray on light fittings. The lamps will explode!)

- Regard most scenic effects as potentially hazardous (e.g. fire, water, smoke, rain, collapsing scenery/wreckage, mirrors – Chapter 7). Don't try out effects by yourself, in case anything goes wrong.

- Avoid using hazardous materials casually in the studio (e.g. sand, salt, or glass).

- When audiences are invited, public safety precautions are essential. Local regulations are usually specific, relative to the type and fixing of seating, safety barriers, fire escape routes, gangways, exit notices, illuminated signs, firefighting equipment, etc.

So you see how the action and production treatment can determine the form of the set. If there are to be other episodes of the show, where emphasis may be on other parts of the room, it might be a good idea to build all four walls of the room initially, and let the action determine which one you omit (as a 'fourth wall') for any given episode.

Furniture tends to follow recognizable positions in most settings. Again, this is partly a matter of:

● *Convention* – we expect furniture to be in certain parts of a room,
● *Practical convenience* – some positions for furniture offer more shot opportunities than others.

5.24 Safety

We all become so preoccupied with getting on with the job that it is easy to overlook, or not bother, about a lot of tedious safety rules and reminders. Larger organizations issue sizeable books of *safety regulations* to guide staff. For some of us it takes the horror of seeing falling scenery crush people and equipment or a fire in the studio to emphasize the need for safety measures.

Many of the hazards are not the direct concern of the scenic designer, such as the electric cable carelessly draped over a ground lamp, or the suspended lamp that could decapitate a passer-by, or the carelessly installed practical lights that could electrocute the unwary. But **you** could be the victim!

In Table 5.1 you will see a very abbreviated list of reminders of typical safety hazards. They are worth thinking over. As the old saw has it, *the life you save may be your own!*

Chapter 6

Shoestring staging

Here we are going to discuss ways of making optimum use of limited facilities, budget and space – yet get high-grade results on the screen.

6.1 Biggest is not best

Scenic design for any television or video program can be costly. But a great deal depends on the ways the director, the set designer, and the lighting director decide to interpret the program.

Let us think for a moment about those television and video shows one sees, in which a simple, straightforward subject such as a solo singer is presented within an elaborate, impressive décor. The treatment we see on the screen is not inherent in the subject but has been decided on by the production group. Does this treatment really heighten the appeal of the program material? It may do. But aren't there times when it tends to overwhelm and diminish the artiste's performance? That can also be true. A singer whose beauteous voice and personality can hold an audience when singing on an empty stage may benefit little if surrounded by an elaborate display of tall columns, imposing drapes, or intricate lighting. On the other hand, it must be admitted that impressive scenic treatment can add a sense of importance or 'occasion' – even to the mediocre.

There are clearly no intrinsic merits in 'impressive' décor as such. In fact there are times when a simpler style can be more persuasive.

6.2 The economical approach

Because a studio is small it does not mean that one cannot tackle sizeable productions. If necessary, a program can be videotaped in sections, changing or revamping the setting, one scene at a time.

Scenic storage can be a problem, but with a little ingenuity even that need not be insuperable.

Quite often, a project that at first sight sounds prohibitively costly can be presented effectively with imaginative yet economical treatment.

Even when scenic design in the studio is quite rudimentary, there is no need for this to be obvious on the screen. It is possible to use very basic effects and yet leave an audience with a sense of luxury and delight. Remember, the camera cannot tell the difference between a genuine gold bar, a gold-painted wooden replica, molded plastic, or a photograph. On the screen they are all gold bars!

Most productions have brief localized scenes, interleaved with others of greater length and importance. The trick is to 'put the money where it will show'.

Let us imagine we have a program for disabled people, showing how various accessories and gadgets can assist them. This could be tackled in various ways:

- The least interesting would be to have *someone behind a table*, picking up each item in turn and talking about it. Requiring only a table and a neutral background, this would be an economical but dull way of presenting the material.
- You might build several *full-scale settings* depicting a kitchen, living room, bathroom, bedroom, and hallway. This could be a major undertaking requiring an appreciable budget and plenty of studio space.
- You could use an *open setting*, showing the items on a number of 'scenic islands'.
- A series of *abbreviated settings*, just large enough to demonstrate particular items, could be very effective. A bed against a wallpapered flat, with a rug and a bedside table, appears to be a bedroom. Some treads against a brick-flat appear to be outside a house. The camera shows a limited area and the imagination does the rest, yet the items we are concentrating on are shown clearly and convincingly.

Of course, the director will have preferences as to which of these approaches is used, but this brief list of examples is a reminder of the variety that is possible, and that the most obvious treatment is not always essential or even the best.

6.3 Low-cost materials

For many program makers, resources are very limited and budgets nominal. But with a little ingenuity attractive scenic treatment is still possible.

Economy begins with the materials you use.

You can recycle clean scrap material to augment or construct scenic pieces. Packaging, cardboard cartons, corrugated cardboard, or expanded polystyrene molding, for example, can be adapted in various ways, especially in the make-believe world of children's programs.

Renovated materials such as lumber or plastic sheeting, mesh, wire, fabric, rope, sacking, angle-iron, etc. can be re-used, formed into structures, painted, and decorated.

This is not 'garbage heap' mentality but making use of perfectly good resources, using one's imagination, and anticipating opportunities. For instance, translucent screens can be made from salvaged bed sheets. Instead of burning small tree-branches use them to produce shadows or as scenic decoration.

Some new materials are not really costly yet they are extremely adaptable. A roll of seamless paper, for instance, will not only provide neutral backgrounds but can be used:

● For graphics,
● Cut into sculptural forms,
● As table covering,
● To clad platforms,
● Decorated and stuck onto flats or panels,
● Made into roller blinds (e.g. pulldown displays).

'Shoestring' scenic design is a long-term concept and, as we shall see, there are a number of basic scenic units such as modular units, screens, flats, or platforms that repay their initial outlay over and over, for they can be adapted and re-used for years.

6.4 Scenic decoration

Because a small television/video unit, campus studio, or local station uses 'shoestring staging' the effect on-air does not have to be crude and amateurish.

For example, you might make a simple frame, stretch cords across it, and intertwine ivy round the cords. A spray-can of gold paint will transform this screen into an elegant, stylish unit. Later, you can remove the ivy and weave 'lathes' of thin card through the cords to change its appearance completely.

You do not even have to be able to paint or draw well. Take a few tree-leaves and pin them to a flat surface. Spray over them and, when they are removed, interesting outlines will remain. You can use wire mesh, netting, trellis, etc. similarly. For extra economy the material that was used to create the outlines can be introduced elsewhere in the setting, as part of the décor!

Stencils provide a very simple way of decorating a surface, with a wide range of decorative motifs: arabesques, acanthus, beading, foliage, garlands, guilloche, etc.

Instead of laborious painting, stretch decorative tapes or masking tape across a surface to form the pattern you want.

All manner of decorative patterns, motifs, and symbols can be made or bought and attached to surfaces. Drawn on adhesive plastic sheet, they can be prepared away from the studio and stuck in positions where they will show to best advantage on camera.

6.5 Realistic aims

The real way to beat low-budget restrictions is to design with imagination.

- Think laterally. If a scene calls for a verandah, do not do the obvious and attempt to build one in the studio when a *skeletal* version would be much more interesting to look at – and cost a lot less (Section 4.31).
- If the purse-strings are tight, why try to build a room when furniture in an *open set* against a black background could be quite as effective on camera (Section 4.5)? Use black-painted or black-draped walls if a cyc is not available.
- Avoid features that you cannot achieve. If a script calls for a setting that is beyond your resources, work out how to get round the problem and yet *convey the same ideas* to the audience.

Suppose, for instance, that the script describes how we are watching a young girl at her first dance, neglected and shy, standing in the ballroom watching the dancers swirl by. We could modify the situation so that we have her standing outside in the night, illuminated by the light from a curtained window, with the tantalizing sounds of the dance ringing in her ears. (One drape frame and one lamp, against black drapes!) To extend the scene we could undercut or superimpose a series of stills ('cutaway shots') showing photographs of a ballroom that represent her imaginings.

- A *cooking demonstration* does not necessarily require a fully working kitchen. Modular units can provide the bench (Section 6.9). If the cook needs running water from a tap, this can be fed from a hidden container (so no main water supply is needed). The sink can drain into a bucket hidden beneath. Examples of the food can be prepared beforehand, and taken from a dummy or unconnected over (so no fully practical oven is needed in the studio).
- As a guitarist plays a haunting melody, and the background is filled with attractive abstract light-patterns, the audience accepts them and listens. They neither know nor care that these patterns are simply reflections from a spotlight shining onto baking foil (Section 4.21).
- A storyteller sits on a log by the campfire, telling us a tale. For the audience it is all real. *We* know that there is just a bit of foliage hung in front of the camera, and someone is gently waving a stick with a row of rag strips, attached over a lamp lying on the ground.

Even these few examples should be enough to show how we can create a lot out of very little. Each situation becomes a challenge, an opportunity to devise convincing décor from simple, everyday materials.

6.6 Minimum scenery

If you are trying to keep the cost of scenery to the absolute minimum then the answer must surely be to make the greatest use possible of a cyclorama, whether it takes the form of stretched cloth or a horizontal run of seamless paper stapled to wall battens or flats.

As we have seen earlier, you can use a plain mid-toned cyc as a background to virtually any kind of show, from a table display to a full-scale drama. Through lighting alone, you can alter the appearance of the background to suit the type of production (Sections 4.14, 4.20, 4.21, and 4.23), and the lamps you need do not have to be particularly sophisticated. Sometimes you can adapt an existing lamp so that it is more suitable (e.g. remove the fresnel lens from a spotlight and its light will cast sharper shadows and spread over a much greater area).

Where there is little space it is not easy to separate the cyc lighting from the *action lighting* that is illuminating the performers. All one can do is to keep them as far away from the background as possible and use sidelighting (from left and right of the camera position) rather than direct frontal lighting (beside the camera) that will fall straight onto the background.

Open sets are obviously a straightforward development of the open cyc background. A few pieces of strategically positioned furniture, and you have created a 'room', a restaurant, a school, etc. (Section 4.5).

Using screens and panels

As we saw in Section 3.46, screens and panels can take many different forms. But what is most important for groups working on a very restricted budget is that they offer an extremely cheap, simple, and flexible way of creating varied and attractive décor.

They are equally valuable, of course, in large-studio productions, where they have been adopted successfully for music, dance, talks, comedy shows, and quiz shows.

6.7 Themes and variations

One can easily underestimate the value of screens and panels. Not only can they be rearranged quickly and easily to present a fresh overall pattern in the acting area but you can alter their appearance in various ways.

The basic unit is a black skeletal framework.

- The *open frame* can have material hung or draped on it. The drape is removed and we see that the frame has a pattern of strings stretched across it, which stand out white against a dark background. The lighting changes, and now light from behind the screen rim-lights the strings, and its patterned mesh falls forward onto the floor to join with the pattern from other screens, forming an overall decorative design.
- A *transparent sheet* is fitted over the frame. The white outlines of seabirds in flight are visible against a black background. But when lit from behind, we see that the panel is painted in translucent colors and becomes a stained-glass window.

Figure 6.1 Panels and screens

Pictorial panels. Large free-standing pictorial panels can be introduced for a wide range of productions. Hand-painted, photo-enlargements, photomontages, projected pictures or patterns, and chroma key inserts offer endless opportunities. A camera can take close shots of the flats to provide a background for titles, illustrate a talk, etc.

Suspended screens. Suspended decorative screens can add a delicate background component in area staging (mesh, painted scrim, translucent panels, etc.).

● Take a *translucent sheet* of frosted plastic and cover it with black adhesive vinyl film. Draw any design and lettering on the vinyl; cut round and remove them, leaving a stenciled graphic which, when lit from the rear, becomes an illuminated sign.
● An *opaque sheet* is decorated with a patterned surface. We turn the frame round and see a different decoration on the reverse side.
● A *translucent sheet* of frosted plastic is lit from the front and appears plain. Lit from behind, we see the silhouette of a pattern attached to its rear face. Alternatively, we can use the screen to display a projected light-pattern.

As we saw in Sections 3.20–3.24, you can decorate solid panels in innumerable ways.

You can attach textured materials, floor tiles, wallpaper, fabric-covered board, wire mesh, artificial leaves/flowers, painted designs, stenciled patterns, or photomontages.

Positioned in front of an open cyc, you can:

● Change the color or tone of the cyc itself,
● Silhouette the screens or panels,
● Cast forward shadows,
● Vary the light intensity on individual screens,
● Progressively shade or change the color on screens,
● Use units of diminishing size, to suggest perspective,
● Have a series of motifs that are continued throughout the units, to form an overall design,

- Use frames faced with black gauze against a black cyc and floor. Then through changes in lighting you can make surface designs stand out, isolated in the darkness, and vanish in a moment.

6.8 Supporting screens and panels

The frames on which screens or panels are mounted can be self-supporting or rear-braced by a jack or stage-brace. They can be attached to tubular poles, which are fixed at the upper end to a ceiling grid or lighting batten, and fitted to a protective floor plate.

In a low-ceilinged studio, spring-loaded poles ('polecats') can be fixed between floor and ceiling or floor and lighting grid to support frames.

You can suspend frames, using stout fishing line, nylon thread, or heavy-duty theatrical hanging line (white or black). But for heavier units, decorative rope or steel cord/wire rope will be necessary. To prevent a lightweight suspended frame from swaying you may need to secure its lower end with cords attached to a short batten or a stage weight on the floor; or perhaps to adjacent scenic units.

6.9 The modular frame

This is an open framework formed from lumber, angle-iron, or slotted steel L-sections (scenic metal or Dexion). The top cross-section can be square, rectangular, triangular, wedge-shaped, trapezoid, or rhomboid. The sizes of modulars can be whatever you find most useful; from a foot or two to several feet long (e.g. 1 ft or 0.3 m to 9 ft or 2.7 m).

The great advantage of these giant 'building bricks' is that they are easily modified to suit your particular needs. You can clip or screw panels of board, plywood, metal, or plastic sheeting onto the faces as you choose, to form 'solid', open, or partially clad units. Low-castered stands can be attached to units to increase their mobility.

You can change or redecorate the panels, intermix textures, tones, and colors, use internally lit translucent panels or modules as skeletal units. Divisions across the framework at intervals can provide shelves or strengthening partitions.

Clad on all sides, we have a *box* unit. Left open on one or two sides, it provides a *shell*. Because a shell unit is hollow it can be used as a desk or for tuckaway storage during a demonstration.

Modular units can be placed side by side, bolted or slotted together, and built up into multi-height platforms.

There are endless applications for modular frames as a basis for screens, tables, shelving, structural units, or lightweight platforms.

- Module surfaces can be solid, translucent, transparent.
- Graphics panels can be fitted with tear-off drawing sheets,

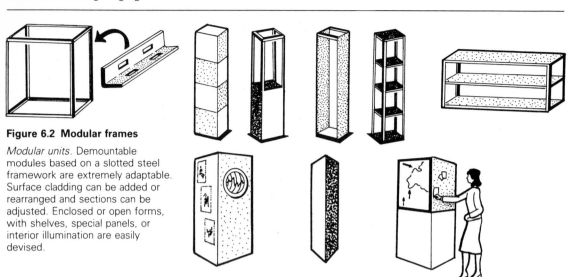

Figure 6.2 Modular frames

Modular units. Demountable modules based on a slotted steel framework are extremely adaptable. Surface cladding can be added or rearranged and sections can be adjusted. Enclosed or open forms, with shelves, special panels, or interior illumination are easily devised.

Combined modulars. Individual modules (box or shell) can be bolted together to form display units, desks, benches, tables, etc.

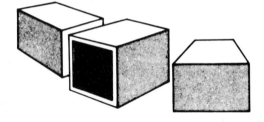

● Wedge-shaped units together form curved assemblies.
● Units can be individually clad or unified with a single piece of facing card or board that hides the joins.

chalkboards, magnetic boards, or plastic-coated for tacky-back symbols.

● Decorative panels can have ornamental motifs, clip-on fabric, texture sheets, etc.

● Blue chroma key panels can enable electronic insertion of titling or graphics.

● Display panels can show maps, graphics, photographs, station or program identification symbols (*logos*).

The art of multiple use

6.10 Multi-use of units

Even standard scenic units have applications that are not immediately obvious.

Figure 6.3 Multi-use of units
Individual scenic units can be used for many quite different purposes:

Two glazed french doors can be end-joined to provide a long wall window or a ceiling-light.

Simple cross-braced wooden rods (doweling) can be used as railings, window bars, or a decorative grille.

An arch head can be turned into a low window or even a throne.

An arch can be filled in to become a bookcase or a window unit.

Movable walls
Large standard flats mounted on castered supports enable entire walls to be repositioned quickly. (Stage weights give them stability.)

Narrow flats up to 2 ft (600 mm) wide that are normally used as *returns*, *jogs*, or *reveals* in room settings can be adapted as shelving, laid on edge to hide groundrow lamps, or coupled together to form square columns. Similarly, they can suggest beams, arches, or cattle troughs.

A shallow scenic arch-unit normally takes the form of a profiled flat, with a board around the opening to give it 'thickness'. With a little work, the opening can be backed, shelves and a cupboard fitted and we have a recessed bookcase. Insert a window frame and block off the base and the arch is now a window flat!

The semicircular 'arch head' that normally rests on side pillars to form a deep scenic arch can be used as a basement window or even an ancient throne.

Fully glazed doors have been pressed into service as decorative skylights or windows.

A set of railings, formed from wooden doweling, can become prison bars or a decorative room divider.

Again, as we saw in Section 6.3, it is a matter of anticipating opportunities.

6.11 Multi-use of settings

If we could re-use the same setting during a production yet have it appear quite different to our audience, this would clearly be a great saving. Happily, there are several ways of doing this.

The simplest is to have cameras shoot the set from *different angles*, including varying amounts of the background in the shots.

You can go further, and make slight changes in the background or the set dressing, reposition parts of the set, or rearrange the furniture to give the picture an entirely different feel.

Figure 6.4 Multi-use of settings
Simply by altering the camera
viewpoint and showing different
parts of the same setting we can
appear to change scene on camera.

Revamping (*redressing*) can be taken a lot further:

● Change the furniture.
● Reposition major furniture (e.g. move a room divider or wall unit).
● Add or remove rugs.
● Add or remove display posters, signs, or notices.
● Replace wall decoration such as maps, mirrors, or pictures.
● *Photographs* of clocks, pictures, window scenes, plaques, etc. can be stuck to cut-out laminates and attached to walls. (At a distance, the camera cannot distinguish between a photograph and the real thing if thickness is not revealed.)
● Use reversible window drapes, venetian blinds, or shutters with different tones/colors on each side.
● A wall's appearance can change according to whether window drapes are open or closed (drawn).
● Imply windows by hanging drapes or blinds from a wall batten.
● For quickly removed rows of books use vertical boards with stuck-on printed card sheets, photographed book backs, or actual book backs.
● Replace minor set dressing on shelves (e.g. substitute the dummy books with a horizontal board that has stuck-on displayed ornaments).
● Hide a doorway with a notice board and a piece of furniture, a drape on a frame, or a folding screen.
● Position indoor plants (e.g. ferns) to break up the background.
● Change apparent architectural features in the setting – attach/ remove dummy fireplaces, doors, windows, or buttresses to the

Figure 6.5 Partial settings

Grouped items. The camera cannot
see the sparseness of the décor and
the short length of fence on its timber
supports. In a fairly close shot the
scene looks complete.

Sky-cloth

Hedge unit

Fiber-glass
tree trunk

Fence section

Small detailed sets. If actors and/or
the camera are going to move around
or different viewpoints are to be
intercut it may be necessary to build
a small setting in greater detail.

Localized setting. You can create an
environment by building an
abbreviated part of the location.

walls of the setting. A sheet of timber-finish laminate with a
plastic-strip surround can be attached to a wall with double-
sided tape to become a 'door'.
- A wall recess can be filled in with lightweight board, on which
  is stuck photographs or dummy replicas of a cupboard,
  bookshelves, equipment, etc.
- Use a drape-frame to cover over part of the background.
- Lighting changes can transform a setting (altered window
  patterns, background tone, wall shading, etc.).

Low-wheeled platforms are useful where a small setting or part of
a set can be wheeled into place or moved to suit the camera
(wagons, floats – Section 3.37). Just replacing or removing some
furniture in the foreground can entirely transform the appearance
of a set.

6.12 Partial settings

In a traditional theater play the action takes place at length, in a
few locations. Film and television drama, on the other hand, tends
to use brief action sequences, in a number of locations. The latter
approach sounds prohibitively expensive, but it can still be
handled on a modest budget with a little ingenuity.

Partial setting

In the studio we see that it is a very abbreviated setting, created with great attention to period detail.

On the screen the camera suggests that it is part of a magnificent room.

If a carefully chosen *part* of the location will suggest the entire situation to our audience why build more?

When there is a lot of action, which cameras are shooting from changing viewpoints, then the setting has to be sufficiently large to suit this treatment. But even in major drama productions there are a surprising number of brief scenes where people move around very little and quite a small setting will suffice.

The technique is to imply the whole by showing a complete but localized part. Build up a section of the scene, complete enough to suit the shot. The wider the shot, the more detail is necessary.

In a restaurant scene, for example, a foreground table, screens, a palm perhaps, and a drape can suggest luxury, with no need for more elaborate treatment. A wider shot would show a large area and need much more extensive décor.

The disadvantage of this technique is that it gives very little leeway for the sort of director who has difficulty in anticipating shots and has to work empirically, and it can lead to a cramped, restricted production style. But for those who are methodical, and plan their production thoroughly, partial settings offer exciting opportunities.

6.13 Selected elements

By using just a few carefully chosen features it is often possible to build up a convincing locale out of very little.

Seeing the door of a house, we assume that the rest of the building exists. A ticket-office represents the entire foyer of a theater.

It is fascinating to see how little is needed at times to create a convincing atmosphere. Show someone holding a fishing rod, backed by a light blue cyc, and we have conveyed the idea that they are fishing. Add the sound of a river, and the audience is convinced. How necessary is it to add the grassy river bank, trees, or water reflections?

Two fugitives are being pursued across moorland (videotaped mute location shots). In the studio we see a close shot of them at ground level, as they lie on the ground speaking, peering through tussocks of grass. That's all there is in the studio – a few tufts of grass! How minimal can you get!

6.14 Permanent sets

The more use one can make of a setting, the more economical it becomes. If a set is used regularly throughout a series of programs, this *permanent set* may need to be made more robust (to stand the repeated handling, transport, and storage) but it will still be a better proposition than décor that is used only once.

If a production is in the studio daily or several times a week it may be left in position as a *standing set*. Other shows can use the rest of the studio staging area, or even 'nest' within the standing set (Section 5.20).

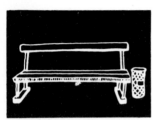

Figure 6.6 Selected elements

Selected minimum. Even a few carefully selected props or scenic elements can set a scene. But these must be unambiguous.
Against black drapes, a bench and a trash basket under dappled lighting become a park scene at night. But the audience must recognize and interpret the situation instantly.

The selective approach. To create a bookshop location you could build up a very complete, extensively dressed setting (1). Clearly, a costly approach. If the set is inadequate there will be too few visual clues (2), and the result is likely to be unconvincing and ambiguous.
By restricting the shot with carefully placed foreground pieces (3) you can limit the setting, enhance the impression of depth, and create a realistic effect at minimum cost. Even a few scenic elements can conjure up an environment when the lighting is selective and localized and much of the setting falls into shadow (4).

Figure 6.7 Permanent sets
With a little ingenuity a permanent setting can be extremely flexible.
1. Roller shade (roller-blind) to provide background-tone variations, to serve as a suggest a window; to serve as a front projection screen for wall-charts, etc. Replace with venetian blind, woven wood, split-bamboo shade, etc.
2. Chroma key surface: for inserted backgrounds (of tone, pattern or texture; pictorial slides, etc.).
3. Curtains on track: double-sided reversible (different tones, textures). To cover all or part of back wall.
4. Overhead projectors: for background patterns, logos, etc. (Further projectors behind back wall provide rear projection.)
5. Series of hook-in, sliding double-sided wall panels. Various forms and finishes, including neutrals, wood veneer, textured materials, fabric, front-projection screens, chroma key blue, etc. Panels can be repositioned, changed, or combined.
6. Ground lamps (trough, strip lights, cyc lights). Removable. Illuminate background from below.
7. Wall screen (removable). For rear-projection of slides (titles, graphics, scenic window, etc.). Screen can be replaced with TV picture-monitor/receiver.

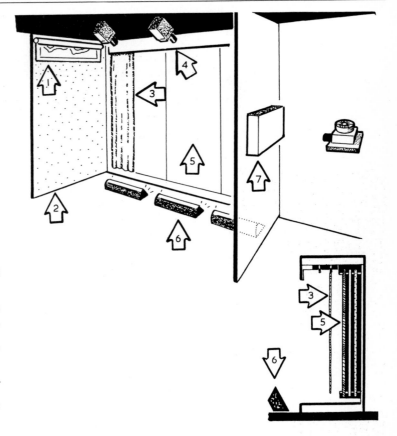

For smaller production units a special *multi-purpose permanent setting* has many advantages, for it can be adapted to suit individual productions. Typical features include:

- *Wall surfaces* – designed to be slid aside, reversed, inverted, removed, or replaced. Their tone, pattern, texture, etc. can be changed.
- *Drapes* – of reversible material on curtain tracks, used pleated or stretched to conceal all or part of the background.
- *Translucent panels* – These can serve as 'windows' and as decorative or architectural features. The panels can be rear-lit in various ways and display shadows, abstract motifs, etc.
- *Lighting treatment* – Lighting changes provide variations in the background tone or hue. Background texture can be emphasized or suppressed. The background can be shaded or display light-patterns.
- *Chroma key* – Panels of suitable hue (blue, yellow, green) can be positioned so that graphics, titling, other cameras' outputs, film, or videotape can be displayed using electronic insertion.

6.15 Stock sets

Where a particular type of set is expensive to construct yet used fairly regularly, such as an aircraft interior, a railway coach, or a courtroom, large film and television studio centers often keep a version in disassembled form as a *stock set*. When required, it is checked over and refurbished for re-use. Where these stock sets can be hired, smaller production groups may find it much cheaper to obtain such a stock set from them than to build their own version.

Chapter 7

Scenic effects

All scenic design is, strictly speaking, an *effect*. But here we shall look at various ways in which the designer can extend and augment normal staging treatment.

The illusion of space

7.1 The divided setting

Any set will look larger than it really is if shot on a wide-angle lens. But suppose there simply isn't room or the scene is too brief to be worth building a sizeable set?

Then the *divided set* can be an effective solution. Instead of constructing a complete room we build a few strategic sections. Let us take an example.

> It is a short scene, showing an episode in a soldier's life. A cadet enters the ancient hall of a military academy and marches up to a table to meet an examining board.
> ● *Set A*: Two examiners sit behind one end of long table in front of a twofold flat with lancet windows.
>   *Set B*: A paneled door flat with backing.
>   *Set C*: The other end of the table and a paneled flat.
> ● *Camera treatment*
>   *Shot 1*: Set A. Examiners discussing the cadet. Door knock is heard.
>   *Shot 2*: Set B. Cadet enters. Walks forward.
>   *Shot 3*: Set A. Examiners greet him. (Sound of extended echoing footsteps suggesting considerable distance.)
>   *Shot 4*: Set C. Cadet at end of table, apparently talking to the examiners.
>   *Shot 5*: Set A. Examiners question cadet.

The sets could be anywhere in the studio. The sequence might even be *re-using parts of existing settings* built for other scenes!

7.2 Foreground planes

Looking at any picture, an audience makes a lot of spatial assumptions.

Suppose, for instance, that they see two people in the foreground of a shot and someone else in the background against a window.

Figure 7.1 The illusion of depth

Foreground planes. Foreground planes can enhance the impression of depth in a picture:

They may arise naturally, from the camera's viewpoint.

The designer may deliberately position items in the foreground to be used for a particular shot.

Even an artificially introduced foreground piece can appear natural in the picture.

Breakthrough pieces. The camera moves up to the foreground piece, which parts on cue as it passes through into the set.
1. A small window (may be hand-held).
2. A doorway on wheeled supports.

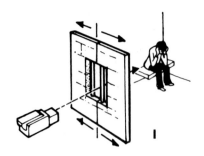
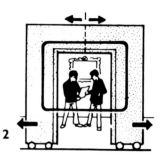

They assume that they are seeing a room, stretching from the foreground to the distant wall. In reality there is no room, just a window flat, some people, and an empty floor. We have *implied* an environment through the use of foreground planes.

Even a single item, such as a tree branch or a vase of flowers, will produce this spatial effect.

You can use part of an architectural feature in the foreground (arch, a doorway, a window frame, or a balustrade) to create an illusion of totality. It might be wheeled into place in front of the camera just for the shot.

A foreground plane such as a window or doorway may be made as a *breakthrough piece*, designed to appear whole but pulling apart as the camera dollies forward 'through' it.

7.3 Exaggerated perspective

In everyday life we are accustomed to the illusion of *perspective*. We see how things appear to get smaller as they move further away from us. Parallel lines in roads and railway tracks seem to converge with distance. We can imitate this phenomenon in scenic design.

The simplest idea is to deliberately adjust set dressing so that larger objects are placed in the foreground of a shot, with

False perspective
Here the designer has used profiled
flats painted to exaggerate
perspective, and created the
impression on camera of
considerable size and distance.

progressively smaller items towards the background. This arrangement has the advantage that it does not look unnatural from other
camera positions.

There are design techniques that can produce a remarkable
impression of distance but, unfortunately, only from the one fixed
camera position for which they were designed:

● A backdrop with strong perspective lines which are continued
  forward into the studio,
● A setting built with emphasized ('forced') perspective, but this
  requires scenery specially constructed for the occasion,
● A *foreground matte* which has a picture containing strong
  perspective and an opening through which we can see people
  in the studio.

7.4 Scale changes

You will seldom need to create the illusion that people are only a
few inches high or are gigantic. But this can be done easily enough
by building the *entire* setting, furniture, and props on a much
larger or smaller scale than normal.

Figure 7.2 Exaggerated perspective

We can deliberately create a false impression of space.

Scenic treatment. 1. Larger objects in the foreground, with progressively smaller ones further from the camera, enhance the impression of depth.

2. A flat background picture containing strong perspective can produce an illusion of depth. But any shadows falling on its surface, any scale errors, or wrong foreground/background perspective can destroy the effect. The camera must remain still.

3. The whole setting may be built in false perspective, exaggerating the way size reduces with distance.

4. Here profiled flats create the illusion of distance.

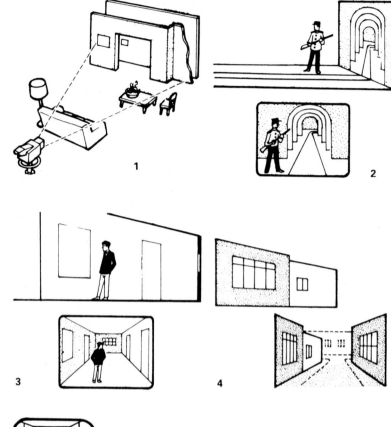

Foreground matte. A scene containing strong perspective is set up as a camera matte. Through a cut-out section action in the studio is visible.

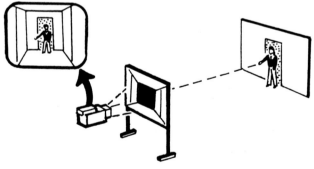

Figure 7.3 Scale changes

1. If the set is built with everything proportionally scaled down people appear gigantic.

2. If everything is scaled up people appear dwarfed.

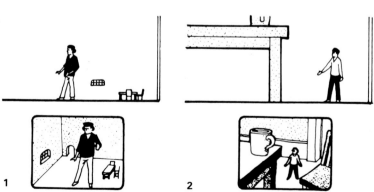

7.5 Using mirrors

Just as wall mirrors in the home can make a room appear more spacious so, too, appropriately used mirrors can enhance the impression of space in the studio set.

When attached to a wall you will need to check that a mirror does not inadvertently reflect lights, cameras, etc. But a small roll of paper tucked behind the frame will usually tilt it sufficiently to overcome this problem.

If the camera shoots via a mirror it will get a laterally reversed picture (which can be corrected by electronic reversal or a second mirror). However, its effective distance from the scene will be increased by the camera-to-mirror distance, so allowing much longer shots in a smaller studio than would otherwise be possible. A foreground camera matte can prevent overshoot.

Mirrors can be used to give the camera a high or low viewpoint. The further the mirror is from the camera, the larger it will need to be. Large glass mirrors are expensive, heavy, and vulnerable, and really need to be *surface silvered* for the highest quality.

Self-adhesive silver-mirror plastic sheeting is more practicable in many situations. Its image is inferior but quite acceptable for many purposes. However, 'shrink-mirror' plastic sheeting (e.g. Rosco's 'Silver Shrink'), is particularly successful. After having been stretched across a frame the material is then shrunk with heat for optical clarity.

Figure 7.4 Using mirrors

Part 1 *Basic laws*. When light strikes a mirror at an angle (I) it is reflected at a corresponding angle (R). So the overall path of the light is changed by I + R degrees.
At the point where the reflection takes place an imaginary plane (the 'normal') can be drawn at right angles to the mirror. (The *incident* and *reflected* rays and the *normal* all lie in the same plane.)
The reflected image appears laterally reversed, and as far behind the mirror as the subject is in front. The camera focuses on the subject's *image*, not on the mirror.

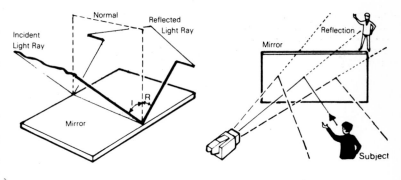

Part 2 *The area seen*. The easiest way to plan a mirror position and judge what it will reflect is to cut out a paper triangle of the lens angle (e.g. 25°), fold it at the anticipated mirror position (or at the point corresponding to the mirror width), and place this on the scale floor plan. This will show the mirror size and its distance from the camera. (*Note:* The smaller the mirror, the closer it must be to the camera.)

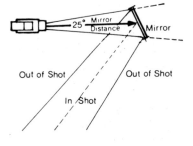

Figure 7.4 (continued)

Part 3 *Viewpoint – single mirror.* You can change the camera's apparent viewpoint with a single mirror.
1. Overhead (top) shot – image inverted and laterally reversed.
2. Reverse-angle top shot.
3. Very low angle shot (inverted).

Part 4 *Viewpoint – using two mirrors.* Mirrors may be mounted separately, fixed in a portable periscope stand, or attached to the camera mounting.
1. Overhead shot.
2. High-angle shot.
3. Low-angle shot.
4. Low-level shot.

Part 5 *Folding the light path.* You can save floor space by folding the light path with a mirror. Using a second mirror, even greater compactness is possible but with further loss of clarity. Surface-silvered mirrors produce less light loss and coloration than normal rear-silvered types.

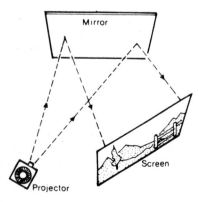

Water in the studio

7.6 Facts and figures

Water is heavy! Check the floor-loading capacity of the studio at an early stage. A typical point loading for a studio might be of the order of 224 lb/ft² (1090 kg/m²), which corresponds to a water depth of 3 ft (900 mm).

- Water weighs 2.2 lb/l. One US gallon (3.7843 liters) weighs 8.33 lb. One Imperial (UK) gallon of water (4.546 liters) weighs 10 lb.
- One *cubic meter* of water (35.32 ft³) is a cube with sides only 1 m (3.28 ft) long. Yet it contains 1000 liters (264.17 gall US/219.97 gal UK). And it weighs 1000 kg or one metric tonne (i.e. 2204.62 lb).
- One *cubic foot* of water (i.e. a cube with sides of only 1 ft long) weighs 62.5 lb. It contains 7.506 gal US (6.25 gal UK); 36 ft³ of water weigh one ton.
- A pool or tank can be filled with water at a rate of somewhere around one minute for 18 gal US/15 gal UK (70 liters).
- Large pools can be emptied at about 240 gal US/200 gal UK (900 liters) per minute, while smaller ones would empty at e.g. 60 gal US/50 gal UK (225 liters) in a minute. The last 6 in (150 mm) or so empties at a much slower rate.

7.7 Water is a hazard!

Do not underestimate the problem you can have with water! It takes no time at all to spill around and a lot of time and effort to clear up. Wherever possible, avoid piped high-pressure water supplies. If anything goes wrong a nuisance can quickly turn into disaster, particularly on painted floors or around electrical equipment!

Where only a limited water supply is needed for a faucet you can gravity-feed it via a hose from a supply in a plastic barrel. The higher the barrel is positioned, the greater the water flow.

Where water cannot be drained away easily, you can:

● Use a bucket or barrel to take the waste water.
● Use a deep tray filled with sawdust, burlap (hessian), or felt. This reduces noise.
● Make a catchment area by laying a sheet of heavy-duty plastic sheeting, supported underneath its edges with a timber framework (e.g. planks), to form a shallow 'tank'.
● Where water is pouring continuously a silent pump may be necessary to take away the drainage water.

7.8 Tanks and pools

Probably the first questions are 'Do you really need it?' 'Could you use a substitute, in the form of a sheet of clear plastic over a floor cloth or a shallow pool of water within plastic sheeting?

If a pool or tank is essential then it is advisable to lay down a protective safety sheet first, and when filling, never leave the water unattended. Continually check that the filled pool is leakproof, for hidden leaks can ruin the studio floor.

If the entire scene is to be flooded with water the director might settle for a narrow, double-sided glass tank positioned in front of the camera lens!

To suggest that there is water nearby, a *ripple tray* on the floor or a *ripple dish* on a lighting stand can provide a convincing illusion. Flickering light reflected from foil or reflective strips attached to cloth may be adequate for some purposes.

7.9 Rain

When you have an 'exterior' scene in the studio that is to depict a rainstorm there is a lot to be said for the time-honored trick of shooting a water spray against a black background then superimposing these pictures on shots of the studio scene. Provided that the scene itself looks 'wet' the subterfuge can be remarkably successful.

Otherwise, having protected floors and arranged catchment areas the most convincing effect comes from using a very fine mist spray on a hose, directed over the action area. At all costs, avoid using wind with rain, because results are difficult to control.

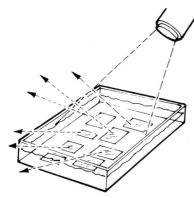

Figure 7.5 Water ripple

Floor tray. Light is reflected from mirror fragments in a tray of water.

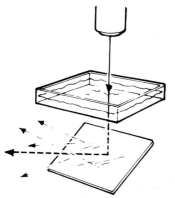

Stand tray. A spotlight shines through a water-filled glass tray. The rippling light is reflected by an adjustable mirror onto the scene.

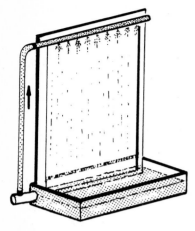

Figure 7.6 Rain
Water pumped from a tank jets out of a perforated pipe and runs down a large clear plastic sheet into the tank. Placed outside a window, the effect is seen as rain on the window panes.

Overhead perforated water pipes are not only unconvincing but provide an embarrassing amount of water to get rid of.

Rain on windows, seen from within a room, is on a much more convenient scale. Because windows in settings are not usually glazed it will be necessary to attach a clear plastic sheet to their exterior side. A fine spray directed at the window may be successful, but water is liable to rebound and cover quite an area around.

Instead, you can use a special gizmo that consists of a perforated pipe fastened along the top edge of a large rigid sheet of clear plastic. A water tray is attached to its lower edge. A small water pump in the tray supplies the pipe and the falling water is collected (hopefully!) for recirculation.

7.10 Fire!

The best advice here is 'If in doubt ... DON'T!'

If flame is essential in any form – candle, flambeau, oil lamp, a fire in a fireplace, or a burning document – ensure that there are always appropriate fire extinguishers at hand and someone checking and controlling it.

Ideally, all materials in the studio should be fireproofed or treated with an appropriate flame-retardant spray. Such treatment will NOT prevent fire but will inhibit flame and reduce the danger of ignition. Paints should be flame-resistant.

Certain materials needed around sets should only be used after being sprayed with flame-retardant solutions (e.g. straw, hay, raffia, grass mats, rags, paper, peat, sawdust).

If a fireplace is to have a visible fire there are several approaches:

● Controlled gas jets on ceramic 'logs' or 'coals' (formerly, asbestos-coated wire mesh versions were used),
● Solid fuel tablets, paraffin-wax firelighters among 'logs' or 'coals',
● Colored orange-red gel and a hidden lamp within a 'fire' of coal, coke, lump glass, or stones,
● Fine-colored silk strips, hanging over a lamp and blown by a gentle fan.

Where possible, a fire-flicker lighting effect (Section 6.5) should supplement the visible 'fire'.

7.11 Smoke

For small quantities of smoke you can use incense, compressed charcoal with oil, or special smoke pellets.

For larger amounts a wide variety of smoke machines and smoke guns are available. The days of eye-stinging, throat-catching oil vapors or overwhelming pyrotechnics in the studio are now long past, and readily controlled smoke with a range of fragrances can be used.

When you want to create a dense fog or a smoke-filled atmosphere in an interior scene it is advisable to switch off studio ventilation systems while using the effect.

Fog or smoke is not just confined to the setting in which it is being used. So if a production has a scene with dense fog and the next scene in a nearby set depicts a different time or place the hangover effect can be embarrassing.

Machines using pieces of 'dry ice' (solid carbon dioxide) in hot water produce extensive clouds of white heavy vapor that serve as mist, fog, steam, or swirling decorative clouds for dancers. You can simply drop pieces into hot water (wear gloves to protect hands from frostbite!). But if the water is not continuously heated its temperature will fall, and the action becomes sluggish.

The mist disappears quite quickly, so it needs to be continually replenished. Unless you only want a low-lying vapor it is best to pour the mist from well above floor level, while fanning it to spread the effect.

Less troublesome, perhaps, where you have sensitive smoke detectors, are fog filters over the camera lens (optical; white nylon net or gauze) and superimposed prerecorded swirling fog shot against a black background.

7.12 Wind

If you only want a gentle breeze, to blow hair or move light foliage, flapping a piece of board may be sufficient.

Wind strong enough to blow trees or bushes is better simulated by pulling attached nylon or fishing line.

Electric fans (wind machines) of various sizes can create winds from a strong breeze... up to storm strength able to blow the scenery over! However, the wind strength falls off rapidly with distance and may be too localized or directional. Fans often prove to be too noisy to use, due to hum and low wind rumble on microphones.

Strong winds are likely to blow dust and paper around the studio. Also, incongruously, you will find them blowing through the glassless windows of nearby interior sets.

Quite often it is better to keep actual wind to a minimum in the studio, to fake it with attached lines and rely on sound effects to add conviction.

7.13 Snow

Snow is fun to apply, provided that someone else clears it up! Rather than use quantities of synthetic snow, large areas can be treated with off-white paint. You can build up 'drifts of snow' from 'sandbags' (filled with polystyrene or sawdust), covered with off-white cloth and scattered with a thin layer of 'snow'. Blocks of styrofoam/expanded polystyrene provide convincing 'packed snow' and can be re-used for other purposes, when the season changes (Section 3.24).

Several types of material can be used to simulate fallen snow. Expanded polystyrene granules and sawdust must be of fire-retardant types. Excellent theatrical snow materials are available, from synthetic snowflakes to aerosol spray snow that melts.

Paper 'snow' is only convincing at a distance and blows around. Salt and gypsum dust are excellent but best avoided. The salt is corrosive for all equipment (cameras, lamps, cable connections, electronics).

Falling snow can be produced from suspended canvas or muslin 'snow-bags' filled with a finely shredded paper material. When tugged, a certain amount falls through the slits in the bag or trough. Confetti is less realistic and is a fire hazard.

A much more controlled, even result comes from 'snow machines'. These are elongated containers filled with small paper or plastic flakes, which are dispensed through slots by a motordriven spiked rod.

For night scenes, projected 'snowfall' lighting effects that suggest falling snow are available. Although rather mechanical and stylized when used on their own, when intermixed with dropping snow they can make a little material go a long way.

As with all loose materials scattered on the studio floor, one needs to take care to continually sweep it back onto the set (it clings to actors' feet when they leave the scene) and to ensure that there are clearways for cameras to move around without picking up debris on their wheels.

Ice can be simulated with frosted plastic sheeting or thin paraffin wax sheets. Clear plastic icicles can be made from strips of thin plastic film dipped in paraffin wax or etched from polystyrene, using an acetone solvent.

The wise designer avoids *blown snow* effects in the studio. Few attempt it a second time! The snow material fouls up the ventilation system and camera equipment and gets into lamps.

If you need a 'blizzard' it is best to simulate the effect by shooting a glass-fronted black box of blown theatrical snow material (e.g. expanded polystyrene granules) and superimposing this shot on pictures of the studio scene.

7.14 The ancient look

Apart from a generous dusting of *fuller's earth* and 'dirt-grimed windows' (excess dulling fluid or wax spray), 'cobwebs' are a must when you want to give an aged, neglected look to an interior.

Having stretched fine cotton threads wherever you want to form cobwebs, you can either use a special aerosol-packed preparation (from theater/film suppliers) or a *cobweb gun* to spin the cobwebs. The 'gun' is a hand-held device in which rubber solution is forced in a jet onto an electric fan and blown as fine filaments. Applied in gentle sweeping movements, cobwebs of any density can be 'grown' from the threads onto nearby surfaces. Blown talcum powder or fuller's earth will make them more prominent.

As we saw in Section 4.29, the set itself can be given various degrees of wear. Walls can be 'water-stained', 'soiled', wallpaper ripped, torn and re-stuck, spattered, or puddled (Section 3.21).

7.15 Skies – day

The skies of exterior settings in the studio need particular care if they are to appear completely convincing.

There are several ways of suggesting cloud in a day sky. Painted skies on a scenic cloth invariably look artificial. The most elaborate effects are produced by flooding a cyclorama with pale blue light and projecting white clouds onto it.

Ellipsoidal spotlights/profile spotlights can project a variety of cloud shapes from stainless-steel stencils ('gobos').

Scenic projectors can provide images from slides of clouds. They can also simulate moving clouds, using a glass disc which slowly rotates behind the projector's lens.

Large metal stenciled sheets with cloud shapes can be clipped in front of fresnel spotlights.

If the cyc is lit by spotlights fitted with blue-colored gel you can cut holes in the color medium to produce white, cloud-shaped light patches.

7.16 Skies – night

For night skies, projected cloud patterns will suggest moonlight. The moon can be provided separately from a semi-circular gobo or an irised-down spot. A word of warning. Although a scrim cyc stretched over the regular cyc (Section 4.37) will help to blur clouds in a daylit sky and improve the effect, it can cause a disconcerting double moon in a night sky.

Stars can be projected (pinpricks in a foil gobo), but because optical defects can misshape the spots and the light output is so low many designers prefer to pin Christmas tree lights (fairy lights, pea-lamps) to the cyc instead.

Obviously, if a black cyc is used for the night sky you cannot project clouds, although you can hang a cut-out moon lit by a spotlight. Against the black background the Christmas tree lights can represent stars, esplanade lights, street lights, airfield landing lights, a distant town, or lights in buildings. (Sequins are sometimes used instead but with rather less reliable results.) They

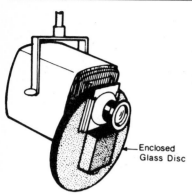

—Enclosed Glass Disc

Figure 7.7 Moving front projection
The scenic projector encloses a large removable glass disc with painted or photographed patterns on its surface. This is rotated at an adjustable speed by a small motor. A lens focuses the passing image onto the background (various lens angles available). Attached to a spotlight, the projector can simulate moving clouds, snow, water patterns, etc. The low image-intensity usually restricts the usable image-size. Images from several projectors can be superimposed on a cyc.

can also be successful if pinned on the *back* of an unlit light-toned cyc.

Normally, lights in city skylines are simulated by cutting small holes in a cut-out/profile flat (Section 3.48) and rear-lighting these 'windows' through a sheet of frosted plastic.

Scenic projection

7.17 Front projection

When you project a slide or film onto a screen you are using *front projection*. Unfortunately, in the television studio it is difficult to prevent ambient lighting washing out the image, so unless used under very controlled conditions any projected color, half-tone, or low-key (dark) images are normally very disappointing.

However, as we have seen, front projection will provide simple light-patterns of decorative shapes, logos, windows, clouds, etc.

The *ideal surface* for a projected image is light-toned, flat, and matte. There should be an uninterrupted light-path from the projector to the surface which is at right angles to its beam. If it is angled we shall see *geometrical* or *keystone distortion*. (Theoretically you can compensate by tilting the surface or using an inversely distorted slide, but that is seldom done.)

The darker the surface, the more powerful will the projector need to be, to provide a strong image. A heavily textured surface will blur the image clarity.

7.18 Reflex projection

Reflex projection (which is also called *front axial projection* or simply *front projection*) is a special-effects set-up that has been used very successfully in television, film, and photography. It is an optical method of undetectably combining a foreground subject with a separate image of a background scene.

Patent problems apart, it is not widely used because the subject/foreground camera *cannot move at all*, and the equipment requires very careful alignment to avoid black border lines around subjects.

The secret lies in the special highly directional beaded 'Scotchlite' screen, which is used for the background. A slide projector and a television camera are mounted on a rigid fitting behind a lightly silvered two-way mirror or pellicle. The background image is projected via the mirror onto the beaded screen. The camera looks straight through the same mirror as it shoots the foreground subject and the reflected background scene.

Although the slide's image does fall on the performer it is swamped by the studio lighting and is not visible. The highly directional screen ignores the studio lighting and reflects an

Figure 7.8 Reflex projection
1. In reflex front projection the background scene is projected along the camera lens's axis via a 'transparent' mirror (half-silvered; pellicle) onto a special, highly directional, glass-beaded screen. Actors' lighting swamps the image falling on them.
2. People appear *in front of* the background scene.
3. If people move behind a surface covered with the beaded screen material they will appear *behind* corresponding areas of the background scene (walls, trees, etc.).

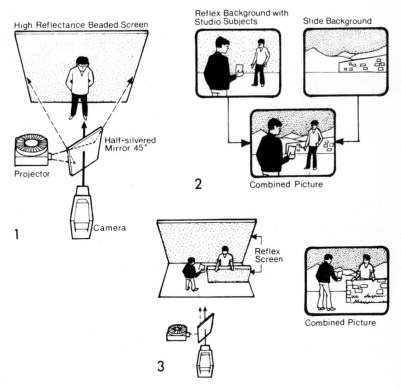

intense image of the background scene. So on camera we see the subject apparently integrated into the background scene.

There are technical problems and matching difficulties, but at best, results can be superb – within the unavoidable limitations.

7.19 Rear projection – patterns

In *rear projection* (*back projection*) action takes place in front of a translucent screen of 'frosted' plastic – either a rigid sheet or sheeting tightly stretched onto a frame.

In simple rear projection the screen is illuminated from behind to display silhouetted patterns, cut-outs, shadows, reflected shapes, colors, graded tone, etc. All this requires is a point light-source such as a lensless spotlight that will cast sharp, clear shadows of items set up behind the screen. The closer the items are to the screen, the sharper the shadows. If more than one lamp is used you will get multiple shadows – and interesting color mixtures if your lamps have different colored gels.

You can, of course, rear-project *gobo patterns* of all kinds using projector lamps/profile spots. But the light-patterns are likely to be unduly small unless the projectors have wide-angle lenses and are quite distant from the screen.

Although you will need a thin seamless plastic medium for detailed or pictorial images, you can rear-project broad light and shadow effects onto any background of thin cloth, linen, or gauze, provided that the projection light is strong enough to penetrate the material.

7.20 Rear projection – pictures

Rear projection was used for decades in film making and later in monochrome television production to provide background scenes for studio action.

Although you can rear-project pictures of moving film or slides successfully today, newer techniques are superior and have largely superseded this earlier method (process work in film, electronic effects in television).

For small-screen set-ups (e.g. up to 4 ft or 1.22 mm wide) a regular slide-projector can be used in the studio to provide rear-projected titles, maps, graphs, illustrations, etc. on a wall display screen. This idea can be particularly useful for talks, demonstrations, weathercasters, newscasters, and decorative effects.

Rear-projected slides can provide a location scene on a small screen positioned outside the windows of a car, a ship's porthole, or even a small house window. For a miniature (model shot) you can project the complete background.

Figure 7.9 Rear projection
1. A slide or film is projected onto the back of a matte translucent screen. At the front, a camera shoots action against the screen image. Foreground lighting must not dilute the screen's image.

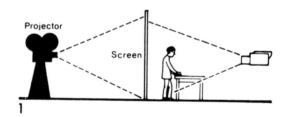

2. You can use the screen as the *complete* background, augmented by foreground pieces or furniture.
3. The rear-projected image can *supplement* the built set (e.g. as a backing).
4. The background can be used to *extend* the built set.

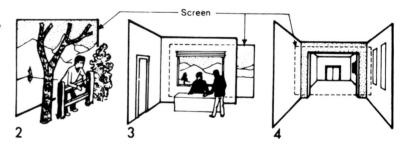

Converting *photographic slides* into television pictures normally requires a special 'slide scanner'. But by using a small rear-projection set-up instead there is the advantage that you can select as much of the slide picture as you require – even zooming in and out and exploring the slide image with the camera.

The camera's shot of the slide-image can either be used directly as a 'slide insert' within the program or fed into *chroma key* video effects equipment to provide a background (total or partial) for the studio action.

Although rear-projection is a simple, cheap, and flexible facility it has its disadvantages:

- It provides a much stronger image than regular front-projection systems but the picture is liable to be brighter in the center than at the edges. (A piece of neutral-tinted gel in the light-beam can reduce this central 'hot spot'.)
- Studio lighting can spill onto the screen, diluting the image and reducing its contrast.

A light blue gel or corrective filter over the projector lens can help to match the color of the projector's light source to the TV cameras' color balance.

The major disadvantage of large-screen rear-projection is the amount of space the whole set-up uses. To fill a 10 ft (3 m) wide screen you would need a high-output precision projector some 20 ft (6 m) away. Performers should not get closer to the screen than about 6 ft (1.8 m) or their lighting will spill onto the screen. So if the camera, which is in front of the screen, is around 15 ft (4.5 m) from the subject we are talking of an overall front-to-back distance of over 40 ft (12 m)!

Chapter 8

Electronic reality

Using an ever-increasing number of electronic effects, the set-designer can create a wide range of scenic illusions, that are often quite impracticable to produce by any other means.

A substitute for reality

8.1 Artifice and art

As you know, since the early years, *film makers* have relied on ingenious photographic trickery to create convincing scenic illusions. Many of the '*impressive vistas*' we see in motion pictures are really combination shots of artwork and reality. But so persuasive are these techniques, that we accept the results unquestioningly as 'the real thing'. For us, '*seeing is believing*'!

The television/video medium has similarly developed ingenious ways of manipulating and controlling pictures, but with an outstanding advantage over film. We do not have to wait for the exposed stock to be processed and projected before assessing the results. The video medium allows us to check and modify pictures (and sound) *immediately*, every step of the way, while watching a monitor screen. Any shot or effect can be altered, copied, filed or revised until we have exactly the result we are seeking. (Now that high-grade video can be transferred imperceptibly to film, and merged with the direct photographic image, many of these same electronic processes are also playing an increasing role in film-making!)

8.2 Electronic effects

We have met two regular ways of creating an environment for the action. Either by constructing a setting from prefabricated scenic units, or by taking the camera to an existing location. But these are both costly time-consuming approaches, which can require considerable resources. Suitable ready-make locales are not always easy to find. Currently therefore, as costs continue to rise, there is increasing interest in a further approach, in which backgrounds are created partially or entirely using *electronic effects*.

The general term '*electronic effects*' covers a wide variety of ways in which the TV picture can be processed and manipulated. Some of them require relatively simple switching circuitry. Others involve extremely sophisticated digitizing processes. While some equipment is quite straightforward to operate, other systems require a specialist operator – particularly for more complex treatment.

Electronic effects offer the designer and the director important creative design opportunities with great practical advantages. And although you will probably not have to handle the actual equipment yourself, you will certainly find that understanding the basics and limitations involved will help you to use these techniques much more successfully.

8.3 Using electronic effects

Electronic effects used in TV/video production fall into three broad categories:

- *Novelty* – These are the endless eye-catching 'magical' effects in which we see subjects contorting and fragmenting, disintegrating . . . forming fantastic mind-blowing eruptions of shape and color . . . undergoing astonishing transformations (*morphing*). Moving pictures suddenly roll themselves up into tubes, turn over, fly around the screen . . .
- *Altering features* – Here various aspects of a picture or a picture sequence are changed electronically. This may involve making subtle alterations in the picture's overall brightness, contrast, sharpness, or color bias (e.g. to ensure that pictures shot under different lighting conditions will match when intercut).

It is even possible to adjust *details* within the picture; to pick out sections and replace them, or duplicate (*paste*) them. A picture sequence can be altered frame-by-frame (*rotoscoping*; *compositing*). A daytime shot of a city, for instance, could be worked on to provide a night scene, with illuminated streets and buildings, and a moonlit sky. People and vehicles might be added. Using similar techniques, one might simulate disasters, the devastation of hurricanes, earthquakes, raging fires, and so on. But in each application, the aim is realism.

- *Augmenting or replacing traditional scenery* – This is the methodology that we shall concentrate on here, in which all (or most of) the background behind the action is introduced *electronically – the virtual set*. The final effect on the screen is usually totally realistic. The studio action appears to be taking place in a shop, on a mountain top, on a sea shore which in fact, may have been photographed weeks before, or extracted from a stock photo library! Occasionally, the background will be *stylized*, by using drawn/painted graphics, computer graphics, etc.

We can use all of these kinds of effects in a range of productions: from straightforward interviews, to opera; from a 'soap' to a musical extravaganza; from a children's show to a serious discussion; from newscasts to weathercasting.

8.4 Electronic picture insertion

The sort of effects we shall be looking at, are all forms of *electronic picture insertion*. They include ways in which:

● *Part(s) of a shot* can be removed (masked out), and another image *matted* in its place,
● Entire *backgrounds* can be provided by graphics, models, film or videotape pictures,
● *Complete graphical environments* can be created for the action, i.e. *virtual sets*.

We use three 'families' of equipment to achieve these wonders:

● A *special effects generator* (SEG). This is the electronic device used to create all those ingenious geometrical wipe patterns between shots.
● *Luminance keying*, where we use a selected *tone* to make the system automatically inter-switch between picture sources.
   – We may choose a particular tonal value *within the master scene* itself to act as this *switching tone*, or
   – Place an area of this tone in front of studio camera or a rostrum camera, or
   – Use an area of tone from some external source, such as a photo slide, titling equipment (*character generator*), or from computer graphics.
● *Chrominance keying*, or as it is usually called, *chroma key*, in which a selected *color* (generally blue) causes the system to inter-switch automatically between pictures.

8.5 Source selection

Selecting the background picture all begins with the *switcher* or *vision mixer* we met in Section 2.23. We use this equipment during studio production and post-production sessions, to:

● *Cut* directly from one source to another.
● *Mix* between sources so that as one image becomes fainter, as another becomes stronger.
● *Superimpose* two or more images, so that they become inter-mixed. (Depending on the picture tones involved, the result may be a *transparent superimposition*, or an apparently *solid 'super'*.)
● *Adjust a picture's overall brightness/intensity* from maximum (full) to minimum (black).
● In addition, the *switcher* usually includes a selection of electronic visual effects (e,g, wipes, chroma key) that we shall talk about in a moment.

The production switcher may be operated *live* during performance, i.e. while the program is on-air or being videotaped. Then any changes will be seen immediately; any errors or misjudgements cannot be corrected, except by re-taping the sequence.

Alternatively, the director can tape each shot in turn, and use the switcher at a later *post-production session* ('*post*'), where the original tapes are copied (dubbed), and transitions, editing, visual effects are introduced.

A range of picture sources can be fed to the switcher for selection:

- *Live* images from several studio cameras.
- *Live* images from remotes (outside broadcast) cameras.
- *Taped* material from videotape machines (VTRs).
- *Film* reproduced from *telecine* channels (film islands).
- *Photo-slide scanners* (holding a selectable store of standard photographic slides).
- *ESS* (electronic still stores) or *servers*, storing numerous video still images.
- Images from *computer systems* (including CD-ROMs).
- *Lettering/titling/text* from character generators. (These provide a range of fonts of adjustable size and shape, that can be used to create text, graphical displays, etc.)

Still images will normally be used for the background material; derived from photographs, paintings, drawings, or graphics. In some cases these will have been specially prepared for the current production. On other occasions, the designer may draw on a selection of stored stills from archives or may re-use a background from a previous production to create the new composite.

Although *moving background* pictures from videotape or film can add reality to a composite, they may introduce complications. A lot depends on whether they are just providing a *general* background (e.g. a seascape), or whether the foreground action needs to be *timed* to suit the moving background (e.g. a moving background outside the windows of a static studio car).

8.6 Advantages of 'electronic scenery'

Let's stop for a moment, and think about some of the advantages of introducing 'electronic scenery':

- *Flexibility* – Scenic effects can be introduced during the original taping session (i.e. during performance), or afterwards during a separate *post-production* session. You can even shoot all the studio action against a blue backdrop, and add the background scenery later!
- *Considerable economy* – You can insert localized studio settings into full-screen photographed or videotaped sequences. Studio and location shots can be combined.
- *Space saving* – Where studio space is very limited, you can build a small partial set, and extend it on the screen by inserting it into a model, artwork, etc.
- *Adaptable treatments* – Backgrounds can be changed instantaneously. As the shot changes, the background can be switched correspondingly.
- *Safety* – Structures that would be cumbersome (e.g. requiring extensive scaffold structures and other support) if built full scale, can be replicated in miniature, and the performers inserted electronically.
- *Impracticable scenic effects* – Where the action calls for scenic effects that would be out of the question in the studio due to cost, scale, time, etc., electronic insertion offers extended

opportunities. For example, a person 'fishing', stands on a small truck which is built-up as a river bank . . . and is keyed into a shot beside a rushing river.

● *Corrective treatments* – You can change the appearance of an electronically inserted subject or background by various computer-generated treatments. For example, parts of a photograph can be worked on, to alter its scale, tones, color. Areas or objects can be duplicated, cut out and 'pasted' onto other parts of the picture. Images can be tilted, reversed, inverted, removed. You can introduce various degrees of sharpening, softening, blurring, etc.

Of course, there are many other considerations too, such as material costs, craft skills involved, labor, storage problems, transport, re-use limitations, studio height and space requirements, lighting complexities, etc. involved when using built settings.

8.7 So why aren't they widely used?

Considering the enormous range of visual opportunities that electronic picture insertion provides, the techniques are surprisingly little used. There are a number of reasons.

Many directors (and set designers) do not even consider the opportunities that electronic effects offer. They think in terms of the *actual*. They like to move around inside a realistic or existing environment, imagining and selecting shots. Their productions are staged in a built studio setting, or on location within a room in a real house. They prefer to work empirically. However, where a director thinks and plans shot-by-shot, and devises complete storyboards, electronic treatments are a welcome adjunct to their techniques, often allowing them to get shots that would otherwise be impracticable. Of course, there are certain inherent limitations and hazards. But with anticipation, care, and experience, these are not unduly limiting in practice, if tackled systematically.

Simple matting

8.8 The special effects generator

The simplest method of combining parts of two pictures into one composite involves automatic switching circuits which instantaneously intercut between two picture sources. This is usually done by a *special effects generator* (*SEG*) in the *production switcher*.

The principle here is simple enough. All the video cameras and other picture sources in the TV system scan the picture systematically line by line, in exact synchronism. Let's suppose that we switch to Camera 1's shot as it starts to scan a picture line by line, and then halfway down the frame, we switch to Camera 2's shot. The transmitted result would be the *top half* of Camera 1's picture, and the *bottom half* of Camera 2's – a *vertical split screen* effect.

Figure 8.1 Special effects generator.
1. A regular setting without a ceiling, simplifies construction and allows free access to lighting. A separate shot of a ceiling can be 'wiped' down into the top of the picture, so that in the combined effect the set now appears extensive.
2. Here a horizontal wipe is moved across the frame, and stopped to provide a 'split screen' combining the left and right of two different shots.

Now instead, let's imagine that we transmit the Camera 1 shot as it starts to scan a picture, then half way through each line, have the system automatically switch to Camera 2's shot for the rest of each scanning line. This time the combined effect on the TV screen will be a composite picture in which the *left* of the screen shows the left portion of Camera 1's shot, while the *right* side of the screen shows the right-hand side of Camera 2's picture. This is the horizontal *split-screen* effect so often used to show people at either end of a phone conversation. Using a vari-position *joystick* control or a *trackball*, you can adjust the instant at which that switching takes place, and the proportions of this split-screen will alter correspondingly. (Moving the joystick while 'on air', produces the familiar moving *wipe* effect in which the first picture is progressively replaced by a corresponding section of another shot.)

Although the various *keying shapes* you can obtain by this method are always essentially geometrical (i.e. round, elliptical, square, rectangular, triangular), they can be adjusted in several ways:

- *Position* – You can move the insert pattern around the frame; up/down, left/right, diagonally, to position the shape wherever you wish in the frame.
- *Size* – You can expand/contract the pattern to adjust its exact size/area.
- *Proportions* – By altering the pattern's height and/or width, you can adjust its shape. So a circle can become an ellipse, or a

square can be made rectangular. Pattern symmetry can be adjusted.

● *Static insert* (*inset*) – You can produce a small '*box wipe*' to insert a selected portion of the master shot into another picture. So you might insert a doorway or window you have built in the studio, into a film or video shot of a busy street.

● *Edge prominence* – The edges of a pattern can be sharply defined, or softened until they merge with the surrounding picture. A black, white, or color border can be placed around the pattern insert.

Even this simple facility can extend the set designer's opportunities considerably, and save a deal of money! A camera taking a long shot of a studio 'interior' setting, *overshoots* the set, and includes a nondescript view of the studio roof with its numerous spotlights. So we use a static *vertical split-screen* to *matte-out* the top part of the picture. Then we insert a corresponding area from another shot (photograph or artwork) showing a ceiling. The result in the composite of the two pictures, is a *room with a ceiling* that avoids all the construction and lighting problems that a real ceiling would involve. A modest setting in the studio is transformed. Our audience sees *an impressive ballroom with a magnificently decorated ceiling and sparkling chandeliers* – none of which actually exist!

Quite often, you can use a routine pattern to mask out an unwanted object which is spoiling the shot, and insert something more suitable in its place. A parked van in a location shot might be matted out, and some bushes introduced in its place! When space is restricted in a studio, and the camera inadvertently reveals other sets nearby, you might matte-in a foreground *masking-piece*, or an appropriate subject from a *photo slide* to disguise the problem.

To create an impressive illusion of the interior of a theater, all you need is a photograph of the real thing, into which you insert a *boxed-in* long shot of the studio action.

8.9 Luminance keying (inlay) ·

Unlike the SEG, which generates its own inter-switching pulses, *luminance keying* systems use a process which relies on a *keying tone*. Three video signals are involved:

● The *master shot* or *program video* into which the effect is to be inserted.

● The *fill signal* or *background video* which is to be inserted. Depending on your system and how it is adjusted, this inserted area may be hard-edged or soft-edged.

● The *key signal* which is generated just to provide the inter-switching action. (It is not seen as such.) This decides the size, shape, and position of the inserted area.

The idea of taking part of one picture and inserting it exactly into a corresponding area in another, is rather like exchanging pieces

Figure 8.2 Matting
The camera matte. A hole in the black card in front of Camera 1 obscures all of the scene except a selected area. Camera 2 has the main scene, with a corresponding black area.
Superimposing the two cameras, the composite shows the matted area within the main scene. (A similar effect can be obtained by using an electronic 'wipe' pattern on Camera 1's shot.)

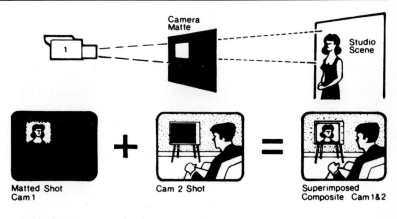

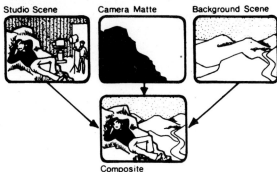

Matted Shot Cam 1   Cam 2 Shot   Superimposed Composite Cam 1&2

The foreground matte. Here a camera shoots through a pictorial graphic (photograph, painting) and sees studio action combined with the foreground matte.

Studio Scene   Camera Matte   Background Scene

Composite

of a jigsaw. There are two practical approaches to this form of insertion:

● *External keying* – Where a *separate* mask or matte is used to trigger the process.
● *Self-keying* – In which the effect is triggered by a tone (usually black) *within* the actual subject picture.

External luminance keying relies on your making a black silhouette of an appropriate size and shape to trigger the *luminance keying* switcher. Its video is used to intercut between the *master subject* and *background* picture sources, and key a selected part into the background picture. (The video from the matting source is used only as a keying signal, and not actually seen.)

There are various ways of creating this shape:

● Placing a black card or painted cel in a special *rostrum camera* equipment,
● Painting a black silhouette on white board set up in front of a studio camera,
● Creating a *computer graphic* silhouette,
● Using a silhouette from a photo slide or titling equipment (*character generator*),
● Passing the video from a normal picture source through a self-keying luminance circuit, to turn the image into a monochrome silhouette.

Let's take a simple example of how this idea can be used:

- Shoot a photograph of overhanging tree branches on one camera.
- Process this picture to derive a corresponding silhouette of the branch, e.g. by routing that video through an SEG to produce a switching matte.
- Shoot an 'exterior scene' in the studio, consisting of someone standing against a 'stone wall' with a sky cyc background. (Bird-song and wind sounds suggest the open air.)

Matting in the tree branches via the silhouette creates a composite shot, in which the person can move *behind* the branches in the photograph, without any of the problems of introducing a large tree into the studio! You can also use this idea to add a branch in a shot that was taken on location, but where there were no trees around!

Luminance self-keying is mostly used to insert titles and logos into a picture. Shoot a title card with white lettering on a black background, and use it to inter-switch between shots of a gold-foil surface and a skyscape. The result would be golden lettering within a cloudy sky. However, this technique is not normally appropriate for scenic insertion.

Chroma key (overlay)

8.10 The principles

Here we have a process with almost limitless possibilities! Instead of using a particular *tone* to produce automatic switching between pictures, this system is controlled by a specific selected *color*. *Cobalt blue* is widely used, for it is found less frequently in typical scenes. But occasionally, where they produce better results, green or yellow may be preferable.

The *chroma key system* can be triggered either by a *separate* blue matte; or more often, by arranging this keying hue *within* the master shot.

We begin the chroma key process by placing our subject in front of a plain cobalt blue backdrop or cyc. This all-color *master* shot is then routed through a special electronic switch. Wherever the system detects *blue* in the master shot, the circuitry will switch, replacing that blue area with a corresponding area of a second picture source (the *background* scene) instead. The combined picture shows the master scene in its natural colors (but usually with an absence of blue), combined with the inserted background. The person in the studio can appear to be walking around in the background scene!

You can use a variety of sources to provide this background image – a second camera, videotape, film, photo-slides, etc. And it does not matter what colors appear in this background picture.

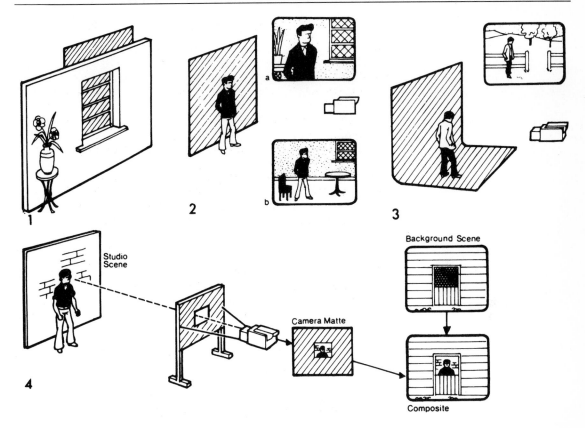

Figure 8.3 Typical chroma key set-ups
1. A chroma key blue backing allows an exterior scene to be inserted outside a window (slide or graphic).
2. Only a simple chroma key background is needed if (a) the floor is not in shot or (b) the studio floor and foreground objects are to be part of the shot.
3. Where people are to appear *within* an inserted background scene, or the studio floor is unsuitable for any reason, a complete chroma key surface is needed behind the action *and* on the floor (separate or continuous).
4. Using a blue camera matte, you can insert part of the studio scene into the main background picture. (Anything moving outside the central matted area will disappear in the composite.)
Long shots normally reveal a large area of the studio, so would require extensive chroma key treatment. Using a blue camera matte, only the area seen within the matte needs blue background and floor in the studio.

8.11 Chroma key mechanics

Let's suppose that you have selected *blue* as the *keying hue* for the system. Then the only blue surfaces to appear in the *master* or *subject* shot should be those intended to trigger the chroma key switches. If any other blue objects appear in the master shot, whether in clothing, props, scenery, or due to reflections, there is a probability that the system will be fooled, causing it to switch when it is not supposed to. In other words, you will see *break-through*. So if for example, a person wearing a blue shirt moves around in the master shot, we shall see the corresponding area of background instead of their body. The effect can be weird!

However, this problem is not as limiting as it would at first seem, particularly when using more sophisticated derivations such as *Ultimatte*. In fact, chroma key inserts have been a familiar feature in TV for many years; regularly providing background graphics behind newscasters, and large-area maps behind weather reporters. But as you will see, its potentials are far beyond simple background use.

How long an electronic insertion effect takes to set up will depend on how elaborate it is, how carefully it has been planned, and on the experience of everyone involved. A good well-organized team takes the job in its stride, and excellent matches are possible.

Simple chroma key equipment can be difficult to adjust accurately. You may find that subject edges appear ragged or prominently outlined, and there may be spurious background breakthrough into the subject image. But in today's sophisticated systems these problems are reduced to a minimum.

Ideally, the blue background in the master scene should be of even tone and hue, without wrinkles or folds, and flatly lit. In practice, as long as it is a strong pure cobalt blue, you can use a blue-painted wall or flat, blue felt, a white cloth lit with blue light, or a translucent blue screen. Again, some systems are more critical than others.

Where an actor needs to hit an exact position in the middle of a chroma key floor, to correspond with a certain part of the background picture, they will need a *location mark*, in the form of a chalked foot position, or a blue disc attached at the critical point. If it's necessary to *look* in a certain direction (remembering that all they can see in reality is a blue backdrop), their eyeline can be guided by using a dim distant colored lamp in a corresponding position.

How large an area of the chroma key surface do you need in the master shot?

● If you want to insert pictures in the wall behind a newscaster, quite a small 4 × 3 blue rectangle attached to background scenery would do the trick, e.g. 3–4 ft or 0.9–1.22 m wide.
● For a scene outside a window, you can use a blue backing flat, or shine blue light onto a frosted plastic sheet behind the window.
● If you are not going to show the studio floor in the shot, or if the studio floor is an acceptable part of the composite shot, then only a vertical blue surface (e,g, a flat) may be necessary.
● However, when you want to place somebody in the studio *within* a long shot of the background scene, both the surface behind the person *and* the floor must be of the keying hue. You can either use a blue backdrop or cyc, and a blue floor covering (painted or floor cloth), or hang a large blue backdrop that extends along the floor.

8.12 Check the chroma key area

When you are staging a chroma key set-up, it is wise to check out the following:

● Is the color of the background appropriate? Ideally, the blue background (and floor if necessary) should be the same overall hue and tone. Some systems are more critical than others. Any blue-painted flats should have a dull, even finish; otherwise their brightness can vary with the lighting and camera positions. Any backdrops, drapes, cyclorama should be stretched, without folds or wrinkles.
● The exact brightness level at which the keying circuits switch from one source to another is adjusted by a *clipping level control*. If set too low, the inserted subject will show severe

Figure 8.4 Chroma key foreground mattes
Using selective foreground mattes, people in the studio can seem to move behind, sit on, or climb items in the background picture!

Matting flat. Studio action normally appears in *front* of the background scene. To walk 'behind' a wall in the photo background, place a flat of chroma key hue in the studio chroma key shot to coincide with it.

Camera matte. Here a specially prepared matte allows people to move 'behind' any chosen object in the photo-background. Three picture sources are involved: studio action shot; background scene; matte. A silhouette is drawn on a white card to correspond with the chosen background object (e.g. a rail fence). The video from this camera matte is fed into the production switcher/vision mixer (as an 'external key') and suppresses normal insertion in the selected area. (The effect can be switched in and out at choice.)

Relating to background objects. Choose an object in the background and place a corresponding blue block, treads, or platform in the studio chroma key set-up. Then in the composite they can appear to sit, climb, or lean on the subjects in the photo-background.

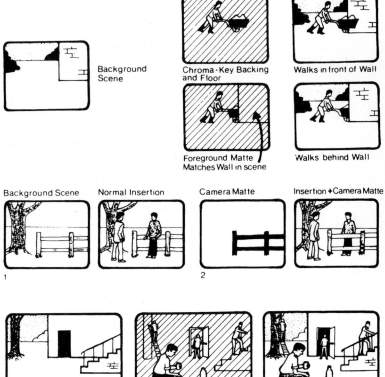

Background Scene

Chroma·Key Backing and Floor

Walks in front of Wall

Foreground Matte Matches Wall in scene

Walks behind Wall

Background Scene   Normal Insertion   Camera Matte   Insertion + Camera Matte

Photo Background   Chroma·Key Backing Floor Matching Areas in Studio   Composite Result

edge ragging around its borders. Set too high, and parts of the inserted subject will be lost. So it is necessary to light the blue keying surfaces reasonably evenly. If there are shadowy areas, or deep shadows fall onto them (e.g. from nearby people, scenery, or furniture), it can be difficult to adjust clipping levels correctly.

● Check for any *accidental* blue areas in the foreground subjects, e.g. clothing, objects, props, furniture, scenery, etc.
● Make sure that there are no shiny surfaces such as glass, mirrors, metallic finishes, that might reflect nearby chroma key color from the blue floor or backdrop.

8.13 Practical problems

As you will have realized, although chroma key can seem to perform miracles, we need to take certain precautions to ensure totally convincing results. There are really two major aspects to look out for: *technical imperfections* (e.g. breakthrough) and *incompatibility* (e.g. poor matching between the subject and its inserted background). Let's look at these problems more closely, and see how they can be overcome. But don't be daunted. You will soon find yourself anticipating these limitations, and taking them in your stride!

- *Breakthrough* – Look out for accidental breakthrough of the background, edge ragging, or parts of the main subject disappearing; particularly because of unexpected reflections or shadows. This error may be due to incorrect adjustment of the clipping level, inappropriate staging or uneven lighting.
- *Fixed camera* – Normally the camera itself must hold a fixed shot. If you pan left or right, or move the mounting sideways (*truck/crab*), the subject will appear to slide across the background. If you move it forwards/backwards (*dolly*) or zoom, you will see the subject appear to grow or shrink. Fine for 'magical' effects, but usually to be strictly avoided!
- *Scale* – The relative sizes of subjects within the subject shot and the background shot should be compatible. Otherwise people will appear unnaturally large or small.
- *Perspective*:
  - *Camera height*: There should be a reasonable similarity between the shooting angles (vertical and horizontal) of the camera shooting the background and the studio camera; otherwise you are likely to see some rather incongruous 'leaning' effects. And if people move towards or away from the camera, there is the possibility that they might appear to sink into the ground or rise above it as they walk. However, as most backgrounds are level shots, these extreme problems seldom arise.
  - *Camera lens angle*: If the subject camera uses an inappropriate *lens angle*, a person may appear to grow noticeably taller (lens angle too narrow) or shorter (lens angle too wide) when walking away from the camera. A lot depends on how strong clues to perspective are in the background shot, and on the amount of subject movement.
- *Image quality* – Ideally, the *brightness*, *contrast*, *tonal balance*, *color quality*, *light direction*, *etc.*, of the subject shot and the inserted background shot should match exactly if they are to blend together perfectly. In practice, you will be surprised how even large discrepancies pass unnoticed!
- *Subject position* – One obvious point that can sometimes be overlooked is the need to check the performers' feet are positioned rationally 'within' the background shot. Otherwise there is a chance that they will appear to be standing in mid-air, or in an incongruous position, e.g. walking on a pond!
- *Subject moves*:
  - *Accidental cut-off*: When you use a straightforward *wipe pattern* on the switcher to blank out part of the frame, any studio action moving into the inserted area will be *lost*. In other words, if a dancer in the master shot leaps high into the area of the ceiling insert, he/she will be decapitated, or even vanish behind the wiped-in area!
  - *Location*: In any regular chroma key set-up, people will normally appear to be moving *in front* of everything in the background picture. If you want them to move *behind* anything shown there, or to sit, climb, move through features in the

background scene, this will involve either using an appropriate matte to cover them at those points, or positioning blue-colored items in corresponding positions in the studio.

When using mattes of any sort, you need to make sure that a subject is not *accidentally cut off or obscured*. Suppose for instance, someone has to walk 'behind' a wall in a photographic background, and later to walk 'in front of it'. The solution is to switch the matting circuits on/off to suit the action. In this case, you begin by switching in the matte corresponding to the wall, then switch it off when they are going to move in front of it.

● *Subject shadows* – In simpler chroma key systems, a person's shadow will not fall onto the floor and nearby surfaces. It will be lost in the chroma key process. As a result, they may appear to be 'floating', rather than firmly connected to the ground. Fortunately, this effect may not be obvious, and will be overlooked. Later systems are designed to insert a totally convincing shadow effect, which adds to the overall realism.

● *Depth of field* – If parts of the foreground shot are defocused due to limited depth of field, yet the background picture depth appears very sharp . . . you have a problem! Slightly defocusing the background shot may be the solution. Otherwise, stopping the lens of the subject camera down a little (smaller aperture) could help.

● *Color fringing* – In some chroma key systems, a blue color fringe may be visible around keyed-in subjects. A *soft-edged* insertion may improve the situation, where special *fringe eliminators* (*hue suppressors, exclusive hue matrix*) are not available. The oft-recommended remedy of using yellow backlighting (i.e. minus blue) seldom alleviates the problem, and is more likely to tint the subject yellow!

● *Window backings* – Imagine that a window in a studio setting has a blue chroma key backing. A background photograph of a street scene is going to provide the window's 'exterior' view. Are there any potential problems?

Yes. Although people can move around in front of the window, the master camera must normally remain fixed. You cannot dolly or zoom on shot when using *basic* chroma key systems. It would spoil the illusion (side-slip and size changes).

If you use a full-screen picture for the background, only a section *corresponding to the blue window area* will be inserted in the composite shot – *not the whole of it*. So if for instance, the subject camera has the window in the left of its shot, and this coincides with where your background photograph happens to have a poster, then all you will see through the window in the composite is the poster – not the entire street scene! The answer, is to arrange the background shot to suit the foreground segment. Perhaps use a smaller localized background picture.

If the subject camera's shot *changes*, so that the blue window is now on the right of its shot, then we will now see whatever coincides with the right of the background shot in the final composite. The view 'outside the window' will have altered! Some advanced chroma key systems include a *tracking facility*, which locks the inserted chroma key area, so that its contents remain unchanged as the master camera's shot varies.

- *Moving backgrounds* – Where you are using a photostill to provide the background scene, it is best to avoid any 'frozen' features (such as waves, people, smoke) which would draw attention to the deception. If there happens to be an unwanted feature in the background photograph, you might retouch the picture, or hide it with a handy tree-branch!

- *Foreground pieces* – With care, you can arrange items in the studio set-up so that they appear to be totally integrated into the background scene. Furniture, pieces of scenery (such as pillars, walls, bushes) can blend into the overall effect.

- *Video build-up* – Having chroma keyed or matted a subject (or a scenic element) into a background scene, it is possible to replay the videotape of this composite, and insert additional new material into *that* version. In this way you could create a multi-layer composite in which shots of a single musician are built up into an entire orchestra, should the need arise! Using the principle, you can also create a multi-layer setting, in which one scenic plane overlaps another. Although in an *analog* TV system, the picture quality deteriorates to some extent at each copying, in *digital* systems the quality is maintained in multi-generation video build-ups.

Table 8.1 Adjusting scale and perspective

To avoid strange scale or perspective effects when inserting someone into a photograph, the following approach can prove helpful:

- Display the background shot on a picture monitor. (Remember, if you are using a drawing, painting, or computer graphic for the background, perspective may not be correct, so adjustments are likely to be a matter of luck!)

- Check this background shot, and choose points where you can make *reasonably accurate guesses* about the sizes of subjects; e.g. beside a car, in a doorway. If there is a brick wall you can probably make quite accurate guesstimates, from counting the number of standard size brick courses. (Don't choose indefinitely sized objects such as bushes of fences.) At these points, using a wax pencil or a wipe-off marker pen, draw vertical lines on the monitor tube face, to represent what you consider the corresponding height of a person.

- Take a long shot of the studio chroma key area using a normal lens angle. Place a person in the master shot, adjust the clipping level, and insert them into the background scene.

- Position the person to coincide with the 'nearest' marker in the background picture. Adjust the camera's distance to fit the person's height to the marker.

- Holding that camera and lens position, move the person further away from the camera to coincide with the marker for a 'distant' object in the background picture. If perspective is correct (i.e. you are using an appropriate lens angle), the person will appear similar enough in height to the 'distant' marker. If disproportionately shorter, zoom *in* a little, and dolly *back* to compensate. If the subject looks too tall at the distant point, zoom *out* a little, and dolly *in*. A reasonable compromise is usually possible.

- If you now find that the camera is over-shooting the chroma key area, or seeing cameras, lights, sound boom, place a chroma key matte in front of the fixed subject camera (a blue card with a 4 × 3 rectangular central hole). Otherwise you could use a localized wipe pattern to cut off unwanted areas.

Virtual sets

8.14 The principles

A *virtual set* is a total illusion, in which build scenery is minimal, and the entire action appears to be taking place in the artificial background scene. There are really two situations:

● *Static* – in which the camera does not move,
● *Dynamic* – in which the camera alters its position or moves around.

Static situations

In many productions (a newscast or an interview) there may be little or no camera movement. The director cuts between fixed viewpoints, and treatment relies on action within the shot.

In these circumstances, with the camera head 'locked off' on a fixed shot and a pre-arranged lens angle, you can use static chroma key backgrounds to provide the entire scenic elements effectively. People can walk around anywhere within the limits of the shot, but it's prudent to check that there is no shadowing (that may cause clipping problems), or any perspective errors.

You can change the background scene where necessary – while on another shot – to suggest that the person has moved to another location. A collection of background shots can be held in a digital still store, computer memory, or a random-access laser disc system. Even where you are aiming at photorealistic results, this technique can be very successful, and entirely undetectable.

In some situations, you might shoot all of the action against a blue (or green) backdrop, and insert the various backgrounds *later*, during post-production!

Dynamic situations

Remembering that you cannot move the camera around without producing some very strange effects, it might seem that virtual sets were restricted to a series of fixed camera shots. But several ingenious systems have been developed to overcome these limitations.

If the subject and background cameras are ganged together electronically through special servo systems, it is possible to make them operate in exact synchronism. Now, although the *camera mounting* (*e.g. pedestal*) itself still *remains stationary*, the foreground camera can turn left/right (pan), tilt up/down, and the lens can zoom. We will see proportional changes in both the shot of the subject, and the size and position of the background picture from the second camera. The combined results in the composite are completely realistic. Using this ganged system, you can follow a person over an arc, so that they appear to be moving around a photographed scene, a graphic, or a miniature (model).

The next development was to extend this idea, so that the subject camera's position is unrestricted. It can appear to *move around 'within' the scene*. And here we come to the most sophisticated forms of *virtual sets*; where scenic backgrounds are created entirely from a camera shooting a photographic display, a three-dimensional scale model, or computer-generated backgrounds.

The subject's camera (which may even be shoulder-mounted) moves around shooting action against a blue (or green) background in the studio. Its exact position is fed to a computer, which provides a corresponding background picture. Whether features such as steps, parallels, furniture, are actually provided in the studio, or substituted with blue-painted items corresponding to those in the background picture, will depend on the situation.

The amount of space and chroma key background needed in the studio will depend on how extensive the action is. It may be only a few square meters. But remember, for a long continuous walk, or where subjects are spaced some distance apart, you will normally need studio space comparable with that in the background scene. There are ways round this of course. Where studio space is limited, you can have the performer walk just a short way, then cut to another camera angle. If you want someone to appear to be standing a considerable distance away, you can shoot them on a wide-angle lens. You might use a multi-layer insert.

To detect the camera's position precisely as it moves around, three electronic systems are available:

- Motion sensors attached to the master (subject) camera, which send data on the camera head's actions and position to the computer controlling the background shot.
- A remote joystick which controls both the position of the motorized subject-camera's mounting, and the background shot.
- Highly sophisticated pattern-recognition computer software, which continually interprets the video output of the subject's camera, and so judges its exact position. From this data, the corresponding section of the background scene is selected.

8.15 Opportunities

We've looked at the practical mechanics involved when creating electronic backgrounds. Let's turn to a couple of examples that show the sort of thing that can be achieved with a little imagination. Built scenery is minimal, and the complications of shooting on location have been avoided:

- *What the viewer saw* – A long shot shows the darkened interior of an ancient church. A cleric walks slowly across the shot from camera left. He is carrying a lighted candle, and passes behind a decorative ironwork grille. He turns towards the distant altar, and moves up the aisle. He lights the large candles on either side of the altar, and exits.

Figure 8.5 Building up a multiplane effect
This example shows how a complete environment can be developed from a series of separate scenic elements. Beginning with a nondescript picture of a landscape, chosen for its striking cloud formation . . . woman and child are inserted to establish scale. To obscure the unattractive land masses, and create foreground interest, a large tree is added. To create a sense of restriction, bushes are introduced into foreground left. Finally, to relieve the stark tree trunk, a broken wall is placed in foreground right.

● *What was in the studio* – A blue cyc and a blue floor cloth. A photograph of a church interior provided the background scene. A silhouette matte had been prepared from a photograph of a period ironwork grille. This was matted in on picture left, over the chroma key 'interior' background. Corresponding with the distant altar in the photograph, a blue-painted table, with a couple of regular candles on tall blue blocks.

In another totally convincing example:

● *What the viewer saw* – We are outside a small country store. A girl cycles into shot, stops, and rests her bike against a nearby tree. She bends down to pat a sleeping dog. Reaching up to pick a blossom from the tree, she walks up steps to enter the store.
● *What was in the studio* – A photo slide provided the background scene, complete with store, tree and sleeping dog beneath it. In the studio (blue cyc and floor) a blue pole on a stand corresponded to the tree in the photograph. (It had a real blossom attached to it by a thread.) The girl patted the air where the photo-dog slept. Blue-painted stock treads were positioned where the store's steps were located in the photograph.

8.16 Digital video effects

Television/video technology is becoming increasingly complex. But fortunately most of the equipment we shall meet is surprisingly simple to use. Understand the basics involved, and much of the 'magic and mystery' resolves itself into straightforward practical techniques.

From the earliest days, video and sound systems relied on *analog* technology, in which picture and sound were conveyed through continuously fluctuating voltages. But this process has various drawbacks. These signals could all too easily become distorted in various ways.

When for instance, you record an *analog* signal, it is difficult to avoid introducing a certain amount of distortion. Make a recording of that tape or disc, and distortion worsens. With repeated copying (dubbing) it can become so bad as to be quite unacceptable. It is not surprising therefore, that as technology advanced, and *digital* methods of transmitting data evolved, these began to replace the older analog systems, for they were not only more 'robust' (i.e. less likely to become distorted), but opened up new ways of correcting and manipulating picture and sound.

The principles of this digital process are not hard to explain. In a digital system, the strength of the continuous analog video (or audio) signal is rapidly sampled at regular intervals, and stored away in coded numerical form. The *binary code* used just consists of groups of on-off pulses. (Rather like the dot and dash patterns of the Morse code, except that each number has permutations of eight on-off samples) These pulses are easily stored magnetically. (They are the basis of computer data, CD recordings, CD-ROM and many other data storage processes.)

Now instead of the fine fluctuations of *analog* video signals, we have a store of numbers representing the brightness and color of each tiny area (pixel) of the picture. These 'quantized' digitally coded signals are readily reconstituted into the original analog picture.

This may all sound pretty tortuous, but now we have independent access to *each stored element of the entire picture!* Normally, we shall want to read out the data from the store in the original order in which it was recorded. But now, whenever we wish, we can manipulate the final video in various ways. We can change the rate and the order in which the filed data is read out. We can just read out selected parts of the data (i.e. edit the picture). Reading it in reverse order, we can flip the picture. Instruct the system to *change* the numbers filed in particular data areas, and this will cause the picture to alter and become diffused, sharpened, hues will change, etc.

In practical terms, that all means that by selective processing, we can alter the appearance of the digitized picture in many different ways – by pasting one feature onto another; altering color and shape; intermixing and editing . . . in short, we have reached the magic of computer graphics and digital effects!

Table 8.2 Techniques summarized

Effect	Method
To insert a subject into an open background scene. *Floor not visible.*	Chroma key background.
To insert a subject into an open background scene. *Floor visible.*	Chroma key background and floor. Shadow insertion?
To insert a subject into a restricted area within a full background (Subject will be naturally cut off when moving beyond that area; e.g. by a wall.)	Localized SEG wipe pattern (e.g. box wipe), or, Localized chroma key insert (e.g. blue patch), or Localized external matte.
Person to move in front of a background subject.	Usual chroma key insertion.
Person to move behind a background subject.	Usual chroma key insertion, with blue scenic elements in studio corresponding with wall, tree, etc. in background. Special localized matte silhouette to inhibit that area of the subject shot.
Person to sit, stand, walk on a background item (furniture, staircase, table, chair).	Usual chroma key insertion, with blue scenic elements in studio corresponding with specific items.
Person to appear abnormally large (e.g. giant).	Adjust size of subject shot relative to background scene.
Person to appear abnormally small (tiny, Tom Thumb).	Adjust size of subject shot relative to background scene.

Chapter 9

Scenic operations

In this chapter we are going to discuss 'putting it up, and tearing it down' – the techniques of safely erecting scenery and 'striking' and storing it afterwards.

As you would expect, most of the terms and techniques used in television and film are derived from the theater. There are variants between studios, but most of the practices are worldwide.

The studio

9.1 The flies

As far as scenic design is concerned, television studios can be divided into a series of distinct areas, although only larger studios are likely to have all of these features.

Starting from the roof, we have the entire upper area above the stage, known as the *flies*.

Here you will find the *grid*, a rigid honeycombed framework floor, fitted over the entire staging area. Walkways (catwalks) allow access to the overhead scenic hoisting facilities and lighting equipment which is housed here. (Because this region is many feet above the studio floor, access to it is restricted. Anything dropped could kill people below!)

9.2 Hoisting scenery

There are several methods of hoisting scenery, either to *support* it from above or to actually *raise* it above the ground (i.e. to 'fly' it):

1. A series of parallel overhead beams (RSJs) or tracks running the length of the studio roof are fitted with a number of wheeled carriages. These can be moved along the length of the beams to any required position.
    For very heavy loads in large studios a 'chain tackle' system may be used. Pulling an endless pull-chain loop operates a gearing system. This controls the load chain, which has a swiveled hook at its end. The load hook is attached to the scenery and secured by a safety catch or mause (securing wire).

2. In a simpler arrangement a pulley system on a wheeled 'skate' is moved along an overhead track. A stout rope (hemp line)

runs through the pulley and is attached to the scenery, while its other end is tied off at an appropriate load-bearing point. (When not used, a small scenic sandbag may be attached to the hook to prevent the rope from running out of the pulley.)

3. A rope may be dropped in from the grid (having fastened one end), attached to scenery, then hauled up and secured to a suitable support (cleat), in the grid, the gantry, or the studio wall.

4. Where pieces of scenery are regularly hung in certain positions in a studio (or on a stage) the pulley-supported ropes may be attached to a counterweight system. The weight of the scenery is counterbalanced by add-on weights (each e.g. 12 lb, 24 lb or 5.4 kg, 10.9 kg) located at the side of the studio. This arrangement makes scenery 'weightless' so that it can be flown in and out rapidly. But like all counterbalanced systems (e.g. lighting battens), accidents can occur if the counterweighting is incorrect.

5. A series of electric scenery hoists may be fitted to overhead tracks. These motor-driven hoists are directly or remotely controlled (e.g. from a wall hoist panel). The hoist's swivel load hook is supported on steel cables and can carry weight of the order of 250–400 lb max (115–180 kg).

Table 9.1   Typical approximate TV studio sizes

			Typical	*Ceiling*
Local TV/campus studios	Small	150 m² (160 ft²)	15 × 10 m (50 × 30 ft)	3.5 m (11 ft)·
	Medium	216 m² (2400 ft²)	18 × 12 m (60 × 40 ft)	7 m (23 ft)
Network studio center	Small general purpose	330 m² (3500 ft²)	22 × 15 m (70 × 50 ft)	9 m (30 ft)
	Medium	672 m² (7200 ft²)	28 × 24 m (90 × 80 ft)	10 m (33 ft)
	Large	1024 m² (10 000 ft²)	32 × 32 m (100 × 100 ft)	13 m (43 ft)

9.3 Wall platform

Some studios have a walkway and working platform or 'gantry' around the studio walls (e.g. 15–20 ft or 4.56–6.08 m) above the studio floor. A rail at the edge of the gantry can be used to tie off suspension ropes and brail lines and support spotlights.

9.4 Studio walls

Studio walls are clearly marked with regular 'footage marks' (grid lines) or similar indicators, corresponding with scale markings on the studio floor plan. These assist accurate positioning of scenery when 'setting'. The individual walls may be identified by number (e.g. Wall 1, 2, 3, 4). So we can specify a point as where lines from 'Wall 1 at 30, Wall 2 at 40' meet. (Walls may be numbered clockwise, from the Control Room on Wall 1.)

Along the walls there may be fittings into which a horizontal scenic brace will fit, cleats for tying off rope lines, and perhaps a load-bearing rail.

9.5 The studio floor

The studio floor has to be treated with care (Section 3.53). Unlike the film studio, where things can be nailed to the wooden floor to give added stability (the film dolly runs on level rails), the TV studio floor is inviolate.

In some TV studios a series of special anchorage floor-bolt points are installed and blanked off until needed. These can be replaced with eye-bolts through which ropes can be looped. Similar bolts may be fitted into the studio walls ('trapeze bolts') and the studio grid ('elephant lugs').

9.6 Studio ventilation

The studio's ventilation systems may be located in the flies or in trunking along the walls (e.g. underneath the gantry).

Ventilation arrangements can affect staging:

● Studio scenery (e.g. cloths) must not cover over the ventilation intake/outlet points.
● Ventilation outlets may need to be redirected if they are near a gauze, cloth, or suspended pattern projector, causing it to move and destroy the illusion.
● When using smoke effects, ventilation may need to be adjusted or shut off.

9.7 Scenic progress

A brief word on the path the scenery takes from drawing board to studio floor in a large studio production.

The scenic designer's studio plans, elevations, and working drawings are received and assessed by the construction shop. There the necessary stock items and newly constructed scenery are prepared and fitted together on a large flat floor. Some materials such as plastic moldings may be bought in or prepared by a separate design group. Surfaces are treated (walls papered, woodwork painted, ageing applied, etc.).

The designer checks the results (perhaps with the production's director and a lighting specialist) and any modifications are made. The set (without any dressing) is as it will be in the studio.

Painted backdrops are prepared by scenic artists, either with the cloth hanging (perhaps being height-adjusted as the artist works) or flat on the floor, depending on local tradition.

Labels on the back of each scenic unit identify the setting with the show title and the setting name (e.g. 'The Big Show'/Lulu's room) and a location number showing where it fits into the set. The setting is then dismantled into its component parts to permit easy handling and transportation.

Low wagons (wheeled platforms) are commonly used to transport the scenery to the studio's *scene dock/scenery dock*, from which it is later taken into the studio and erected in the planned position ('built') (see Section 2.20).

Once the set is 'on the floor' it will be checked over for damage during transportation or setting (tears, breakages, dirty marks). These will be remedied by a standby team (carpenters, painters, etc.), who may also do jobs that can only be carried out on the completed set: cladding and painting platforms, last-minute alterations, extra wall supports, and so on. The floors can now be painted or treated (Sections 3.55–3.61).

Whether the lighting for the show is rigged before the set is built or afterwards will depend on the size of the show and the local facilities.

Now the properties ('props') are brought into the studio and the process of set dressing begins (Sections 4.54–4.58). The practical lamps decorating the set are installed (Sections 4.59–4.63). The studio lighting is set up for the rehearsal (lamps aimed and adjusted, cues organized, etc.).

Camera rehearsal begins, and any scenic adjustments that prove necessary are made as time allows.

After the show is over the setting is systematically disassembled ('striking' or 'breaking' the sets), and then removed to a scenic storage area. There scenery is assessed and put into stock or material is salvaged for re-use while unusable items are destroyed.

As always, there are differing names for the people doing the various jobs, but typically:

- The *set crew* erects the sets.
- The *stage crew* dresses the sets.
- *Stagehands* carry out all action cues (e.g. rocking a boat), setting up camera title cards, operating any crawl titles, and sundry other routines in the studio.
- Sometimes the props will be arranged by a *property specialist*.

9.8 Scenic support

Scenic units come into several broad categories:

- Those needing total support,
- Those that need support aid for safety,
- Those that are self-supporting.

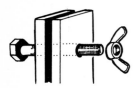

1. Securing bolt with wing-nut.

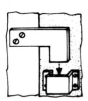

2. L-plates.

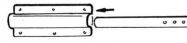

3. Extension plug.

4. U-plate.

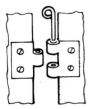

5. Pin hinge.

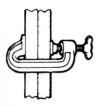

6. C-clamp.

Quite often the scenery has not only to be supported but to be held rigidly in place. If a door, for instance, is not erected correctly it may not close properly or may stick or continually come open. We want to avoid walls that shudder as a door shuts or a handrail that shakes when held. Also, if the script calls for very violent action, such as battering a door down, the unit's bracing will need to be suitably reinforced.

Setting flats

9.9 Fastenings for flats

The walls of most settings are made up from a series of standard flats, securely fastened together to form a firm, stable structure. It is not normally acceptable to nail flats together, for this will damage and shorten the life of units. So a series of special fittings have been devised for this purpose.

Lashing is a simple flexible system in which a length of attached cord is wound round alternating projections on the units (brace cleats), then pulled tight and tied off with a quick-release knot. This gives support along the entire edge of the flat (see Section 9.10). Edge-location devices are often fitted to ensure good edge-to-edge alignment (locating pins, aligning blocks, stop cleats), which allow flats to be set up quickly and accurately to a 'setting line' on the studio floor.

Various other systems are widely used to fasten units together:

- *Securing bolts* through the vertical stiles, fastened with wing-nuts,
- *L-plates* which drop into a metal socket,
- An *extension plug and socket*,
- A *U-plate* which attaches to a protruding bolt,
- *Loose pin hinge* and loop pin.

They all work effectively enough, particularly with lightweight flats, but they do have disadvantages:

- Units have to be mated together carefully to ensure that the fasteners come exactly into position. Adjustment can be critical.
- They give little overall support to heavier units (which may lean off the vertical).
- Some of these fasteners are easily damaged and liable to damage other scenery during transportation.

Some studios favor the use of *C-clamps* which have adjustable jaw-widths and can clamp together structures of various shapes and sizes very firmly. Both screw types and quick-fix forms are used. But again, support is localized. Good C-clamps are detachable, costly fittings, comparatively heavy, and readily mislaid – particularly as they have many other applications!

Box flats (Section 3.16) may be fastened together with either securing bolts or C-clamps.

9.10 Lashing

This is a regular theatrical method of fastening flats together edge to edge.

Let's suppose we are going to lash together flats 'A' (on the left of Figure 9.2) and 'B' (on the right):
● Near the top-right stile (upright) or flat 'A' you will see that a *lash eye* is fitted. From it hangs a length of *lashline* (e.g. jute sash cord) reaching to the floor.
● Holding the right-hand side of flat 'B' a little nearer you than flat 'A', take this lashline around the upper *lash cleat* (throwline

Figure 9.2 Lashing
Scenic flats lashed together by cord (lashline; line; throwline).

Part 1
1. Lash eye to which lashline is attached.
2. Lash cleat guides line, and pulls flats together.
3. Brace cleat/brace eye to which stage brace is attached (screw eye, plate, or cast fitting).
4. Stop cleats, fitted to keep flats in line.

Part 2
Taken round the bottom pair of tie-off cleats, the line is tied in a slip knot/jerk knot. This holds firmly but is quickly released on pulling the line end.

Part 3
Where flats are larger or heavier than normal, additional lashing may be needed.

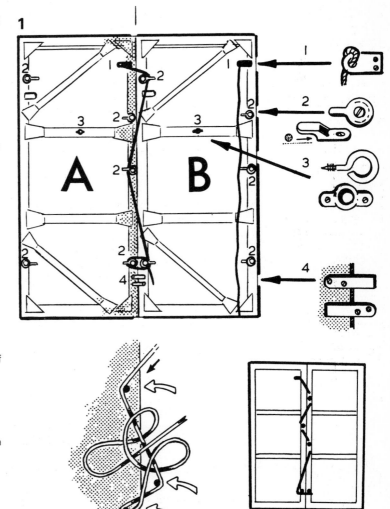

cleat) on 'B' and jerk the line sharply so that it bites into the cleat.

● Pulling the line taut, take it similarly around the next lowest lash cleat on flat 'A' and then on to flat 'B'.

● At the bottom, take the line round adjacent *tie-off cleats* and tie it with a *slip knot/jerk knot*.

● Then push flat 'B' into line with 'A'.

When lashing 'returns' (Section 3.18), place the short return flat behind the main flat. This will not only provide better support but will conceal the join more effectively. *Stop cleats* or *blocks* at the edges of the flats ensure a firm 90° join. When tightly lashed, the returns will add to the stability of the structure.

9.11 Stage brace

A *stage brace* comprises two wooden struts, held together by metal bands. The brace is extendable and can be locked at any chosen length with a thumb screw on one of the bands.

At its upper end the brace has a *claw-hook*, a *C-hook*, or a *bar* which goes into a *brace eye* fitting or a large *screw eye* attached to the back of the flat (on a *cross-toggle* or *stretcher*). On large flats, with an extra central stile, the point may be about one-quarter of the flat height from the top, for better balance.

At its lower end an angled *brace-iron* is fitted which, in use, is trapped beneath a *stage weight*. Alternatively, it may have a right-angled rod which hooks into a bracket on the studio wall (for horizontal bracing).

Figure 9.3 Stage brace
After fitting the top of the brace into the brace cleat on a toggle rail (stretcher) the brace is extended to floor level and the thumb screw tightened. The lower end (brace iron) is securely weighed with a stage weight or sandbag (seldom a stage screw).
Brace design varies. At the *top*, a claw hook, C-hook, or bar is fitted. At the *lower* end, a flat brace iron or a round bar (rod) is fitted. (The bars are primarily for horizontal bracing; e.g. to studio wall.)

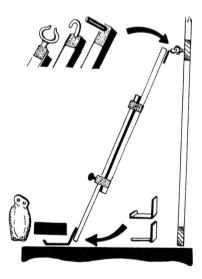

Stage weights (brace weight), in square or round form, have central hand grips and perhaps an underside recess for firm location. Raised location lugs allow weights to be stacked safely (four max).

A *stage weight* (*brace weight*) is made of cast iron, typically weighing 1.1 lb (0.5 kg), 28 lb (12.7 kg), or 33 lb (15 kg). Both circular and square forms are used and are fitted with a central hand grip. Up to four weights may be stacked safely, thanks to their raised location lugs which fit into recesses beneath the weights. As well as weighing down stage braces, the weights can be used to secure the bottom of cloths, cycloramas, isolated scenic pieces, trees, free-standing units, etc.

9.12 Jacks

The *jack* (*french brace*, *hinged brace*) is a vertical triangular strut, fitted at 90° to the lower part of a flat. It may be attached by a pin hinge or, less reliably, a hook-on contour or simply tied to the toggle.

The jack can be weighed down with a sandbag or stage weight (occasionally, an H-counterbalance weight).

Sometimes the jack is rigid and the unit castered for easy movement.

9.13 Stabilizing scenery

Certain structures are inherently unstable, particularly if they are high, narrow-based, top-heavy, or relatively unsupported.

There are, of course, various degrees of stability. You may only want to ensure that the structure will not fall over. But if someone is going to climb up it, that is a different matter. In an extreme case it may have to withstand someone battering against it, bursting through a locked door!

Bottom weighting with stage-weights or sandbags is sufficient to hold small isolated units stable (e.g. pillars, small trees, panels, screens).

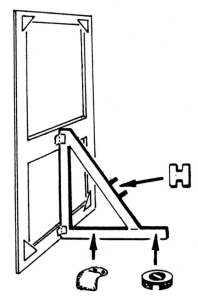

Figure 9.4 Jacks
Stored folded, the hinged strut is opened 90° during setting and weighted with a stage weight or sandbag (sometimes an H-counterweight).

Table 9.2   Comparing methods of support

Stage brace	Jack/french brace	Hinged flats
Advantages Adaptable to scenic units of all sizes and types. Easily readjusted. Lightweight. Braces can be used for various other jobs including unhooking or adjusting cables, drapes, or lines; adjusting lamps; forming barriers; etc. *Disadvantages* A separate component. Requires a heavy stage weight to hold it rigid. Can be incorrectly adjusted or loose.	*Advantages* Simple to fit. Easily made. May need less bottom weighting than a stage brace. *Disadvantages* Large, heavy, cumbersome. Not adaptable. Only really suitable for lightweight flats.	*Advantages* Two- or threefold hinged units, may be self-supporting (require no braces). Useful with lightweight (canvas) flats. Pin-hinged fastenings are quickly dismantled. *Disadvantages* Permanently combined hinged units are heavier than separate flats. Alignment problems when fitting together pin-hinged units. Little strength in hinges compared with other methods. Limited applications. The pins get lost.

Figure 9.5 Stabilizing scenery

Methods of stabilizing

1. Some scenic units are sufficiently stable to be self-supporting.

2. Items that are lightweight, top heavy, or unbalanced may only need bottom weighting to make them stable.

3. Suspension lines (wire slings or ropes) may be needed to support or stabilize units.

4. Timber bracing struts to nearby scenery can anchor an isolated unit (e.g. a pillar, screen, or pole).

5. Corner bracing with lumber struts can add stability to right-angled flats.

6. Various 'standard' fittings are screwed or bolted to scenery to attach lines which support or suspend units: (a) *Hanging irons* (fixed to rails/battens) – inward or outward loops. (b) *Ring plate*. To suspend light scenery or as a grummet. (c) *Flying iron*. Alternative to hanging iron. May be fixed to stile. (d) *Fixing iron*. Attached to any flat surface for suspension or stabilizing line. (e) *Grummet*. Holds flying cables in position. Secures knotted end of lashing line on flats.

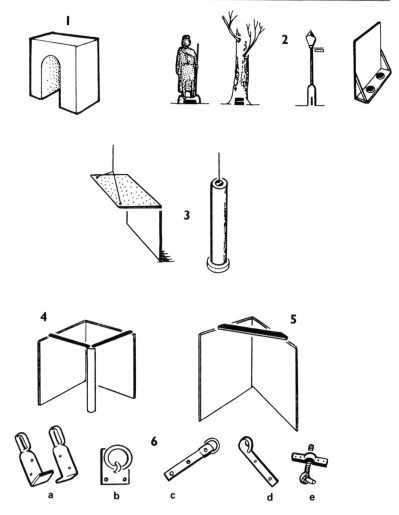

Brailing. The suspended flat would normally hang at position (1) below. It is required in a slightly different position (2), so is pulled over with attached brail lines, which are secured (tied off) to a suitable wall or catwalk point.

If brailing is excessive (3), much of the weight of the flat would be taken on the brail lines, which could break. The suspension line might come off its hoist pulley. (Note that the flat's height above the floor increases with brailing.)

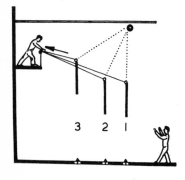

Where scenery is top-heavy or unbalanced, normal bracing may not be enough. Then you can drop *suspension lines* (steel cables or ropes) from the studio's grid or a scenic hoist to take the strain or to steady the scenery. These lines are tied or clipped to *hanging irons/fixing irons* (metal straps with loops and rings) fixed to the top rails of flats and scenic units. Typical applications include high walls, ceilings, roofs, large trees, tall columns, and long staircases.

As well as being used to suspend more obvious scenic units (e.g. panels, backdrops, tubular bars for drapes, tab tracks/curtain tracks), lines are also used for a variety of general purposes – to hang chandeliers, shadow gobos, snow bags, equipment (e.g. loudspeakers).

In large studios suspension lines may be used to fly a cloth or a piece of scenery up to the grid during a show, either to clear the studio floor or to allow it to be dropped in when required.

The position in which a suspended unit hangs naturally may not be exactly where it is required. Lightweight units may sway about or may be hanging at the wrong angle. So, using *scenic cord/brail line*, we brail them into position, tying the line to a securing point on the studio wall, the gantry, or the grid (by a bowline knot). More extreme brailing (e.g. over 10 ft or 3 m) can be dangerous, especially where the thin brail line begins to take the weight.

Where a rope or a brail line is likely to hang near a lamp and to be burned a short steel-wire 'bond' or 'strop' should be inserted instead at that point.

Bracing struts of 3×1 in (75×25 mm) lumber are sometimes fixed to the built set to give it added stability. They may be nailed across the tops of flats in the corners of a composite setting where stage braces cannot be used. Bracing struts can help to hold an unbalanced door flat upright or anchor an isolated pillar. But they should really only be introduced in collaboration with the lighting treatment, for they can cause distracting shadows.

9.14 Rope and knots

For many people 'a rope is just a rope'. But where scenery is concerned it is as well to use the right sort and to secure ropes correctly. Someone's life may depend on it. Even where motorized scenic hoists are installed in a studio, additional ropes are needed.

Rope is usually assessed according to its *safe working load* (e.g. $SWL = 250$ lb or 113 kg), a fraction of the minimum breaking load. These ropes or 'lines' may be:

Figure 9.6 Rigging knots and hitches
Various knots and hitches are used regularly when rigging scenery. (See Table 9.1.)
1. *Bight hitch*: By taking a turn round a firm support, a rope can be controlled during hoisting/lowering and when tying off.
2. *Bowline*: For tying off suspended scenery; providing a loop at a rope end; for attaching sandbags to loose lines.
3. *Clove hitch*: General-purpose knot; tying lines to bars/battens/rails; tying off brail lines.
4. *Half hitch*: A final securing hitch used after a clove hitch or figure-of-eight knot.
5. *Reef knot/thief knot (US)*: Secure knot for joining two lines.
6. *Sheepshank*: For shortening ropes; must be kept taut.
7. *Sheet bend*: Joins two ropes of different thickness.
8. *Draw hitch*: Method of securing a rope, to be undone and recovered from a distance. L bears the load. R releases the rope.
Ends must be identified, so put a knot in R end to distinguish them.

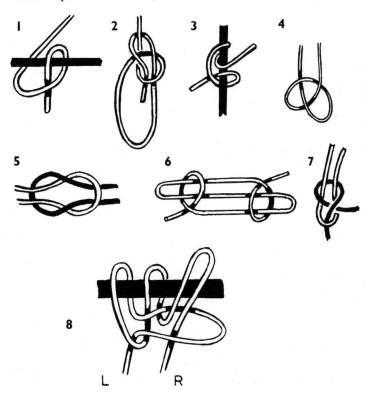

Table 9.3   Rigging knots and hitches

Bight hitch	Provides control while hauling a load.
Bowline	For tying off suspended scenery.
Clove hitch	For tying ropes to tubular bars or wire-rope bonds.
Draw hitch	A double-rope arrangement: one supports the load, the other instantly releases and recovers the complete rope. Dangerous if the lines are confused!
Half-hitch	Used to finish off a clove hitch or secure line tied in a figure-of-eight round a securing cleat.
Thief knot (US)/reef knot	Ties rope ends together. (Difficult to release if heavily loaded.)
Sheepshank	Shortens the length of a taut rope.
Sheet bend	Joins ropes of differing sizes.
Slip knot (jerk knot)	Easily released knot, used to secure cleating lines on flats, or to tie cloths to battens/bars.

- *Natural fiber* – manila hemp for hand hauling and general lifting; jute sashline (No. 8), for lashing and brailing lines,
- *Man-made fiber* (polyester and polypropylene) – unaffected by humidity; for flying, suspension, and hauling lines,
- *Galvanized wire rope* – for hoists, slings, and control cables.

When pulling on a rope to lift an object you should generally raise it just above the required 'dead' position and take the rope round a securing bar with a *bight hitch*. You can then ease the load down into position without strain and avoid suddenly releasing it.

Typical knots and hitches used in rigging scenery are listed in Table 9.3 and Figure 9.6.

9.15 Tubular bars

Long wooden battens are widely used to support drapes, back-drops, cycloramas, gauzes, scenic cloths, etc. as well as to weigh down stretched cycs and cloths.

Many studios, however, now use rigid lightweight metal tubes of various lengths instead (e.g. 10–20ft or 3–6 m long), for tubular bars are safer, more durable, and more adaptable than timber battens.

This tubing can be joined together firmly with removable couplers, and long continuous lengths can be built up, including curved sections (e.g. 45°, 60°, 90° bends), for wrapround cycs or cloths.

9.16 Rigging the cyc

Most studios suspend the cyclorama, black drapes, chroma key cloths, or gauzes from a permanent, heavy-duty curtain track/cyc rail. The upper edge of the cyc has a series of eyelets which clip onto hooks on wheeled runners (bobbins). These enable the cloth to be pulled along the track. (In some systems a section of the track can be lowered to fit the cyclorama.)

Where there is no track (or it is in use) the cloth may be tied to battens or tubular bars suspended by ropes.

The suspended cloth may be allowed to hang 'dead' (with natural folds and wrinkles) or 'stretched' by applying tension from below. Tension smooths the surface.

To stretch a cloth vertically it may be provided with a series of tie-tapes along its bottom edge, which are fastened to a floor pipe or batten, or a pipe may be fitted into a skirt pocket sewn along its lower length. Alternatively, the free bottom edge may be trapped under a floor batten or bar, pulled taut and weighted with stage weights (e.g. every 18 in (450 mm)) working from the center outwards. The excess cloth is rolled.

There is much to be said for having excess material in the initial *height* of any cyc or cloth to allow for subsequent shrinkage. It is embarrassing to find that the weather has changed and your regular cyc now ends several inches above the studio floor!

Where a cyc is not *long* enough it may be joined to another reasonably successfully by sandwiching their adjoining edges together between vertical wooden battens, using C-clamps.
To stretch a cyc horizontally a vertical barrel is needed, fixed in a floor plate at its lower end (a 'tree stand' will do) and the studio grid or gantry rail at the upper end. The end of the cyc is tied to this barrel using a series of edge-eyelets. Alternatively, *cyc clamps* can be used, so that when sufficient of the cyc has been stretched the remainder can be tied off and bunched. To shorten a cyc, or neaten its unstretched end, its edge can be folded back on itself, and clamped or rear-hung on the suspension hooks.

9.17 Suspending backdrops

Artist-painted backdrops or scenic cloths are normally prepared on a heavy-duty canvas cloth. Repainted over and over, the thick paint layer is liable to crack or flake if handled carelessly.

Figure 9.7 Tumble cloth
The cloth/backdrop hangs from a batten. Pulleys on the batten guide topes wound round each end of the cloth's bottom tumbler (L: clockwise; R: counter-clockwise). Pulling the combined ropes (RL knotted together), the tumbler turns and winds up the cloth to leave it suspended out of sight.

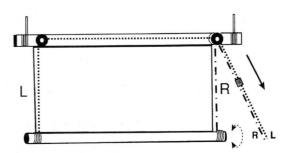

The upper edge of the cloth may be attached to a flat batten, while its lower one is fastened to a wooden pole or tumbler (e.g. 4 in or 100 mm diameter), around which it is rolled for storage. The upper batten may be tied to a tubular bar, which is raised to unroll the cloth. The tumbler serves to weigh the cloth down.

The cloth should hang level and vertical, without bulges. A short length wrapped round its tumbler keeps it stable, but add bottom weight if necessary. If hung just touching the floor, the cloth is liable to sway.

Where a cloth has to be raised out of sight but there is insufficient headroom to fly it vertically you can *tumble* it, i.e. hang the cloth rolled up and, using ropes at either end of the tumbler, unroll it when required.

Unlike 'aniline cloths' which have been coloured with aniline dyes, painted cloths must never be folded. Needless to say, the painted face of the cloth must not be allowed to touch the floor.

Setting up scenery

9.18 Preliminaries

Setting begins with a careful study of the staging plan and the elevations. Strategic setting points are then marked on the floor, guided by studio wall markings and overhead lighting battens. Setting lines are then laid out, showing main wall positions.

Building the settings
The various scenic pieces are being assembled and the sets built during the setting period.

As we saw earlier, the scenery carries identifying labels at the rear, showing the set each unit belongs to and where it is located in that set. These unit numbers will also have been marked on the setting plan. The next move is to group the units into their corresponding sets, with their labels visible, and confirm that all the parts have arrived!

9.19 Setting priorities

There are priorities in the setting process:

- Establish the *access routes* needed for everything that is to be brought into the studio, i.e. scenery from the scene dock, props, and, later, the technical equipment. Leave these clear. Otherwise you may find cameras, sound booms, monitors, etc. trapped in their store rooms after the setting has been completed!
- Build any *large platforms* or *scaffolding work* first.
- Anything that is to be *suspended* (or *flown*) (e.g. large scenic cloths, cyc cloth, drapes, or ceiling pieces) should be hung early but moved out of the way while positioning scenery.
- Position any *large floor cloths* before their respective settings.

9.20 Building sets

There are advantages in beginning with the sets furthest from the scene dock so as to leave optimum floor space at all times. Select a major unit in the set (e.g. a fireplace in the center of the upstage wall), locate this accurately, and then build out on either side of it.

It is safest to secure and brace each scenic unit as it is added. Do not, for instance, assume that lashing alone will make a run of flats secure, but brace them as you go. If in doubt, use extra ropes or braces temporarily. Although a structure may be quite rigid when complete, it could be unsafe at intermediate stages.

Isolate working areas as far as possible, so that, for example, there is no danger of someone fixing a door while other people are lowering a ceiling above.

Some studios have more stringent safety/fire rules than others, either from bitter experience or due to local regulatory bodies. There it is obligatory to keep the safety-lane/fire-lane (Section 2.13) clear at all times, free of braces or stored scenery. Flats positioned right at the edge of the staging area are braced (above head height) to brackets on the studio wall.

9.21 Handling scenery

Good handling is a matter of technique and coordination rather than brute strength. Good hand positions and proper balance are essential.

Figure 9.8 Moving flats
With two people. The flat is best handled from the rear undecorated side. With upper hands balancing the flat, and lower hands supporting it, the person in front steers and the other at the rear adds strength and helps to maneuver.

With one person. Using a similar technique, a single person can handle moderately sized flats alone with care.

Lifting scenery. When moving scenery up stairs it is particularly important to have both lower hands on the same side of the flat to avoid unbalance. Never readjust hands during movement.

Figure 9.9 Cradling a flat
A technique for moving awkwardly shaped flats (e.g heavily profiled, contoured). Also used to invert a flat.

Figure 9.10 Handling a flat
A flat that was resting on its side edge is turned onto its base edge (or vice versa). Only suitable for relatively small light flats.

To upright a heavy flat one person anchors the base edge while two others walk forward, progressively raising the top edge.
If a flat is lying face up on the floor push it up to a firm support (e.g. a nearby wall) and 'walk it' to a vertical position before moving it.

Working from behind a flat, place one hand as high as possible for best balance and grasp the edge of the flat at waist height with the other. Lean the flat towards you a little.

If two people are running a flat they adopt similar positions, the upper hand balances and the lower hand does the work. The front person steers and the rear one adds strength to the operation – taking care not to have a shoulder behind the edge of the flat in case the person in front stops suddenly.

If a piece of scenery is awkwardly shaped (e.g. heavily contoured) it may be more convenient for two people to move it *cradled* in a horizontal position, holding opposite edges.

To invert a flat, a similar technique can be used ('circusing').

Where a flat is resting on its side and is to be rotated so as to rest on its base edge, this can be done with two people. One steadies the top corner at that end while the other grasps the lower corner at the other end of the flat and walks forward, progressively raising the lower edge of the flat.

For a heavy flat a third person is needed. The unit is flat on the floor and one person places his feet in the center of its base edge. The other two take the far corners and walk forward, lifting the flat as they go.

9.22 Lifting

Although back injuries do arise from lifting something that is too heavy, more often they are the result of bad techniques.

In Table 9.4 you will find a summary of the lifting code.

Table 9.4   The lifting code

- Check the weight of a load before trying to lift it. If necessary, get assistance or divide it into smaller loads that can be carried separately.
- Stand close to the load with your feet apart, facing the direction you are going to take. Do not twist or bend your body.
- With equal weight on each leg, and keeping your back straight *all the time*, bend your knees and hips.
- With your elbows close to your thighs, grip the load firmly with your whole hands (not just the fingers). If possible, have one hand below it and the other to one side. If there is nothing with which to hold it, use a container, a sling, or a rope.
- With straight back and arms close to your body, lean forward a little while straightening your knees and hips. With head raised and chin tucked in, lift the load slowly and progressively (do not jerk), keeping it close to your body all the time.
- Carry the load close, never with arms stretched out.
- When lowering the load, do the reverse. Keeping your back straight, bend your hips and knees.
- Do not bend over to lift items near floor level. Kneel rather than stoop and keep a straight back.
- Lifting loads from floor level, begin the lift by putting one hand on a nearby support (e.g. a chair) to serve as a lever, or kneel on one knee and rest your free arm on the other.

Figure 9.11 Lifting and carrying techniques
Part 1 *The lifting code*
- Check object's weight. Check your route.
- Stand close to object, facing route. Bending hips and knees, crouch down to the load. Always keep your back straight. Elbows tucked into thighs, grip load either side if possible, above and below. (Use all of your hand, not the fingers alone.) If there are no handholds, place a rope round object.
- Raised head and chin in. Equally balanced on either leg, begin to lift the object (keeping a straight back!) with arms close to body and leaning forward slightly. Smoothly straighten legs, keeping object close to body. Carry object close to body, with your lower arm straight.
- To put the object down, reverse the lifting process with a straight back and bending at the hips and knees. Do not bend over!
- If lifting with one hand, place the other on a nearby bench, table, chair; or kneel on one knee, using it as a support.

Part 2 *Carrying weights*. Carry weights on your shoulders where possible, not in front of you with extended arms.
Always avoid twisting or bending your back when lifting or carrying.
- Wherever possible, do not carry heavy weights, but use a wagon, trolley, castered skids, etc.

9.23 Disguising joins

Unless you take precautions, butt joins between flats can be very pronounced. One may even be able to see studio lights through them!

Apart from minimizing the effect by tight lashing (cleating) and overlapping, joins can be disguised by pasting long strips of paper or fabric over them (e.g. 3 in (75 mm) wide)), a process known as *stripping*. (These strips are occasionally also called 'dutchmen' or 'rhinoceros hide'.)

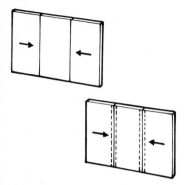

Figure 9.12 Disguising joins
When scenic units are fastened together, the joins between them can usually be seen on camera, unless disguised in some way. With varying success, paper or fabric strip ('stripping') may be pasted over joins to make them less visible.

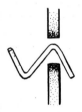

Figure 9.13 Wall attachments
A thick wire Z-hook passed through a hole in a flat can support quite heavy objects (wall-mirrors, pictures, etc.).

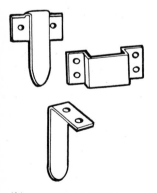

If items such as pelmets, battens, pictures, shelves, etc. are fitted with *pelmet clips* (upper two clips) or *L-irons* (lower clip) they are easily attached to sockets screwed to a flat.

The strip is then painted to match the wall tone and color. When flats have a plain light-toned finish the divisions may still remain slightly visible. If wallpaper has been used to decorate the flats the stripping may need to be done in the same material and patterns carefully matched.

Stripping can, of course, only be applied in the studio once the set has been erected, and it may be destroyed if adjacent flats are later re-angled for any reason.

9.24 Set-dressing mechanics

Although the walls of a setting look solid enough on camera, when dressing a set we need to remember that they are, after all, only a thin plywood surface.

We need quick reliable methods for attaching items to flats, methods that do little or no damage and allow the set dressing to be removed quickly and easily.

A *staple hammer* (*hammer tacker*) or *staple gun* (*gun tacker*) will fire staples of various lengths (e.g. ¼–½ in or 6–12 mm) to attach light drapes, posters, foliage, plastic molding, wire, or fishing line to flats. Staples are often more convenient than thumb-tacks or tacks.

When heavier items are to be attached to a flat, a thick wire 'Z-hook' can be passed through a small hole in the flat to provide a V-support for pictures, wall mirrors, etc. Sometimes it is preferable to drop a heavy-duty fishing line (or two) from the top of a flat to support a large wall map, a tapestry, or a climbing wall plant.

A metal *back-plate* behind the flat will give strength when attaching a larger item to a wall (e.g. a trophy). A *pelmet clip* can be screwed to shelves, pictures, and, of course, pelmets. It fits into a socket screwed on the flat and allows items to be attached and removed rapidly.

Where a decorative 'practical' lamp-fitting is to be attached to a flat a rear metal back-plate support is again desirable. The lamp's wiring is connected to a small insulated junction block placed just behind the flat and the supply cable taken to a fused circuit. It is essential that the fitting is grounded (earthed) correctly. The supply cable should be secured and suspended or taped to the backs of flats, well away from cameras and passing feet.

Gaffer tape (duct tape) is a waterproof-cloth sealing tape for which there are always fresh uses. This is a polyethylene-coated cloth, available in matt, gloss, and double-sided forms, 1 in and 2 in (25 mm and 50 mm) wide. A range of colors includes silver, black, brown, white, beige, green, yellow, red, and blue. It will hold light items in position, stick cables or small lamps to walls, make temporary repairs, identify rope-ends, tie back drapes, provide floor-marks, and so on.

Table 9.5   Attached detail

There are several regular methods of attaching labels, symbols, posters, etc. to walls:

- Small items of paper, card, or thin plastic can be attached to flats with *plastic putty* (e.g. Blu-tak) or with *double-sided adhesive tape* or *rubber solution*.
- To attach and remove large symbols, arrows, or data to a wall chart or map, back them with strips of *magnetic plastic sheeting* or *small magnets*. Use sheet steel behind the background.
- Use *Teazlegraph/Velcro*. Stick a small multi-hook nylon strip behind the shape and a multi-loop strip on the background.
- *Masking tapes* of adhesive crepe paper will secure corners and edges of objects to the wall. They can also be used for general repair jobs and to form decorative patterns. (Stick to a surface which is then color-sprayed. Remove the tape to leave a clean narrow line.)
- *PVC tape* can also be used to attach details and to form decorative patterns on walls, screens, or floors (widths ¾ in, 2 in; 19 mm, 50 mm).

9.25 Striking the scenery

Photographs of the décor for a show are important for any designer, not only as a record of work done and part of a personal *curriculum vitae* but also a reference for others. If a show is repeated or part of the setting is to be re-used, a photograph, coupled with plans and elevations, tells it all. Make sure that you have a series of photographs of the settings taken from several angles, showing any particular features in detail. If lighting or effects have made a major contribution, then off-tube pictures may also be useful.

The designer normally supervises operations when settings are being struck. There may be items that need to be put to one side for re-use; items that are delicate or on special loan; items that are on hire... that one does not want to see whisked away by an overenthusiastic crew (or ruined!).

Once the technical equipment has been moved out of the way into storage (cameras, sound booms, loudspeaker units, floor monitors, lighting equipment on stands or on the floor, etc.) the strike can begin.

It normally starts with the removal of props, drapes, rugs, furniture, practical lamps (after disconnection!), and so on. These should be placed separately and safely in special props baskets, bins, or wheeled cages, ready to be returned to their storage area for sorting.

Anything that could impede work around the floor is generally removed next (e.g. tubular bars around the bottom of cyc cloths, which are then pulled back). Any studio lighting clamped onto settings is disconnected and removed. Vehicles, plants, foliage, and built-up areas' sandbags progressively vanish, until the bare sets stand alone in an empty studio.

Scenic attachments are usually removed next (e.g. half-arches, plugs, bolt-on pilasters or molding, etc.). (It may not be possible to do this until the associated flat is removed from the main structure.)

Secure any doors or windows to prevent them from moving or becoming displaced in transit.

Even if the set was erected only a few hours before, various additions and changes have probably been made since. Reinforcing struts and extra bracing may have been added. Extra ropes or lighting cables may now be stretched across suspended units that were not there when the set was built. So it is a good idea to check how the various units in a set are now secured. Some may be fixed in more than one place (e.g. a suspended ceiling piece attached to adjacent flats or corner bracing struts added). Decide which fastenings should be released first.

Any stripping will need to be cut before parting the flats. With one person supporting a flat, another removes any nails, top braces, bolts, clamps, and pin hinges and then unties the lashing/ cleat-line. The weights or sandbags are removed next and neatly piled, then the jacks or braces are taken off.

If the flat is ready to be moved (i.e. no loose lash-line, flapping parts, overlooked fittings, or nails that might be dangerous) it can be taken to storage in the studio scene dock or stacked on a scenic truck ready for transport.

If more than one set is being cleared at the same time, make sure that there are unobstructed areas for the crew to work and to remove the scenic units.

9.26 Scenic transport

Scenic construction is a compromise. The more robustly a unit is made, the longer it is likely to last. But it is also likely to be heavy and bulkier. A lighter, flimsier unit is easier to move around but more vulnerable.

If a unit is heavy the effort involved in moving it can result in accidental damage to both the unit and other scenic pieces with which it comes in contact. Crushing, tearing, breakages, and dirtying in transit are not uncommon. So careful handling, transport, and storage are imperative.

How durable scenery needs to be can depend on its long-term value:

- *Once only* – destroyed after the show,
- *Short term* – needed for several episodes then no longer required,
- *Stock* – refurbished and re-used for other productions. (This includes both individual units and 'permanent stock sets'.)

Today, an increasing amount of scenery is constructed from fiber glass, which is lightweight and resistant to damage. Typical units include flats, masonry, fireplaces, statuary, pillars, columns, balustrades, walls, paving, tree trunks, windows, archways, shop fronts, and roofs.

A scenic wagon (trolley) in the form of a low-wheeled platform with fixed tubular support rails has proved to be an adaptable method of transporting scenery near the studio. Small battery-powered units can tow the wagons and maneuver them into limited parking spaces.

9.27 Storage

In most TV stations space is at a premium. Yet daily program requirements continually add to the number of settings and properties used.

By renovating or restyling units they can be re-used many times, so reducing the actual number of items being held and keeping the quantity of unused (*dead*) stock to a minimum. On the other hand, if the same old stock is overused it can stultify creative design.

Clearly, there is a delicate economic balance when you decide whether to

● Make a new unit,
● Use a stock piece,
● Junk a new unit after using it once (perhaps salvaging some material), or
● Retain a unit in expensive storage space until someone is able to integrate it into a future setting.

Some items can be re-used frequently without being recognized; others are too distinctive for more than occasional use.

9.28 Storage methods

Storage, identification, and classification can be an ongoing problem. If items are to be re-used they must be found easily. If something is not clearly cataloged it is virtually lost – yet occupies storage space. Stock indexes *with reference photographs* help to ensure that usable stock is not forgotten or overlooked.

Whatever method of storage is chosen, it needs to be protective (to stop the items deteriorating or becoming damaged) and secure from theft or accidental misplacement.

Bigger props and furniture are usually kept under covers on large multi-tier shelf units or racks. Smaller items are transported in cages or bins and kept in coded bins, closets, or shelved containers.

Methods of scenery storage depend on the type of unit involved:

● Although a few *flats* may be rested against a wall for a while (*piling, wall pack*) they are best stored in vertical tubular frameworks (*scenic rack, bin*). Preferably, these racks should

Figure 9.14 Storage

Furniture. Furniture and large properties are stored under protective sheeting on multi-tier shelf units. Small items, drapes, etc. may be kept in storage boxes (hampers), bins, or closets.

Scenery. Various forms of storage (temporary and permanent), are used for scenic units. This figure shows typical features of a *scene dock*.
1. Stock flats resting against a wall (wall pack) while being selected for a production. (Permanent wall packs are cumbersome, selection is difficult, and units become damaged.)
2. Wall racks for rolled backdrops, cloths, etc.
3. Boxes containing cyc cloths, drapes.
4. Scenic racks/bins for storage of stock flattage. Flats are fitted into individual slots for rapid selection. Coding on each unit (color, alphanumeric) denotes particular sizes, styles, types, and finishes.
5. Suspended bulky or difficult-to-store items.
6. Storage rack.
7. Scenic wagon for transporting scenic units. Various sizes of rails can be fitted to suit the size/type of scenery. The wagon/truck may be towed manually or by a small battery-powered unit ('tug').

Properties. A metal-framed mobile unit, used to house and transport the properties required for a production. The mesh covering protects and secures items. For large productions, bigger double-door cages may be used.

have separate 'stalls' with slots, separators, or dividers to enable individual flats to be slid out easily. Edge labels can be color-coded to show the type, size, color, and surface treatment.

● Small rigid *platforms* must be stacked. But with demountable units the bases are usually folded and stored on end, while tops are stored separately.

● A *painted scenic cloth* is rolled on a large round wooden batten and supported in a horizontal wall rack, with data clearly visible.

● *Aniline cloths* may be folded, and can be kept in containers, baskets, partitioned shelves, etc.

● *Scrims/gauzes* can be folded gently in a concertina fashion ('fanning'), but without compression. Rolling is liable to produce pronounced creases.

● *Other materials* (e.g. rayon) are better stored rolled, preferably onto a round batten as they are lowered from their suspended position – *not* allowing them to rest on the studio floor.

● *Cycloramas* are best left hanging or pulled back and bunched out of the way if necessary, because any stains or creases are likely to be difficult to remove. If the cyc is to be stored it should be folded as large drapes or other cloths. The material is lowered so that it is stretched out with its *back* on a clean surface (presumably a freshly swept studio floor). One edge is brought over to meet the opposite one. The folded edge is then brought over to join the pair of edges, and so on, until you have a fairly narrow strip. One end of the strip is taken to the other end, then the fold is taken to the two ends. The resulting folded cyc or cloth is then bagged or placed in a container or basket. As usual, this all sounds more complicated than it really is.

Chapter 10

The designer on location

Television, video, and film productions today are made under a wide range of conditions and the designer's contributions can vary accordingly.

10.1 Away from the studio

As equipment becomes more mobile and studio staging costs rise, an increasing proportion of television/video productions are being shot *on location*. In practice, this broad term 'location' covers anywhere away from the studio – from a castle to a coal mine or a desert to Disneyland.

The director may accept the location as it is, using the camera very selectively, showing just the parts of the scene that suit the purpose, and avoiding anything that would be inappropriate or likely to distract the audience. The impression a camera conveys depends very much on the way it is used and the lighting that prevails.

Design effort on location can range from the odd alteration or two to major changes in a landscape. In extreme cases the location is so disguised that it becomes unrecognizable.

10.2 Eye and camera

Going into any room, we form an immediate impression – of its tidiness, disorder, its feeling of casual comfort, authority, poverty... But although *we* see it this way there is no guarantee that the camera will convey the same feeling.

A colored vase that our eyes pass over casually may dominate the screen. An impressive citation on the wall can become just a defocused blur in the shot. We may ignore activity outside the window but on the screen it becomes an interesting distraction. An attractive table-lamp shade may rest on top of a guest's head, like a crown! Your audience may be too busy reading titles on the bookshelf behind the speaker to listen to what is being said! There are many reasons for making temporary changes for the camera.

10.3 Improving an interior

In this situation the idea is to enhance the appearance of a scene on camera to avoid distracting or unbalancing features without changing its ambiance.

Sometimes even a slight change in camera position will alter the impression of size, distance, or proportions that the shot conveys.

Would a judiciously placed foreground item improve the sense of depth in the picture?

Would careful lighting change or improve the appearance of a room (e.g. lightening or darkening walls)?

Window
- Do the window coverings (curtains, blinds, etc.) reduce the amount of daylight getting into the room, making it look dingy?
- If sunlight is strong, would closing or partially closing window draperies/curtains/blinds improve the overall effect and the lighting balance?
- Are the curtains (window coverings) overbright?
- Do the curtains/drapes have a pattern that is overprominent on the screen?
- Is the scene outside the window distracting on camera?

Furniture
- Are any of the furnishings interfering with the shot or the action?
- Would picture composition be improved by repositioning any of the existing furniture?
- Do the existing chairs, sofa/settee cause talent to sit badly on camera (e.g. do they need cushions)?
- Would there be any benefit in removing any furniture, or replacing it with other items (e.g. from an adjacent room)?

Wall decorations
- Are any wall pictures overpowering or distracting on camera? Are there any light reflections in pictures?
- Is any mirror showing unwanted reflections (of lamps, equipment, or people)? Would it be better replaced with a wall picture?

Lighting fittings
- Would the effect be more attractive if lighting fittings were lit (wall brackets, table lamps, floor lamps)? Or would they be distracting or incongruous?

Ornamentation
Scattered around most interiors are various articles such as vases, books, papers, plants, knick-knacks, bric-à-brac.
- Are any items in shot distracting or overprominent? Often, just re-angling an article (e.g. a small picture on a desk) will make it less prominent. If an article is obtrusive try placing another in front of it to break up its mass, leave it in shadow, or mask it with another item to make it less visible.

Doorway
● Is anything seen through the doorway that would be distracting?

Equipment
● Is any of your lighting equipment visible (e.g. lamp stands, cables)? Reroute cables out of shot. Run cables neatly along bottom of wall. Hide cables behind furniture or rugs. Tape cables high on walls out of sight.

10.4 Modifying an interior

Here we are using the location as a *basis* for a scene in a drama, retaining anything that suits the story line, removing inappropriate features, and *adding* any new ones you need.

This is an extension of the 'revamping principles' we met in Section 6.11. Often just a few alterations to furniture and props can ring the changes, transforming an office into a living room, a waiting room, a restaurant, a classroom...

With subtle set dressing what might otherwise become a very artificial rearrangement becomes a 'real' working place. Instead of orderly empty surfaces and overall tidiness, you can introduce the casual newspaper, magazine, and coffee cup, and the scene comes to life.

However, it is not enough to just scatter things hopefully. It is a matter of choosing the right kind of bits and pieces and having them where they would be found in reality. For instance, few busy garages have sets of tools lying neatly arranged along benches. They are in use, grouped with tins of lubricant, cleaning rags, and other miscellaneous items. Many advertisements for modern kitchen design fail to look convincing because they are bespattered with bric-à-brac that no self-respecting cook would permit in the place!

You can even alter major features of the room comparatively easily and economically without damaging the existing décor.

As well as blocking off windows, adding dummy doorways, or windows, etc. you can hide existing wall treatment with background paper, wallpapered lightweight board, or drapes on frames, or introduce false wall structures (flattage, buttresses, arches), and so on.

Within reason, even a derelict room on location can be made to appear habitable, perhaps luxurious on camera.

A ruined mansion, for example, could, as far as the camera is concerned, be restored to its former glories with a little cunning. Walls can be covered temporarily in 'tapestry' (painted hessian) and wood paneling (plastic laminate). Rich-looking furniture (hired or borrowed), carpets, drapes, and ornaments develop the atmosphere. In a night scene, lighting can be localized to avoid showing the less attractive aspects and highlighting the quality features. Remember, at a distance a peeling, decaying, decorated ceiling can still look impressive on camera.

10.5 Modifying an exterior

This can be as straightforward as placing a stock dummy fire-hydrant or postbox in a real street to building an entire 'village' in the open fields!

Although large-scale design work on location is confined to film making, it is possible to provide very convincing changes on a more modest scale by relatively simple means:

- *Masking*. By placing something (or someone) in the foreground of the shot you can mask off an unwanted feature in the scene. A carefully parked truck might prevent a roadside stall from being seen. A leafy branch suspended in front of the camera can prevent our seeing unwanted overhead lines or a TV antenna in the shot. A fake foreground bush, wall, plastic statue, noticeboard, sign, or even a convenient nearby cow have served as effective masking pieces for this purpose!
- *Night scenes*. 'Night scenes' are usually shot in daylight ('day-for-night') to avoid lighting problems. Lens filters and considerably reduced exposure can create the illusion of 'darkness'. Under these conditions black panels can be used to hide unwanted features. You could even add 'new features' by introducing painted or photographic panels (e.g. photo cut-outs) into the scene. They will look convincing enough on camera if well done.
- *Selective camera position*. Using a carefully chosen camera position you can often keep unwanted items out of shot, seeing the wooded landscape but not the busy highway.
- *Covering over*. It is often practicable to cover over an unwanted feature. A temporary dummy shop sign can be stuck over the existing one. In an historic drama modern markings on a road may be covered over temporarily with a generous spread of tanbark or powdered peat.
- *Added features*. There is really no end to the dummy features you can add to a scene to disguise it. Put a sign outside a period building and on camera it becomes an apothecary's or the local jail. Stick a new street name over the real one and a renumbered doorway becomes the non-existent home of a fictional character! There is no street telephone booth? Then add one for the shot. A signpost beside a country road can suggest that it is the pilgrims' route to ancient Canterbury or the way to magical Oz!
- *Special effects*. You can use various optical and electronic masking processes to manipulate the picture and create apparent changes in the scene. Unwanted features can be removed and new ones inserted as you wish. Some of these methods require specialized equipment, but even surprisingly basic facilities often allow us to make dramatic changes.

10.6 Matching location to studio

Sometimes in the course of a drama production a director needs to suggest that there is direct continuity between a location shot and a setting in the studio.

For instance, we see someone walking along a street (taped or filmed on location), pause outside a shop, then walk in (studio setting) to buy something.

Several things can cause the audience to assume that the shots are consecutive when they are edited together:

- The studio set appears similar to the building seen in the location shot.
- Something in the location scene (e.g. a sign) is visible through a window of the studio scene (on a photo backdrop).
- Background sounds are similar.
- Dialogue connects the two places ('I am just going into this shop').

Wherever possible, it is best to avoid having to make a *direct match* between the location and the studio set. Rather than cut from action outside a shop on location to a direct replica of that shopfront in the studio(!) it is preferable to use some sort of subterfuge to disguise the differences between the scenes.

If you cannot avoid a direct match between shots of location and the studio setting try to introduce a simple feature at that point that is easily imitated in the studio (e.g. a bush or a brick wall). You could even, perhaps, take your own 'brick wall' with you to location, to make sure that the match works!

On the odd occasion it might be practicable to bring something from the location into the studio to help establish the continuity (e.g. borrow a pavement sign from outside the shop or make a convincing copy of it to use in the studio scene). On-the-spot photographs and scale drawings can provide a valuable guide for matching the studio setting to the location scene.

It is far better, though, to use entirely different camera angles in the two shots so there is no direct match (e.g. by cutting from someone outside a door to a reverse shot showing them coming through it). We might even cut from the exterior to a shot showing them inside the shop, and avoid the dilemma of actual continuity altogether ('filmic time').

10.7 Faking the studio 'exterior'

Although the location scene itself may have been a busy one any attempts to copy this activity in the studio by showing people and vehicles passing the window of the setting are usually doomed to failure.

Where there is hypothetically a 'busy exterior scene' outside the window there are several ways of getting round the problem.

In some situations the director can help by avoiding revealing through-shots that look straight out the window. Instead, the window is seen only in obliquely angled shots. Background sound effects (traffic, crowds) will convey the idea of activity outside without actually having to show it.

Perhaps you can stretch nets/ninon drapes across the window or swag the drapes so that little of the exterior is visible beyond them.

You may be able to position items in the window so that there is no clear view through it. A shop window may have large display objects; in the home, several plants may obscure the window.

There are often simple ways of getting round what would otherwise be a costly or space-occupying situation.

Chapter 11

Controlling tone and color

The pictorial effect on the screen is the combined result of scenic design, camera and video adjustments, and lighting treatment. It is important to appreciate how other people's judgements can alter the appearance of your settings.

Controlling tone

11.1 Exposure

If you point a video camera at a scene containing a wide range of tones the resulting picture can sometimes be very disappointing.

We can see subtle tonal gradations in those whitewashed walls, yet in the *camera's picture* they are only reproduced as blank white areas. Similarly, details that we can see in the shadows are lost on the screen as they merge into blank black areas. That is because the video camera can only reproduce a comparatively limited range of tones.

A TV color system can reproduce tonal gradations accurately over a contrast range, in which the lightest area is up to 30 or 40 times as bright as the darkest – i.e. 30:1. The human eye, however, can interpret variations over a range of 1000:1 in fairly bright conditions (although its range can fall to 10:1 or less in dim surroundings).

Using the piano keyborad as an analogy, you can think of the camera as only being able to span an 'octave'. Anything above or below that octave is lost. You can pick out an octave anywhere on the keyboard (down among the lowest notes or up in the highest), but it can still only handle an octave.

By adjusting the *aperture* (*iris, diaphragm, f-stop*) of the camera's lens we can control the average brightness of the image it is focusing onto the camera tube. (In our keyboard analogy we are choosing whereabouts on the overall tonal scale we select the octave.) Opening up the aperture, we can see shadow detail more clearly. Closing the lens down enables it to reproduce the lightest tones more effectively.

If the tones in the scene itself do not exceed a range of about 30:1, and the lens aperture is correctly adjusted, the camera should be able to show them all clearly.

But if there is excessive contrast in the scene then we have either to accept the results or make a judgement as to which part of the wide tonal range we want to see most clearly.

By adjusting the camera lens' aperture we get clear tonal gradation in those subject tones that are most important to us – or, as we say, *adjust the exposure*.

We usually expose a shot to get attractive face tones. But if, for example, a girl wears a very white lace dress while standing in front of very dark wooden paneling we might have to decide which area we wanted to see most clearly in a particular shot – the face, the dress, or the paneling – and adjust the exposure to suit that subject. We cannot normally expect to get optimum modeling over the whole tonal range.

We have the options of:

- Exposing for good reproduction of *facial tones* and accepting any merging ('crushing') in lightest and darkest areas.
- Exposing for good tonal reproduction in the *lightest tones* and allowing all other tones in the shot to reproduce correspondingly darker. Lower tones will be 'underexposed', poorly modeled, undetailed, and probably marred with 'picture noise' (random scintillating specks or grain). The lowest will merge into black.
- Or we can expose for good tonal reproduction in the *darker tones*, and allow light tones to be 'overexposed', paled out (desaturated), perhaps crushed out to white.

Even when a scene has a wider tonal range than the camera can handle, we can often find that we are getting subjectively attractive pictures. But that is because we are looking at the correctly exposed, well-modeled faces, and not noticing that there is no detail in the underexposed dark clothing and that the snow in the distance is overexposed and reproduced as blank white.

If we 'stop down' the lens (reduce its aperture) to improve reproduction of a white wall poster the wall it is attached to will reproduce much darker. Aperture adjustment affects *all* tones in the picture.

If the next shot shows dark furniture against the same wall we can 'open up' the lens (increase aperture) to improve its clarity, but now this wall will appear very light.

So you see that if the camera's exposure is continually adjusted in an attempt to compensate for extreme tones in the scene all tonal values and the atmospheric effect are going to vary from shot to shot.

Exposure adjustments can be made either *manually* by turning the lens 'aperture control' or electronically with an 'automatic iris' system. The latter is a valuable device for preventing gross overexposure, but artistically, the results are entirely fortuitous!

11.2 Tonal restriction

Even if a modern TV camera can handle a tonal range of 30:1 to 40:1, it is wisest to work to a much lower contrast range when choosing tones in a setting (e.g. 15:1–20:1).

Under flat shadowless lighting, contrast comes primarily from the actual *surface tones* in the scene. But under the light and shade of more attractive lighting treatment the effective tonal contrast in the scene becomes considerably increased. Dark parts of the scene fall into shadow and appear darker; strong lighting falls on light-toned areas, which appear lighter.

When the scenic contrast is too high for the camera we can try, within limits, to adjust the lighting to compensate, illuminating the darker areas to make them lighter while shading off the light-toned areas. But this is really only a palliative, and not always practicable. However, when coupled with careful exposure it can sometimes do quite a lot to improve the overall picture quality.

11.3 Reflectance

If a surface reflects all the light that falls on it we say that it has a *100% reflectance*. If no light is reflected (i.e. an ideal 'black') it has 0% reflectance.

In practice, we are likely to meet reflectances ranging from the 93–97% of fresh snow to the 0.3–1% of black velvet. Skin tones are typically: Caucasian, 30–40%; mid-brown skin, 20%; black skin, 10%.

11.4 Gray scale

To assess how well a system can distinguish between different tonal values a standard *gray scale* was devised. You can see an example of this in Figure 11.1.

This tonal scale has ten apparently equal brightness steps, from a minimum of 3% reflectance ('TV black'/Munsell 2) to 60% reflectance ('TV white'/Munsell 8). It covers a contrast range of 20:1. A tonal standard with more half-tone steps would be confusing to match, while one with fewer could be too arbitrary.

Above the maximum (TV white) and below the minimum (TV black) tonal gradation is generally lost.

The eye does not judge changes in surface brightness accurately. Double the amount of light falling on a surface and it will not appear twice as bright, because our eyes respond logarithmically to variations. The scale of the *step wedge* takes this into account (each step is $\sqrt{2}$ times the brightness of the next). The steps of the wedge *appear* equal but compare their relative light reflectances as shown in Figure 11.1 on the right in percentages. You

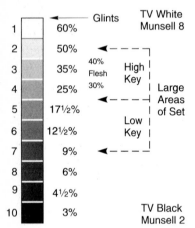

Figure 11.1 Gray scale
In a calibrated photographic version of this tonal wedge each step appears proportionally darker than the next.
Studio paints and materials can be compared on camera with the standard gray scale and classified accordingly, to identify and interrelate tonal values.
Ideally, scenic and subject contrasts should not generally exceed around 2:1 for large adjacent areas; 5:1 for large non-adjacent areas; 20:1 for small adjacent areas.
In practice, the final tone seen on the screen depends on many additional factors (light levels and contrast, exposure, video adjustment, surface angles, surface finish, perception effect, monitor/receiver adjustment, etc.). But careful control of scenic tones and finish does ensure optimum picture quality.

will see that the middle of the scale (mid-gray) is not the 50% you might expect but only 17.5%. That is why one often has to increase the amount of light on darker tones considerably (e.g. when lighting dark foliage) to make any appreciable change in the picture.

As well as being used for checks of the video system the gray scale serves as a tonal reference for scenic designers. The reflectances of all paints and materials regularly used in the studio can be checked and rated:

● To help them to avoid exceeding the camera's tonal limits,
● To help them to anticipate how effectively various materials would contrast,
● To help them to avoid juxtaposing colors that have distinctly different *hue* but reproduce with similar gray-scale values in a monochrome picture.

11.5 Reproduced tones

Although we have discussed the *camera's* ability to differentiate between tones, how well are these tones reproduced on the *TV receiver* or *picture monitor*?

A high-quality picture monitor will usually be able to display all the tonal steps in the gray scale quite clearly. However, many home receivers can have difficulty in reproducing even seven steps well. (Lightest tones merge; darkest tones merge.) Also, where room lighting or daylight dilutes the lower tones only as few as five gray-scale levels may be visible overall. Consequently, some organizations prefer to use a seven-step 'standard' gray-scale, as more realistically representing what their audience will be seeing.

So what does all this amount to for the designer?

● Very subtle tonal variations can be lost in the transmission process.
● A good range of tonal values is desirable in a picture to give it a dynamic impact. But if extreme tones go beyond the camera's contrast limits (or are over- or underexposed) they will merge.

In addition to care with tones, pattern may also pose problems. It is always wisest to avoid close stripes (vertical, horizontal, or diagonal), herringbone, and closely checkered patterns. When sharply in focus, they are very likely to 'strobe' and produce a distracting, dazzling moiré effect. When defocused, they degrade to become a neutral gray.

11.6 Video basics

Before we discuss *electronic adjustments* that can alter tonal values in a picture let us look briefly at the *video* or *picture signal* from the camera.

The image from the lens falls onto a CCD imaging device within the camera. Here a charge-pattern builds up, which is propor-

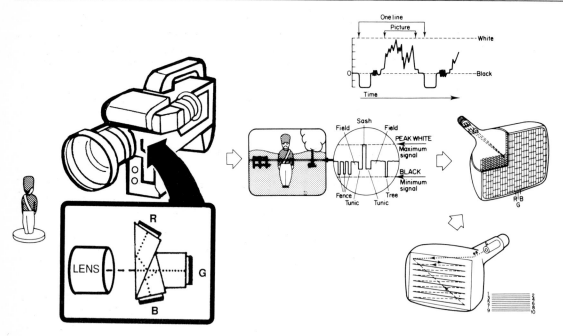

Figure 11.2 Video basics

Inside the camera, a prism splits the lens' image of the scene into three light paths. Each has an image sensor (usually a CCD — charge coupled device — but sometimes a camera tube) with respective red, green, and blue filters. The image of the scene is focused onto the light-sensitive surface of each sensor. There a charge pattern is built up, on many thousands of tiny independent elements, corresponding with the scenic tones. These charges are systematically read out line by line,

to produce a fluctuating video signal. Taking a single line of the picture, you can see how the video varies with picture tones. Regular synchronizing pulses (sync pulses) are then combined with the video so that the entire picture system, from camera to receiver (or picture monitor) scans the picture in exact step. This scanning is done in an 'interlaced' pattern, first tracing all the odd lines, and then the even lines. (This reduces picture-flicker.) The screen of the TV picture tube has three separate patterns of

phosphors. Each glows red, green, or blue depending on its material, when struck by the picture tube's scanning electron beam. The brightness of each tiny phosphor area corresponds with the video strength from the respective color channel at that point. Our eyes cannot resolve the adjacent individual phosphor points, but blend them together, so that their separate red, green, and blue images mix, and form a natural colored picture.

tional at each point to the light and dark there in the image. This pattern is systematically read out ('scanned') to produce a 'video signal'. The maximum of this fluctuating signal corresponds to white points in the picture and the minimum relates to the darkest areas. This is the essence of monochrome TV.

Unbelievable as it may seem, all the colors of the rainbow, the entire light spectrum, can be reproduced simply by mixing together appropriate proportions of red, green, and blue light ('additive mixing'). Blended equally, they produce white light. The color camera relies on this fact.

Shooting through red, green, and blue filters it analyzes the scene, and produces three corresponding video signals. These signals are used to activate the red, green, and blue phosphor dots on the screen of the receiver's picture tube, where they blend to re-create the original color.

Few subjects reflect pure color. Green grass, for example, actually reflects colors over quite a wide range of the spectrum. So as the camera scans different hues in the scene it produces video signals proportional to the color mixture at each point.

The entire TV system, from cameras to home receivers, is made to scan in step, thanks to special 'sync pulses' that accompany the video signals.

11.7 Black level

We come now to the way in which the person controlling the camera performance behind the scenes ('*Shader*'; '*Vision control*') can lighten or darken the entire picture tones.

As the signals from the camera pass through the video system they need to be adjusted to ensure optimum picture quality. They must not, for example, exceed the system's limits. If they do, then the lightest tones will 'clip off' to peak white.

As well as ensuring that the whitest tones in the picture do not 'overmodulate' the video operator adjusts the *black level* (*sit*) of the picture, so that the darkest tones reproduce as black on the screen.

By adjusting a *lift* control all the picture tones can be moved up or down the tonal scale. By 'setting or sitting the picture *up*' all tones will be correspondingly lighter. But the very lightest tones will now be clipped off to peak white. Although the darkest tones will be reproduced lighter, shadow details will not become clearer.

The effect is to 'gray-out' the picture, producing a higher tonal key – very suitable for enhancing the illusion of misty daylight, fog, or an aethereal atmosphere.

On the other hand, moving all the tones *down* the scale (i.e. 'setting or sitting the picture down') the reverse happens. Lightest tones move down towards mid-gray; mid-tones become darker; and the darkest tones will be clipped off to solid black.

This is a useful device when you are using a black background behind a subject or in a graphic, and want the surface to appear completely black. A judicious amount of 'sit' can improve a low-key scene or a night scene, and produce denser shadows.

When you want these special atmospheric effects, careful adjustments to the video can considerably enhance scenic treatment and lighting.

11.8 Gamma

Gamma is a measurement of reproduced contrast. If a system has a *high gamma* the tonal contrast will be coarsened; fewer tonal steps will be discernible in the picture, lightest tones will crush, darkest will merge. Very high gamma pictures have a 'soot and whitewash' tonal crudity.

A *low-gamma* picture will produce a thin, low-contrast picture quality. A very low-gamma picture could appear as a delicate notan or a washed-out, lifeless effect.

Gamma can also be selectively adjusted in order to improve shadow detail or highlight gradation.

Controlling color

11.9 Color impact

In many productions the cameras only show an occasional view of the complete setting, sometimes only at the beginning and end of the show or from limited viewpoints. Much of the time we are watching people in close shots, and only part of the background is visible. (Even that may be soft-focused).

What appears to be an interesting localized splash of color in a long shot can actually dominate the background of a close one, in which it fills most of the frame. Similarly, an attractive combination of wide blue and yellow stripes may provide a totally blue

Table 11.1 Color terms

Achromatic/gray scale	Intermediate tonal steps (*values*) from black to white.
Brightness	Our subjective impression of the amount of light received from a surface. (This may be very different from the true amount being reflected – *luminance*.) *Brightness* is often used to denote *luminosity*.
Complementary colors	In *light*, two colors which, when added together, produce white light (e.g. blue + yellow; cyan + red; magenta + green). In *pigments*, two colors which add to produce black.
Hue	The predominant sensation of color (i.e. red, blue, yellow, etc.).
Luminance/brightness/value	A color's apparent brightness (lightness or darkness).
Luminosity	The perceived brightness of light sources.
Monochrome	Generally refers to 'black-and-white' (achromatic) reproduction. (Strictly, it means varying brightnesses of *any* hue.)
Primary colors	Three spectral colors which, when mixed in correct proportions, produce any other colors of the spectrum. (For light: red, green, and blue.)
Saturation/chroma/ purity/intensity	The color strength; how far it has been 'diluted' (paled, grayed-off) by the addition of white light. 100% saturation represents the pure undiluted color. Desaturation produces pastel colors, such as pink
Shade	A hue mixed with black.
Tint	A hue diluted with white.
Tone	A grayed white.
Value	In the Munsell system indicates subjective 'brightness'.

The terms *hue*, *chroma*, and *value* are used in the Munsell system of color notation.

background behind one person and a totally yellow one for their neighbor's close-up. An impressive sun motif in the center of the back wall of the set may look great in a wide shot, but be seen throughout most of the show as a few meaningless rays crossing the background or a large blob of color that unbalances the composition of shots.

Although in a monochrome system something that is defocused tends to blend into the background behind the subject, in a color picture it can remain dominant, even although it is not clearly seen.

11.10 Compatibility

We have always to distinguish between the *hue* of a surface (Table 11.1) and its *tone*. You can have a multi-color graphic that is pleasing to the eye but contains areas which all have exactly the same tonal or gray-scale value! In this situation the color picture would be fine, but the monochrome version would have the same

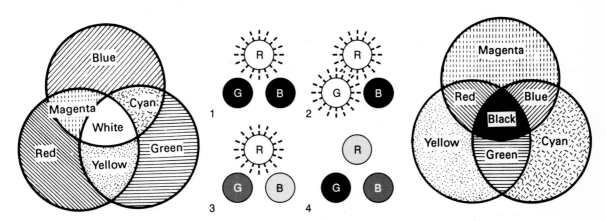

Figure 11.3 Color mixing

Additive primaries. When white light is analyzed it is found to cover a continuous wide visible spectrum from red, orange, yellow, green, blue, and indigo to violet.
Surfaces around us reflect different ranges of the spectrum, which we interpret as their particular 'colors'. (They are really color mixtures; seldom pure colors.)
Conveniently, any light mixture can be analyzed into its respective red, green, and blue components. Mixtures of these *additive primaries* can reproduce most colors. Equal proportions of two light primaries produces a *secondary* color – magenta (purple), cyan (blue-green), or yellow (also know as *subtractive primaries*).

Color mixing. What we call the *hue* results from the *proportions* of red, green, and blue present. The brightness of the mixture (*luminance*) depends on the *quantity* present.
1. If only one set of phosphors is activated, the screen appears of that primary hue (e.g. green).
2. Two or three active phosphors produce additive color mixtures (e.g. R + G = yellow).
3, 4. If all three primary phosphors are activated, but with different brightnesses, we shall see various shades or degrees of saturation (dilution) on the screen (e.g. diluted red = pink; dim orange or yellow = brown). Equal quantities will produce a 'white' area.

Subtractive primaries. Most light covers a range of spectral colors. When it falls onto a surface colored with *pigments* (ink, paint, dyes) much of this light spectrum is selectively absorbed by these pigments. What we actually see, therefore, is *what is left of the original light's component colors*. We call this the surface's 'color'. So the mixing process when using pigments is described as *subtractive*. These facts explain effects that arise when using colored light on colored surfaces.

shade of gray overall! The picture is not 'compatible' for both the color and monochrome receivers.

On a map an island was exactly the same tone as the sea surrounding it! A salutary reminder that it is good practice to work with at least a two-step difference between the tones of a subject and its background, after lighting. This is an extreme case, perhaps, but it has happened.

Fortunately, with experience you can squint at a scene through nearly closed eyes and get a very good idea how relative tonal values will reproduce. (We use the same trick when assessing the contrasts and balance of lighting treatment.)

11.11 Color fidelity

Today's TV cameras achieve much more accurate color quality than hitherto. But there is still a tendency for certain color mixtures to be reproduced inaccurately; blue-greens (cyan) and purples may seem too blue, deep red too dark. A plum-colored dress could appear quite violet on the screen. A tastefully designed blue costume may look rather garish on camera if the reproduced color is too pure (saturated). Green can appear desaturated and darker than normal.

Strong reds can also be troublesome, owing to their propensity to reproduce as noisy, poorly defined areas that 'bleed' into neighboring colors.

Also, of course, if the color balances of two cameras differ we may see the color of a subject change on switching from one shot to another.

Add to that the fact that *picture monitors* can drift as time passes (becoming lighter, darker, redder, or bluer), and the overheard question 'Which of these versions is *correct?*' is not entirely unexpected.

Careful consistent adjustments and advanced circuit design keep such anomalies to a minimum.

11.12 Staging for color

Color is attractive! Color is dynamic! Color has associative impact!

True, but, on the other hand, color can distract. When we want to create delicate, subtle, subdued effects, color can be too prominent. Color too easily becomes brash, vulgar, cheap, tawdry, exaggerated, or tiring to watch.

Most staging for color TV falls into two broad categories – stylized and naturalistic:

● In *stylized* situations you can fully exploit the vigor, excitement, and persuasive potentials of color, to create a vivid background to the action (with pop groups, for example).

However, even there it is best to avoid large areas of unrelieved color. Instead, break them up with scenic elements (columns, screens), or lighting variations (shading, patterns).

● In *naturalistic* situations color needs to be used very selectively, to avoid overemphasis. Here you do not want to overglamorize, arouse false associations, or create the wrong ambiance. Background hues should complement the foreground performer, not dominate the scene.

You will probably make extensive use of paled pastel colors of grayed and darkened hues. For many naturalistic types of production color emphasis is achieved through the use of color in costume, set dressings, and props rather than through large scenic areas of background color.

As a good working principle it is best to choose the surrounding décor to match the unalterable elements of a scene. It is very easy to create strong color effects, but it needs a sensitive interpretative skill to achieve subtle color blends. There is a temptation at times to play safe and resort to gray-scale neutrals.

It can be difficult to simulate sordid, slummy, rundown, drab environments in color, because any pronounced hues immediately add attractiveness to the scene.

11.13 Color illusions

There are a number of psychological effects that we regularly experience when using color. The designer can turn them to advantage.

● The color of smooth surfaces appears more saturated than identical matte ones. Their brightness can change considerably with camera position.
● Specular reflections from studio lighting obscure surface color. They will have the hue of the luminant or, if bright enough, will crush out to a white, detailless patch.
● Under *diffuse light* the color of a surface will appear less saturated and of more even brightness from different angles than when lit by hard light.
● By comparison, a matte surface of the same hue will look desaturated (paled-out) even under directional lighting, with similar brightness from all camera positions.
● Warmer hues (e.g. red, orange) look closer than cooler ones (e.g. blues). Settings finished in warmer colors tend to look smaller, while those in cooler colors appear larger and further away.
● A background color can modify the apparent color of a foreground subject and vice versa. Even a neutral tone can appear modified against a strong color. White, for instance, can appear reddish, bluish, or yellowish, in sympathy with its background.
● Colors appear lighter against black and darker against white. So an orange area against a black background will appear paler

and less intense, while against a white background it will appear more strongly colored.

- Colors have strong mood associations (e.g. the more vibrant, vivacious, upbeat hues, such as red, orange, yellow; the quieter, more contemplative greens and blues). Broadly speaking, the less saturated a color is, the less powerful its effect.
- Some colors have greater attraction than others (yellows and reds, compared with greens and blues). Primaries tend to be more arresting than mixtures, saturated colors more than desaturated (pastel) shades.
- Prominent hues can distract. Where there are several different prominent colors the audience's attention can become divided and compositional unity upset.
- Saturated colors can appear vibrant, forceful, or dynamic. But they can equally well appear gaudy, strident, or obtrusive.

Chapter 12

Lighting and the designer

Scenic design and lighting together create the environment for the action. With a good basic knowledge of lighting principles and techniques a designer can anticipate both opportunities and problems.

12.1 Why light the scene?

Away from the studio there is usually light of some kind around. There is nothing to stop us shooting action using that existing lighting. But whether the resulting pictures are successful or unattractive will be a matter of luck. The light direction may be wrong, resulting in half-lit faces or hot tops to heads. There may be no shadow detail, distracting blobs of light, ugly shadows, prominent picture noise...

Rearranging the subject or shooting from another direction may improve the situation.

By introducing suitable lamps we can overcome such problems and control light direction and picture contrast to suit the shots the director wants. We can enhance the tonal and color quality of the pictures.

In the studio there is no illumination (apart from overhead 'working lights/house lights') until we switch on studio lighting.

12.2 Lighting aims

What are we aiming at when lighting a show? A lot depends on the type of production.

At the most basic level we usually want the performers and the setting to be clearly visible and to create an impression of solidity and space. We need sufficient light for the camera to produce clear, noise-free pictures. At the same time, we must avoid such distractions as hot spots, strong reflections, and ugly shadows.

Lighting is designed to provide an attractive, atmospheric, persuasive picture, with an appropriate ambiance from all camera viewpoints.

Techniques are varied to suit each type of production. In some, emphasis may be on portraiture, while others are more concerned with an impressive spectacular effect. But the underlying principles we shall be looking at remain the same for them all.

Figure 12.1 What lighting can do
Light can conceal and reveal. It can suppress texture.

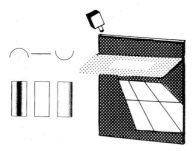

Through shading, it can suggest form that does not exist.
A flat surface can appear curved.
A light-pattern on the wall suggests that there is a window and a ceiling... that do not exist!

The impact of lighting
Under flat lighting we can see all the details of the setting; but the situation is completely lacking in any sort of atmosphere.

12.3 What lighting can do

The appearance of most subjects varies considerably as we alter the angle and intensity of the light falling upon them. It will change, too, with the quality of this light – whether it is diffused ('soft light') or casting strong clear-cut shadows ('hard light').

In fact, simply by adjusting a few lamps we can often make the same setting look alluring, ugly, stark, rich, crude, depressing, or mysterious.

Depending on the lighting treatment used, it can seem on camera to be lit by daylight, firelight, or localized table lamps, or be in 'darkness'.

We can transform the visual impact of the scene slowly and imperceptibly, or instantly on a switched cue. Yet this may only involve readjusting the relative intensities ('balance') of the same set of lamps.

Let's look at typical opportunities lighting can provide. Depending on how we light the scene, we can:

● *Reveal* form, texture, detail – subtly or strongly,
● *Overemphasize* form, texture, detail,
● *Conceal* form, texture, detail,
● *Suggest contouring* where none exists,
● *Imply that features exist* that are not really there (e.g. the shadows of foliage suggesting a nearby tree),
● *Influence the audience's interpretation* of size, distance, space,
● *Provide color* on neutral backgrounds,
● *Modify* existing colors,
● Concentrate on a subject's *outline* and suppress surface contouring and detail (*silhouette*),

With appropriate lighting the setting becomes a real place. This pair of pictures reminds us of the interdependence of good set design, and sympathetic lighting design, to create the final illusion.

- Concentrate on *surface detail*, suppressing surface contouring (*notan*),
- Emphasize *solidity and form* (*chiaroscuro*),
- Create *compositional relationships* (i.e. forming and adjusting tonal masses),
- *Concentrate the audience's attention* on particular features,
- *Move their attention by lighting changes*, subtly or abruptly,
- *Imply the time of day and weather* (e.g. sunny day, moonlit night),
- Develop an *atmosphere or mood*,
- *Create environmental associations* (e.g. bar shadows falling across someone to suggest imprisonment – actual or symbolic),
- *Create visual isolation* (e.g. a series of separately spotlit subjects),
- *Create visual continuity* (e.g. using light to unify a series of separate subjects).

Tone, form and texture

Looking at a flat, two-dimensional picture we get impressions of form, distance, and scale from a series of visual clues. Some of these clues are reliable, others are very subjective, and can fool us at times.

12.4 Tone

Tonal values can strongly influence how an audience interprets a picture.

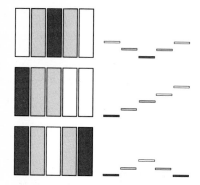

Figure 12.2 The illusion of distance
Tone can influence the apparent distance of a surface. Lighter tones appear more distant. On the screen, a line of identical flats illuminated with different light levels (or painted different tones) will seem to advance and recede, as on the left.

Tones interact. Against a dark background a light area looks lighter and larger than normal.

Tone influences our impressions of *size*. Looking at a picture of two identical boxes side by side, one light- and one dark-toned, we will usually feel that the lighter appears larger than the darker box.

Tone influences our impressions of *distance*. Lighter planes appear further away than darker ones. Consequently, you can enhance the impression of depth in a scene by ensuring that planes are progressively lighter as they get further from the camera.

A setting with light-toned walls will appear more spacious than the same set with dark-toned walls.

We can take advantage of all these phenomena in scenic design; but *light* has a particular advantage. It is *dynamic*. We can emphasize or change tonal impact. In a moment, a mid-gray background can be transformed into a near-white or a black one simply by adjusting the intensity of the lamps illuminating it.

12.5 Surface contours

Looking at a picture of a well-shaped object such as a ball, we see that its surface tones are not even but progressively shaded. These visual clues help us to estimate its form.

What we interpret as 'shading' is simply variation in brightness at each point on the surface, depending on its angle to the light. Where the surface is more oblique to the ray of light it appears less bright from that viewpoint.

Lighting from around the camera's position reduces visual clues of surface contour and texture to a minimum. Where we can see no shading we tend to assume that the surface is flat! As the lighting angle increases, contours become more emphasized.

Bearing all this in mind, it is not surprising to find that we can arrange lighting to create an *illusion* of contours by deliberately varying light intensity, simulating shading, and introducing false shadows.

12.6 Texture

How clearly we can see texture on camera will depend on:

- *Its prominence* – Whether it is slight or pronounced.
- *The surface tone* – It is less easily seen on darker surfaces.
- *The lighting quality* – Texture is most sharply defined under 'hard' light and may virtually disappear under diffused, 'soft' lighting.
- *The angle of the lighting* – Texture is hard to see when light strikes the surface straight-on at right angles and sharpest when light skims along the surface from a shallow angle.
- *Sharpness of focus* – If the surface is not sharply focused, texture tends to disappear.

Basic lighting

12.7 Light-fittings

For all practical purposes, you can assess the various types of light-fitting used in television production as:

- Soft light sources,
- Hard light sources,
- Projection spotlights.

Soft light is simply diffuse, shadowless illumination, the sort of thing you get under an overcast sky, from North light, or a ceiling of fluorescent lamps.

Some lamp designs achieve reasonably soft light by using heavy diffusers over the bulbs, some by internal reflection, while others use multi-lamp clusters. Although illumination from most soft light sources can still cast discernible shadows under certain conditions, in practice these are usually very diluted.

Hard light is the general term for any directional lighting that produces well-defined shadows. It comes from concentrated 'point' light sources, whether these are as powerful as the sun or as feeble as a candle or a match.

The lightweight 'lensless spot' is a typical hard light source. Here a small open bulb is set in a very efficient reflector which focuses its light into a beam of adjustable width (and intensity). Other spotlight fittings have a special 'stepped' or 'fresnel' lens, as well as a reflector system.

Projection spotlights (*ellipsoidal spotlights*, *profile spots*, *effects* or *pattern projectors*) have an optical system that enables them to project a precisely shaped beam of light, patterns of metal stencils ('gobos'), or slides.

12.8 Lamp suspension

Most of the lighting in a television/video studio comes from suspended lamps. This avoids floor space becoming cluttered by lamps or cables, leaving it free for camera movement.

There are various methods of fixing overhead lamps, depending on the design of the studio:

- *Lighting grid.* This is formed from a pipework lattice or ladder beams fixed below the ceiling, some 15–18 ft (4.5–5.4 m) above the studio floor. The piping is typically 1.5–2 in (37–50 mm) in diameter, spaced about 4–6 ft (1.2–1.8 m) apart. Lamps are clamped to the grid or suspended from it as required.
- *Battens/barrels/bars.* In many studios overhead *battens* (e.g. 15–20 ft (4.5–6 m) long) are suspended in a regular pattern, over the staging area. Their heights can be adjusted with rope-and-pulley systems (wall-weights counterbalance the lamps attached to each batten) or by using motor or hand winches.

Figure 12.3 Lamp suspension
Lamps in the studio are supported in a number of different ways. (In this illustration a ceiling 'pipe-grid' is fitted instead of suspended battens, bars, barrels, or telescopes.)
1. Soft light clamped directly to the ceiling pipe-grid (with a C-clamp).
2. Lowered from an extendable hanger (sliding rod, drop arm).
3. A movable trolley holding a vertically adjustable spring counterbalanced pantograph (extends from e.g. 2 to 12 ft or 0.05 to 3.6m).
4. Telescopic hanger on trolley (skyhook, telescope, monopole).
5. In a confined space a spring-loaded support bar can be wedged between walls or floor/ceiling (polecat, baricuda).
6. Telescopic floor stand (1.5–9 ft or 0.45–2.7 m).
7. Clip lamp (spring clamp) attaches lamp to scenic flat.
8. Bracket attached to top of flat supports small lamp.
9. Low-power lamp fitted to camera (headlamp, basher), for eyelight or local illumination.
Safety bonds (wire or chain) should be fitted to all lamps and accessories.

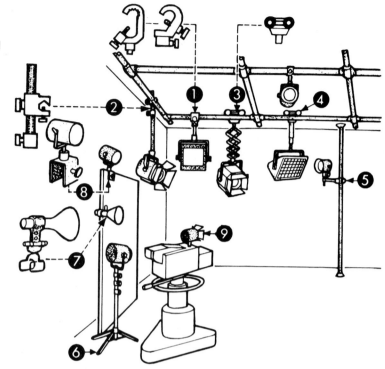

As an alternative, a large number of independently adjusted *barrels* or *bars* (e.g. 4–6 ft or 1.2–1.8 m long) are hung over the staging area, each with its quota of lamps.

● *Separate hangers.* Lamps may be suspended individually on adjusable hangers, telescopic tubes ('telescopes'), or spring-counterbalanced 'pantographs' hung on overhead tracks.

● Additional lamps may be positioned on telescopic floor stands, clamped to the top of scenery or resting on the floor.

The lamp-rigging arrangements in a studio directly affect lighting flexibility. In some studios only a very limited number of lamps are available, and one needs to climb a step-ladder (treads) to attach fittings to the overhead suspension system and adjust them.

In other studios a generous supply of lamps and adaptable supply routing ('patching') cut down rigging time and give greater lighting opportunities. Overhead bars can be lowered to attach lamps. Suspended lamps can be adjusted from the studio floor. A telescopic pole is used to focus and direct the lamp (tilt and pan) and to adjust barndoor shutters.

12.9 Using soft light

We use soft light:

● To illuminate without casting shadows (e.g. where shadows would be inappropriate or confusing),

Figure 12.4 Soft light fittings

Typical units. Examples of typical light fittings producing soft (diffused) light:
1. *Scoop.*
2. *Small broad* (may have barndoor flaps).
3. *Floodlight bank* (*cluster, nest, mini-brute*) consisting of multi-lamp groups of internal-reflector bulbs.
4. Portable bank of fluorescent tubes.

Internal reflection. Some *large broads* rely on internal light scatter to produce diffused illumination.

Cyclorama lighting. The (1) *ground-row* (*trough*) and the (2) *strip-light* (*border light*) are used to illuminate cycloramas and backgrounds upwards from ground level. They are usually hidden behind scenic groundrows.
Suspended forms (3) of cyc/background lighting include single, double, and multi-unit fittings (in-line or grouped), fitted with color media (gels) for color mixing. Certain fittings provide *even* lighting intensity over the entire background. Others require a combination of suspended and floor lamps (Figure 12.9).

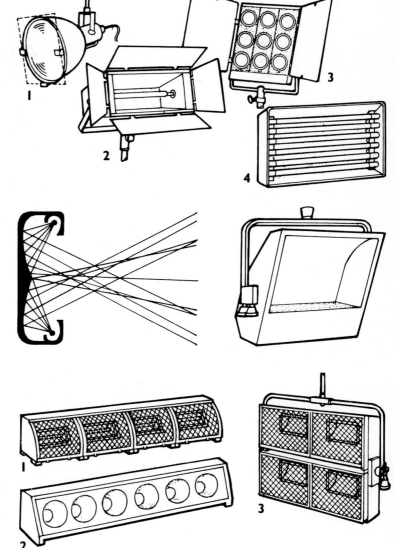

- To reveal detail in shadow areas without creating further shadows,
- To reduce or conceal surface modeling or texture,
- To ensure that no part of the scene is insufficiently illuminated to be visible in the picture,
- To reduce the overall contrast in a scene (i.e. prevent other lighting from exaggerating scenic contrast).

Soft light has disadvantages:

- Its intensity falls off rapidly as the subject moves away from the soft light source.

- Soft light is not easily restricted. It spreads around over a wide angle.
- A subject lit entirely with soft light can be very subtly modeled with delicate half-tones. But the video medium does not reproduce such fine tonal gradations, and instead, the picture appears flat and featureless.

12.10 Using hard light

Hard light forms the basis of most good lighting practice, for it reveals form, modeling, and texture. Depending on how it is used, hard light can create a vigorous, well-defined impact or a crude, harsh effect.

Cast shadows can be attractively decorative, as when the tracery of a grille spreads over the floor. They can reveal subjects that are not visible in the picture (e.g. a person hidden behind a wall).

Hard light has a number of advantages:

- It is easily controlled and directed. A beam of light can be restricted with shutters or flaps (barndoors) attached to the lamp. It is easily shielded off a surface.
- Hard light 'carries well', i.e. its intensity does not fall off badly with distance.
- You can use reflective surfaces to redirect or to soften a beam of hard light.
- Diffuser material over the lamp (spun glass, wire mesh, frosted media) will soften the hard light and also reduce its effective intensity.

Figure 12.5 Hard light accessories

Part 1 *Diffusers* of spun-glass sheet, wire mesh, or frosted plastic can soften the spotlight's beam (overall or locally) and reduce its intensity.

Part 2 *Barndoors* have independently adjustable flaps (two or four) on a rotatable frame to cut off the light beam selectively.

Part 3 A *flat* is a small metal sheet (gobo) to cut light from a selected part of the beam.

Part 4 A *cookie* (*cucaloris, cuke*) is an opaque or translucent cut-out sheet that creates dappling, shadows, light break-up, or patterns.

Part 5 A *reflector* is a white or metallic sheet reflecting light, either to redirect or to diffuse it.

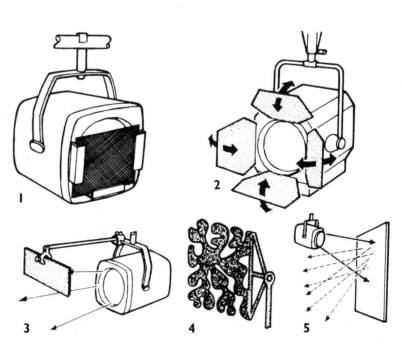

12.11 The effect of light direction

The effect of lighting alters with its angle relative to our viewpoint. If we move round the subject the effect of the light will change.

Because light direction can have a considerable effect on a subject's appearance it might seem that lighting techniques must necessarily be very arbitrary. Fortunately, we can summarize the basics quite simply.

The closer to the lens a light source is located ('dead frontal'), the less will we see tonal and shadow formations that give us clues to surface contours and texture (in other words, the flatter the subject will appear in the picture).

As the frontal light is moved off the lens axis (e.g. by about 10–50°) we shall see shadows and shading form, developing in the direction opposite from the light move.

If you light a surface at a very shallow angle it will emphasize any texture and irregularities, whatever the actual direction of that light. Located to the sides of the subject it is often called *side light*, while from directly overhead it is termed *top light*.

Edge lighting of this kind is fine for throwing into sharp relief the texture of paper, fabric, wood, stone, etc. and for showing up the details of low-relief carving, coins, etc. But conversely, it's obviously something we want to avoid wherever it might show up

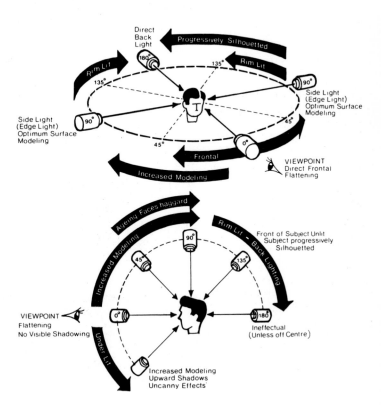

Figure 12.6 Light direction
The lighting angle chosen depends on the particular aspects of the subject you want to emphasize or suppress.
If the camera's viewpoint changes, the effective direction of the light changes correspondingly (i.e. a back light can become a frontal light if the camera moves to the rear of the subject).

and exaggerate any surface irregularities we would prefer to hide (e.g. revealing creases and wrinkles in the surface of a cyc!).

As we move a light source further round the subject the areas facing our viewpoint fall into shadow and its rear surfaces become lit. This *backlight* from behind the subject, pointing towards the camera, appears in the picture as a rim of light along the top and side edges of the subject – hence the term 'rim lighting'.

If the subject is transparent or translucent this backlight will reveal its structure and show the material most effectively.

12.12 Three-point lighting

For many subjects, including people, the most successful lighting approach is to use an arrangement of three lamps – often called 'three-point lighting'.

The strongest is the frontal *key light*, which is normally a spotlight located anywhere from around 10° to 50° off the lens axis (laterally

Figure 12.7 Three-point lighting
There are normally four basic functions in a lighting set-up:
Key light. Generally one lamp (spotlight) in a cross-frontal position.
Fill light: usually a soft-light source illuminating shadows and reducing the lighting contrast. (May not be needed.)
Back light: A spotlight (or two) behind the subject, pointing towards the camera.
Background lighting: Backgrounds are preferably lit by specific lighting, but they may be sufficiently illuminated by the key or fill-light.

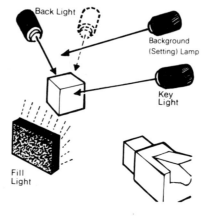

and vertically). This not only illuminates the subject but reveals its modeling and texture. The optimum direction depends on the subject's features and which particular aspects we want to reveal.

On the other side of the camera, diffused lighting from a *fill light* (*filler*) illuminates the shadows cast by the key light, without itself adding more, and confusing the modeling. It is of lower intensity than the keylight.

Finally, there is the backlight, which, as we have seen, provides a rim of light around the subject, revealing edge contours and helping to separate it from the background tones.

12.13 Lighting people

The most exacting part of the lighting process is undoubtedly in providing attractive portraiture for the performers from a number of camera positions. As we have seen, the effect of a given lamp will change as the director switches to a different viewpoint. What was a frontal key for one camera can become a backlight for another! Add to that the fact that people move around and face various directions and the problems in selecting the optimum light directions for the action are not to be underestimated.

When lighting people we usually follow three-point principles. These can be applied equally well to areas (e.g. for a group set-up) or to specific individual positions. Lighting may be varied during action to suit different shots or performer positions.

12.14 Background lighting

Lighting for the setting will usually be of two kinds:

● Areas that are to be lit evenly to provide a similar tone overall,
● Sectionalized lighting, in which specific parts of the set are lit separately by carefully restricted spotlights.

Figure 12.8 Surface brightness

1. The apparent brightness of a surface depends on both the surface tone and the amount of light falling on it. Each of these examples could appear equally bright (i.e. low light on white surface, strong light on darker one).

2. The light is almost completely absorbed by the surface (e.g. black velvet), and so little or none is reflected. The surface appears dark from all directions.

3. A rough irregular surface produces *diffuse reflection*, so light scatters in all directions and the surface appears fairly dark from all positions (a)–(c).

4. A glossy surface produces *spread reflection*. The surface appears fairly dark at (a); fairly bright at (b): and bright from position (c).

5. A shiny surface causes *specular reflection*. From positions (a) and (b) the surface looks fairly dark, while from position (c) it looks very bright.

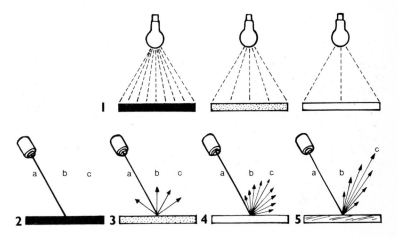

Evenly lit areas (e.g. backdrops, cyc) may be illuminated with soft light units (suspended, on the floor, or both) or by joining together the light from a series of spotlights, to form continuous, even illumination.

Elsewhere in the setting, localized spotlights are used to emphasize carefully chosen features of the setting and build up an appropriate atmosphere.

Effects lighting, such as sunlight through windows, wall shadows and light-patterns, is introduced to suit the situation.

12.15 The need for compromise

In the studio, where scenery and lighting are under our control, it would seem reasonable to assume that difficulties are minimal and that one can easily avoid substandard or unattractive picture quality that changes from shot to shot.

Figure 12.9 Background lighting

Soft overall lighting. Suspended soft lights and soft groundrow lighting combine to provide even overall lighting.

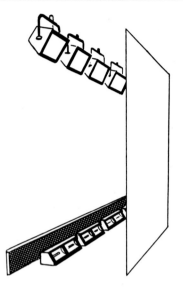

Merged spotlights. A series of spotlights with soft-edged beams merge to provide reasonably even illumination on a background. Fitted with *cookies/dapple-plates* (Figure 4.5), they can produce an overall dappled effect. You can 'spot' (focus) lamps to obtain pools or blobs of light. Barndoors can restrict light into columns, squares, etc.

Localized spotlights. In addition to specific portrait lighting arranged for people (shown here as 'back', 'key'), the set itself is lit with a series of spotlights picking out various features. Ideally, the combined effect of these local lamps should produce an environmental lighting effect, appropriate for the situation (e.g. sunlight).

In practice, though, it is not always possible to put lamps in their optimum positions. A lot depends on the complexity of the show, the construction and form of the setting, how elaborate the camera treatment is, and, of course, the facilities available.

Compromise is inevitable in many situations. Suppose, for instance, we are lighting an 'office setting' and want to cast a shadow on the far wall of a room from the setting sun. We may be able to position a lamp on a floor stand outside the window to do exactly that. No problem.

But what if we have not anticipated this during planning?

● We may find that there is insufficient space for the lamp.
● Or we might discover that the director is going to cross-shoot with a camera that will be looking straight into the lamp!
● Or drapes that have been added over the window, to prevent a camera overshooting the backing, are going to block off all sunlight effects.
● Or the sunlight effect is fine, but now the sound boom is casting an obstrusive shadow from it across the actors!

Do we do without the sunlight, or alter some other aspect of the staging, or the shot itself, to enable the lamp to be placed for the maximum effect? It is then that teamwork pays off, with compromise rather than battle.

It is very frustrating for a designer to find that a set which was very effective in one scene seems to be providing considerable lighting difficulties in another. That is usually because shots and/ or action have changed, and now require quite different lighting treatment.

If, for instance, someone sits at a table beneath a low ceiling it may be simple to light them perfectly from a lamp hidden behind a piece of furniture. But if the camera now moves in close to them (shadowing the lamp), or the person faces the other way, it may be impossible to light attractively or appropriately!

In these circumstances it is not just the lighting director's worry but a problem that the production team has to solve. Clearly, the earlier it is anticipated and overcome, the better, preferably during initial planning.

Glossary

(For other terms see Index)

Abacus. Flat slab at the top of a column, usually bolted on.

Achromatic. Lacking color. Neutral tonal values (white, grays, black) without distinct hue.

Acoustic flat. Flat designed specifically to absorb or reflect sound.

Act drop. In a theater a drape (often front stage) lowered between acts, usually to permit scene changes.

Acting area. The region within a setting in which performance/action takes place.

Action. General term for performance, movement. Usually begins on hand cue from floor manager (FM). (Cue can be taken from light cues, sound cues, action, monitor pictures.)

Ambiant light. General uncontrolled light spilling onto a surface. It tends to illuminate shadows and reduce contrast. Especially refers to random light falling on TV picture display, reducing contrast and degrading its image.

Apron. In a theater an extension of the stage, projecting towards the auditorium (audience area).

Architrave. Plain or molded wooden frame surrounding a door or window.

Arena. A large open acting area, usually with an onlooking audience.

Aspect ratio. The relative proportions of the horizontal and vertical aspects of a rectangular shape (graphic, opening, flat). The TV screen has a 4:3 format (i.e. proportions of 1.33 to 1).

Audience drapes. Drapes hung around audience seating areas.

Audience rostra. Specially prefabricated, stepped platforms, fitted with seating, safety rails, etc. Collapsible for storage.

Baluster. An upright or pillar in a series supporting a handrail to form a *balustrade*.

Batting down on blacks. Adjusting video signal to crush the darkest picture tones to black, particularly to obliterate unevenness in areas required to appear as dense black.

Bight. Loop or slack part of a rope.

248

Black level. The level below which the video system reproduces all signals as black.

Blackout. To switch all lights off (or fade to a blank screen) for effect. In a theater, to make a surprise exit or entrance or alter scenery.

Blocking. The process of rehearsing (or working out) the moves and action of performers/actors, camera shots, positions, etc.

Bloom. (*Burn out*) Area reflecting light beyond the video system's capacity and reproducing as blank white. Due to overlight tone, specular reflection, overlighting, lighting angle, overexposure.

Boat-truck. British term for wagon. Low castered platform supporting scenery to allow easy repositioning or striking.

Bond. Stainless steel wire rope used to support scenery, particularly when very heavy or near lamps.

Book wing. Wing constructed as book flats.

Break. A brief pause during operations/rehearsal. *Also* to dismantle (e.g. to break or strike a set).

Breakaway. (*Break-up*) Prop or scenery designed to shatter easily on impact or to break on cue.

Bridge. A suspended walkway or tubular-scaffolding fixture providing a position for following-spot operation or for rigging lighting equipment.

Busy. Too full of detail, cluttered, overdressed, overdecorated.

Burn in. A retained image from an excessively bright area remaining on the camera tube long after the shot has changed perhaps permanently). (Not normally with CCD image sensors.)

Burn out. See **Bloom**.

Butt joint. Joined edge to edge, without overlapping.

Buttress. Timber or masonry support projecting from or built against a wall to provide additional strength.

Camera mounting. Equipment on which a camera unit (head) is supported: *Dolly* – Any wheeled camera mounting. *Tripod* – Three-legged static mounting. *Rolling tripod* – Camera tripod on wheeled/castered base. *Camera crane* – Large counterbalanced boom on a mobile base, allowing the camera height to be freely adjusted from e.g. 2 ft (0.6 m) to a maximum of 7–9 ft (2–2.7 m) or more above floor level. Particularly used for mobile 'elevated' (high) shots.

Camera rehearsal. Period during which action is rehearsed in the settings while the production team (cameras, sound, lighting, scenic crews, etc.) goes through the planned production treatment which the director assesses.

Camera right. Right-hand side of the picture (performers' left side).

Camera tower. Metal framework with a raised platform (e.g. 9–12 ft or 2.7–3.6 m high) on which a camera can be positioned for high shots.

Canopy. A projecting hood or roof over a door, window, niche, etc.

Catwalk. Walkways allowing access (e.g. in flies).

Ceiling plate. A metal plate with ring, used to suspend ceilings and light scenic pieces.

Center stage. A position in the center of the acting area.

Cheat. To rearrange something from a previously established position in order to improve the composition or mechanics of a subsequent shot (hoping that the alteration will not be detected by the audience!).

Chiaroscuro. The most familiar pictorial style, using light and shade to convey an impression of solidity and depth.

Cladding. Sheets of prepared board, plywood, etc. attached to a structure (e.g. platforms) to provide a smooth and/or decorative surface.

Cleat. A fitting round which a rope can be passed and made fast.

Cleat line. A length of cord used to tie (lash) two scenic units together.

Clew. A steel clamp used to hold several ropes together, and allow them to be hauled as one.

Cloth clip. (*Top batten clip*) When a backdrop has been partly rolled up to shorten its height this metal clip secures surplus material on the support batten and provides a lifting point for flying lines.

Color cast. An overall color bias in a system, causing all hues to be inaccurately reproduced. Particularly noticeable when reproducing neutral gray tones. Due to imbalance between the color primaries.

Comet tail. Camera-tube limitation, producing a trailing smear of light behind a moving specular reflection.

Compatible picture. A color picture that is equally effective in monochrome (black and white).

Concave. Inward curving.

Contrast range. (*Subject brightness range*) The ratio of the lightest and darkest tones in a scene that a *system* can accommodate while still reproducing intermediate tones well (e.g. 30:1). *Also* used to describe the range of tones present in a scene.

Contrast ratio. The relative 'brightness' of any two tones. Given as a luminance ratio (e.g. 2:1).

Contrasty. A picture with extreme tones and few half-tones.

Convex. Outward curving.

Cookie. (*Kuke; Cucalorus*) Large cut-out pattern placed in front of a spotlight to break light into random shadow shapes.

Corbel. Projecting stone or wood block supporting a beam, arch head, ceiling, or other horizontal member.

Cornice. Ornamental molding around the top of a room just below a ceiling.

Costing. The economic assessment of materials, effort, man-hours, equipment, facilities, hire, labor costs, etc.

Crawl. Titles which move vertically up the screen, or across the screen. Used mainly for travelling titles, credits, etc. Produced by a special character generator, or computer program. (Formerly by a hand or motor-driven *caption machine* using titling printed on a long roll of paper.)

Cross-shot. A camera viewpoint that is oblique to the action area as opposed to a *frontal* or *head-on shot*, in which the camera looks straight onto the scene.

Cue. An indication that action is to begin. See **Action**.

Curved cyc. Cyc cloth arranged in a shallow 'C' form for spacious panoramic effect. See **Wrapround cyc**.

Cut cloth. Suspended canvas scenic cloth with *uneven edges* (e.g. profiled to simulate foliage), or *cut-out* (e.g. stenciled for window openings, or to reveal another drop behind it). Large cut-out areas are backed with scrim/gauze.

Cyan. A blue-green hue. Minus red (i.e. white light minus its red component).

Dead. No longer required (of props, scenery), either having been used or found unnecessary. *Also* when suspended scenery is raised/lowered, its required final position is its 'dead'.

Depth of field. Variable range of distances from the camera within which a subject appears to be sharply focused. The depth increases with focused distance, with smaller *f*-stops, and as lens focal length is reduced (i.e. lens angle widened). Often wrongly called 'depth of focus'.

Dipping. Lightly dyeing white or very light-toned fabrics (e.g. coffee or blue tints) to reduce reflectance and avoid 'blooming'/ 'crushing out' on camera. White shirts, blouses, sheets, coats, dust covers, or lace curtains are frequently dipped before use.

Directional lighting. Illumination from a clearly defined direction, usually casting sharp shadows.

Double. Scenery duplicating whole or part of another set (e.g. for 'before-and-after' transformations).

Downstage. In a *theater*, refers to the part of the stage area near the audience or proscenium arch. In *TV*, usually indicates a position *nearer the camera* – whatever the camera position. Hence 'Come downstage a little' means 'Move slightly nearer the camera.'

Drop. Large sheet of painted canvas used for a scenic background. Any curtain lowered from above.

Drugget. A floor cloth of coarse fabric used to reduce foot noise.

Dulling spray. Wax spray, used to reduce shine on glass, metal, polished surfaces. 'Anti-flare'.

Fall-off. The rate at which brightness diminishes over a surface. Gradual shading has a 'slow fall-off'; coarse shading a 'fast fall-off'.

Fascia. Plain horizontal band under eaves or cornice.

Fascia board. A wide board set vertically on edge, above head height.

Festoon border. Border hung in a series of even, U-shaped folds.

Festoon tabs. Curtains opened by drawing the bottom upwards towards the top and/or the sides.

Fill light. Light used to illuminate shadow areas without creating further modeling.

Fire backing. Three-sided hinged board structure placed behind a fireplace flat opening.

Flag. Sheet of metal placed in front of a lamp to block light off a specific area.

Flies. Roof space above staging area. Area above stage where scenery, scenic cloths, lighting equipment, etc. can be raised by lines and held suspended, out of sight of audience.

Flood. General term for soft light source. *Also* adjustment of a spotlight to provide a wide light-beam (hence 'fully flooded').

Floodlight. Light fitting producing soft, diffused light.

Floor lamp. Lamp fixed to an adjustable metal stand, consisting of concentric tubes in a castered tripod base. *Also* a lamp resting on the floor.

Floor monitor. High-quality *picture monitor* on wheeled stand, used in studio to check shots, display film and videotape, show studio output, etc. It has no sound channel.

Floor wash. The process of removing water-soluble paints (hand or mechanical scrubbers) that have been used to tone or decorate the floor.

Flying iron. Hinged ring on metal plate used to suspend scenery.

Free perspective. Design in which normal perspective has been exaggerated in order to enhance the impression of depth in a shot.

French flat. Several flats battened together and flown as one unit.

Gantry. Walkway around upper part of studio wall. Gives access to tying-off points for suspended scenery, lighting, and sound outlets.

Gel. (*'Jelly'*) Colored gelatin or plastic sheeting placed over lamps to produce colored light.

Grummet. Fitting which fixes at the top of a flat to hold flying cables in position, or the knotted end of a lashing line.

Guard rail. Safety handrail around an elevated area beside treads, etc.

Hanging iron. Metal fitting with a square loop fixed to the bottom rail or the stile of a flown flat or frame.

Header. A horizontal surface above head height, simulating a beam or lintel.

High-key scene. Predominently light to mid-tones. No deep shadows.

Hoist. A remotely winched or motorized mechanism controlling a ceiling-located wire cable, used to suspend or support scenery and suspend lighting equipment.

Hot. Any overbright area. It may appear to pale off or reproduce as a blank white patch ('bloom').

Hot spot. Overbright localized patch of light, usually due to specular reflection. *Also* in *rear projection* uneven illumination causing the center of the screen image to be brighter than its edges.

House lights. Powerful ceiling lights used to illuminate the studio for general working purposes (e.g. during rigging, setting, etc.). Switched off when specific production lighting is in use.

Irons. Various attachments permitting flats to be supported by line, suspended or flown – hanging irons, flying irons, fixing irons.

Jelly. Color medium (see **Gel**). *Also* used to indicate 'diffuser'.

Jog. To move a flat forwards or backwards from its original line. *Also* narrow flat used to create a short *return* and suggest wall thickness.

Kelvin. Measurement of the color quality of light; its color temperature. Lower color temperature sources have warm yellowish-red quality (candles, dimmed tungsten). High kelvin sources have cold bluish light (e.g. North sky light, carbon arcs). Typical interior lighting 3200–3400 K: daylight 5600 K.

Key light. Main lamp lighting a subject, responsible for establishing modeling and light direction.

Kill. To remove unwanted props or scenery.

Lag. (*Trailing*) Camera-tube limitation. Persistence or smearing after-image following a moving object. Particularly evident with light-toned subjects in very dark scenes.

Leg. Vertical narrow length of material (usually black) hung at side of stage to mask off wings.

Leg up. To raise the height of scenic unit by adding supports at floor level.

Lens angle. The camera lens sees a 4×3 shaped wedge of the scene. The *horizontal* coverage angle of a lens is simply termed the 'lens angle'. In a zoom lens this can be varied from 'narrow (telephoto)' (e.g. 10°) to 'wide' (e.g. 50°). The lens angle can be drawn on scale plans to show what a camera will see from any given postion. The *vertical* lens angle is three quarters of its corresponding horizontal angle and can be used on scale elevations. HDTV systems use a 16:9 aspect ratio, so that their horizontal and vertical coverage angles are in those proportions.

Lens aperture. (*f-stop*; *iris*) Adjustable diameter diaphragm within the lens housing. Altering its size simultaneously affects the image brightness ('exposure') and the 'depth of field'.

Library shots. (*Stock shot*) A library of filmed or videotaped shots of particular action, subject, location, etc. (e.g. view of Mount Everest) that can be inserted into any program requiring this illustration.

Light level. Intensity of illumination falling on or reflected from a scene. Measured with a light meter in *lux* (formerly 'foot-candles').

Light setting. The process of directing lamps, adjusting their precise angle, coverage, light quality, color, and intensity to suit their individual purposes.

Lighting balance. The relative intensities of lamps that together produce a specific effect.

Line beating. (*Strobing*) A localized rapid flickering effect, as a fine pattern in the scene coincides with TV scanning lines in the picture. Particularly visible on engravings, close horizontal lines, close mesh.

Lintel. Small beam over a door, window, or opening.

Live. An event transmitted as it is happening. *Live-on-tape* is a straight-through recording of continuous live performance.

Louver (louvre). Structure consisting of series of sloping slats (fixed or adjustable) in window or opening.

Luminance. The true measured brightness of a surface. Doubling the illumination produces double the luminance, unlike the impression received by the eye. Snow has a high luminance: black velvet, extremely low luminance.

Man-hours. A unit used in estimating/calculating labor requirements and time for a project (e.g. scenic construction). The theoretical work-effort achieved by a man in one hour.

Marks. (*Floor marks*) Small L-shaped marks crayoned or taped on the floor to indicate the position of furniture, scenery, props, actors' (toe marks), etc. to ensure accuracy in repeated positioning.

Masking. Any surface positioned to prevent the camera from seeing a particular area.

Matte. (*Mask*) Graphic or electronically generated shape used to obscure part of one picture in order that a corresponding area of another shot can be inserted there.

Mause. Safety binding across a suspension hook to prevent a slack line from slipping off.

Miniature. Small realistic replica scene (often called 'model').

Mirror (verb). To reverse a graphic, setting, composition, etc. left to right as if seen in a mirror.

Mirror ball. A suspended motor-rotated ball, completely surfaced with a pattern of tiny mirrors. Lit by a spotlight, numerous points are reflected and traverse the scene.

Model. A construction for demonstration. It may be diagrammatic, symbolic, facsimile; scaled down, full-size; working, demountable, etc. (see **Miniature**).

Move. A planned rearrangement of props or scenery at a given moment. *Also* any repositioning by a performer (e.g. making a move from the door to a chair).

Munsell system. A system of color notation in which pages of sample chips methodically analyze progressively varied hues. Each hue is displayed at varying saturation (chroma) and luminance, so enabling each aspect to be numerically classified or identified.

Narrow-angle lens. A camera lens with a narrow coverage (e.g. <10°). The shot appears to bring subjects nearer, compressing distance, reducing depth and thickness.

Niche. Decorative wall recess.

Notan. Pictorial style primarily concerned with surface detail, color, and outline rather than an illusion of solidity and depth.

O/P side. (*Opposite prompt*) The left side of the stage seen from the audience or camera position. (*Stage right.*)

Off stage. A position outside the acting area. To move 'off stage' is to move away from the center of the acting area.

On stage. A position inside the acting area. To move 'on stage', is to move towards the center of the acting area.

Overnight set. Practice of erecting scenery at night in readiness for early daytime camera rehearsals.

Overpiece. General term for suspended vertical plane or wide arch.

Pack. A series of scenic units stacked in order, ready for setting.

Parapet. Low wall around edge of balcony, bridge, roof, etc.

Pea light. (*Pea lamp*; *Christmas tree light*) Tiny lamp used for decorative effects to simulate stars, etc.

Pedestal. Base of a column, statue, or superstructure. *Also* wheeled camera mounting with central column of adjustable height ('Ped').

Pelmet. Decorative cloth border hung above window curtains to hide supports.

Perch. Platform built to the side of a stage close to the proscenium arch.

Pilaster. A rectangular pier projecting from the face of a wall as a buttress.

Pin hinge. A two-part hinge held together with a removable loop pin (or bent wire nail!). Allows scenery, doors, parallels, etc. to be securely locked together yet instantly dismounted by withdrawing the pin.

Plumbicon. Type of camera tube.

Podium. A continuous low wall or base (e.g. supporting columns). *Also* small raised platform (e.g. for a conductor).

Pre-record. To videotape a section of a show *before* the main recording session. This may be replayed during the main taping session and re-recorded on the master tape or inserted later during *post-production* editing.

Prompt side (PS). The right side of the stage seen from the audience or camera position. (*Stage left*, actors' left.)

Proscenium. In a theater, the space between the curtain and the orchestra ('apron'). Hence the 'proscenium arch' at the front of the stage area.

Rake. To set at an angle. *Also* the slope of a floor.

Ramp. A sloping surface joining two different levels.

Recording break. A period during a videotaping session when recording ceases briefly to allow rehearsal, scene changes, camera moves, etc.

Reflectors. Boards or sheets used to reflect light. In the studio, to obtain very diffused light. In open air, to reflect sunlight (as key or fill light).

Retake. Repeating and re-recording a sequence to improve or correct performance, camerawork, sound, etc.

Reveal. The side of an opening (e.g. door, window) between the outer edge and the frame, simulating wall thickness.

Revolve. A rotatable circular platform built into a stage or raised floor.

Rig. To set up (e.g. to rig a lamp). *Also* a temporary contrivance.
Ring plate. (*Ceiling plate*) A fixing enabling lightweight scenic units to be suspended.
Ruche. To hang material in folds or pleats.

Safe area. Most TV receivers cut off the edges of the picture (up to a 10% margin around the frame). So it is advisable to keep important information within the remaining central safe area.
Safety bond. A wire strop attached to equipment or scenery to ensure its stability, hold it erect, or prevent parts falling off.
Sandbag. A small sand-filled canvas bag hung on unused hanging ropes (to prevent them running back through pulleys). Used to weigh down lighting stands, stage braces, cloths, etc.
Scaffold boards. Planks laid across scaffolding to provide walkways. Cut sheets of prepared board may be screwed to them to form continuous, smooth flooring surface.
Scene dock. Scenic storage area, usually adjacent to the studio.
Scrim. Diffuser (spun glass or wire) placed in light-beam to diffuse it and/or reduce its intensity.
Setting line. A line drawn on the studio floor showing exactly where a setting is to be built. *Also* a floor line showing the boundary limits for staging.
Shot. The picture sequence between two transitions (cut, mix, etc.). *Also* a description of a specific camera set-up (e.g. image size, height, etc.).
Shrink mirror. Metalized plastic sheeting attached to a support frame then heat-shrunk to tauten.
Silhouette. Pictorial style concentrating entirely on subject outline, filled in with solid color (usually black).
Skid. A small movable trolley attached to a ceiling girder. Fitted with e.g. pulley and rope to hoist or suspend scenery or lighting equipment.
Skip. Wheeled basket or container, used to transport props, drapes, etc.
Slashed curtains. An ornamental curtain made from vertical PVC strips (e.g. 0.25–3 in or 5–75 mm wide).
Soffit. The horizontal undersurface of a beam, arch, vault, stair, cornice.
Special effects. Specialists responsible for the creation and operation of a very wide range of physical illusions, including catastrophes, destruction, fire, gimmick apparatus, 'impossible' monsters, etc.
Specular reflection. Localized, very intense reflection of a light source.
Spill light. Accidental illumination (e.g. light falling onto adjacent walls as distracting streaks or blobs).
Spot. General term for spotlight. *Also* concentrated area of light. *Also* adjustment of a spotlight to provide a narrow light beam.
Spotline. A single, specially rigged line (rope) (e.g. from the flies) in addition to regular scenic hoists.
Stage cloth. A large canvas or plastic sheet used to decorate or protect the floor.

Stock shot. See **Library shot**.

Stop, lens. See **Lens aperture**.

Streaking. Picture defect in which spurious horizontal bars spread across a picture from high-contrast scenic features.

Strike. To dismantle scenery.

Subtractive color mixing. White light covers the entire color spectrum through red, orange, yellow, green, blue, indigo, and violet. When it falls on a colored surface each color pigment there absorbs (i.e. subtracts) light over its own part of the spectrum. What we see is a reflected mixture of the remainder of the spectrum. The pigment color primaries are magenta, cyan, and yellow. If mixed, each subtracts part of the white spectrum and little remains to be reflected (i.e. the surface appears black).

Swag. ('*Festoon*') Material hung in decorative loops – often of uneven depth – in hung curtains, borders, legs.

Swivel clew. A swiveled device enabling several suspension cables to be hauled with a single line.

Tabs. See **Traveler**.

Tablature. Flat surface with design, inscription, or painting.

Tap mat. Mat used to emphasize the sound of tap dancing. Made of narrow wooden slats fixed to a canvas backing.

Teaser. Overhead material strip used to hide lights and studio and avoid overshooting.

Throwline cleat. Attachment for guiding a line when lashing flats together.

Tie-off cleat. Attachment for guiding and trapping lashing line in order to pull it tight.

Tormentor. Flat or curtain projecting either side of the proscenium stage to conceal the wings and backstage from the audience and to reduce its effective width.

Track. Any overhead rail enabling suspended curtains to be moved along on runners.

Trailer drapes. Background drapes that open and close on a horizontal track.

Trailing. Picture defect in which a smeared image persists behind a moving object.

Traveler. ('*Tab track*') Overhead rail suspending curtains on rolling or sliding carriers. A pulley system allows curtains to be operated from side-hanging lines.

Trip. When there is insufficient studio height to *fly* a suspended drop or horizontally hinged flat (i.e. pull it vertically out of sight) its lower edge may be raised by attached lines, folding it back to about half its original height.

Tubular. Light, general-purpose metal tubing used to suspend scenic units, drapes, etc.

Tumble. A drop/cloth wound round a pole and rolled up/down with an attached pulley system.

Tumbler. Pole or batten attached to bottom edge of a drop/cloth for storage and to bottom-weigh the suspended drop.

Turntable. Horizontal circular table slowly rotated to display the subject.

Upstage. Strictly speaking, the area near the back walls of a setting. In *TV*, usually indicates a position further from a particular camera. Thus 'Go upstage a little' means 'Move away from the camera.'

Valance. Short curtain or drape hanging from the edge of a shelf, table, etc. often to the floor. *Also* short drapery or board hiding curtain rods, etc. ('pelmet').

Velour. Cotton fabric with deep pile; very light-absorbent; rich appearance. Mainly used for impressive drapes.

Videotape (VT). System for recording picture and sound simultaneously on magnetic tape. There are several incompatible systems. The tape can be replayed instantly and re-used. Editing involves replaying and re-recording tape on another recorder.

Wall brace. Scenic brace used to support scenery. Attached to a fitting in the studio wall.

Wide-angle lens. A camera lens with a wide coverage (e.g. $>45°$). In the shot, subjects look further away than normal; space and distance appear exaggerated; depth and thickness emphasized.

Winch. A drum or cylinder on which rope or cable is wound. Used to hoist or suspend scenery. Manually cranked or motor operated.

Wind machine. Large electric fan of adjustable speed used to simulate wind effects.

Window, bay. A three-sided window structure jutting out from the wall-line of a building and forming an alcove within.

Window, bow. A curved form of **bay window**.

Window, casement. Window opening on side hinges; often a centrally opening pair of windows.

Window, french. (*French door*) Casement door. Long window reaching to floor level, centrally opening on side hinges.

Window, sash. Vertically sliding windows within a frame, balanced by side counterweights.

Wing. Vertical drape or flat used at either side of an acting area to conceal the wings.

Wings. Working space offstage to left and right of main stage or acting area.

Working light. Any light introduced to enable craftsmen, performers, etc. to see what they are doing when there is insufficient lighting (e.g. behind scenery).

Wrapround cyc. Cyc arranged as a straight rear wall with straight side walls at right angles.

Zoom lens. Specially designed camera lens with a continuously adjustable lens angle (focal length) between certain limits (e.g. 10–30°; a 3:1 ratio).

Further reading

If you want to explore further aspects of television/video production in greater detail the following companion books by Gerald Millerson are available from Focal Press.

The Technique of Television Production
An established standard textbook used in universities, broadcasting organizations, TV and film schools throughout the world. This is a detailed practical discussion of the mechanics, techniques, and aesthetics of the medium. It explains the power to persuade and the nature of audience appeal.

Video Production Handbook
This realistic, practical guide to low-cost video program-making explains how to achieve professional standards with limited facilities and a restricted budget.

Effective TV Production
This is a 'succinct but thorough overview of the production process' (*American Cinematographer*) distilled for rapid study into a single volume.

Video Camera Techniques
A quick, lucid guide to the essentials of handling video cameras.

The Technique of Lighting for Television and Motion Pictures
An internationally established source-book, discussing in detail the principles and techniques of the art of lighting.

Lighting for Video
A rapid guide to the practical lighting techniques in television and video production.

Index

PALETTE EIGHT: IRIDESCENT

Holograph
in design

PALETTE EIGHT: IRIDESCENT

ACKNOWLEDGEMENTS

We would like to thank all the designers and companies who were involved in the production of this book. This project would not have been accomplished without their significant contributions to its compilation.

We would also like to express our gratitude to all the producers for their invaluable opinions and assistance throughout this entire project. Its successful completion is also owed to the many professionals in the creative industry who have given us precious insights and comments. And to the many others whose names are not credited but have made specific input in this book, we thank you for your continuous support the whole time.

FUTURE EDITIONS

If you wish to participate in viction:ary's future projects and publications, please send your website or portfolio to submit@victionary.com.

P08 IRIDESCENT

First published and distributed by
viction:workshop ltd.

viction:workshop ltd.
Unit C, 7/F, Seabright Plaza, 9-23 Shell Street,
North Point, Hong Kong
Url: www.victionary.com   Email: we@victionary.com

@victionworkshop
@victionary_
@victionworkshop

Edited and produced by viction:ary
Concepts & art direction by Victor Cheung
Book design by viction:workshop ltd.

ISBN 978-988-77747-2-3
Printed and bound in China

PRE
PREFACE
PREFACE
FACE

From sublime applications of simple black-and-white contrasts to designs finessed with in-your-face fluorescent tones, our PALETTE series to-date has explored the inspiring possibilities of popular flat-colour ranges through artist and designer work that push creative boundaries.

In pushing our own, we conceptualised PALETTE 08 by going back to the basics of colour itself. Based on its general attributes and variations, we challenged ourselves to discover what its ultimate manifestation would be, and how it could change the means with which artists and designers ideate and create.

Iridescence can be likened to both a colour and a palette existing in a single form. It is a phenomenon that occurs when certain surfaces appear to change colours depending on where the light hits or where the viewer looks, due to how the surfaces' microscopic structures interfere with illumination and pigments. The word 'iridescence' itself originates partly from the Greek word 'iris', which means rainbow, and derives from the name of a goddess in Greek mythology.

Even though human beings have been known to fascinate themselves with the interplay of light and colour since birth, iridescence in the design world has only become more ubiquitous over the recent years. In an interview with Meg Miller of Co. Design, executive director of the Pantone Color Institute Leatrice Eiseman traces the rise of translucent designs back to where it all started: Philippe Starck's renowned Louis Ghost Chair in 2001. Although its alluring attributes have continued to be harnessed and refined for new creations, the popularity of iridescence today is mostly owed to the rise of technology that has made the sky the limit.

As there is no uniform process to artificially produce iridescence, artists and designers like the ones featured in this edition have been finding much room for experimentation and play. From using glazes and colour-changing films for a multidimensional illusion to manipulating materials such as plexi-glass, acrylics, and plastics to build innovative products and environments, the compelling purpose, impact, and raison d'être of iridescence in their work often outweigh the costs of trial and error.

Like its own kaleidoscopic character, iridescence carries multiple roles in design. To create depth, balance, and points of interest on a monochromatic base, holographic foil is a weapon of choice. While the result can be subtle yet meaningful, as in Design Ranch's 'Lux Naturalis' invitation cards for the Spencer Museum of Art, it can also capture the viewer's attention in a bold and gripping manner. Vanja Golubovic and Tibhaud Tissot's flyers for Homériade exemplify this effect by using it to embody The Illiad and The Odyssey's symbolic tumultuous sea.

For editorial, fashion, and packaging designs, the reflective and refractive qualities of iridescence can serve to reveal or conceal the essence of a project in intriguing ways, such as Noviki's psychedelic cover for the Encyklopedia Polskiej Psychodelii, Evin Tison's crystallisation of the female form through clothes, and Daniel Barkle's print work for Holography., an underground music exhibition. Furniture by Patricia Urquiola for Glas Italia and Saerom Yoon also tap into the same transformative properties to shift perceptions and renew appreciation of the pieces at every angle.

In the art and sculptural domain, iridescence can evoke surreal and dreamlike connotations as well as atmospheres that could be deemed futuristic. While selgascano's structure for the 2015 Serpentine Pavilion is a clever combination of light and shadows that invites viewers into an intergalactic cave of wonders, digital artists like Six N. Five and YUNGBLD masterfully apply holographics onto their 3D canvases to depict new multichromatic realms.

As much as we would like to think that we have found the most powerful palette of all, this edition might merely be scratching the surface of what tomorrow could bring. In showcasing the malleable nature of iridescence as brought to life by our talented contributors in ways that stretch the imagination, we can only look forward to more line-blurring colour concepts in the years to come.

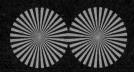

"Iridescence has always fascinated us and captured our attention. To us, it is like a breath of fresh air."

The design industry is changing, and the means and methods with which we express ourselves today are inevitably changing along with it. We are constantly evolving from old-school practices that are becoming less and less relevant; saying goodbye to things like letterheads on paper. In fact, we have not sent documents by fax in a long, long time.

In leaning towards new materials and experimentation over the recent years, creative entities like ours have been continuously exploring to go far beyond designing just a logo or business card. By tapping into inspiration that can now be found anywhere and anytime from anyone, a simple spark is all it takes to strengthen an ideal or point of view and propel ourselves further.

Futura was founded in 2008 by Vicky González and Iván García. The intersection of two different backgrounds and working methods gave the studio a unique way of approaching projects by finding the balance between stiffness and rebellion. What they both had in common was key to laying the groundwork and forming the values that drive us to this day, whether it is being fearlessly obstinate when it comes to good design or always choosing great people and projects over monetary rewards.

At Futura, we value intelligent provocation. By believing in the atypical — function before form — we celebrate clarity of content. We strive to make each identity we design timeless. We want to create brands that are authentic and take you by surprise through provocative images, beautiful objects, ergonomic spaces, and friendly interfaces. In doing so, we have had to ditch past rules and paradigms, opening new doors to experimentation in the process.

With this ethos in mind, iridescence has always fascinated us and captured our attention. Part of the reason why it is experiencing a boom in design today is the extreme minimalism, super-clean aesthetics, and excessive use of neutral colours such as white and black that have become all too prevalent in everything else out there. To us, it is like a breath of fresh air. Coupled with our love for colours and textures, particularly metallic ones, we have been ready for a brighter and shinier palette like this for a long, long time.

WORD
FOREWORD
FORE
FOREWORD by
FORE
FUTURA

Thanks to technological advances, there are many new ways of creating iridescence. There are also no rules as to how to achieve the perfect effect, which is interesting to us, as we do not even have to stay on a two-dimensional plane. By experimenting with an infinite combination of materials such as acrylic, glass, and plastics, we can manipulate and play with light and volume as many architects, industrial designers, fashion designers, and artists are currently doing. Consequently, iridescent materials and finishes have become a lot more accessible — challenging us to see how far we can go with them.

Lately, there has been a revival in the Finish Fetish and the Light and Space Movement. Exhibitions and installations by artists like James Turrell, Craig Kauffman, and Robert Irwin are enjoying impressive turnouts all over the world. While appreciating their work, it is impossible not to become immersed in the concepts of technology and futurism, such as the way a Turrell piece is bound to evoke a certain kind of melancholy towards the unknown. There is something about the colours and the dim light he uses that transport the viewer to a completely different world; an amazing world that we, too, hope to be part of creating.

We are fortunate to live in Mexico, an amazing country where design is vibrant, organic, and everywhere. More and more people have been showing interest in good design, good architecture, and good art in recent times; which is why the city is home to some of the best international fairs like Zona Maco, Salon Acme and the Material Art Fair. Amidst this setting, Futura wants to change the world. We want to make objects that go far beyond their purpose and intrigue our audiences. Through our specialisations in art direction, brand development, interior design, and architecture, we will continue approaching things differently, experimenting, and creating memorable and easily recognisable brands with personality. There are always new trends in the design world, so why not come up with something different than what you are expected to?

HIGHLIGHTS

Black & Bone

Black & Bone is an edgy womenswear label that brims with attitude. To appeal to its young and style savvy audience, Parámetro Studio designed a fresh and modern branding suite that anchored on a solid sans-serif type. Holographic foil was merged with black and white to create both contrast and balance between all the materials.

Parámetro Studio

Client: Black & Bone

Joaquin Homs

Using typographic hierarchies as the guiding concept, Anagrama's brand identity project for renowned architect Joaquin Homs exemplifies his diverse skillsets in a timeless way. The customised logotype is a stylish touch that represents his studio as a fashion design house would, while the neutral colour palette allows for the variety in his portfolio to be distinct. Holographic and metallic details highlight the contemporary touches prominent in his work.

Anagrama

Client: Joaquin Homs • **Photo:** Caroga Foto

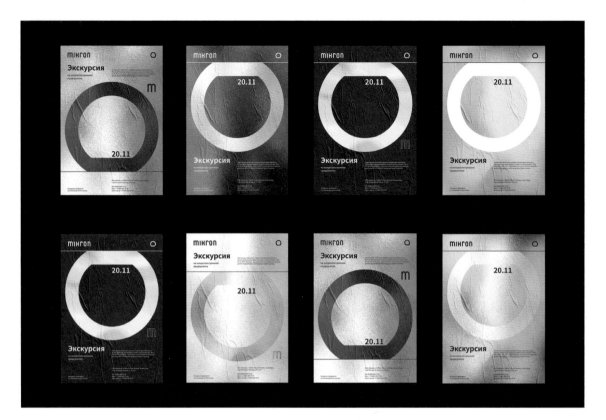

mikron

JSC mikron is a leading manufacturer in the Russian semiconductor industry, and one of the top five micro-electronic enterprises in Europe. Radmir Volk built its identity suite upon an accurate grid that reflects the process of producing microchips in 'clean rooms', where even a speck of dust can disrupt operations. Holographic foil was used to manifest the form of crystalline silicon on which microchips are grown.

Radmir Volk

Client: JSC mikron • **Art Direction:** FRESHBLOOD

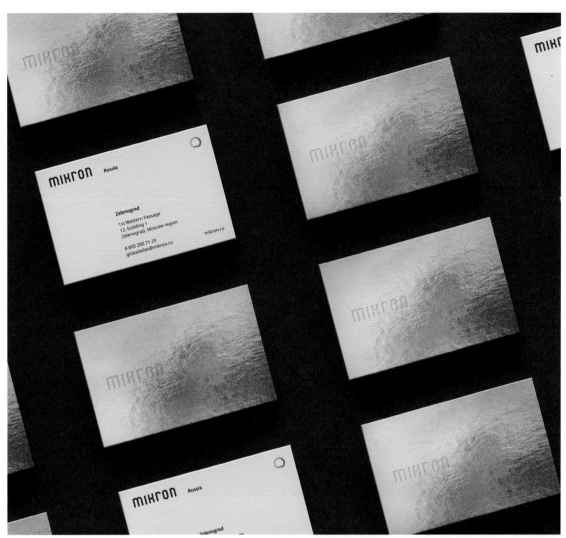

Selected Europe

For Selected Europe, a two-day event focusing on visual creativity and inspiration across different design disciplines in the region, Mubien created a schedule based on Style Wars, a documentary featuring the 1982 anti-graffiti campaign in New York. Using different stamping prints, they turned the actual campaign slogan into graffiti itself to invert the message; making it more meaningful with the added context of the event.

Mubien

Client: Selected Europe

PONYO PORCO GAME CALENDAR 2018

PONYO PORCO's 2018 calendar doubles as a playable retro handheld console, where each month is a different game. The fluorescent and holographic hues coupled with the LCD displays, control buttons, and knobs evoke a sense of nostalgia and child-like fun.

PONYO PORCO, Chu Ling

Printing: 33print

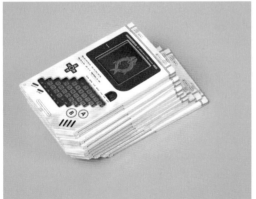

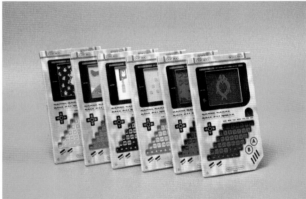

"Compared with gold and silver, the rainbow is young and lovely."

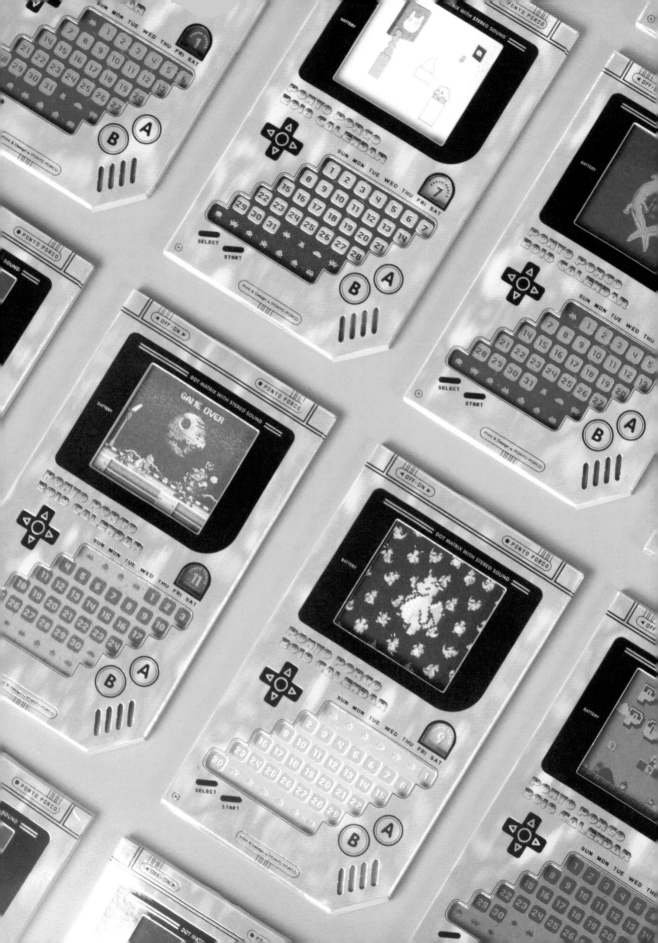

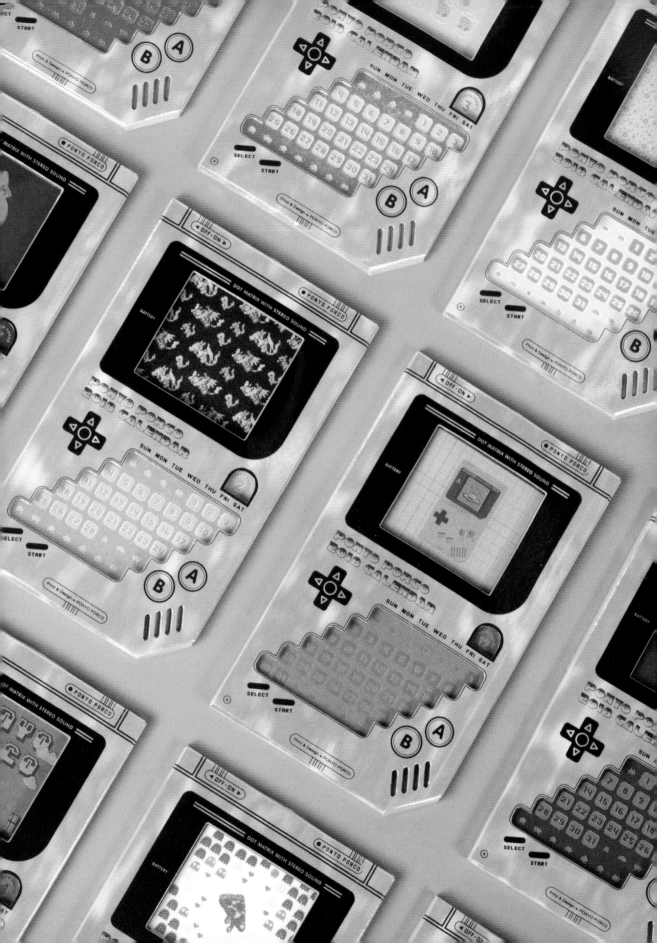

Sphynx

As a brand that seeks to modernise and simplify existing beauty routines, Sphynx's visual language needed to convey accessibility, friendliness, and a pop of fun. Anagrama achieved that by using intense colours, dynamic textures, and holographic foils to convey modernity, vibrancy, and a sense of joy through its communication materials.

Anagrama

Client: Sphynx • **Photo:** Caroga Foto

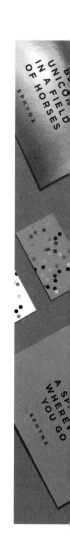

Material Art Fair

Material Art Fair is a contemporary art fair in Mexico City that is dedicated to emerging practices. Anagrama's design work conveys the essence of the event in a conceptual but careful way, where each piece is unique without overpowering the overall brand personality. The combination of elements adds a sense of spontaneity and dynamism, while the colours and compositions reflect the merging of street art and modern art.

Anagrama

Client: Material Art Branding •
Photo: Caroga Foto

Cocofloss

For Cocofloss's branding and packaging project, Anagrama used vibrant visual language to highlight the company's fun approach to promoting dental floss. The interplay of various graphic elements results in an eye-catching distinction from the age-worn clinical white hues of common oral care products. A holographic finish from metallic foil contrasts against pastel tones to enhance the association to liveliness and cleanliness.

Anagrama

Client: Cocofloss • **Photo:** Caroga Foto

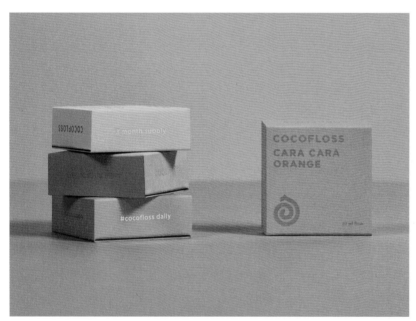

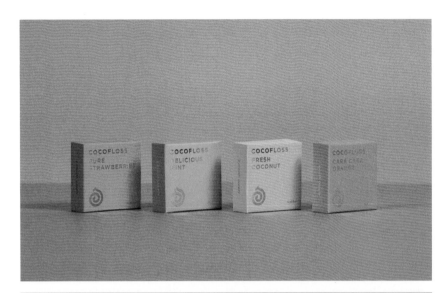

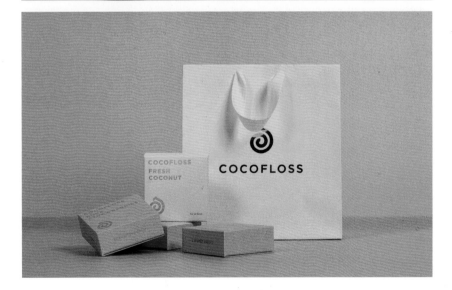

EAT ME

To make a set of small-square chocolate bars stand out on the shelf amongst other brands, Packvision used a textured, iridescent finish in its packaging design work. By harnessing the unpredictability of holographic material with geometric patterns to produce interesting and unexpected effects, a simple everyday product was made bright and fun.

Packvision

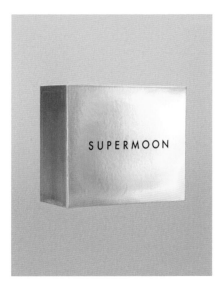

Supermoon Bakehouse

Supermoon Bakehouse offers various croissants and doughnuts with decadent fillings. To reflect its adventurous flavours and over-the-top pastries, co-owner Aron Tzimas conceptualised fun and flashy designs for the bakery, including iridescent boxes and a cheeky neon sign that would appeal to the new generation of foodies who love sharing their food on social media.

Aron Tzimas

Photo: Drex Drechsel

Identity 2018

For the launch of his new portfolio site, Daniel Barkle refreshed his identity suite using a type-led design approach. Besides hand-embossing the face logo that he had previously been known for, he also created a new logotype and used holographic paper stock for an updated and fun aesthetic.

Daniel Barkle

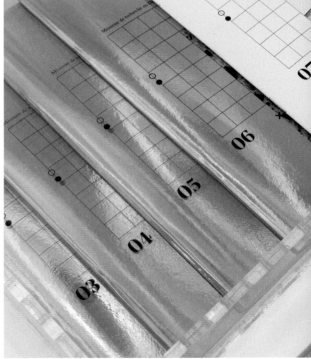

Dealing with the Book — Order and Disorder, Shaping as In-between

There is more to a book than its physical form, and how it came to be is a result of over 21 centuries of transformation. Alycia Rainaud explored what codex is as a symbolic form, an ordinal form, and an open form in her thesis, using a transparent and holographic layer as the cover to embody a book's hybrid nature. She also sought to crystallise how order and disorder can be parts of a book's shape.

Alycia Rainaud

"Iridescence is about manipulating or contemplating by searching for the right angle to catch the right light."

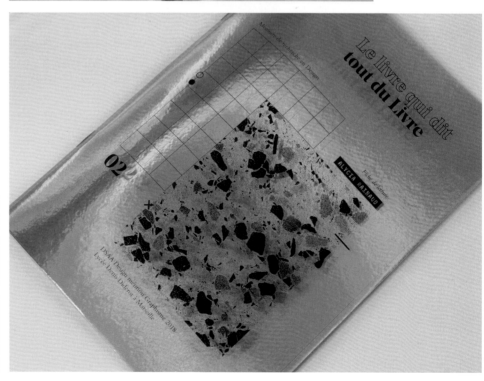

Note and Annual Book

Alexia ROUX gave her self-produced notebook and annual book a personal and artisanal touch by layering a transparent holographic sheet over a pink cover to produce a distinctive effect with visual interest and dimension.

Alexia ROUX

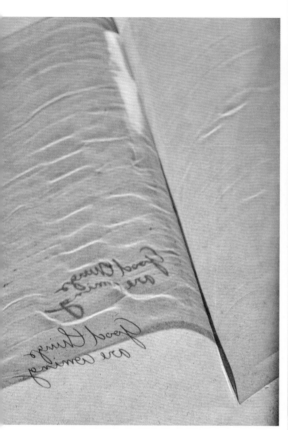

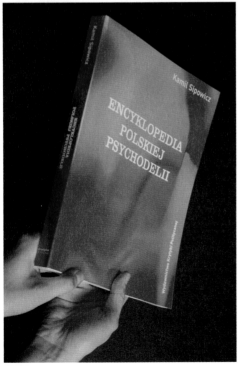

Encyklopedia Polskiej Psychodelii

Noviki's psychedelic cover design for the Encyclopaedia of Polish Psychodelia cleverly encapsulates the book's comprehensive content. By using a holographic sheet as the backdrop for the title's serif type, they found a balance between the kaleidoscopic nature of the subject matter and the function of the book as a repository of facts and forgotten episodes from the lives of artists and writers.

Noviki

Client: Political Critique • **Text:** Kamil Sipowicz, Jaś Kapela

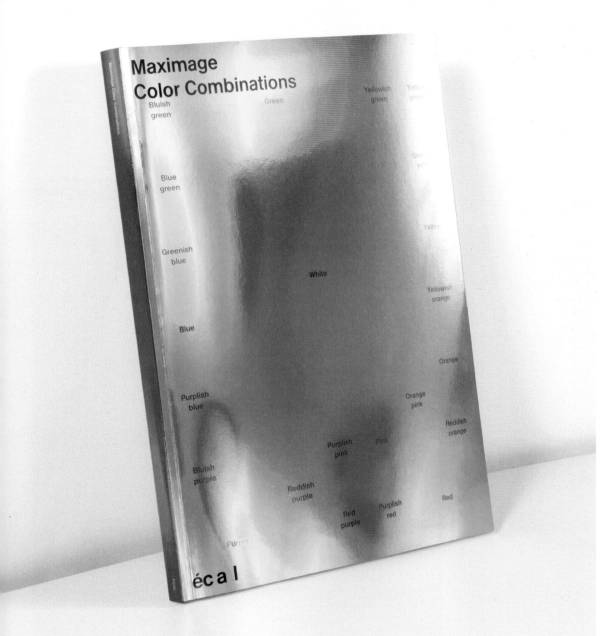

Maximage Color Combinations

Maximage Color Combinations explores how different colours interact and merge from one to another without chapters or formulas to form personalised palettes. Each book contains a set of totally unique colour combinations created directly in the offset press by interfering with the ink unit, with a holographic cover representing its essence. This publication is part of 'Workflow', a research project led by David Keshavjee, Guy Meldem, Tatiana Rihs, and Julien Tavelli (Maximage).

ECAL/University of Art and Design Lausanne

Printing: Benjamin Plantier, Thomi Wolfensberger, Maximage

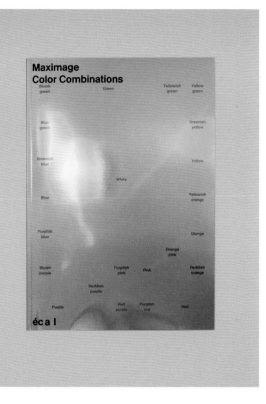

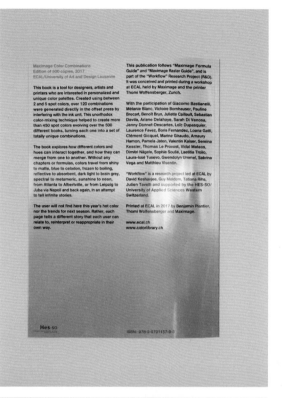

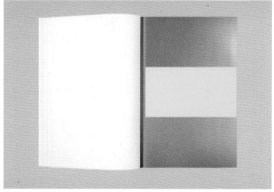

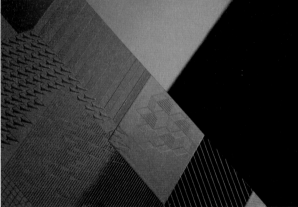

NOVUM Magazine 3/18 — Golden City Lights

To mark 7 years since designing their last cover for NOVUM, Paperlux Studio equated all the unique adventures and experiences the magazine has shared over time with a 'golden moment'. This idea was translated via a new printing technique that pushed the boundaries of colour and movement within a printed object called Scodix, where foils and varnishes could be 100% digitally transferred onto paper. Matt and shiny effects were used to achieve a special effect for a very special edition.

Paperlux Studio

Client: NOVUM Magazine • **Photo:** Michael Pfeiffer

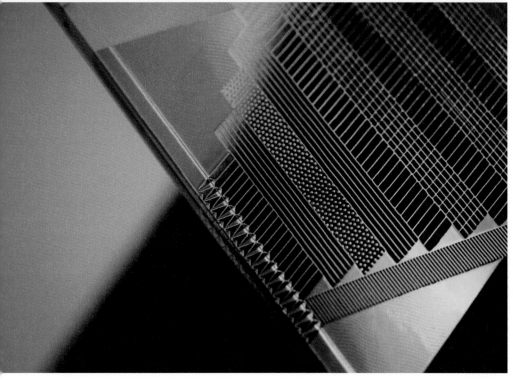

From A to Z: The Alphabet Poster

For his 2018 self-promotion exercise, Mateusz Witczak
custom-made a folder containing an alphabet poster,
envelope, letterhead, and business card. Everything was
designed from scratch with a pencil, and carried through
the graphic design process using the highest quality
of craftsmanship and printing techniques available.
The hot-stamping finish sheds light on his impeccable
attention to detail.

Mateusz Witczak

"[Iridescence] allows one to create a new visual universe still little-known to the general public."

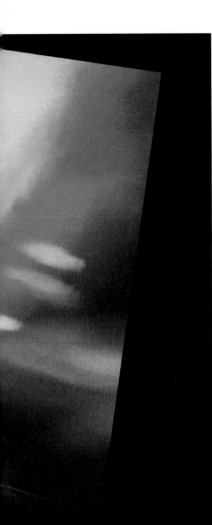

Cycladic

bonjour garçon studio designed a flexible visual identity for Cycladic Label after being inspired by all the artists and musical styles that the company represents. They used a photograph of a piece of holographic paper as the base of the branding suite, so that its prism-like colours would showcase the multifaceted aspects of the company.

bonjour garçon studio

Client: Cycladic Label

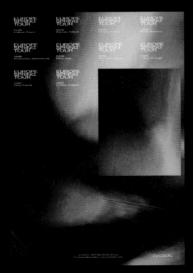

Young Black Youth

For a clothing label that 'dresses in black and white, but thinks in colour', Studio Band designed a branding system and website using holographic hues, bold typography, and eye-catching imagery. Through the clever composition of luminescent text against a black backdrop, the name cards express a sense of youthful confidence that Young Black Youth emanates.

Studio Band

Client: Young Black Youth

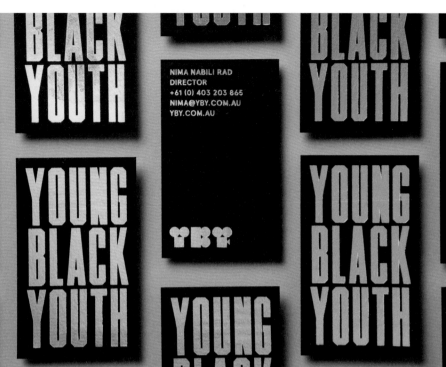

Homériade

Homériade was a play directed by Alexa Gruber based on Homer's classics, The Iliad and The Odyssey. To match its contemporary interpretation of the poems, Vanja Golubovic and Thibaud Tissot applied silk-screen print on holographic paper to update the symbolic visual of ships on a tumultuous sea. The reflective effect suggests crashing waves on a misty night in a compelling way.

Vanja Golubovic & Thibaud Tissot

Client: Alexa Gruber

HaslerWein Panorama

Swiss wine producer Lukas Hasler thinks of wine as the zest of life itself captured in a bottle. For the launch of his new wine and tasting bar, Selina Gerber designed invitation cards reflecting his ethos, based on the concept of 'a glass full of life'. Through the die-cut, coloured papers evoke different landscapes, people, and meanings, while holographic gradient sheets result in a more vibrant, dynamic, and playful look.

Selina Gerber

Client: Weinkellerei Hasler AG • **Agency:** In Flagranti AG

"Holographic designs captivate through their play of colours."

Book, Tale, Page, Read

Book, Tale, Page, Read is a series of hot-foil bookmarks that were created for and during the 2018 Open Days of ECAL. Designed by teaching assistants Amaury Hamon, Eilean Friis-Lund, and Thomas Le Provost, each of the four visuals represent concrete poems depicting the process of reading and designing books. They also experimented with various foils in collaboration with printer Benjamin Plantier for an eye-catching finish.

ECAL/University of Art and Design Lausanne

Typeface: Eddy by Eliott Grunewald & Anna Toussaint

Forward Consulting — 2018 Notebooks

Nonverbal Club were commissioned by their long-term printing partner to design a series of notebooks that showcased special finishing processes, where ink could be printed directly over metallic and holographic foils, and 3D varnishes could be applied at high levels of precision. They were inspired by their partner's global network to illustrate projections of the Earth and expanded typography; leveraging on the finishing processes to change the colours, brightness, and materiality of the notebook covers.

Nonverbal Club

Client: Forward Consulting • **Printing:** Estúdio Gráfico 21 • **Photo:** Dinis Santos

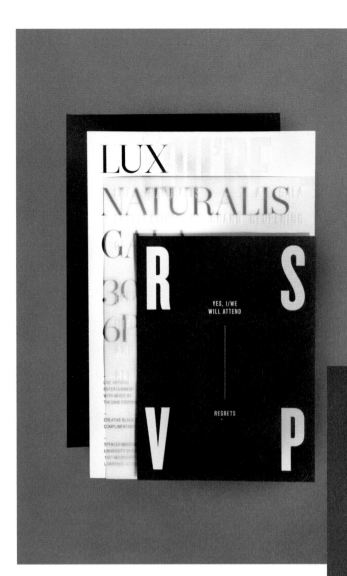

Lux Naturalis Invitations

For Spencer Museum of Art's grand re-opening gala, Design Ranch were inspired by changes to the building itself. They revolved their design work around interesting type, and then let unique processes and details take over. A clear holographic foil was used to get recipients to see the invitations from new perspectives; reflecting the way that visitors would be experiencing art in the newly renovated museum.

Design Ranch

Client: Spencer Museum of Art

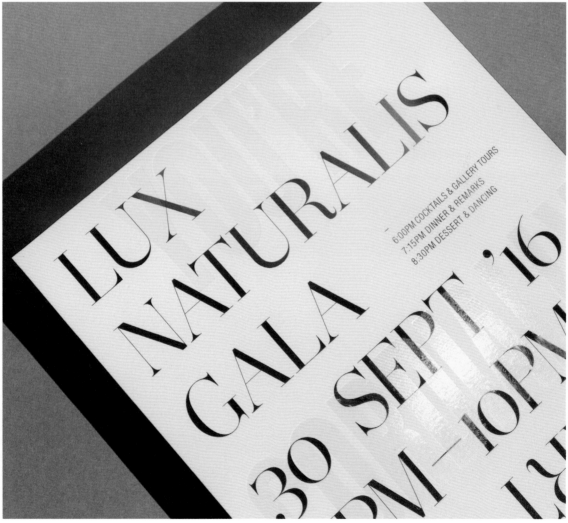

Derek Jarman 'Chroma. Księga Kolorów'

Derek Jarman's book not only proposes a colourful anthropology of culture, but also unofficially functions as the autobiography of the father of new queer cinema. Marcin Wysocki designed a minimal but meaningful cover that reflected the book's content using holographic details instead of a flat colour.

Marcin Wysocki

Client: Instytucja Filmowa Silesia Film •
Printing: Centrum Usług Drukarskich Henryk Miller

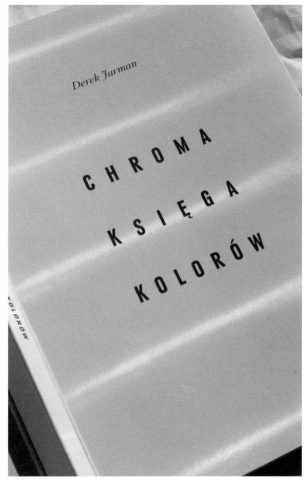

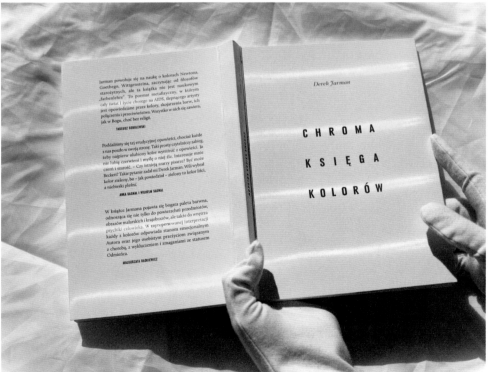

Pola Foster

Pola Foster is a designer and entrepreneur of handmade shoes with artistic sensibilities. To create her brand, Futura based their design concept around her fun, young, and trendy personality. Besides capturing her character through type, colours, and textures, holographic material was used to add a sense of playfulness and allude to modern art.

Futura

Client: Pola Foster • **Photo:** Caroga Foto

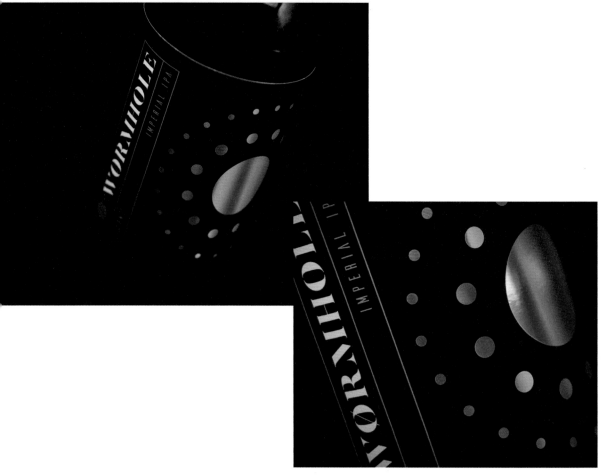

SZPUNT Craft Brewery

Flov Creative Agency were asked to design some unusual labels for SZPUNT Craft Brewery's new product line. Deriving inspiration from astrology and black magic, they set striking holographic details against a strong and dark background with elegant typography, so that the labels could make the beers stand out in the Polish craft beer market.

Flov Creative Agency

Client: SZPUNT Craft Brewery

Project Charisma

BLOW aims to create bold, fresh, and contemporary design solutions for brand identity, packaging, print, and web design work. To that end, Project Charisma was launched to showcase Polytrade Paper's wide range of products through cosmetic packaging. Using various paper types and finishes, each letter of 'CHARISMA' was derived to represent a different woman with her own personality. Holographic foil was added to inject texture as well as hints of modernity and delight.

BLOW

Client: Polytrade Paper

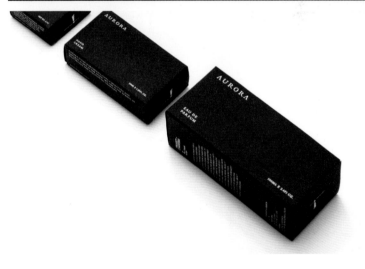

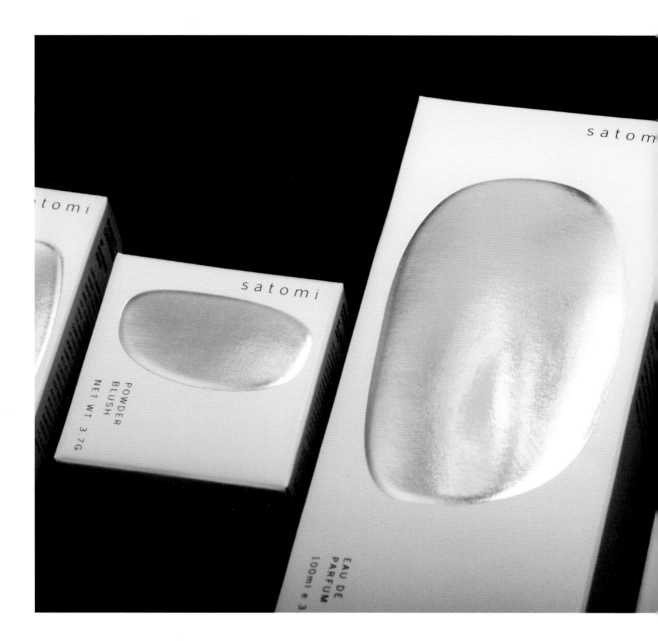

satomi

satomi

POWDER
BLUSH
NET WT 3.7G

EAU DE
PARFUM
100ml e 3

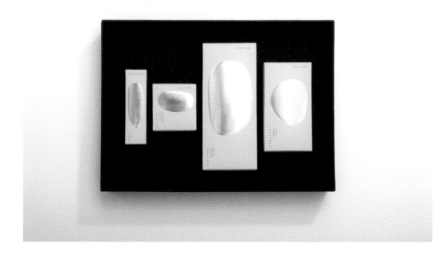

HAND CREAM

PROJECT—
CHARISMA

S

satomi

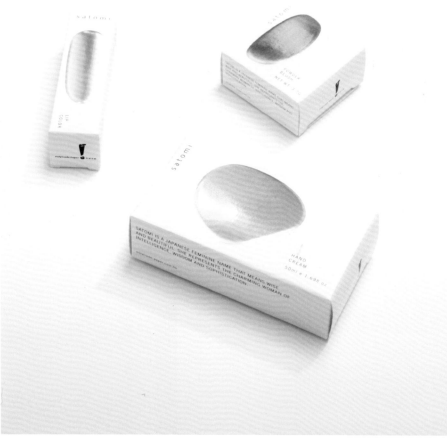

satomi

LIP
COLOR

satomi

PURPLE
BLUSH

satomi

HAND
CREAM

SATOMI IS A JAPANESE FEMININE NAME THAT MEANS WISE
AND BEAUTIFUL. SHE REPRESENTS THE CHARMING WOMAN OF
INTELLIGENCE, WISDOM AND SOPHISTICATION.

Nike Vapormax

For the global launch of Nike's new full-foot air technology, Hovercraft Studio were inspired to create a box that bent the rules in form and finish to match the ingenuity of the product. The 23-sided box features an origami-inspired opening, exterior tessellation graphics, and holographic foil; stylish details that highlight the complexity of the box structure.

Hovercraft Studio

Client: Nike Inc.

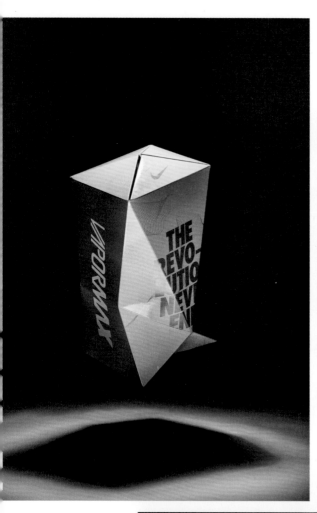

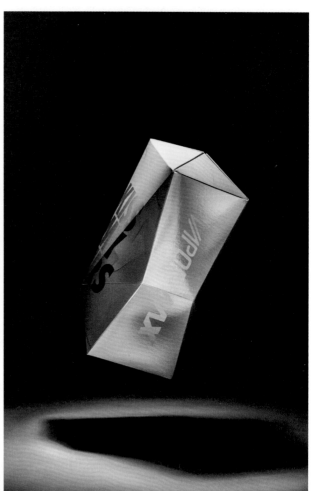

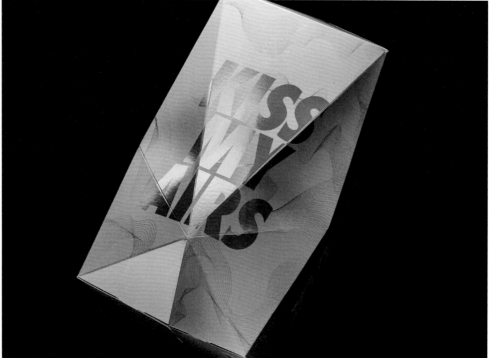

Fenty Galaxy Collection

Following the success of their work for the core Fenty beauty line, Established was asked to design a limited edition capsule collection for the 2017 holiday season. They used indulgent iridescent finishes on the primary packaging to refer to Rihanna's Caribbean heritage, and evoke the festive party spirit. The graphic language of the core line was extended into glitter foils to showcase its flexibility.

Established

Client: Kendo

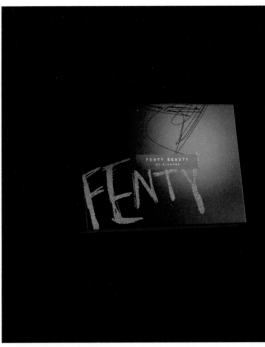

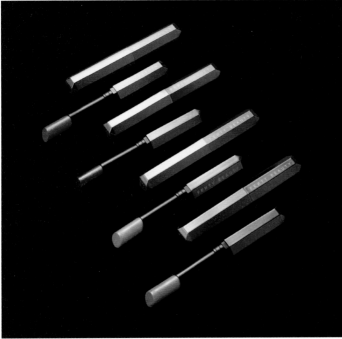

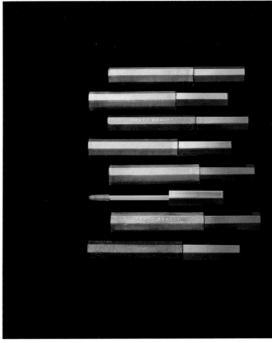

Boreálica

Boreálica is a clinic that specialises in whole-body cryotherapy. Anagrama drew inspiration from the coldest places on Earth and used a frosty colour palette of white, grey, and holographic foil to communicate the nature of Boreálica's glacial services. The monogram was designed based on the traditional symbolic representation of temperature to convey the values of health, technology, and hygiene through the work as a whole.

Anagrama

Client: Boreálica • **Photo:** Caroga Foto

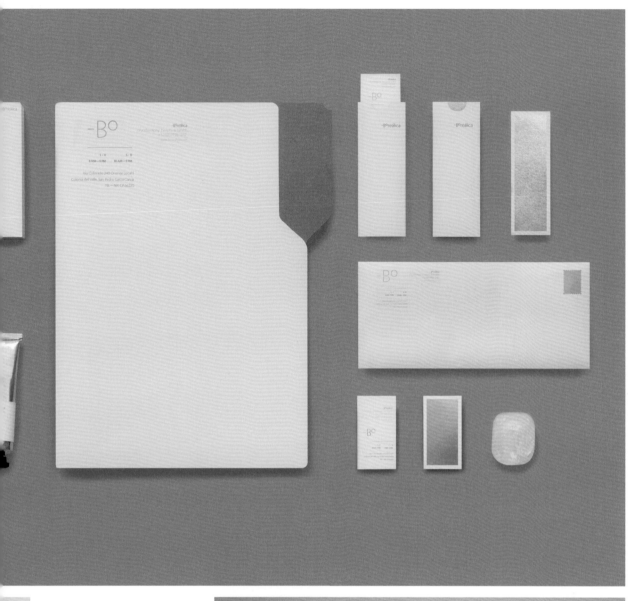

Stellar Beauty

Stellar is an inclusive, high-performance make-up brand that delivers across all skin colours, with a particular focus on medium tones. The brand's black-and-white palette reflects the product's quality and ability to be worn all day and into the night. A secondary opalescent palette vibrates across the full spectrum of light, speaking to the brand's sense of inclusivity.

Bruce Mau Design

Client: Stellar Beauty • **Photo:** Adrian Armstrong (Fuze Reps)

K11 Taste From The Moon

For the mid-autumn festival, Not Available Design's packaging work for K11 Mooncakes involved the use of abstracted graphics and contemporary colours to represent the lunar cycle. The pastel palette was derived from the hues often seen as a halo around the moon in the sky or reflected in bodies of water. Shiny silver foil was added as a celebratory element.

Not Available Design

Photo: Jimmy Ho

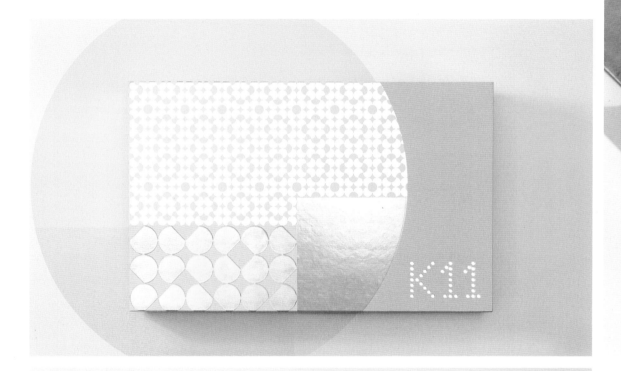

"An iridescent
colour is all about
happiness."

Studio South Identity

In conjunction with the launch of their new name and website, Studio South refreshed their brand identity suite by paying close attention to material choice and execution. Clean combinations of black and white were accented with dyed boards and holographic foil to reflect the progression of the studio's portfolio and approach.

Studio South

Bombay Electric Identity

Mumbai's most exciting fashion select store needed a new identity that embodied the utilitarian nature of its name in a modern and exciting way. Besides using minimal typography and a simple grid to offset vibrant colour gradients drawn to look like blurry abstract photographs, Michael Thorsby vibrated the letter 'I' in the logotype to infuse the company's restless curiosity into the result.

Michael Thorsby

Client: Bombay Electric

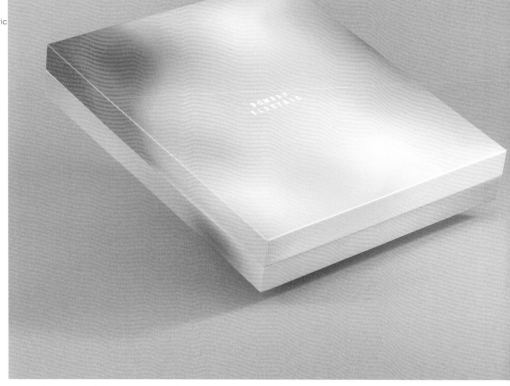

Roksanda Ilincic
Nicholas Kirkwood

ntzou
Pilotto

5 British designers reimagine the most timeless of all Indian silhouettes: the Sari. Made in a limited edition of 20, and available only at Bombay Electric London and Mumbai, this special piece can be collected and worn with pleasure. A percentage of profits goes to Elephant Family, a charity dedicated to protecting Asian elephants and their habitat.

www.bombayelectric.in

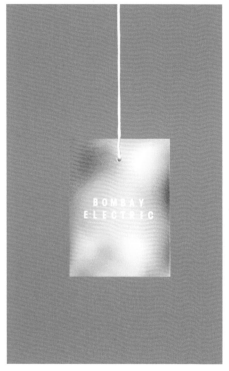

BOMBAY ELECTRIC

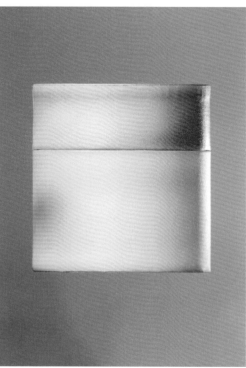

Giorgia Zanellato

Studio AH—HA were inspired by Giorgia Zanellato's fascination with fluorescent light and her keen eye for combining geometric shapes in designing her brand identity. They centred on the colour palette that is ever-present in the designer's body of work; mixing several tones in iridescent textures that were then used as filters or backgrounds throughout all the communication collaterals.

Studio AH—HA

Client: Georgia Zanellato • **Photo:** Diogo Alves

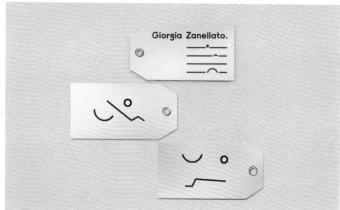

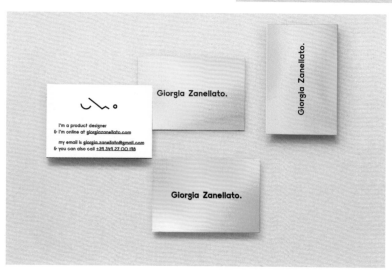

Hey Name Cards

Hey designed name cards for their studio using a vibrant holographic spectrum as the main element. The unique finishes on each card due to different parts of the spectrum used serve to reflect and highlight the unique strengths and personalities of each employee.

Hey

Photo: Enric Badrinas

Hey
Eva Vesikansa
Senior Designer & Art Director
Pallars 141, 3B
08018 Barcelona
+34 936 762 400
eva@heystudio.es

Hey
Gemma Fajardo
HeyShop Manager
Pallars 141, 3B
08018 Barcelona
+34 936 762 400
gemma@heystudio.es

Hey
Verònica Fuerte
Founder & Creative Director
Pallars 141, 3B
08018 Barcelona
+34 936 762 400
veronica@heystudio.es

Hey
Adrià Molins
Designer
Pallars 141, 3B
08018 Barcelona
+34 936 762 400
adria@heystudio.es

Hey
Adrià Molins
Designer
Pallars 141, 3B
08018 Barcelona
+34 936 762 400
adria@heystudio.es

Hey
Eva Vesikansa
Senior Designer & Art Director
Pallars 141, 3B
08018 Barcelona
+34 936 762 400
eva@heystudio.es

Hey
Verònica Fuerte
Founder & Creative Director
Pallars 141, 3B
08018 Barcelona
+34 936 762 400
veronica@heystudio.es

Hey
Adrià Molins
Designer
Pallars 141, 3B
08018 Barcelona
+34 936 762 400
adria@heystudio.es

Hey
Adrià Molins
Designer
Pallars 141, 3B
08018 Barcelona
+34 936 762 400
adria@heystudio.es

Hey
Paula Sánchez
Project Manager
Pallars 141, 3B
08018 Barcelona
+34 936 762 400
paula@heystudio.es

Hey
Verònica Fuerte
Founder & Creative Director
Pallars 141, 3B
08018 Barcelona
+34 936 762 400
veronica@heystudio.es

Hey
Verònica Fuerte
Founder & Creative Director
Pallars 141, 3B
08018 Barcelona
+34 936 762 400
veronica@heystudio.es

Hey
Eva Vesikansa
Senior Designer & Art Director
Pallars 141, 3B
08018 Barcelona
+34 936 762 400
eva@heystudio.es

Hey
Adrià Molins
Designer
Pallars 141, 3B
08018 Barcelona
+34 936 762 400
adria@heystudio.es

Hey
Eva Vesikansa
Senior Designer & Art Director
Pallars 141, 3B
08018 Barcelona
+34 936 762 400
eva@heystudio.es

Hey
Eva Vesikansa
Senior Designer & Art Director
Pallars 141, 3B
08018 Barcelona
+34 936 762 400
eva@heystudio.es

Hey
Eva Vesikansa
Senior Designer & Art Director
Pallars 141, 3B
08018 Barcelona
+34 936 762 400
eva@heystudio.es

Hey
Adrià Molins
Designer
Pallars 141, 3B
08018 Barcelona
+34 936 762 400
adria@heystudio.es

Hey
Adrià Molins
Designer
Pallars 141, 3B
08018 Barcelona
+34 936 762 400
adria@heystudio.es

Hey
Verònica Fuerte
Founder & Creative Director
Pallars 141, 3B
08018 Barcelona
+34 936 762 400
veronica@heystudio.es

Hey
Eva Vesikansa
Senior Designer & Art Director
Pallars 141, 3B
08018 Barcelona
+34 936 762 400
eva@heystudio.es

Hey
Gemma Fajardo
HeyShop Manager
Pallars 141, 3B
08018 Barcelona
+34 936 762 400
gemma@heystudio.es

Hey
Paula Sánchez
Project Manager
Pallars 141, 3B
08018 Barcelona
+34 936 762 400
paula@heystudio.es

Hey
Verònica Fuerte
Founder & Creative Director
Pallars 141, 3B
08018 Barcelona
+34 936 762 400
veronica@heystudio.es

Hey
Adrià Molins
Designer
Pallars 141, 3B
08018 Barcelona
+34 936 762 400
adria@heystudio.es

@heystudio
heystudio.es

"...because iridescence can only be revealed with motion, it invites the viewer to actively engage with the design object."

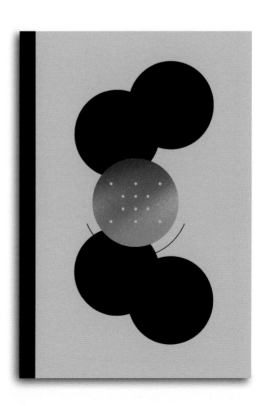

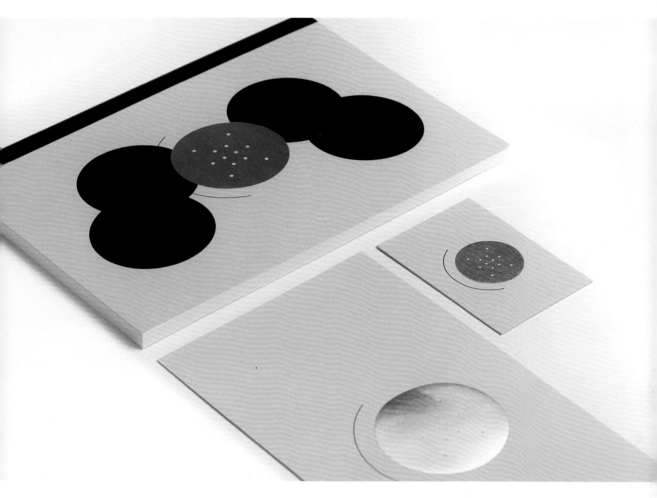

Katerina Kagia Dental Facility

Semiotik Design Agency developed an original and eye-catching brand identity for Katerina Kagia's unique dental facility. Using clean grids and simple graphic lines with black and holographic circles, a distinctive visual system was created to embody the clarity, expertise, and consistency that the facility's patients would experience.

Semiotik Design Agency

Client: Katerina Kagia • **Photo:** Stefanos Tsakiris

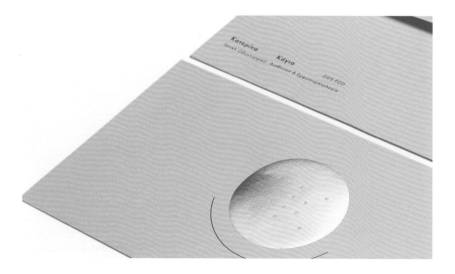

Dawn Creative Rebrand

In line with their move to a new studio space, Dawn Creative decided to rebrand themselves. They created a clean and simple identity using the sunrise and their initials as inspiration. Holographic foil was applied across the printed assets as a living gradient that moved through the different spectrums of their brand colour palette to convey the concept of changing light.

Dawn Creative

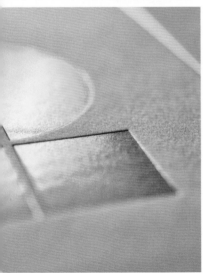

Dave O'Hearns
Creative Director

0161 711 0610
07739 102 308
dave@dawncreative.co.uk

dawncreative.co.uk

Dawn Creative

Dawn Creative

Rendez-vous des créateurs 2017

Balmer Hählen pushed the limits of graphic design techniques in this Type Directors Club prize-winning invitation for Rendez-vous des créateurs in 2017. Using cut-outs, textures, and a glossy varnish with an almost-holographic effect, they distorted the typography to create new dimensions and the illusion of print taking over the design itself.

Balmer Hählen

Client: Rendez-vous des créateurs • **Production:** Hinderer + Mühlich Schweiz, Kurz AG, Sonderegger •
Paper: Papyrus Schweiz

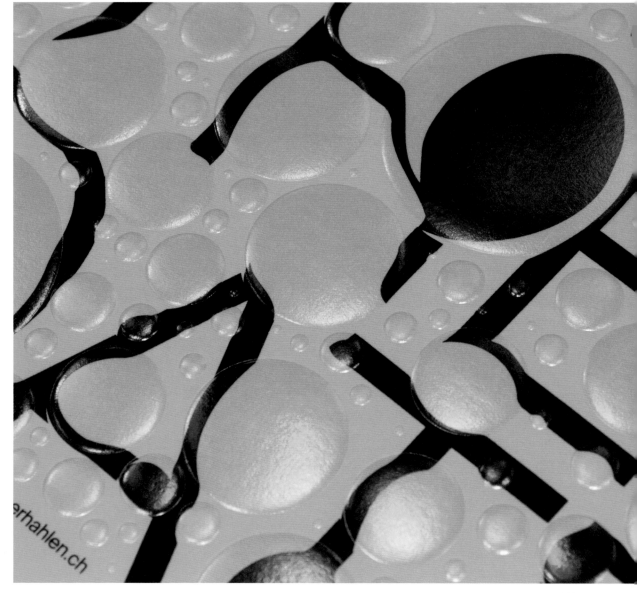

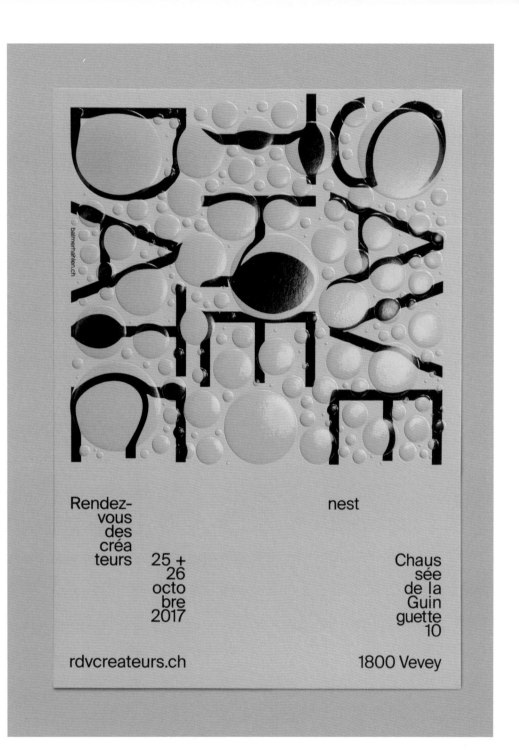

Rendez-
vous
des
créa
teurs   25 +
         26
         octo
         bre
         2017

rdvcreateurs.ch

nest

Chaus
sée
de la
Guin
guette
10

1800 Vevey

TDC

COLLINS sought to find the future of form in their campaign for the Type Directors Club (TDC), a renowned global organisation that promotes excellence in typography. Based on the concept of 'a new generation', they created bespoke software that generated real-time typographic expressions online. The application of holographic details on the printed materials complements the futuristic design elements in the digital space.

COLLINS

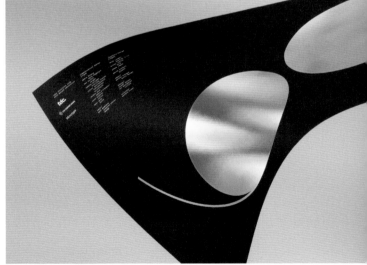

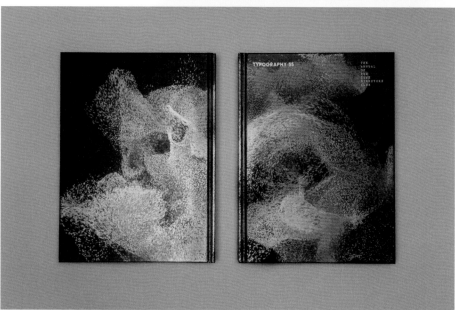

Five — 2015 Hey's Christmas Poster

Hey created unique prints that came in different combinations of flat colours and coloured foils. The multi-coloured sheen on the number '5' that was used as the main visual element added a celebratory touch to the posters when combined with the bright but matted hues.

Hey

Photo: Roc Canals

Halocyan — Universal Quantifier

For Halocyan Records' double-CD pack, Build used a mirri board slipcase with minimal typography in holographic foil to emulate the nature of the music compiled. The futuristic palette and clean composition complemented the 24 tracks on the discs by exploring the future of techno and showcasing the impact that the genre has had so far.

Build

Client: Halocyan Records

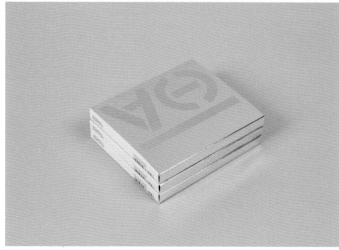

Holography.

For an exhibition-driven campaign that celebrated underground music without explicitly revealing the genre, Daniel Barkle used holographic sheets and Grotesk type on printed materials to mask the details of the subject matter and yet, give the content depth. The visual treatment served to block preconceptions or stereotypical judgements about the genre with its indistinguishable form.

Daniel Barkle

"Iridescence particularly acts as a powerful tool to metaphorically represent diversity. When placed in different environments, it transforms and mixes colours so uniquely that you cannot control the outcome."

29th Summer Universiade Taipei 2017 Commemorative Token

In 2017, Metro Taipei and the 29th Summer Universiade Taipei jointly launched 2017 commemorative token sets. Midnight Design played with the outlines of existing mascots to keep them as the main graphic elements, and added geometric touches to enrich the visuals. Hot stamping and laser foil printing were adopted, so that the changing colours of refractive lines would symbolise diversity and youthful vitality.

Midnight Design

Client: Taipei Rapid Transit Corporation • **Photo:** Mo Chien

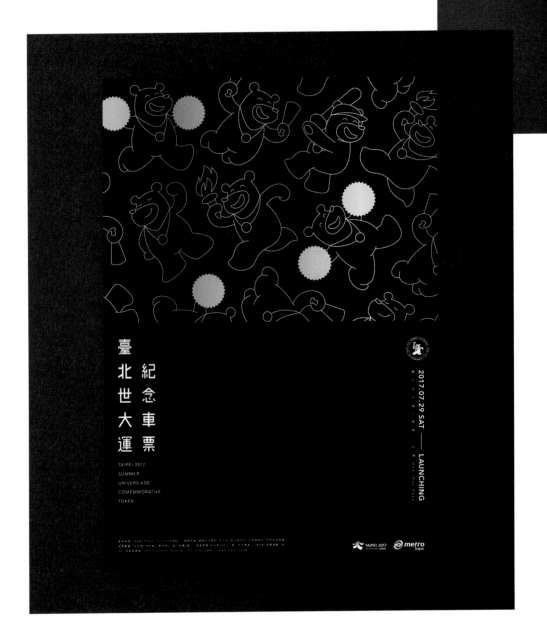

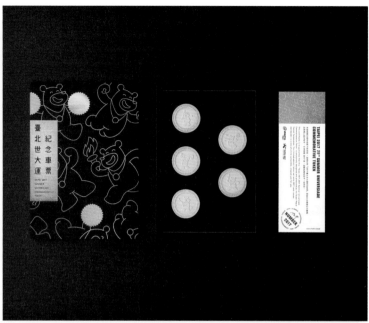

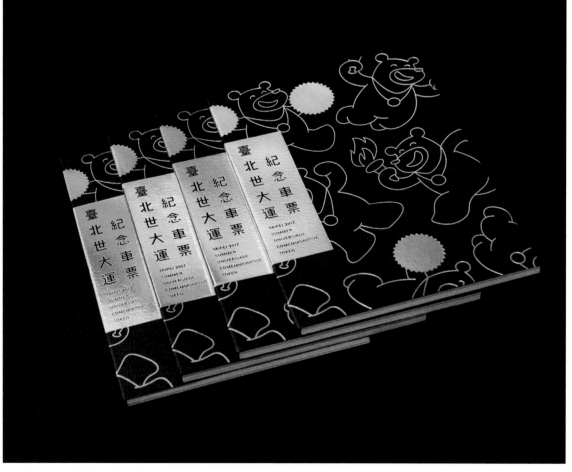

Ethan Lee Photography #2

Inspired by the sense of tranquillity that emanates from Yi-Hsien Lee's work, Sion Hsu designed name cards for the London-based photographer using dark tones as a base. The graphic lines in silver foil represent dismantled camera parts like the viewfinder and shutter; functioning as holographic accents that make the result more abstract.

Sion Hsu Graphic

Client: Ethan Lee Photography • **Photo:** Ben Chen, Ethan Lee

"Iridescence gives new possibilities to graphic design."

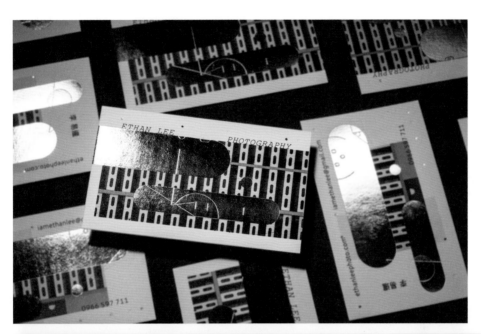

Holographic & Letterpressed Hot-stamping Business Cards

For Paulina Zbylut's business cards, Kolory set out to push the boundaries of print technologies and paper. Besides playing around with colours and layers, they also set themselves free to see what would develop as a result. After a series of experiments, they ended up combining cotton paper, letterpress printing, and hot-stamping with a transparent holographic film for a minimal look with a futuristic edge.

Kolory

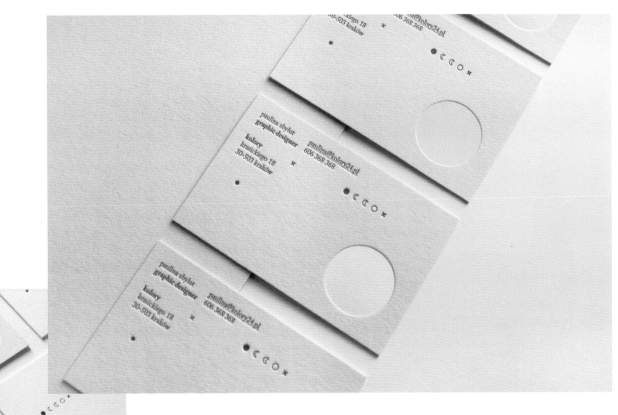

Jennifer Young Studio

Jennifer Young is a lifestyle, portrait, and travel photographer fond of human connection, the art of everyday, juxtaposition, and finding beauty in the simple. For her identity suite, she wanted something minimal, modern, and unique that would best represent the essence of her work. Kati Forner used holographic foil to infuse life into the clean and modern suite she designed.

Kati Forner Design

Client: Jennifer Young

Pink and Holographic

Alexia ROUX designed her business cards by contrasting holographic details on light pink cards with simple typography to embody the combination of fresh femininity and modern edge that permeates her work.

Alexia ROUX

sound:frame Agency AV Art

sound:frame connects audio-visual artists across different disciplines and contexts for creative experimentation and outcomes that break boundaries. For its business cards, 101 used holographic hot foil to represent the infinite possibilities that multifaceted partnerships can bring, along with a plain letterpress border to frame its new focus.

101

Client: sound:frame Agency AV Art • Printing: The Infinitive Factory •
Photo: Daniela Trost, Lupi Spuma

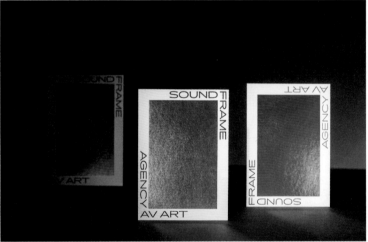

WE ARE SOUND:FRAME

Sauvage.tv Business Cards

Mubien designed and handcrafted exclusive business cards and matching cardholders with holographic hues for Sausage.tv, a creative audio-visual production house. By applying foil-stamping and debossing techniques, they added depth and dimension to the entire aesthetic.

Mubien

Client: Sausage.tv

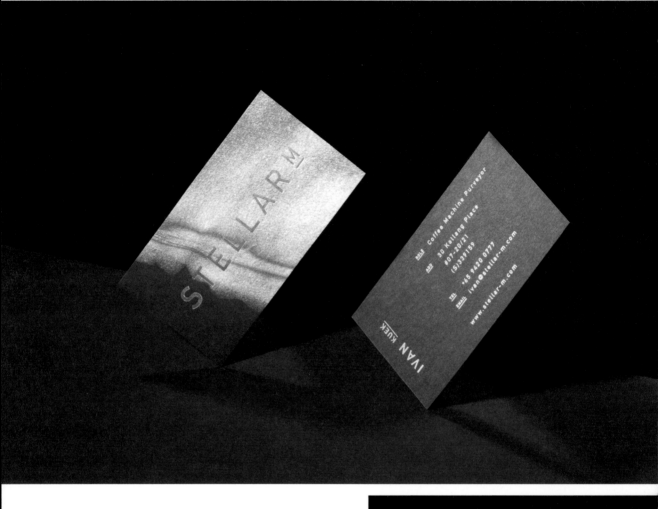

Stellar M, Singapore

To reflect Stellar M's resolve to relentlessly serve the needs of
coffee enthusiasts with stellar coffee equipment, Foreign Policy
Design Group adopted long exposures and gradients inspired
by Angelo Secchi's stellar spectograms to form the core of its
branding suite. The reflective surfaces serve to highlight the
quality, brilliance, and heart behind the company's products and
technical team.

Foreign Policy Design Group

Client: Stellar M

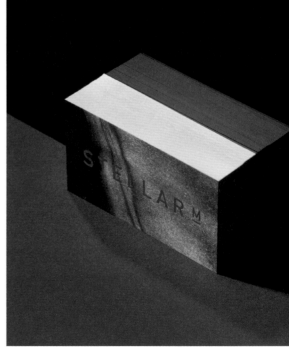

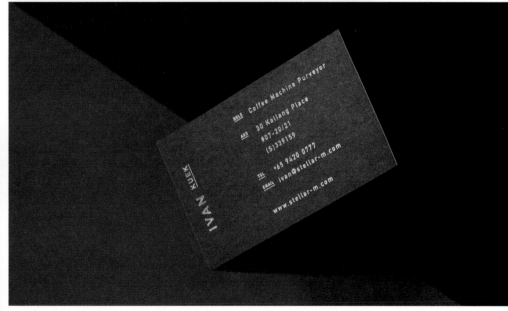

nativeye

nativeye specialises in visual production and exhibition design. For its name cards, HOUTH were driven by the company's main purpose and passion for conveying the primitive view, idea, or story of the client in an intriguing way. Instead of paper, they used transparent, hard-to-recycle brightness-enhancement film to materialise nativeye's ethos.

HOUTH

Client: nativeye

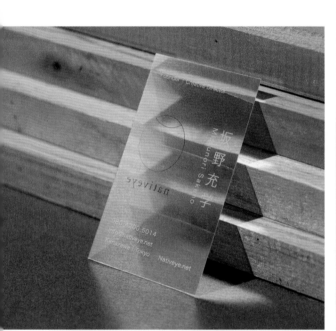

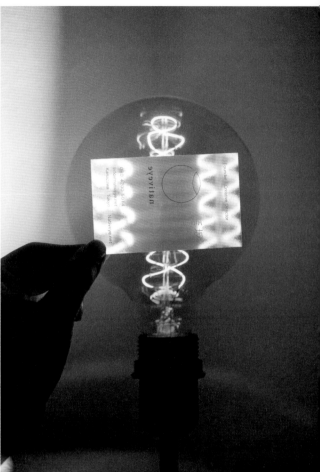

Antalis / Promo Letterpress Card

To promote the WILD paper that Antalis offers, Kolory were inspired to create kitschy animal drawings on cards and print them with a 'rainbow roll' letterpress. The vibrancy of the holographic hues shines through the intricate illustrations; showcasing the impeccable quality of the paper.

Kolory

Client: Antalis Poland

Galaxies

Fundamental designed a series of postcards that fused intricate illustrations and iridescent foil for Galaxies, an on-going zine project that uses graphics, paper, and printing effects to deliver positive messages. By pairing Risograph and letterpress printing techniques with hot foil stamping, they managed to create striking yet meaningful pieces of work.

Fundamental

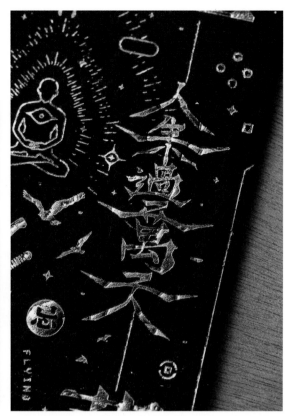

Much feeling little thinking

For singer Ivana Wong's album, Fundamental created a holographic aurora that flowed throughout the cover and parts of the booklet. By applying a hot-stamping effect, the multidimensional line graphics mirrored the ethereal nature of the album title and photography within the sleeve.

Fundamental

Client: Media Asia Music

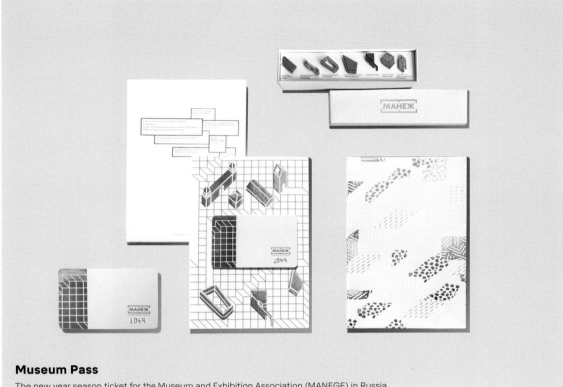

Museum Pass

The new year season ticket for the Museum and Exhibition Association (MANEGE) in Russia enabled access to all 7 exhibitions being held at the time. Dasha F drew inspiration from the rainbow and applied its colour scheme in holographic foil on all the passes. Besides entry, these passes also allowed their holders to gain commemorative pins at each exhibition hall.

Dasha F

Client: Moscow Manege Museum

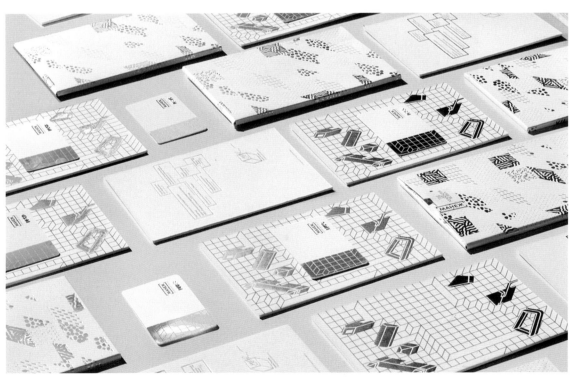

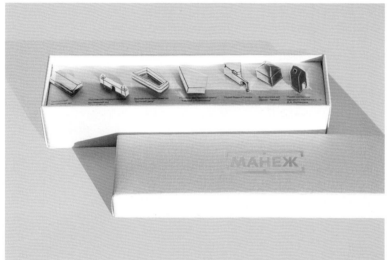

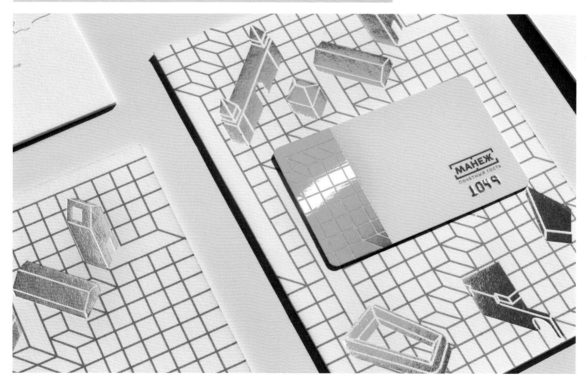

NeuroTribes: The Legacy of Autism and the Future of Neurodiversity

Author Steve Silberman wrote a book hoping that the world would make accommodations for autism, and not the other way around. Tsai Chia-hao designed a befitting book cover using multiple colours and gradients of holographic film to represent the wide spectrum of the condition. He was also inspired by its reflective effect to emphasise how important it is to understand and respect pluralism within society.

Tsai Chia-hao

Client: The Walk Publishing

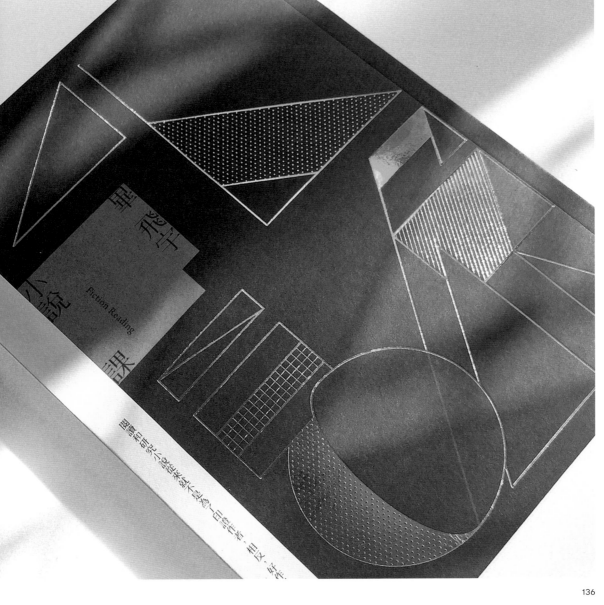

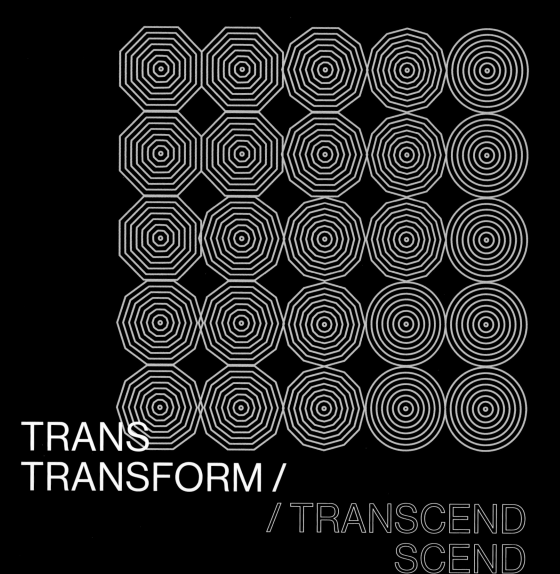

TRANS
TRANSFORM /
/ TRANSCEND
SCEND

While technology has enabled the creation and application of
iridescence onto anything from identity suites to product and furniture
design work, their multidimensional, maleable powers seem to truly
come to light when they are used within the ever-evolving digital space.
This special section features an inspiring selection of 3D artists who
have opened the doors to mind-bending new forms, realms, and artistic
expressions through holographic hues — armed with a whole lot of
imagination, curiosity, and the tenacity to try.

Catello Gragnaniello

Davy Evans

Machineast

PALAST PHOTOGRAPHIE
– Julien Palast

Peter Tarka

Siddhant Jaokar

Six N. Five

The Acid House

YUNGBLD

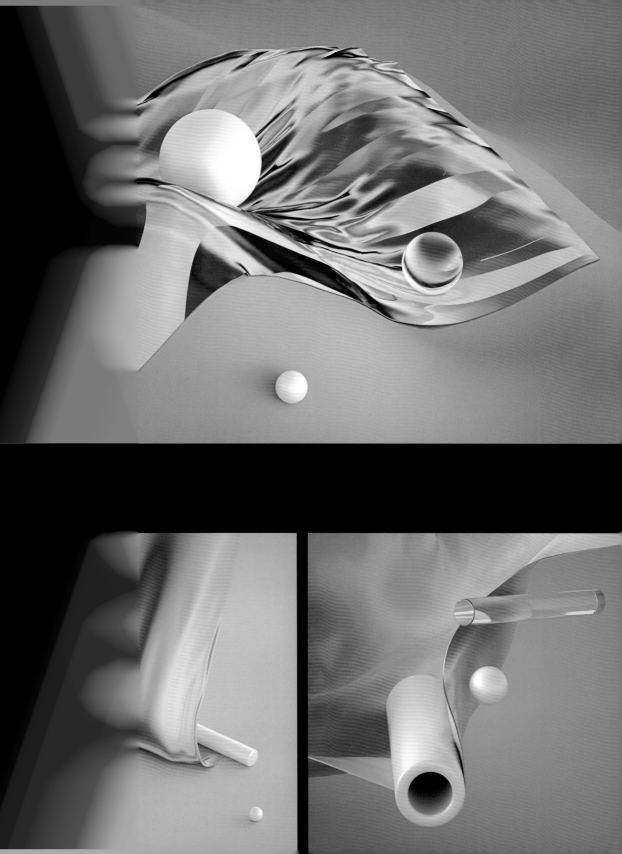

Translucent Iridescent

Machineast were inspired to recreate the unique fusion of coldness and warmth that they felt during a trip to Japan in autumn. They created the Translucent Iridescent series using a holographic ribbon and pearl as the main visual elements to crystalise the atmosphere at the time onto a digital canvas.

Machineast

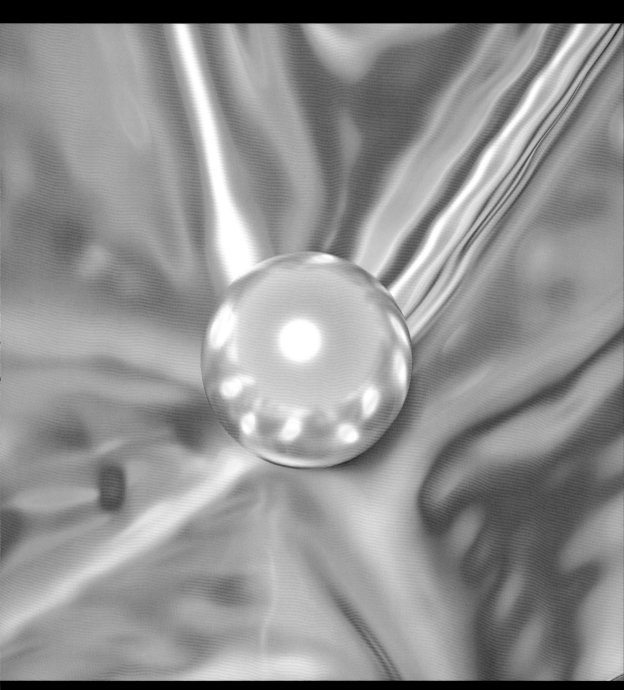

SOMA for Catalogue Fashion Book

Six N. Five were invited by Catalogue, a fashion magazine from Buenos Aires to create a series of visuals based on the concept of a mermaid. The finished work is a successful manifestation of their imagination, after exploring the different possibilities of fusing holographic colours, waves, tiles, and shapes.

Six N. Five

Client: Catalogue Fashion Book •

Art Direction: Six N. Five, Jimena Nahon • **Photo:** Jimena Nahon

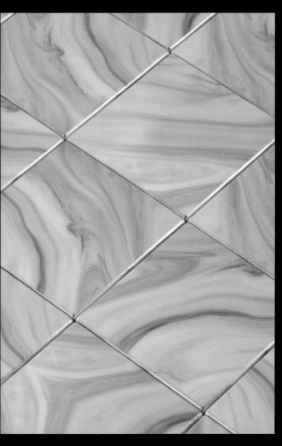

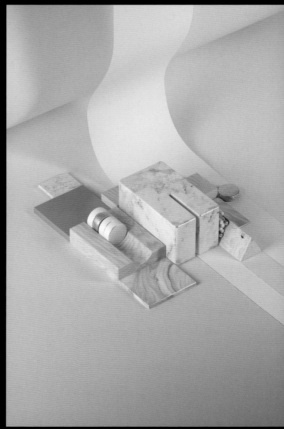

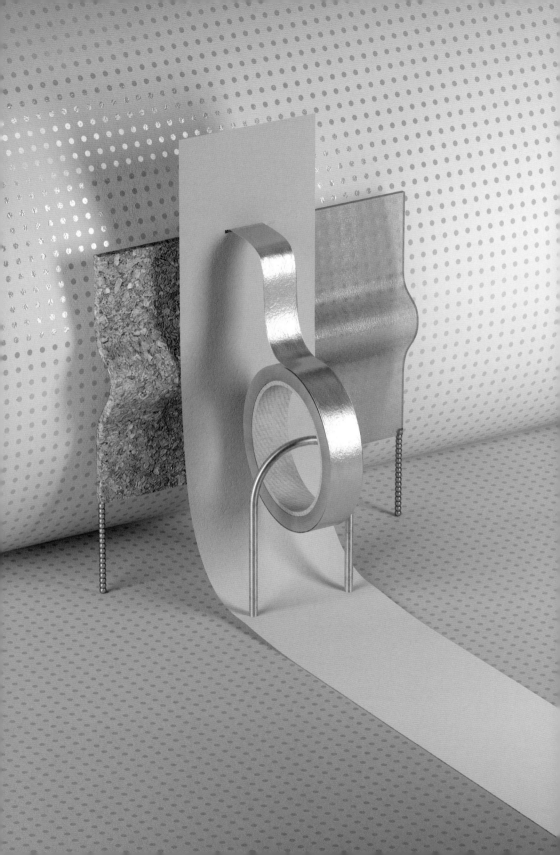

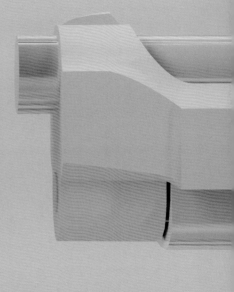

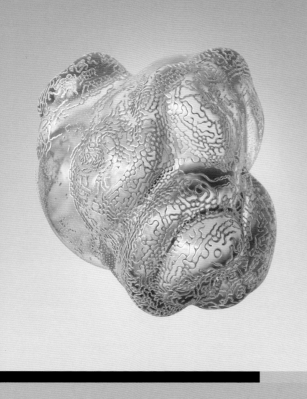

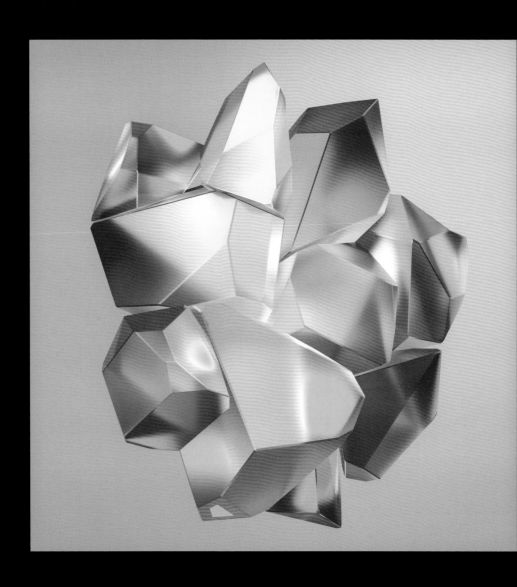

Untitled

Peter Tarka's talents in art direction and illustration are clearly demonstrated in this series of 3D illustrations that he created over the course of a year. His keen eye for colour and pattern combinations, the interplay of light and shadows, as well as the intricacy of details shine through the neon and holographic spectrum used.

Peter Tarka

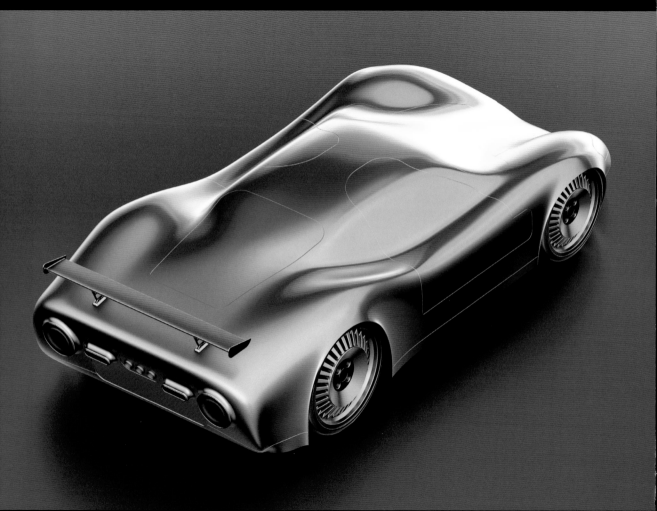

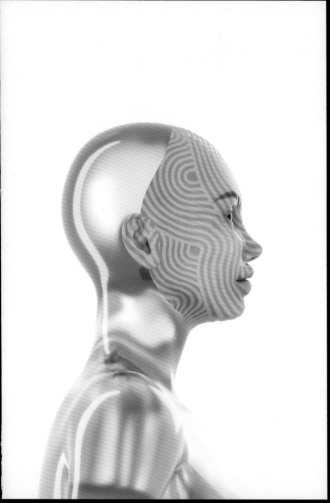

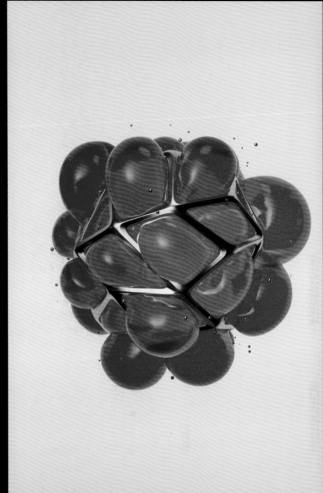

FUSION MK1 / Untitled

For Fusion MK1 (left page), Siddhant Jaokar experimented with Fusion360 and Cinema 4D software techniques to reinterpret the classic FORD GT40 in different ways while retaining its sleek form. In one of the iterations, he coats the car in a holographic sheen, enhancing its clean lines in a futuristic way. Using the same techniques, he has also been experimenting with different visual projects (this page) that play with surreal landscapes and futuristic details.

Siddhant Jaokar

Cosmic Machinaria / Nightcall

Cosmic Machinaria (left page) is a set of performance visuals that The Acid House created for Bassnectar's 2016 festival tour. There are a total of 16 loops, which shows a massive galactic engine capable of constructing stars, planets, and other heavenly bodies in the cosmos. Nightcall (this page) was a series of visuals inspired by Kavinsky's song 'Nightcall', which is from the Drive original soundtrack.

The Acid House

For Cosmic Machinaria — Client: Bassnectar

SkullDeep

Julien Palast conceptualised a contemporary
version of 17th century Memento Mori paintings to
represent the shortness and fugacity of life. He used
the SkinDeep technique to shrink-wrap a skull in an
electrifying and colourful environment, creating a
synthetic skin layer resembling the iridescent shell of
certain cockroach species.

PALAST PHOTOGRAPHIE — Julien Palast
Retouching: Bassnectar

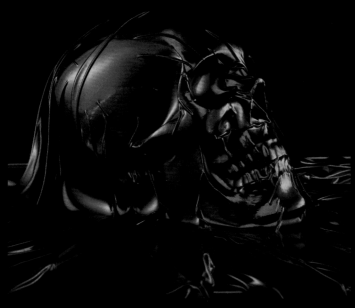

Bug / Cassini / Apple

Davy Evans created Bug (this page) by collaging various elements of macro photography textures to bring a fictional alien-esque plant to life. The iridescent colour palette was based on an actual one that certain real-life plants thrive on. For Cassini (right page), he digitally enhanced macro photographs of household chemicals to create a graphical composition with organic lines and textures. The colours and gradients evoke a dreamy, surreal, and meditative feel. Apple (after page-turn) showcases the improved colours and brightness of the new iMac Pro screen launched in 2017 through macro photography.

Davy Evans
For Apple — Client: Apple

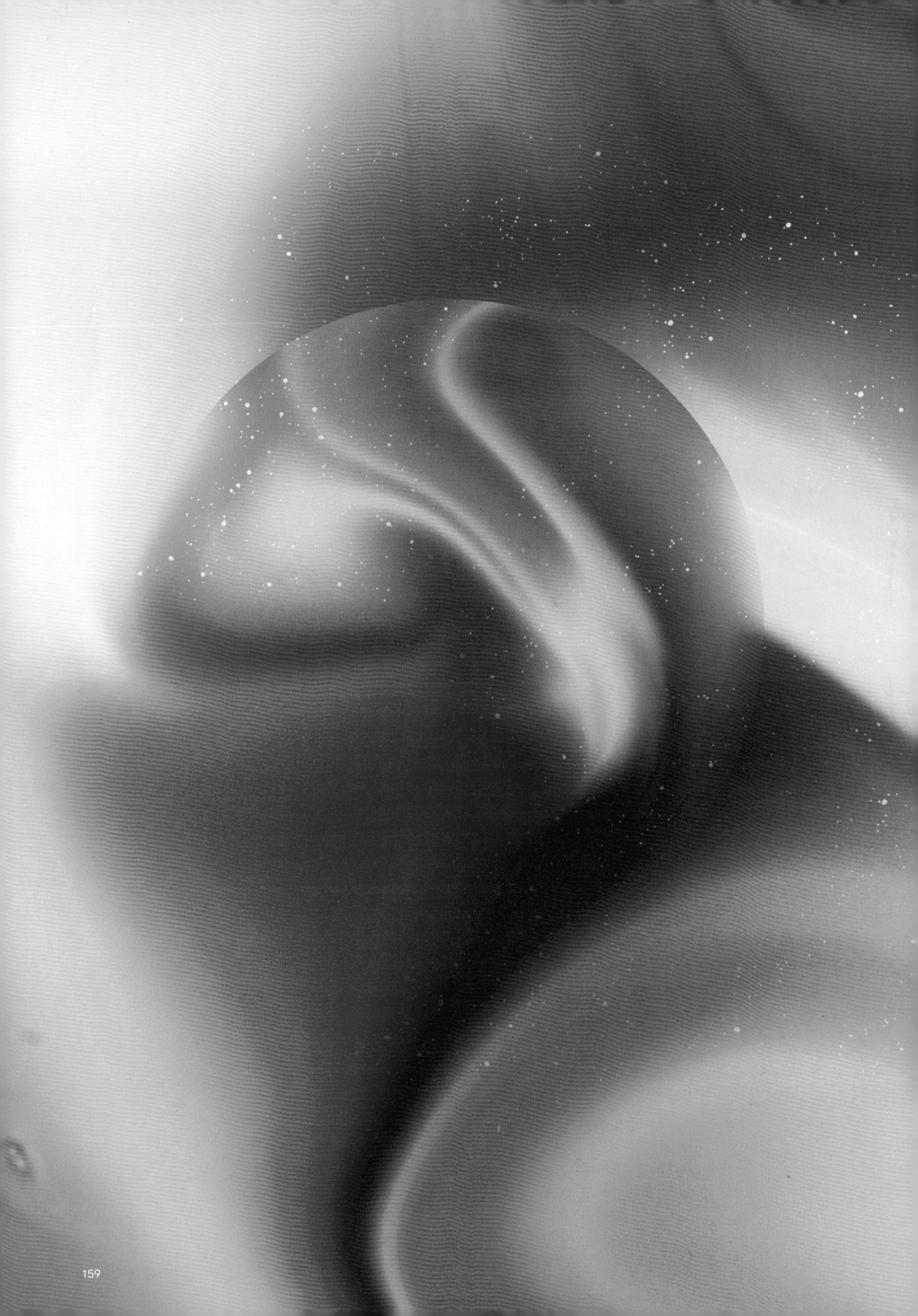

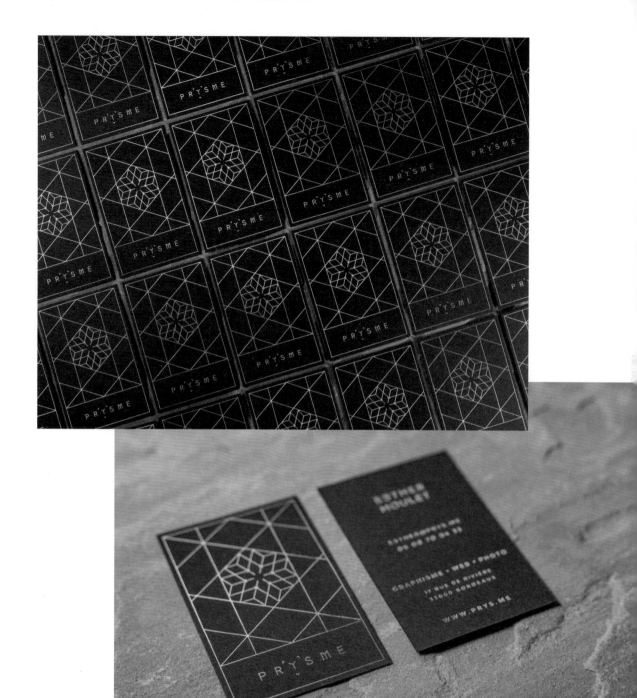

PRYSME

To evolve from their previous branding system, PRYSME decided to try
something new for their identity suite by creating a faceted pattern using
thin lines. They printed this pattern on dark and raw paper, and added
contrast and visual interest using light and glossy hot foil to bring the
meaning of their name to life.

PRYSME

Strelka Summer Closing Party 2017

The Summer Closing Party is a special event celebrated by the Strelka Institute, a non-profit international educational project in the fields of media, architecture, and design. Anna Kulachek was inspired by an installation that was to be put in place during the 2017 party to apply iridescence into her designs and reflect the vibrant mood of the festivities.

Anna Kulachek

Client: Strelka Institute

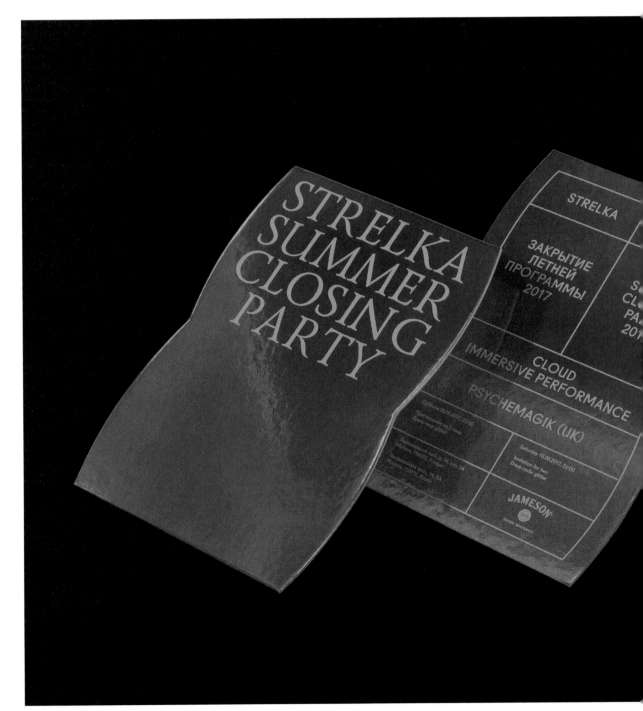

STRELKA
SUMMER
CLOSING
PARTY

MARK SCHEDRIN

16.09.17
22:00

14, Bldg. 5A,
Bersenevskaya Embankment
Moscow, 119072, Russia

INTERACTIVE PERFORMANCE

PSYCHE-
MAGIK
(UK)

#strelkasummer
strelka.com

JAMESON
J.J·S
IRISH WHISKEY

CLOUD

This exhibition is a conceptual representation of heat in its most immediate expression, temperature.

A curated experience through a series of artistic and sensory installations which "give shape" to the most widely used means to transfer heat. This gallery of multi-cultural creative visions is conceived by the international team of young designers of Fabrica and Daikin, a firm that has always been committed to provide the "climate for life", promoting the responsible use of energy in harmony with nature. The domestic environment thus becomes design thanks to Daikin.

HOT & COLD

FABRICA

FELL IN LOVE WITH

DAIKIN

HOTANDCOLD.ORG
#HOTANDCOLD
#FABRICALOVESDAIKIN

Hot & Cold

For this project, Studio AH—HA aspired to provide an experiential journey through a series of multi-sensory artistic and sculptural installations that 'give shape' to air. They did so by inviting visitors to participate in an immersive laboratory of hot and cold experiences, where there were conceptual representations of temperature. Graphics were built upon iridescent materials to portray all the different hues associated with heat and the lack thereof.

Studio AH—HA

Client: Fabrica for Daikin • **Special credits:** Shek Po Kwan, Fabrica

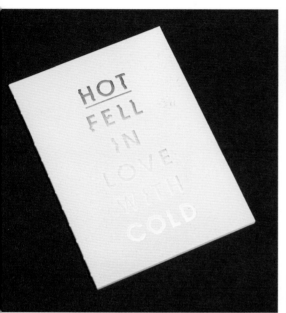

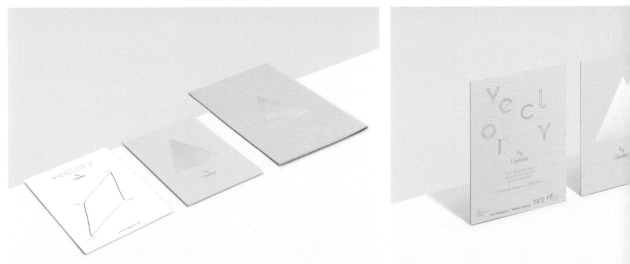

Baguera

Baguera is a jewellery brand owned by artist Branca Cuvier, where she explores the elasticity of juxtapositions by adding different layers and colours of lasered plexi-glass. For the launch of her first collection Vectory, Studio AH—HA designed a catalogue and invitations with iridescent hot-stamping to reflect the properties of the mirrored materials she used. The triangular design element is also a strong visual reference to her pieces.

Studio AH—HA

Client: Baguera • **Photo:** Diogo Alves

The Lost Fingers - Wonders of the World Album

The award-nominated Wonders of the World recording package is a stellar mix of photography, art direction, and design work by Caroline Blanchette and Martin Tremblay. White, grey and silver tones form the canvas for holographic details and surrealistic imagery, giving the album cover art, posters, and other materials an ethereal feel that encapsulates the essence of wonder.

Caroline Blanchette, Martin Tremblay

Client: The Lost Fingers

THE
LOST
FINGERS
WONDERS OF
THE WORLD

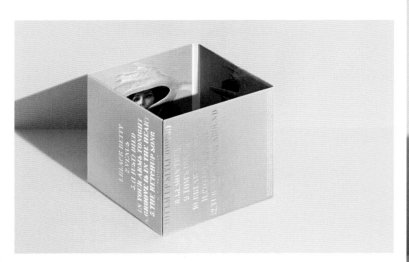

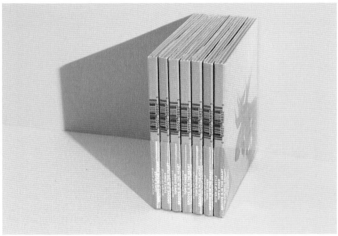

SIMIAN GHOST — The Veil

Drawing inspiration from the name of Simian Ghost's album itself, Pyramid layered transparent blue-pink 'veils' on top of ethereal black, white, and grey shots of natural landscapes for the band's double-vinyl pack, Digipak, and single artwork. The combinations produced a haunting holographic effect that complemented the release.

Pyramid

Client: Simian Ghost • **Photo:** Alan Harford

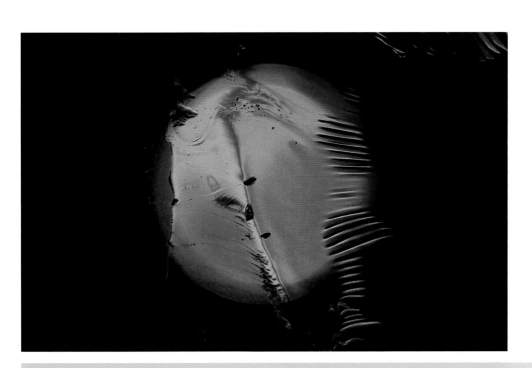

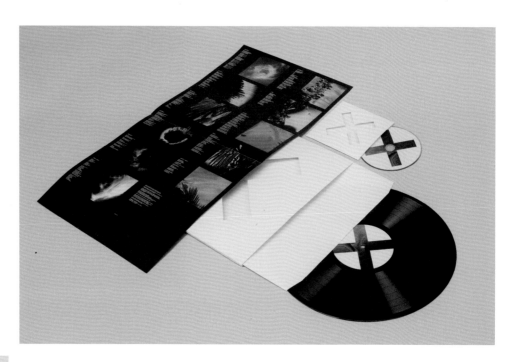

The XX

For the cover of The XX's album Coexist, Davy Evans created a range of macro photographs; each with its own piece of moving imagery to accompany every track. Motion was used for visualisers online, on applications, and in live visuals to add dynamism to the designs. To mirror the organic production of the record, all effects were created in-camera.

Davy Evans

Client: XL Recordings, Young Turks • **Art Direction:** Romy Madley Croft, Davy Evans • **Design:** Phill Lee

Nightcap/ROOM SERVICE

For synth-pop band Nightcap's new ROOM SERVICE album, Tsai Shu-yu was inspired by the idea of escaping from reality and entering a dreamland. She used holographic tones to create liquid-like patterns suggestive of floating, and drew planet surfaces that evoke the sensation of drifting. The alphabetical letter 'Z' formed the design basis of both the wine glass and sleep icons (i.e. 'zzzz') that represent what the phrase 'night cap' means.

Tsai Shu-yu

Client: Linfair Records Limited

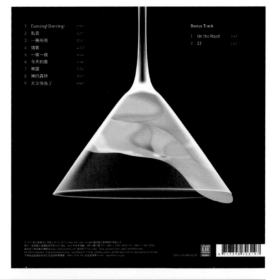

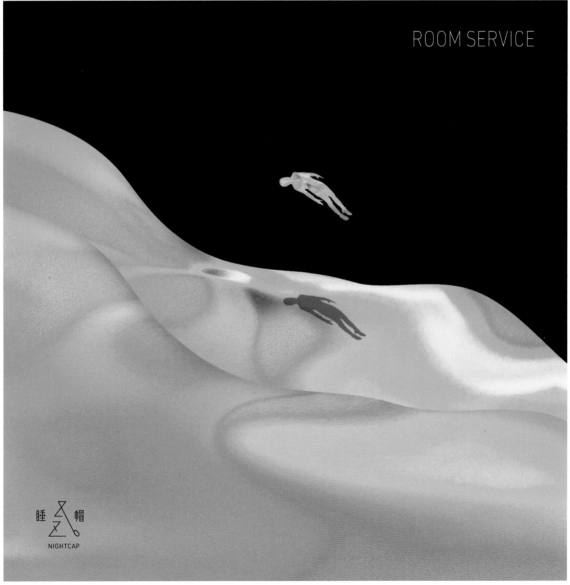

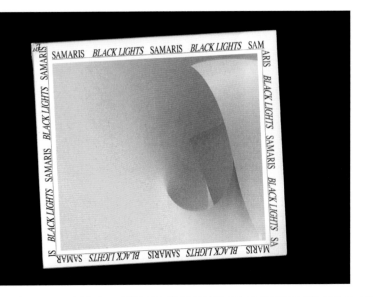

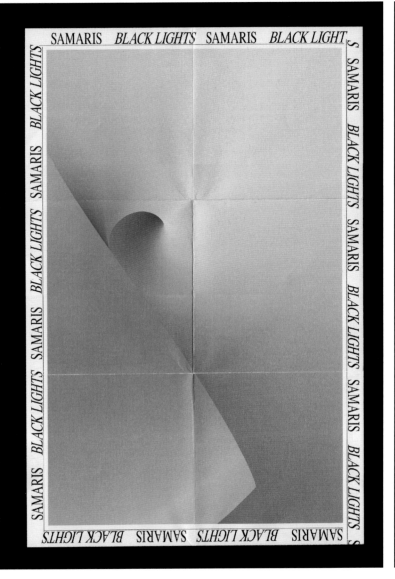

SAMARIS *BLACK LIGHTS* SA

1 WANTED 2 SAY Heavy growth, hard die. It's the pressure of ours. Got the sh things we have. It's the treasure of ours. right. This is the thing I wanted to say. W all. Pleasure is ours. **2 BLACK LIGH** Black lights when they close down. Whe falls. Washes away the tar. But it won't un to the thought impaired by the feeling. N you. Come back to me. Once more. All isn seeing things when you know you can't when you want them to (find you). **3 G** you were back then. 'Cause I only know this one. Hard to grasp your slippery ha don't be like someone else. 'Cause I only one. **4 T3MPO** I am speedy from the b I move no faster than you see. I can't feel po? Can you keep up with the driving forc Underwater. I can't feel your tempo. Wha thought I'd given you all. I thought there wa I will. I thought you had taken my breath. I now I know. I will. When you reach the p weight. I thought we made each other wa and hide at nightfall. With nerves more al cover every inch. We're blinded by glimps path. From the core to the stars. Shoot h back towards the sun. Never face what closed, no need to see straight. Dreams a constant fight, it's a constant conquer. . tion. **7 3Y3** I know what they say abou not one with it. Your eyes won't talk abou darkness stays dark). **8 T4NGLED** Yo whispers are soft as silk. Surround me wit You always say. But the only thing that I quick as you can. Your arms were wide op easy for you to think that you do. That yo you promise. And I want to believe you. T ing sign. Run as quick as you can. It's ea you do. It makes the reality vanish from y don't know how. **9 IN DEEP** In deep is easiest way to discomfort me. The tinies me off. In deep is the current that contro washing me. Up high is the heaven that wa ing an eye on me. Makes it so no one sets

Black Lights LP by Samaris

After listening to Samaris' first full-length studio album, Greta Thorkels was moved by the feelings of sadness and heartache reminiscent of break-ups and downward spirals. To convey those themes, she designed a cover that alternated lightness and darkness, with the main illustration being a spiral 3D shape. The wireframe mesh represented a suffocating darkness, while the iridescent pink material embodied the bright moments in between.

Greta Thorkels

Client: Samaris

"Iridescence navigates within nostalgia and can therefore call upon powerful responses from viewers."

S BLACK LIGHTS

read the water, or you
the wave. It's the only
the point of making it
nted to say. Nothing at
lights in the distance.
ults open and the rain
e back to me. Attached
as carved as deep as
hen it's sunny. It's hard
y. It's hard to disguise
T SKY Please be like
. 'Cause I don't know
en if I want to. Please
e. 'Cause I only know
my heart. But with you
npo. What is your tem-
fade into slow motion.
matter? 5 I WILL I
g left. But now I know.
I was given yours. But
hought we carried the
R4VIN Days we sleep
ever. Darkness sheets
ver. We can chase the
d hit harsher. With our
away from. Eyes are
re vivid than ever. It's
y that has no destina-
I'd relate to it. but I'm
ot theirs to tell. (Their
got me tangled. Your
You'll build me a fort.
a siren shout. Run as
grip on me strong. It's
or me. No matter how
hing I hear. Is a warn-
u thinking. And saying
words tangled. And I
that unravels me. The
unsettles me. Or sets
e moon is constantly
e. The mother is keep-
on me. Or sets me off.

THE PEACOCK SOCIETY

THE
PEACOCK
SOCIETY
FESTIVAL

FESTIVAL
DES CULTURES
ÉLECTRONIQUES
WAREHOUSE VISUAL ARTS CLUB FILMS TALKS

VENDREDI   SAMEDI
7   JUILLET   8
2017

PARC FLORAL DE PARIS | 22H > 7H

ARTWORK: ATELIER IRRADIÉ

SOCIETY

INFOS & PRÉVENTES
SUR THEPEACOCKSOCIETY.FR

The Peacock Society

The Peacock Society Festival is a celebration of electronic cultures through different manifestations of the digital arts. Irradié was commissioned to create the visual identity for its summer edition in 2017. Their design concept takes inspiration from retro-futurism, abstract art, and the iridescent colour scheme of net art.

Irradié

Client: The Peacock Society

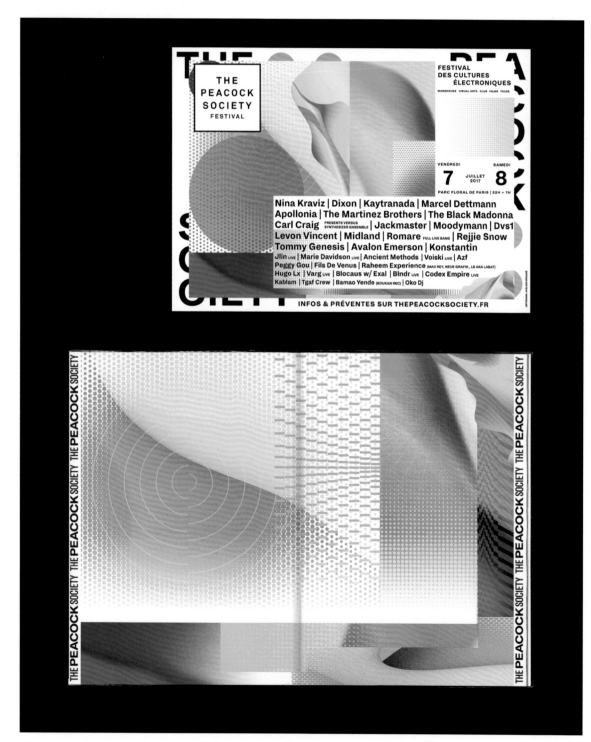

"Iridescent colours and the structures that produce them have unique properties. It is interesting to have colour distortions in design."

Design for Dance 2017

twomuch materialised the fluidity of movement in a modern and exciting way by manipulating the multidimensional nature of holographic hues in Design for Dance's identity. When in motion, the gradation of colours on the main visual element captures forms and shadows like a fabric. This concept was carried forward from the digital space onto print materials with a dynamic result.

twomuch

Client: Central Saint Martins

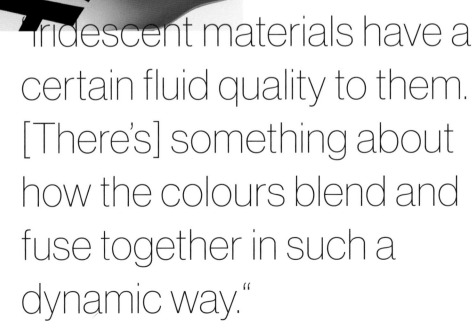

"Iridescent materials have a certain fluid quality to them. [There's] something about how the colours blend and fuse together in such a dynamic way."

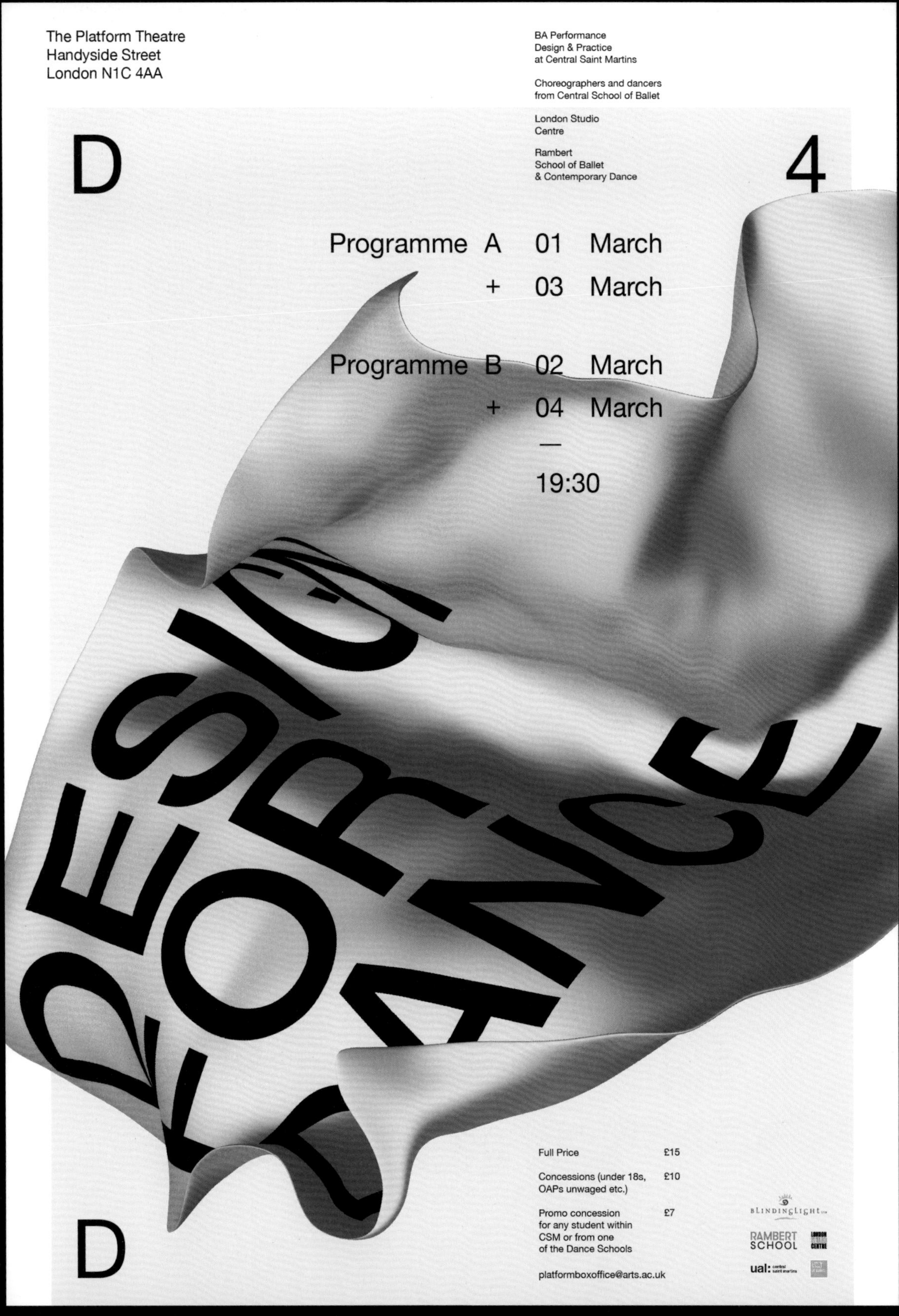

The Platform Theatre
Handyside Street
London N1C 4AA

BA Performance
Design & Practice
at Central Saint Martins

Choreographers and dancers
from Central School of Ballet

London Studio
Centre

Rambert
School of Ballet
& Contemporary Dance

D

4

Programme A   01   March
+   03   March

Programme B   02   March
+   04   March
—
19:30

DESIGN
FOR
DANCE

Full Price   £15

Concessions (under 18s,   £10
OAPs unwaged etc.)

Promo concession   £7
for any student within
CSM or from one
of the Dance Schools

platformboxoffice@arts.ac.uk

BLINDINGLIGHT...

RAMBERT
SCHOOL

LONDON
STUDIO
CENTRE

ual: central
saint martins

D

"YSHOW" THE 1ST

The Y Show is a joint exhibition that gathers the works of local and international art and design graduates in Macau. It strives to be an integrated and appealing platform to showcase Macau's design industry. For its first edition, Chiii Design tapped into the sense of tension and used trendy fashion colours as visual design elements to represent vibrancy and youth.

Chiii Design

Client: Chiu Yeng Culture Limited

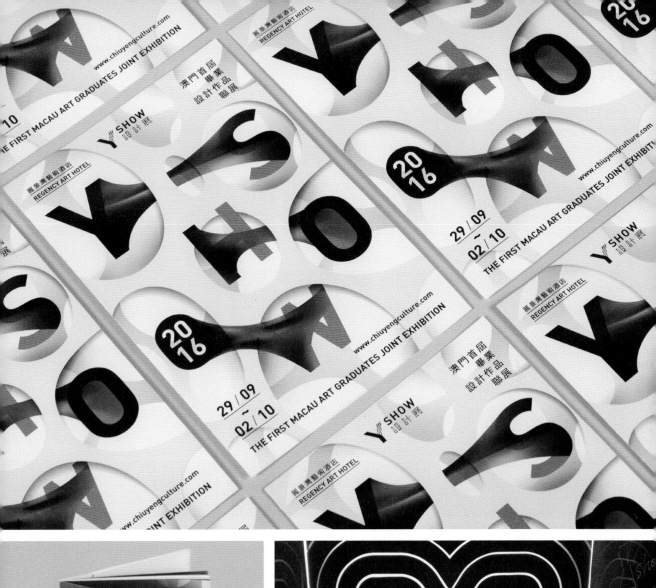

"Iridescence as a means of communication is far older than humanity."

Photos of Wave Garden Installation at the Cosmos Exhibition at Daejeon Museum of Art South Korea

Although Paul Friedlander has always dreamt of building his own spaceship since his youth, his art has become the vessel for his imagination in adulthood. The Light Harp is a continuation of a series of artworks and his fascination with waves; generative forms arising from the interaction of forces within the piece. Luminous colours change dynamically and endlessly in response to algorithmic software that controls the chromastrobic lights which are arranged on the ground in a way that shines up into the wave patterns.

Paul Friedlander

Special credits: Carole Purnelle, Nuno Maya, Laurie Spiegel

White City Place

To celebrate White City Place as the crucible for creative ideas, dn&co. based their design work on the idea of 'Networked for Creative Thought'. They created a kinetic identity that expressed the fluid nature and power of networks, where different paths cross to form something new, exponential, and limitless. The colour scheme takes a cue from how 'white' light can be broken down into a spectrum, while the blend of colours reinforces the dynamic nature of the place itself.

dn&co.

Client: Stanhope plc, Mitsui Fudosan, AIMCo • **Photo:** Guy Archard, Tian Khee Siong

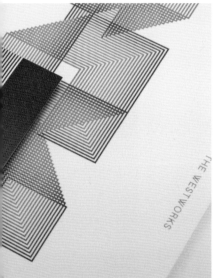

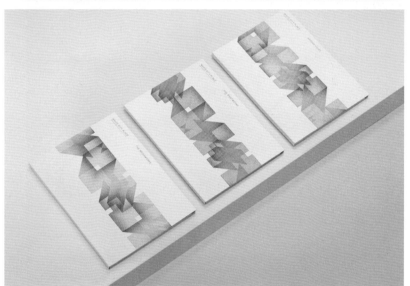

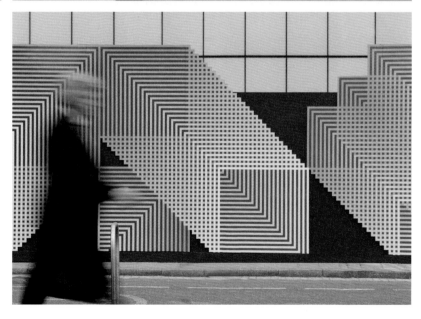

"It is easy to induce an interaction by using iridescence even when designing on stationary materials."

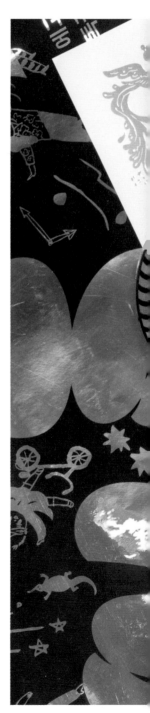

Ego Function Error

Kimgarden designed the concert poster for Seoul-based rock band Ego Function Error's new album release. To represent the nature of the band's punk and psychedelic music which is fun yet difficult to explain, they combined holographic paper with youthful and playful illustrations.

Kimgarden

Client: Ego Function Error • **Illustration:** Choi Jin Young

2016헌나1
-
11 / 04
2016

박근혜 화법

내가 이러려고 대통령을 했나라는
자괴감이 들정도로 괴롭기만 합니다

박근혜 - 최순실 게이트
관련 2차 대국민 사과에서

Swing's Voice

Inspired by the way ciphers often hide the true meanings of messages, Lee Chulwoong used holographic hues and ambiguous forms to represent the incoherent speech style of Park Geun-hye, the 18th president of South Korea. Based on her key quotes, he created an abstract visual language to amplify the sense of distraction and disruption in a satirical way.

Lee Chulwoong

Matías
Elichabehere

R h u m

Matías
Elichab

Matías Elichabehere — Rhum

Alexis Jamet visually translated French producer and singer Matías Elichabehere's new song about 'jellyrish, rum, and drunkenness' into metaphorical blurry images. These images were then printed and scanned to keep them looking naturally vaporous and granular, after which the prints were digitally animated with foam effects and gelatinous moves. The resulting holographic palette complements the meaning of the song.

Alexis Jamet

Client: Matías Elichabehere

Matías Elichabehere

Rhum

here Rhum

Matías
Elichabehere

Rhum

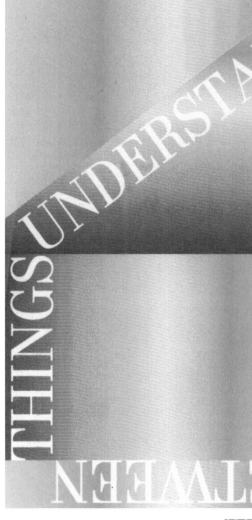

Self Motivation

Marina Lewandowska created a series of posters that experiment with colour composition, geometric shapes, and bold type. Based on motivational phrases that were most important to her, she played with typography to visually reflect the meanings of the phrases themselves. The resulting overall effect is a fresh take on retro-futuristic art.

Marina Lewandowska

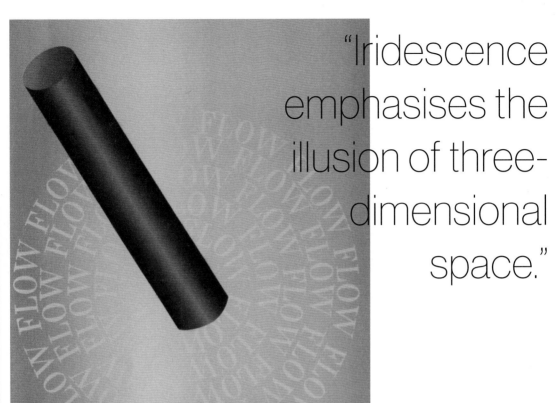

RELATIONSHIP

"Iridescence emphasises the illusion of three-dimensional space."

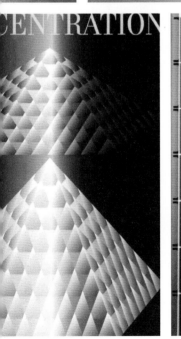

CONCENTRATION

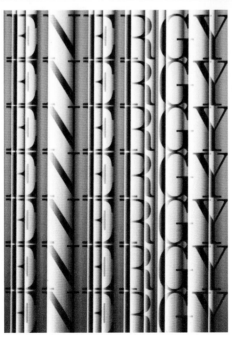

ENERGY

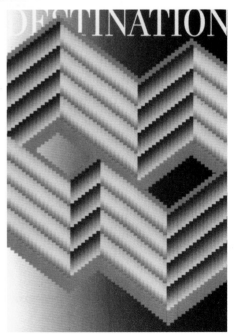

DESTINATION

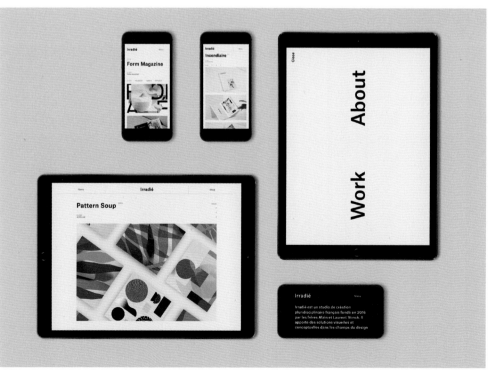

Irradié Identity

Irradié's own brand identity design is based on the French word 'irradié', which means 'the spreading of light'. True to their essence and design aesthetics, the studio applied this concept throughout all of their communication materials. Holographic hot foil and debossing were used to explore the propagation of light and colour further, giving the work additional depth and movement.

Irradié

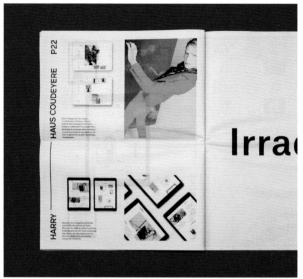

"Iridescence is part of our studio's visual identity. We wanted to play with the reflections of light and shadows on our business cards."

London Fashion Week 2017

Pentagram designed a visual and graphic system that tied together a series of leading fashion events, namely the London Fashion Week, London Fashion Week Men's, and London Fashion Week Festival. They focused on providing a coherent voice while retaining the individuality of each event by manifesting the creative process that fashion designers typically go through. Holographic touches on a monochromatic palette infused dynamism and movement into the work.

Pentagram

Client: British Fashion Council •
Outdoor Screen Photo: Ocean Outdoor

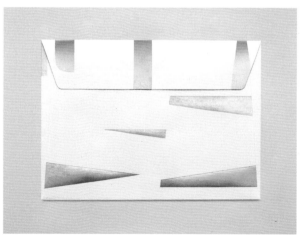

LONDON FASHION WEEK
15–19 SEPTEMBER 2017

The British Fashion Council
invites you to

_____

Date

_____

Time

_____

Block   Row

_____

The BFC Show Space
The Store Studios
180 Strand, London
WC2R 1EA

#LFW

Please present this invitation upon
arrival at London Fashion Week.
Strictly by invitation only.

"The movement
found in iridescent foil
illustrates the feeling
of energy in fashion
creation."

British Higher School of Art & Design Brochures

To depict the atmosphere and education one can expect at the British Higher School of Art & Design in Moscow, Shuka Design created a series of vibrant brochures using multiple colours and patterns to differentiate the courses. All the brochures were held together by a clean layout system and the school logo on the cover embossed in gasoline foil. The foil's holographic nature, coupled with the play of graphic shapes and lines, embodied dynamism and diversity.

Shuka Design

Client: British Higher School of Art & Design

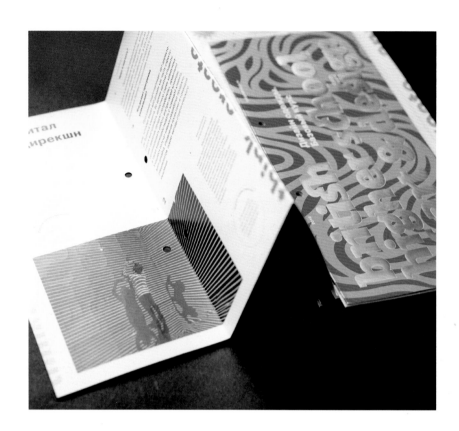

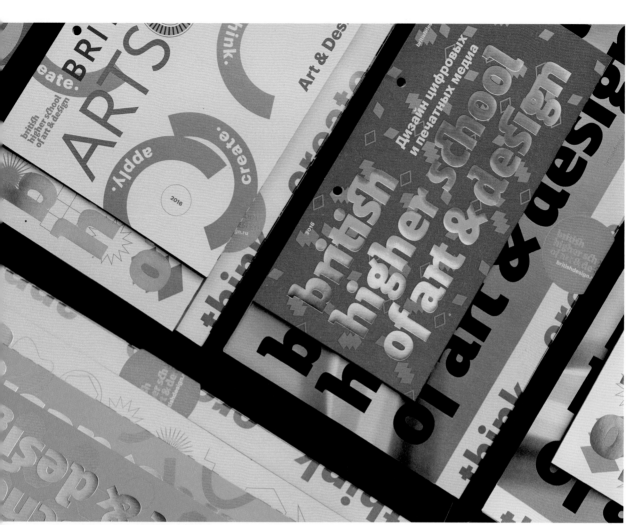

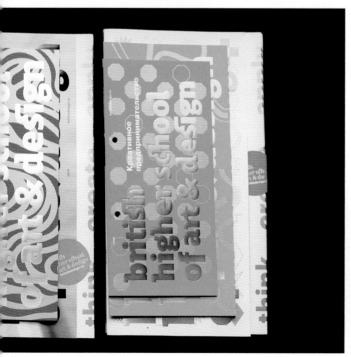

VR Fest

VR Fest celebrates virtual reality, augmented reality, and mixed reality through immersive art, media art, and technology. For its festival identity, Futura explored new processes and tools through software to create volumetric shapes that represent physical environments around the world. A synthetic colour palette was adopted to represent modern pop culture, while strident colourimetry was applied to different materials for visual impact.

Futura

Client: VR Fest • **Photo:** Rodrigo Chapa

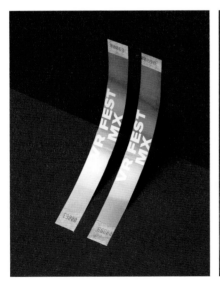

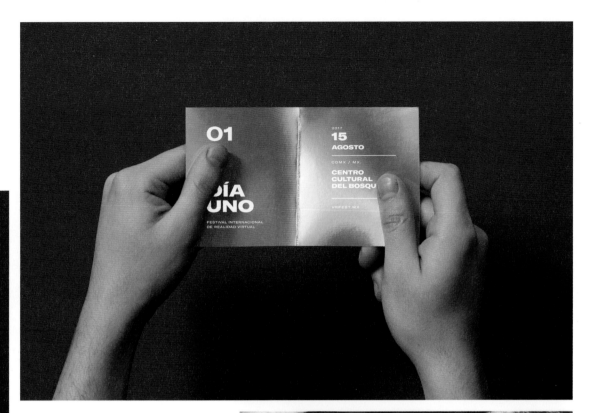

Sam Fox Lecture Series Calendar

The Sam Fox School of Design and Visual Arts' Public Lecture Series is well known for its influential and inspiring speakers and programmes. For its 2016 fall edition, Amanda Reiter created a fresh and exciting mailer that doubled as an informational calendar on one side and a fun poster on the other. She focused on colour by setting a simple layout grid against a saturated red, blue, and green spectrum.

Amanda Reiter

Special credits: Sam Fox School of Design and Visual Arts, Baugasm

9.09
*Museum Exhibition Opening & 10th Anniversary Celebration ***
Real / Radical / Psychological: The Collection on Display
6–10p | Kemper Art Museum

Celebrate the 10th anniversary of the Mildred Lane Kemper Art Museum building and the founding of the Sam Fox School of Design & Visual Arts.

9.10
*Gallery Talk ***
Sabine Eckmann
1p | Kemper Art Museum

Sabine Eckmann, William T. Kemper Director and Chief Curator, will discuss works in the exhibition Real / Radical / Psychological: The Collection on Display.

9.14
Artist Talk & Book Signing
Charlie le Mindu
4–6p | Kemp Auditorium

Hosted by Barrett Barrera Presents
Paris-based visual artist Charlie le Mindu will deliver an artist talk, followed by a book signing of Haute Coiffure.

9.15
Spotlight Talk
Allison Unruh
5p | Kemper Art Museum

Allison Unruh, associate curator, will discuss Carrie Mae Weems's Untitled (Colored People God) (2009–10).

9.19
Public Lecture Series
Dario Robleto
6p Reception | 6:30p Lecture - Steinberg Steinberg Auditorium

Arthur L. and Sheila Prensky Island Press Visiting Artist Lecture
As the Arthur L. and Sheila Prensky Island Press Visiting Artist for Fall 2016, Houston-based artist Dario Robleto will deliver a lecture titled The Polar Armed With a Pen: An Unknown History of the Human Heartbeat.

9.21
Discussions in Architectural History and Theory Lecture
Robin Middleton
Noon | Kemp Auditorium

Robin Middleton, professor emeritus in the Department of Art History and Archaeology at Columbia University, will deliver a lecture titled Flashpoints, or Yet Another Attempt at a History of Twentieth Century Architecture as part of DISCUSSIONS in Architectural History and Theory.

9.23
Film Screening
Frei Otto: Spanning the Future
6p | Steinberg Auditorium

The Sam Fox School Student Council presents a free public screening of Frei Otto: Spanning the Future, a documentary about the life and works of Frei Otto, told in his own words and by those he inspired.

* In conjunction with Real / Radical / Psychological: The Collection on Display

9.26
Public Lecture Series
Martino Stierli
6p Reception | Kemper Art Museum
6:30p Lecture | Steinberg Auditorium

Harris Armstrong Fund Lecture
Martino Stierli, the Philip Johnson Chief Curator of Architecture and Design at the Museum of Modern Art, will deliver a lecture addressing photomontage as a quintessential means of representation in modernity.

9.27
Dedication of the Douglas B. Dowd Modern Graphic History Library
10a–Noon Open House | West Campus
1–4p Symposium | Brown Hall
6p Reception, 6:30p Lecture | Steinberg Auditorium

Chancellor Mark S. Wrighton announces the dedication of the Douglas B. Dowd Modern Graphic History Library, a division of Special Collections. Made possible by an endowing gift from Ken and Nancy Kranzberg.

9.27
Thinking the Museum: Exhibition Design
Sabine Eckmann, Frank Escher, Ravi GuneWardena, Angela Pang, & Jan Ulmer
6p | Kemper Art Museum

Since the beginning of the twentieth century artists have employed exhibition design as an experimental new art form to intervene in existing institutional structures and art historical canons.

9.28
Public Lecture Series
Wangechi Mutu
6p Reception | 6:30p Lecture

Artist Wangechi Mutu, whose work is concerned with questions of self-image, humanness, and representation, will speak as part of the Sam Fox School Public Lecture Series. Sponsored by the Office of the Provost and the Law, Identity & Culture Initiative in the School of Law.

Thorsten Deckler

10.4
*Kemper Art Museum Film Series ***
Pollock (2000)
7p | Tivoli Theatre, 6350 Delmar Blvd.

Directed by and starring Ed Harris as Abstract Expressionist painter Jackson Pollock, the film looks at the career and the tumultuous life of the man who has fittingly been called "an artist dedicated to concealment, a celebrity who nobody knew."

10.5
*Kemper Art Museum Film Series ***
Moulin Rouge (1952)
7p | Tivoli Theatre, 6350 Delmar Blvd.

In his Oscar-nominated role, José Ferrer portrays Henri de Toulouse-Lautrec, whose work embodies the spirit of bohemian Paris in the 1890s.

10.6
*Kemper Art Museum Film Series ***
The Mystery of Picasso (1956)
7p | Tivoli Theatre, 6350 Delmar Blvd.

Through a combination of stop-motion and time-lapse photography, director Henri-Georges Clouzot films Pablo Picasso at work in his studio, emerging with a quiet documentary that captures the revolutionary artist's creative process.

Kemper Museum Image

10.6
*Kemper Art Museum Film Series ***
The Mystery of Picasso (1956)
7p | Tivoli Theatre, 6350 Delmar Blvd.

Through a combination of stop-motion and time-lapse photography, director Henri-Georges Clouzot films Pablo Picasso at work in his studio, emerging with a quiet documentary that captures the revolutionary artist's creative process.

10.7
Opening Reception
Ontology of Influence: Ron Leax and Alumni Exhibition
6–8p | Des Lee Gallery, 1627 Washington Ave.

In honor and celebration of his remarkable thirty-year tenure as a professor of art at Washington University, the Des Lee Gallery presents Ontology of Influence: Ron Leax and Alumni Exhibition, featuring artwork by Leax and thirty-seven alumni with whom he has worked closely.

10.13
Spotlight Talk
Elizabeth C. Childs
5p | Kemper Art Museum

Elizabeth C. Childs, Etta and Mark Steinberg Professor of Art History and chair, Department of Art History & Archaeology in Arts & Sciences, will discuss Paul Gauguin's Te Atua (The Gods) (1899).

10.19
Public Lecture Series
Shelley Rice
6p Reception | Kemper Art Museum
6:30p Lecture | Steinberg Auditorium

Women and the Kemper Lecture
Shelley Rice, Arts Professor in the Department of Photography & Imaging and Department of Art History at New York University, will deliver the inaugural Women and the Kemper Lecture, titled "Rio de Janeiro and the World: Marc Ferrez, Photographic Mobility, and International Modernity".

10.20
Public Lecture Series
Amale Andraos
6p Reception | 6:30p Lecture Steinberg Auditorium

Ruth Kahn Lynford Lecture
Amale Andraos, dean of Columbia University's Graduate School of Architecture, Planning and Preservation (GSAPP) and co-founder of WORKac, a New York based architectural and urban practice with international reach, will deliver the Ruth Kahn Lynford Lecture, titled Five Year Plan.

10.21
Informal Cities Workshop Lecture
Amale Andraos
6p Reception | 6:30p Lecture Steinberg Auditorium

Architect Thorsten Deckler will deliver a public lecture titled Armed Response—architectural nonsevens in Johannesburg to kick off the Informal Cities Workshop.

10.24
*Performance ***
Art Inspiring Music: New Morse Code
5p | Kemper Art Museum

The Kemper Art Museum partners with the Department of Music in Arts & Sciences to welcome the cello / percussion duo New Morse Code, performing music inspired by the exhibition Real / Radical / Psychological: The Collection on Display.
Presented with the Department of Music in Arts & Sciences

10.24
Public Lecture Series
Seymour Chwast
6p Reception | 6:30p Lecture Steinberg Auditorium

Graphic designer Seymour Chwast will deliver a lecture titled God/Sex/War as part of the Sam Fox School Public Lecture Series.
Co-sponsored by Modern Graphic History Library

10.24
Public Lecture Series
Seymour Chwast
6p Reception | 6:30p Lecture Steinberg Auditorium

Graphic designer Seymour Chwast will deliver a lecture titled God/Sex/War as part of the Sam Fox School Public Lecture Series.
Co-sponsored by Modern Graphic History Library

10.27
*Gallery Talk ***
Allison Unruh
5p | Kemper Art Museum

Allison Unruh, associate curator, will discuss works in the exhibition Real / Radical / Psychological: The Collection on Display.

10.29
*Family Fun Saturday ***
11a–3p | Kemper Art Museum

Celebrating the Museum's ten years in the current building, this Family Fun Saturday will have interactive artmaking experiences inspired by the Museum's renowned permanent collection.
Funded in part by the Women's Society of Washington University and Women and the Kemper.

11.7
Public Lecture Series
Tom Friedman
6p Reception | Kemper Art Museum
6:30p Lecture | Steinberg Auditorium

Art on Campus Lecture
American artist Tom Friedman is known for works that often make unconventional use of ordinary materials, exploiting earnest visual perception, logic, and humor.

11.9
Public Lecture Series
Philippe Rahm
6p Reception | 6:30p Lecture Steinberg Auditorium

AIA St. Louis Scholarship Fund Lecture
Swiss architect Philippe Rahm, principal in the office of Philippe Rahm architectes in Paris, will deliver the annual AIA St. Louis Scholarship Fund Lecture, titled Gradient pneumatics: recent work by Philippe Rahm architectes.

11.10
*Gallery Talk ***
Meredith Malone
5p | Kemper Art Museum

Meredith Malone, associate curator, will discuss works in the exhibition Real / Radical / Psychological: The Collection on Display.

11.14
Public Lecture Series
Henry L. and Natalie E. Freund Visiting Artist Lecture
6p Reception | 6:30p Lecture Steinberg Auditorium

John Douglas Powers
John Douglas Powers will deliver the Henry L. and Natalie E. Freund Visiting Artist Lecture, titled Movement and Meaning.

12.1
Spotlight Talk
Jennifer Padgett
5p | Kemper Art Museum

Jennifer Padgett, PhD candidate, Department of Art History & Archaeology in Arts & Sciences, will discuss Stuart Davis's Flying Carpet (1942).

12.2
Opening Reception
Parabola 2016
6–9p | Des Lee Gallery, 1627 Washington Ave.

festival techno audiovisual

25__27
/11 / 16

Ciudad Cultural Konex

SUB

festival techno
audiovisual

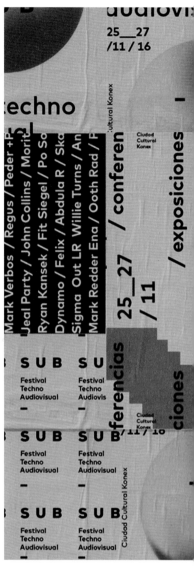

SUB-Techno Audiovisual Festival

Mariana Cecilia Iriberri worked on a themed design project that would bring an electronic music-driven festival to life. To portray an immersive aural and visual experience in a factory environment, the festival's hypothetical venue, she set bright hues against a muted greyscale palette as well as a mixture of minimal typography and layouts to convey the ambivalence between darkness and light.

Mariana Cecilia Iriberri

Special credits: FADU-UBA (Universidad de Buenos Aires), Cátedra Gabriele, Diseño III

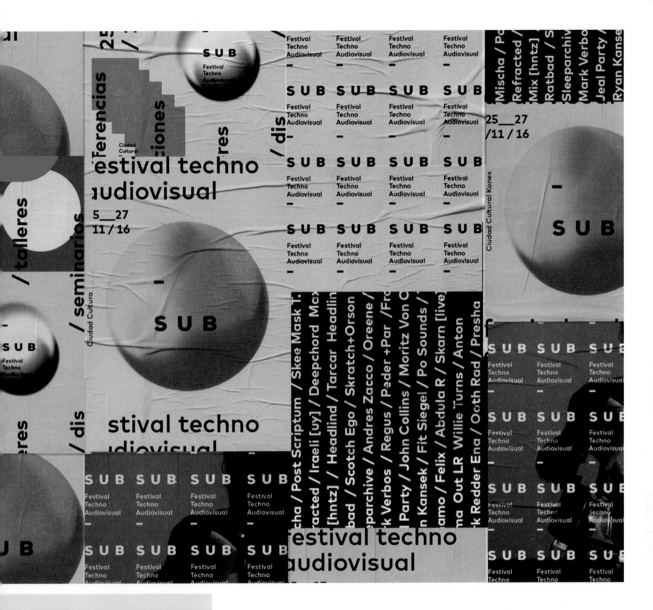

"Besides being an abstract way of communication, [iridescence] has the power of transmitting different sensations."

Adobe InDesign CC2018

Adobe has always been known as the creative platform of choice for designers all over the world. For the Adobe InDesign CC 2018 splash screen, My Name is Wendy collaborated with Ruslan Khasanov to create eye-catching artwork by pairing geometric patterns in monochrome with organic holographic splashes. The colourful combination of contrasts embodies a fusion of the software's fluidity and precision in function.

Studio My Name is Wendy, Ruslan Khasanov
Client: Adobe

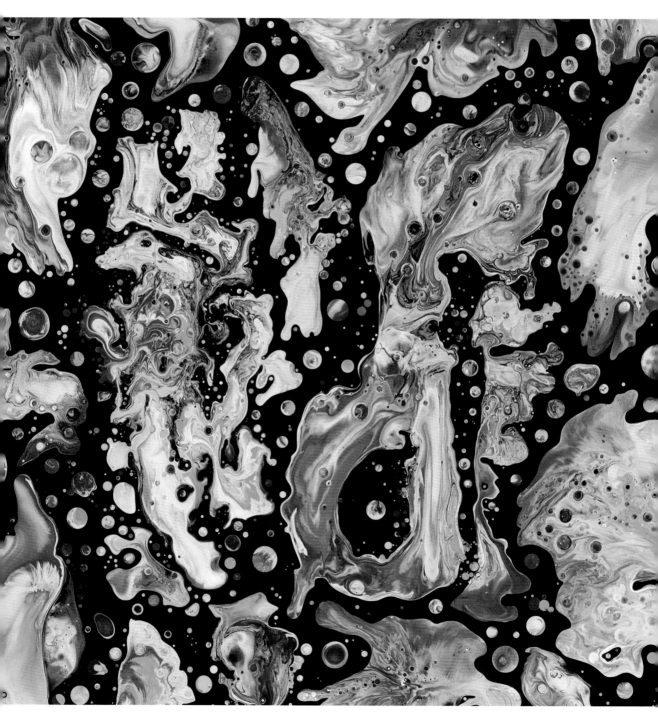

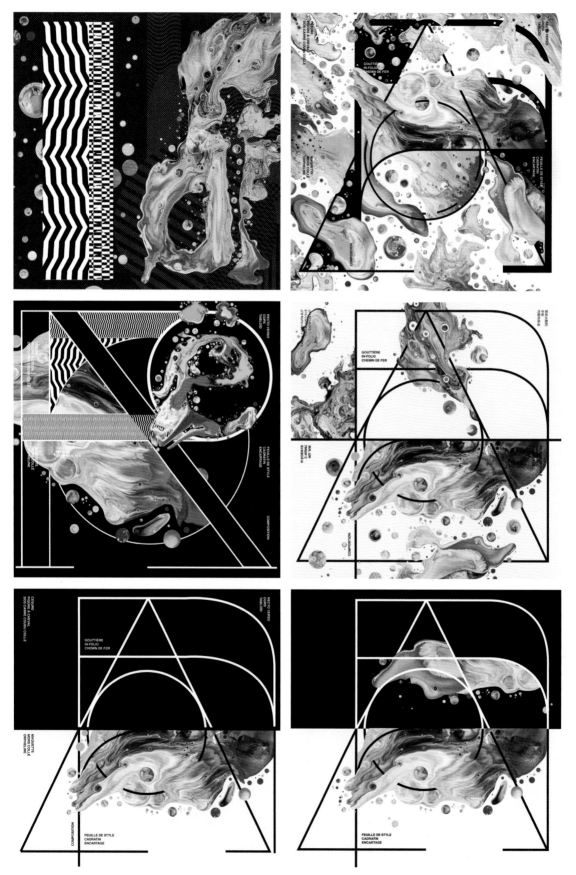

"Iridescence was a good way to create a new visual [for this project]. The context of creation motivated this particular choice."

CESURA
PIQÛRE À CHEVAL
KANSIPAPERII

RECTO VERSO
小口
SCHUTBLAD

GOUTTIÈRE
ΑΠΡΟШ
RISGUARDI

BUCHFORMAT
EM DASH
スタイルシート

ШМУЦТИТУЛ
페이지 레이아웃
CHEMIN DE FER

COMPOSITION

Holland Festival 2017

The Holland Festival is Amsterdam's most important international performing arts festival, with a rich heritage in poster design. For its 70th anniversary, thonik took a radical approach by drawing inspiration from and applying digital code onto their on-ground work instead of the other way round. The coding turned images and film clips provided by the theatre groups into organic and colourful abstractions.

thonik

Client: Holland Festival

"[Iridescence] radiates optimism and pleasure. It is a way to show all colours, to express inclusiveness."

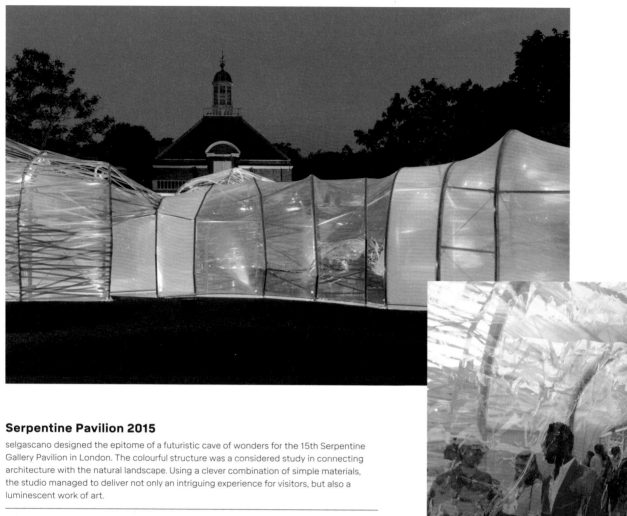

Serpentine Pavilion 2015

selgascano designed the epitome of a futuristic cave of wonders for the 15th Serpentine Gallery Pavilion in London. The colourful structure was a considered study in connecting architecture with the natural landscape. Using a clever combination of simple materials, the studio managed to deliver not only an intriguing experience for visitors, but also a luminescent work of art.

selgascano

Client: Serpentine Galleries • **Photo:** Iwan Baan

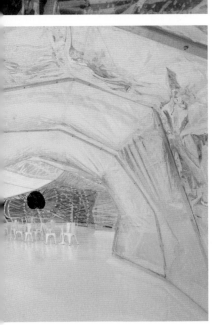

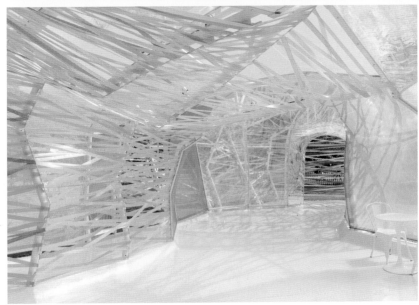

"We sought a way to experience architecture through its most common, simple elements: structure, light, transparency."

Internal Mutation

Evin Tison's Internal Mutation collection showcases a woman with both the 'perfect' aesthetic and a non-conventional personality: a free and eccentric spirit who is not bothered by prejudices. By playing with volume and materials like semi-transparent latex, iridescent PVC, liquid vinyl, and sulphured plastic sheets, she reflected the mutation of her subject's outward appearance into the inner self.

Evin Tison

Photo: Robin Lempire, Gaetan Caputo

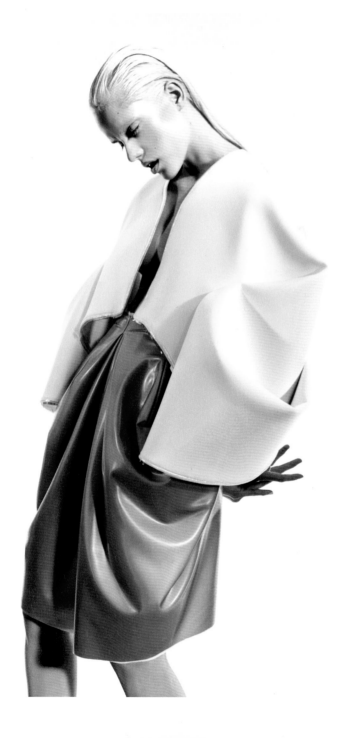

"I love to imagine that the consciousness, dreams, thoughts, and ideas within us are materialised by iridescence."

Under The Sea

In collaboration with accessory designer brand Wiggle Wiggle, Sydney Sie staged a bright and playful photo shoot to showcase their new luminescent clamshell phone case. Using summery props like tropical leaves and scuba gear with holographic sheets that complement the case, she captured the brand's fun and youthful vibes.

Sydney Sie

Client: Wiggle Wiggle

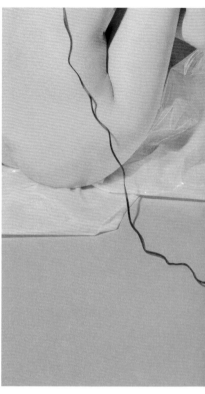

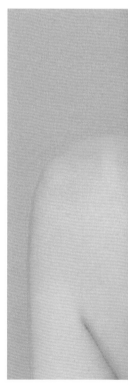

Mellow Collection

The Mellow Collection is a series of 'living' products that respond to light in a unique way. Inspired by late-19th century art print impressionism and techniques, blurred and transparent finishes were used to create different atmospheres. As a result, the colour gradations on the surfaces induce subtle changes that transform the aesthetics of each product.

HATTERN, UMZIKIM

"Colours are very powerful communication tools for people around the world, without the need for words."

Soft

For Glas Italia, nendo created three low tables using frosted glass and brightly coloured joints that created a gradation effect when bonded. By printing a pattern on the reverse side of the frosted glass, they evoked a natural and soft effect that expressed a delicate blurriness; an appearance that contradicts the conventional image of glass, which is a hard and sharp material.

nendo

Client: Glas Italia • **Photo:** Kenichi Sonehara

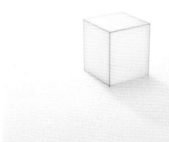

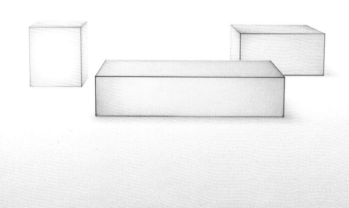

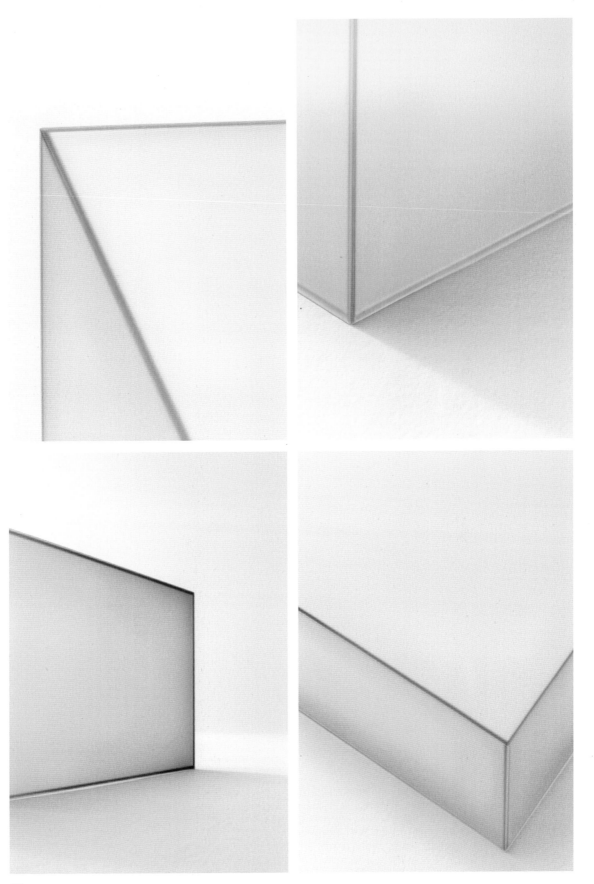

Crystal Series

Saerom Yoon was inspired by the sky's rich and beautiful colours to create the Crystal Series. He dyed acrylic material to maintain its transparency and create an optical illusion within to express the sky as a concept of space and time. The overall shapes of the furniture appear distorted from various angles due to the reflections and refractions within the transparent surfaces.

Saerom Yoon

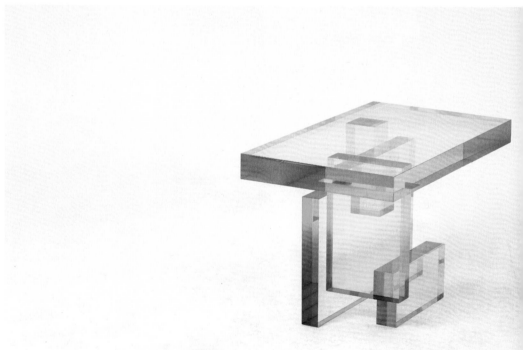

Shimmer

Patricia Urquiola designed a luminous collection for furniture brand Glas Italia in laminated and glued glass characterised by a special iridescent, multichromatic finish. The nuances of each piece in the collection change depending on the light source and vantage point.

Glas Italia, Patricia Urquiola

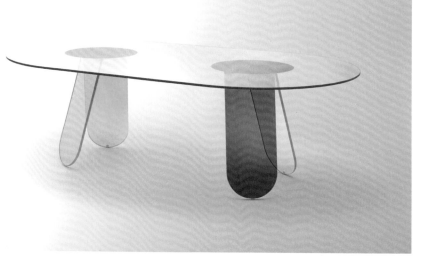

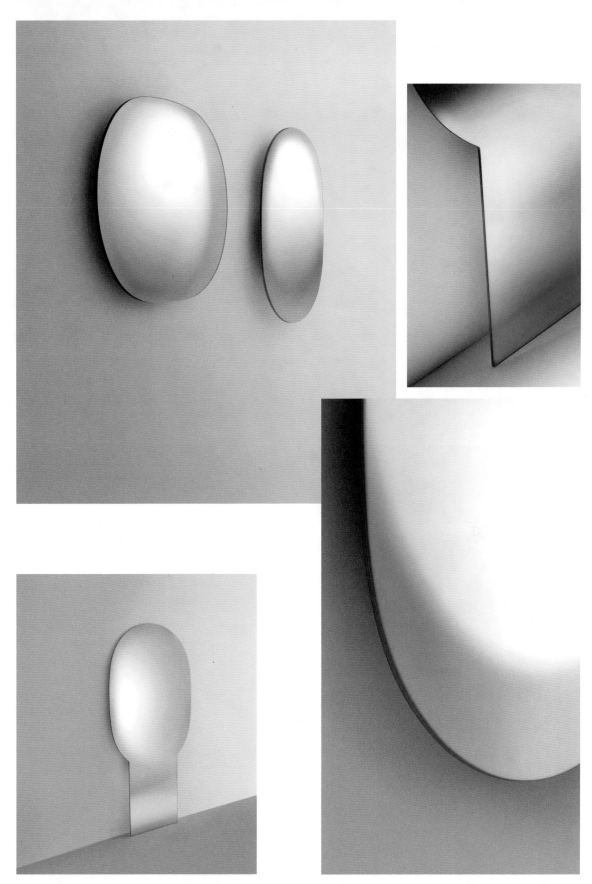

101

101 is a coding and design agency that believes in the power of a good concept. They work with, and not for, their clients, as they are convinced that in meeting eye-to-eye, the best results can be achieved. By seeking challenges in every project, they aim to surprise their clients and themselves with ideas and solutions.

Anagrama

Anagrama is an international branding, architecture, and software development firm with offices in Monterrey and Mexico City. Their client list consists of companies in varied industries from all around the world. They create the perfect balance between a design boutique and a business consultancy by focusing on the development of creative pieces and providing perfect solutions based on the analysis of tangible data.

Balmer Hählen

Balmer Hählen was founded in 2011 by Priscilla Balmer and Yvo Hählen. Currently based in Lausanne, they are involved in various collaborative projects with designers, stylists, artists, photographers, and printers. They pay special attention to the quality of their prints for outstanding outcomes.

Barkle, Daniel

Daniel is a London-based graphic designer whose skills lie in typography, print, and music design. He is the co-founder of the Dank Type, a curated design platform that gives exposure to the highest forms of typography.

Blanchette, Caroline

Caroline is an award-winning graphic designer and art director based in Canada. She has worked with multiple international advertising agencies for leading brands from all over the world.

BLOW

BLOW is a Hong Kong-based design studio founded by Ken Lo in 2010. They specialise in branding, packaging, print, and website design. As part of their creative ethos, they provide clients with simple and inspiring work powered by great ideas and executed with a high level of craftsmanship.

bonjour garçon studio

bonjour garçon studio is a Paris-based creative studio that was founded by Romain Fritiau and Pierre Tostain, a graphic designer and photographer respectively. Their works often embody their vision of the contemporary landscape through creative direction, graphic design, print, editorials, and fashion photography.

Bruce Mau Design

Bruce Mau Design brands organisations that are shaping the future of their respective industries worldwide. Their passion lies in bringing compelling ideas to life, invigorating brands, and helping businesses grow through their unrelenting commitment to leading-edge design. Their creative work is recognised for its depth of thought, clarity of purpose, and boldness of vision.

Build

Build is an award-winning creative studio with an international reputation for creating strong visual narratives. Utilising art direction and graphic design, they create brand identities, websites, packaging, and books for design-led clients around the world.

Chiii Design

Chiii Design specialises in integrating commercial elements with arts and culture. Headquartered in Macau, the studio provides consultancy services that focus on brand image and packaging design. Through their international vision and unique style, they are making waves in Asia, the U.K., the U.S. and beyond.

BIOGRAPHY

COLLINS

COLLINS is an independent, brand experience design company based in New York and San Francisco. They design products, environments, and communications that transform brands, drive businesses, and improve people's lives. Their clients include some of the world's leading companies, including Spotify, Facebook, Nike, Instagram, Target, Airbnb, and The Coca-Cola Company, among others.

102-103

Dasha F

Dasha F is an artist from Moscow who loves the colour pink.

134-135

Dawn Creative

Dawn Creative is a branding, design, digital, and motion agency. They wake up and shake up brands to make them fit and ready for the day ahead — like a shot of espresso. They are 'where stories are born and ideas shine brighter'.

098-099

Design Ranch

Design Ranch has been creating and reinvigorating forward-thinking brands for years. They drive results with sincere, compelling, and creative messages that are designed to build brand presence, awareness, and mindshare.

064-065

dn&co.

dn&co. is a brand and design consultancy inspired by culture and place. They have worked with some of the world's leading architects, developers, planners, and cultural leaders to create meaningful destinations and neighbourhoods.

190-191

ECAL/University of Art and Design Lausanne

ECAL or the École Cantonale d'Art de Lausanne is a university of art and design based in Renens, and is one of the top 10 in its field. ECAL's influence is reflected in numerous press articles and awards, exhibitions in prestigious venues, collaborations with well-known companies as well as the success of its graduates.

046-047 / 060-061

Established

Established was set up in 2007 by Sam O'Donahue and Becky Jones. A full-service boutique agency, they offer graphic design, branding, art direction and packaging design services, with a track record of creating highly-successful, award-winning global brands for a wide range of clients.

078-079

Evans, Davy

Davy is an award-winning multi-disciplinary artist and designer based in Brighton. Armed with his background in graphic design, he fuses analogue and digital techniques to create ethereal, abstract imagery. He often uses experimental photographic methods combined with light and liquid in an attempt to replicate colour, form, and distortions found in the natural world.

158-160 / 174-175

Flov Creative Agency

Flov Creative Agency is based in Wroclaw. They are a part of NOMONO, a strategic brand consultancy, design studio, and production company that fuses strong conceptual thinking with rigorous attention to detail to create timeless and effective work.

070-071

Foreign Policy Design Group

Foreign Policy Design Group is a team of idea makers and storytellers who help brands evolve via the creative and strategic deployment of traditional and digital media channels. Helmed by Yah-Leng Yu and Arthur Chin, they work on a smorgasbord of projects spanning from creative direction and design to digital strategy, research and marketing campaign services for a variety of clients.

124-125

Friedlander, Paul

Paul is a London-based scientific artist who first trained as a physicist with a degree from Sussex University, where his personal tutor Tony Leggett subsequently received the Nobel prize for his works on superfluids. He continues to have a lively interest in the sciences, which inform and shape his creative work.

188-189

Fundamental

Fundamental is a Hong Kong-based creative studio with the belief that substantial communication is the key to creating and providing the best designs and solutions to clients.

130-133

Futura

Futura was founded in 2008 by Vicky González and Iván García. The intersection of two different backgrounds and working methods has given them a unique way of approaching projects, while finding balance between stiffness and rebellion.

068-069 / 212-213

Gerber, Selina

Selina is an aspiring graphic designer who loves to experiment with colours, shapes, and typography. She also enjoys expressing her talent for drawing with illustrations that range from the witty to the ambitious.

058-059

Glas Italia

Glas Italia was established in Brianza in the early 1970s. Driven by an unbridled passion for glass manufacturing, they produce modern pieces of furniture, door-wall partitions, and accessories in crystal glass — drawing from years of experience and technical know-how.

Golubovic, Vanja

Vanja graduated from the School of Applied Arts in Geneva. She first worked in several advertising and branding agencies before starting her own practice as an independent graphic designer. In 2016, she co-founded Onlab, a graphic design studio with a strong focus on content, narrative, and visual quality.

Gragnaniello, Catello

Catello was born in Naples, where he currently lives and works. Driven by his passion for technology, he began dabbling in 3D graphics and motion graphic design after bouts of experimentation. His recent work is the result of exploring new perspectives and means of expression.

HATTERN, UMZIKIM

Hattern is a product brand that exemplifies the beauty of ombre colours and material combinations. It was brought to life under the art direction of Jae Yang, who currently works between Seoul and Milan under UMZIKIM.

Hey

Hey is a graphic design and illustration studio based in Barcelona. They work on finding the right solutions for each project by overseeing every aspect of the design process and working closely with their clients. Their style is defined by geometry, colour, typography, and bold graphics, which the owners also carry over into their personal projects as a means of breaking down barriers and finding new ways of doing things.

HOUTH

HOUTH is a creative studio based in Taipei that flexibly integrates ideas, creativity, strategy, design, and resources to create fresh solutions and stories for clients.

Hovercraft Studio

Hovercraft Studio is an independent creative studio with offices in Portland and Denver. Their work is brand-centric and focuses on environments, retail and interactive experiences as well as site-specific installations.

Iriberri, Mariana Cecilia

Mariana is a graphic designer from Argentina who graduated from Universidad de Buenos Aires (UBA). She considers herself to be a curious and observant person with a constant need to learn and search for new experiences. Her passion lies in music and visual expressions.

Irradié

L'atelier Irradié is a multi-disciplinary creative studio founded in 2016 by brothers Alain and Laurent Vonck. They offer visual and conceptual solutions in graphic design, art direction, and digital design. Their focus is on branding, graphical systems, publications, and digital interfaces for a variety of clients —always with the same intellectual curiosity and passion.

Jamet, Alexis

Alexis is a French graphic designer based in the U.K. His diverse work ranges from conventional identities to bright and charming illustrations. He shares his time between graphic design, art direction, and drawing.

Jaokar, Siddhant

Siddhant is an industrial designer-turned-visual artist based in Mumbai. He believes in creating human experiences.

Kati Forner Design

Kati is a Los Angeles-based creative director with years of experience in print and digital design. Rooted in classical design and forms, she creates a blend of minimal yet impactful work.

Khasanov, Ruslan

Ruslan is a designer and visual artist whose work is driven by the motto 'beauty is everywhere'. The ability to express strong emotions through visual art, experimentation, and improvisation plays a central role in his creative process. At the heart of his work is the desire to show synergy between art, science, and design; that these disciplines are not separated by academism, but can be organised through mutual reinforcement.

Kimgarden

Kimgarden is a Seoul-based graphic design studio founded by Lee Yun Ho and Kim Kang In. They work with companies, museums, artists, and publishers in various fields. Fuelled by their strong interest in gardening, they have also designed gardening-related products.

Kolory

Kolory is a design and print studio based in Kraków. They aim to create designs that audiences would 'want to keep holding in their hands', or cannot take their eyes away from. Besides veering towards things that are light, clear, and well designed, they enjoy experimenting with print by combining seemingly incompatible materials, textures, and techniques.

Kuiachek, Anna

Anna is a graphic designer from Ukraine. After her residency at Fabrica in Treviso, she became an art director at the Strelka Institute for Media, Architecture and Design, where she currently oversees all the visualisation of public and educational programmes. She also works for the Strelka Press, a publishing house at the Institute.

162-163

Lee, Chulwoong

Chulwoong has a master's degree in communication design from Kookmin University. He seeks design expressions that extend beyond the two-dimensional. His interest in abstractness, fortuity, and infinity rather than delivering a clear message drives him to explore the true role of a designer, supported by technological developments.

194-195

Lewandowska, Marina

Marina is currently working as a graphic designer in Vienna. After graduating in 2017, she was an intern at Eduardo Aires Studio in Portugal. She also worked at the Oskar Zięta-run Zieta Prozessdesign studio while she was studying at the Wrocław Academy of Art and Design.

198-199

Machineast

Machineast is an independent creative design studio that focuses on 3D typography and graphic design. Over the course of many years in the motion graphic, advertising, and design industry, they have collaborated with many creative studios, advertising agencies, and brands worldwide. Driven by a great passion for making things aesthetically pleasing, Machineast always does its best to offer creative solutions to clients and collaborators.

140-143

Midnight Design

Midnight Design consists of a team of talented designers from various fields. They devote themselves to brainstorming and interweaving creative ideas all through the night for extraordinary designs. To accomplish their mission through unique perspectives and dynamic analysis, they dedicate their time to solving client dilemmas.

110-111

Mubien

Mubien is a design and handmade production studio-workshop based in Santander. Besides specialising in branding, corporate identity, and handmade productions, they enjoy researching new formulas, combinations and techniques to apply onto their work.

020-021 / 122-123

nendo

nendo was founded by its Chief Designer Oki Sato in 2002, who has been named one of 'The 100 Most Respected Japanese' by Newsweek magazine. He has also won many 'Designer of the Year' awards from major publications around the world. The studio is involved in multifaceted work, spanning from graphic and product design to designing furniture, installations, windows, interiors, and architecture. nendo designs can be found in the Museum of Modern Art in New York, as well as Musée des Arts Décoratifs and Centre Pompidou in Paris.

240-241

Nonverbal Club

Nonverbal Club is a design studio, based in Porto and Berlin. They focus on providing custom design solutions and communication consultancy to clients looking for work that goes beyond their expectations. Every project that they undertake is a dedicated balancing act between craft and technology, rationality and poetry, as well as expectation and surprise.

062-063

Not Available Design

Not Available Design is a multi-disciplinary studio focused on branding, design strategy, and space design. Founded by Kit Cheuk and Billy Sung, they serve innovative and creative clients who love to inject playful and unexpected twists on everyday simplicity. Their philosophy is NOT following a set routine AVAILABLE in the market, and daring to be different.

084-085

Noviki

Noviki lives in a graphic utopia. The studio's signature style is a context-driven approach based on the idea of design as a source for searching and exploring fields of contemporary artistic expression. Their works span across various media formats, from books and typefaces to exhibition design, videos, and applications.

044-045

Packvision

Packvision is a design studio from Russia that specialises in developing packaging and labels. They actively apply holographic materials onto their designs and think of them as the basis for new ideas.

032-035

PALAST PHOTOGRAPHIE — Julien Palast

Julien is a French photographer based in Paris, France. His artistic work revolves around the body-object, reification, and fetishisation. His studio work revolves around still-lifes with retoucher Thierry Palast, for clients such as Baccarat, Clarins, Roger&Gallet, and Caudalie.

156-157

Paperlux Studio

Paperlux Studio was established in 2006, and consists of an unconventional team of branding experts, purebred designers, material fetishists, and project wizards in Hamburg. Their creations constantly evolve in an environment that combines a studio, office, and workshop for German and international brands.

048-049

Parámetro Studio

Parámetro Studio is a multi-disciplinary design practice based in Mexico. They are all about becoming something new and iconic.

010-013

Pentagram

Pentagram is the world's largest independently owned design studio. Their work encompasses graphics, architecture, interiors, products, packaging, exhibitions, installations, digital experiences, advertising and communications.

204-207

PONYO PORCO

PONYO PORCO is a brand that focuses on hand-painted printing. Launched in 2015, it was named after the founder's two axolotls, which are also featured on its logo to reflect the harmony and differences between individuals, as well as the brand philosophy.

022-025

PRYSME

PRYSME is a Bordeaux-based graphic design studio that values aesthetics, quality, and customisation. They base their creative ideas on their passion for beautiful papers, photography, and tailor-made websites.

161

Pyramid

Pyramid is a visual communication and sound design studio working for the music, arts, and culture sectors based in London and Lisbon. They are committed to using graphic design as a tool to always inquire about the world.

172-173

Rainaud, Alycia

Alycia is a French graphic designer based in Marseille. Influenced and driven by publishing and hybrid books, she has also started working as a digital artist known as Malavida to experiment with new technologies, digital painting, programming, and visual effects.

040-041

Reiter, Amanda

Amanda is a graphic designer whose approach is rooted in visual research and conceptual thinking. With a background in neuroscience and psychology, she wishes to use design to shape meaningful human experiences for her audiences. She focuses on branding, illustration, packaging, art direction and everything in between.

214-215

ROUX, Alexia

Alexia is a graphic designer based in Montpellier. She designs visual identities for various types of projects, including branding and publishing. Her skills lie in art direction as well as print and web design, where she attaches particular importance to the uniqueness of a brand image via its signs, shapes, and colours.

042-043 / 118-119

selgascano

selgascano is an intentionally-small atelier that has worked on a wide variety of projects with nature at the core of the programme. Established in 1998, their work is focused on research into the construction process, where they 'listen' to the largest possible number of elements involved at every stage. They strive to seek beauty that is comprehensible to any human being.

226-229

Semiotik Design Agency

Semiotik Design Agency relies on simplicity, functionality, and effectiveness strongly associated with emotional responsiveness. Their design methodology is research-based and aligned with the objectives of each project. This forms the foundation for being truthful to the content, sets the pace for successful outputs, and expands the creative opportunities.

096-097

Shuka Design

Shuka Design is a cosy design studio based in Moscow that tailors visual identities and illustrations, produces websites and makes books. They are renowned for creating the controversial London World Chess Championship 2018 visual identity.

208-211

Sie, Sydney

Sydney uses design, photography, animation, and video as a way to present art. Her creative approach to photography is based on a need to create a strong impression of the external form with an implied narrative buried within. She employs colour gradients, surreal imagery, the female body, and other graphical elements to construct ambiguous, two-dimensional worlds in her photographs.

234-235

Sion Hsu Graphic

Sion Hsu is a designer from Taiwan who is devoted to redesigning rural culture. Based in a small village called Tun Yuan Zih, he tries to show the world how beautiful his hometown is through his work. He believes that design should be accessible and everywhere.

112-113

Six N. Five

Six N. Five is a contemporary art duo based in Barcelona. Founded by Andy Reisinger and Ezequiel Pini, they specialise in still-life visuals with a clean, modern aesthetic that explore the frontier between art and design. Aside from working on advertising and editorial commissions, they also find time to create experimental work that legitimises CGI as the new medium for creative self-expression.

144-147

Studio AH—HA

Studio AH—HA was founded by university mates Carolina and Catarina after working with some of their design heroes. Currently based in Lisbon, they pursue varied creative interests, ranging from brand strategy, identity work, advertising, new media, traditional and fine print, retail and product design, photography, and illustration to interior design. With an ever-changing cast of collaborators, they have a holistic approach towards design, working together with clients through every stage of the process and filtering their inspirations into fresh, engaging and compelling brand messages.

092-093 / 164-167

Studio Band

Studio Band believes in brutally beautiful design. Their ethos is based on communicating and resonating with their clients and audiences. They offer creative yet effective solutions that are reached through intelligent understanding of the task at hand.

054-055

Studio My Name is Wendy

Studio My Name is Wendy was founded in 2006 as the result of a collaboration between graphic designers Carole Gautier and Eugénie Favre. They produce visual identities, typefaces, formal principals, pictures, patterns and printings for a variety of projects. It is their aim to create forms with cogency and expression.

218-221

Studio South

Studio South is a small design practice in the fields of brand identity and visual communication. They emphasise producing thoughtful, conceptually driven work that comes from a close understanding of their clients and their audiences. They seek to deliver ideas that not only resonate, but also endure with people.

086-089

Tarka, Peter

Peter is an art director and illustrator who creates CGI work that has viewers leaning in for a closer look. Having previously worked with commercial clients and agencies such as Nike, BMW, Audi, Google, Airbnb, Red Bull and many other renowned brands, the London-based creative has recently completed personal projects that showcase his talent for creating 3D illustrations.

150-151

The Acid House

The Acid House works on various concoctions of static and moving imagery. They are directors, designers, illustrators, animators, and sound designers rolled into one formidable team that takes a project from its conceptual and developmental stages to final renders of the work.

154-155

thonik

thonik is an Amsterdam-based design collective led by lauded designers Nikki Gonnissen and Thomas Widdershoven. Specialising in visual communication, graphic identity, interaction, and motion design, they offer their clients a visual voice that sets them apart from the rest, and places them at the top. They have their roots firmly planted in society, and seek to change the world, one design at a time.

222-225

Thorkels, Greta

Greta is an Icelandic-born graphic designer based in Berlin. She graduated with a BA degree in Visual Communication in 2016, with a background in Fine Arts. Currently, she focuses on art direction, editorial and music design.

178-179

Thorsby, Michael

Michael is a Paris-based graphic designer originally from Sweden. Having travelled across a variety of cities, he has picked up a myriad of creative influences to develop a style that is unique to his background and experiences.

090-091

Tison, Evin

Evin is a young fashion designer who specialises in womenswear. She seeks to materialise the vision of a new couture in collaboration with art. Out of the usual codes, Evin's work is sculptural and provides audiences with a conceptual way to appreciate clothes.

230-233

Tissot, Tibhaud

Tibhaud is a Berlin-based designer and art director at Onlab, a graphic design studio with a strong focus on content, narrative, and visual quality. He was born and studied in La Chaux-de-Fonds.

056-057

Tremblay, Martin

Martin has an exceptional eye for the play between shadow and light, making him a master at constructing hyper-realistic images. He is an award-winning photographer whose work has been recognised all over the world and published in prestigious international magazines such as Zink New York, Schön! London, NOI.SE Australia and Highlights Australia, to name but a few.

168-171

Tsai Chia-hao

Chia-hao is a graphic designer whose passion lies in book design, packaging, typography, the performing arts, and exhibitions. His work has been nominated for various design awards.

136

Tsai Shu-yu

Shu-yu is a designer originally from Taiwan. Her work can be seen on a variety of music-related output.

176-177

twomuch

twomuch is a newly formed collaboration between Benjamin Chan and Malone Chen. They are currently studying graphic design at Central Saint Martins. Their work focuses on using contemporary and upcoming digital techniques to form intriguing visuals and playful outcomes.

184-185

Tzimas, Aron

Aron is a New York-based designer working on everything from UI/UX app design to restaurant design and branding. Originally from Melbourne, he has founded many projects around the world and is currently the Chief Creative Officer of Knotch Inc.

036-037

Volk, Radmir

Radmir specialises in brand design and is based in Moscow. He is a member of the AIGA and focuses on simple, clean, and timeless aesthetics.

016-019

Witczak, Mateusz

Mateusz is a self-taught lettering artist and graphic designer currently living in Warsaw. Besides specialising in highly detailed hand-drawn lettering and typography designs that combine traditional methods and tools with the latest digital applications, he is experienced in the fields of branding, packaging, textile design and illustration.

050-051

Wysocki, Marcin

Marcin is a designer who graduated from the Academy of Fine Arts in Katowice. His portfolio includes visual identification projects, books, posters, web applications, and video clips. Besides working as an art director over the years, he has been managing the publishing department of the Centre for Contemporary Art (Kronika) since 2011.

066-067

Yoon, Saerom

Saerom is an artist based in Seoul. His work is inspired by the effortless beauty of nature, particularly the colours of the sunset and sunrise. To that end, he aspires for his sculptural furniture to have the appearance and feel similar to a watercolour painting. He also hopes to materialise natural textures; such as the interplay of clouds, calm water, rippling waves, frozen ice, and the bark of trees.

242-245

YUNGBLD

YUNGBLD or Young Blood is a creative and design studio founded by Laura Miller in 2015. They use the creative box that everyone strives to think outside of as a foot rest.

148-149

PALETTE No.1:
BLACK & WHITE
New Monochrome Graphics

With eyes on graphic schemes
that incorporate no colour, Black
& White is the first of PALETTE
which manifests how recent
design projects leap out in simple
black and white. The book collects
130 monochrome projects, ranging from graphic solutions, spatial
installations to textile prints.

PALETTE No.2:
MULTICOLOUR
New Rainbow-hued Graphics

Looking at visual experiences
founded on a rich palette, Multi-
colour lends a striking perception
to what makes colour a powerful
communication tool in today's
design. The title examines how
colours become a new vocabulary
in profusion and elicits emotions in
various context and use.

PALETTE No.3:
GOLD & SILVER
New Metallic Graphics

Digging into the lustrous shades
that incite mesmerising glares,
Gold & Silver surveys how the
metallic duo interact with colours
and surfaces in visual communication design. The title focuses on
application and production, with
techniques spanning gilding, pure
gold plating and metallic coating.

PALETTE No.4:
NEON
New Fluorescent Graphics

Snazzy, aggressive and intrinsi-
cally captivating, neon transmits
more than verve. As special
paper, spot colour inks, paint or
even lighting installations, this
artificial colour lets designs pop
with attitude in the crowd. With
110 recent projects, NEON reveals
fluorescent colours' full potential
with six-colour print.

PALETTE No.5:
PASTEL
New Light-toned Graphics

Pastels are visually sweet, soft,
tender but not weak in its expres-
sive energy. The 5th volume of
PALETTE, Pastel sets to reveal the
diverse character of this soothing
colour range through more than
100 recent visual experiments and
thoughtful solutions spanning
brand identities and fashion
photography.

PALETTE No.6:
TRANSPARENT
Transparencies in design

Spawning a sense of presence
and absence, transparencies lure
viewers into exploring what lies
beneath and beyond. Through 110
select works, Transparent demonstrates how the beguiling layer
is interpreted anew in design,
whether it's a tangible element or
a conceptual idea that deceives
the eyes.

PALETTE No.7:
MONOTONE
New Single-colour Graphics

Monochrome designs have the
power to stand out in the midst of
visual noise with their distinctive
simplicity. This seventh edition of
PALETTE explores how designers
create variety out of singularity
through 110 creative projects that
capitalise on a sole colour or a tonal palette to make a lasting impact.